The Constitution on
the Campaign Trail

The Constitution on the Campaign Trail

The Surprising Political Career
of America's Founding Document

Andrew E. Busch

ROWMAN & LITTLEFIELD PUBLISHERS, INC.
Lanham • Boulder • New York • Toronto • Plymouth, UK

ROWMAN & LITTLEFIELD PUBLISHERS, INC.

Published in the United States of America
by Rowman & Littlefield Publishers, Inc.
A wholly owned subsidary of The Rowman & Littlefield Publishing Group, Inc.
4501 Forbes Boulevard, Suite 200, Lanham, Maryland 20706
www.rowmanlittlefield.com

Estover Road
Plymouth PL6 7PY
United Kingdom

Copyright © 2007 by Rowman & Littlefield Publishers, Inc.

British Library Cataloguing in Publication Information Available

Library of Congress Cataloging-in-Publication Data:
Busch, Andrew.
  The Constitution on the campaign trail : the surprising political career of America's
founding document / Andrew E. Busch.
     p. cm.
  Includes bibliographical references and index.
  ISBN-13: 978-0-7425-4848-0 (cloth : alk. paper)
  ISBN-10: 0-7425-4848-1 (cloth : alk. paper)
  ISBN-13: 978-0-7425-5901-1 (pbk. : alk. paper)
  ISBN-10: 0-7425-5901-7 (pbk. : alk. paper)
  1. Constitutional history—United States. 2. Electioneering—United States—History.
I. Title.
  KF4552.B87 2007
  342.7302'9—dc22   2007011519

Printed in the United States of America

∞™ The paper used in this publication meets the minimum requirements of
American National Standard for Information Sciences—Permanence of Paper
for Printed Library Materials, ANSI/NISO Z39.48-1992.

To Joe and Charlotte, to whom I owe so much

~

Contents

~

Acknowledgments

I would like to acknowledge the assistance and support of many people without whom this project would not have been possible. I wish specifically to thank the Institute for Public Policy, Chris McLemore, and Rebecca Swanson at the University of Denver; the Salvatori Center for the Study of Individual Freedom in the Modern World, the Gould Center for the Humanities and the Rose Institute at Claremont McKenna College, along with Anne Johnson, Miles Staglik, and Dan Mitchell; Hans Hassell; and Jonathan Miller and the Social Philosophy and Policy Center at Bowling Green State University. In particular, Miles Staglik's aid was indispensable in making sense of Microsoft Excel. I would also like to acknowledge the thoughtful comments and guidance offered by my friends and colleagues Ralph Rossum, Charles Lofgren, John Dinan, Charles Kesler, Steve Bragow, Mark Hull, Bob Stacey, and others, as well as the very helpful suggestions made by the anonymous reviewers of my manuscript. As always, the folks at Rowman & Littlefield—Michael McGandy, Asa Johnson, Molly Ahearn, Nancy Barry and the rest—were extremely helpful. Of course, no acknowledgement is complete without thanking my wife Melinda, who patiently allowed me to spend several years muddling through this project.

Introduction

The United States Constitution establishes the framework for American government and elucidates the fundamental principles and values of the American order. Its structural provisions guard against a dangerous concentration of power, its enumeration of rights serve as a standard around which to rally citizens in the defense of their freedom. It is, in the abstract, venerated by an overwhelming proportion of the American people.

A number of prominent scholars, including Keith Whittington, Louis Fischer, David P. Currie, J. Mitchell Pickerill, Bruce G. Peabody, Susan Burgess, and John Dinan, lay out a powerful argument for the importance of the elected branches to constitutional interpretation and construction.[1] In this view, Congress and the president frequently stake out constitutional positions and seek to shift Americans' understanding of what the Constitution requires, sometimes in conflict with each other and sometimes in conflict with the courts. Even in modern times, on issues such as war powers, congressional control over the power of the purse, and impeachment, constitutional debates have extended well outside the judiciary. As Keith Whittington argues in *Constitutional Construction*, "The Constitution penetrates politics, shaping it from the inside and altering the outcomes. Along the way, the Constitution is also made subject to politics."[2] In the view of presidential scholar Sidney Milkis, "Presidents who enjoy prominent places in history have justified their reform programs in constitutional terms, claiming to restore the proper understanding of first principles, even as they have attempted to transfuse the Declaration of Independence and Constitution with new meaning."[3] John Gerring, in his study *Party Ideologies in America, 1828–1996,* went so far as to argue that "few issues in American history have *not* been framed in constitutional terms."[4]

Yet the Constitution's place in government and politics is surprisingly uncertain today. In recent decades, a variety of analysts have contended that the Constitution has fallen on hard times. Voices ranging from Barry M. Goldwater, Ronald Reagan, and the *National Review* to John Kerry, Ralph Nader, and *The Nation* have protested that the federal government has at times acted without due consideration of the Constitution. Some scholars have decried a "deconstitutionalization" of government—that is, a decline in the degree to which government officials have made the Constitution a significant factor in their deliberations and decisions, or in the degree to which citizens defend the institutional restraints on the power of government necessary for democracy to prosper rather than self-destruct.[5]

In this view, which also has much to recommend it, some crucial moments in a process of deconstitutionalization can be proposed: the Civil War, the Progressive Era, and the New Deal. After the first, federalism and enumerated powers lost some of their power to motivate political action. By 1890, one U.S. Senator lamented that "It has come to the point in our country, that the man who attempts to question anything under a constitutional grant of power is looked upon as an effete and worn-out fossil who lives in ancient history, and is unfit for the active life of today."[6] While this might have been an exaggeration, there is no doubt that Appomattox put an end to at least the most extreme form of argument for states' rights.

The Progressives' governing vision included, among other things, dismissal of a number of key constitutional principles, including separation of powers, limited government, property rights, and a constrained presidency, complemented by a view of the Constitution as a "living" document that could be molded by policymakers to fit new social circumstances. Woodrow Wilson, for example, argued that separation of powers was a counterproductive mechanism invented in a Newtonian era; rather, government was an evolving organism that required unity of purpose. Progressive devices of direct democracy, such as the initiative, referendum, recall, and (to a lesser degree) primary election and popular election of senators, were efforts to bypass the principle of representative government at the heart of the Constitution. More broadly, it is impossible not to notice the degree to which progressivism was grounded in a deliberate attempt to downgrade veneration for the Constitution and its framers.[7]

New Deal governance, amplified in the Great Society, further diminished concern for once-prominent features of American constitutionalism. Enumeration of powers was swept aside with an extremely broad conception of the commerce power; scores of governmental functions once left to state and local governments became federal responsibilities; separation of powers was bypassed as Congress delegated rule-making authority to executive agencies. First the elected branches, then the courts, increasingly applied the notion of the Constitution as a document without fixed meaning.

In this narrative, ultimately appearing alongside the deconstitutionalization of policymaking and logically connected to it, came the rise of *judicialism*—the national embrace of an outsized role for the federal judiciary as the sole arbiter of constitutionality. If the first threat to constitutionalism was the result of a general constitutional carelessness in the elected branches, the second took the form of the ghettoization of the Constitution, an attempt to force it within the narrow precincts inhabited by lawyers and judges. The two phenomena have worked symbiotically, and toward the same result: the steady decline of constitutional deliberation among the people and their elected representatives.

This transformation was driven by events: the violence of secession, the rise of urbanization and industrialization, the intractability of the Depression, and (as far as judicialism goes) the moral imperative of civil rights. It was also driven by the ascendance of new ideas, especially in the cases of the progressives and of the New Deal, which drew heavily on both progressive ideology and Franklin Roosevelt's vision of a large and active central government administering a welfare state of positive economic rights.

Altogether, Max Lerner observed in 1937, contemplating the Constitution as a symbol, that industrialism "creates a climate in which a symbol has to be hardy to survive. There is an erosive power in the machine-process which makes men think increasingly in matter-of-fact terms and before which legends tend to crumble away."[8] Arguing that those governing no longer look to the Constitution, law professor Stephen M. Griffin contended shortly after the bicentennial of the Federal Convention that in the modern world "the political branches alter the Constitution in the course of ordinary political struggles, often without much attention to what the legal profession would surely claim are independent constitutional values."[9] Others point to the loss of constitutional discourse in the polity. Harvey C. Mansfield noted near the bicentennial of the Federal Convention that "we find that Americans no longer speak of their Constitution as frequently and as enthusiastically as they once did," as social movements of left and right came to view the Constitution as a means of getting what they wanted rather than as a binding form of government.[10] Charles Kesler, some years later, observed that today

one seldom hears about the Constitution in connection with our political parties . . . the Constitution itself has been under running intellectual and political attack for about a hundred years. As a result, the Constitution no longer provides a clear raison d'être for our parties. . . . Whereas once the parties stood or tried to stand on the solid rock of the Constitution, now they struggle to gain a footing amid the sinking sand of post-Constitutional doctrines.[11]

Most starkly, legal scholar Sanford Levinson predicted that "the 'death of constitutionalism' may be the central event of our time."[12]

The Constitution and American Political Campaigns

If true, there could hardly be a more serious specter for the well-being of the American Republic than the death of constitutionalism. But is it true? Is constitutionalism in the polity really in sharp decline? And how could we tell if it is?

This book will propose that one crucial way of assessing that prospect is to focus on the extent and character of constitutional rhetoric in American elections.

Just as the role of the elected branches in constitutional application has been the object of considerable analysis, the general content of federal campaign rhetoric has also been widely studied by scholars such as Gerring, Gerald Pomper, Harold Lasswell, and many others.[13] However, the intersection of those topics—the role of the Constitution in electoral politics—has received little scholarly attention. Sidney Milkis's book on the parties and constitutional government explores ways that the structure and mission of the parties has affected the tenor of campaigns and of government. Similarly, a volume edited by Peter W. Schramm and Bradford P. Wilson—*American Political Parties & Constitutional Politics*—examines the connection between parties and the Constitution.[14] In *Campaigns and the Court*, Donald Grier Stephenson, Jr. offers a rich history of key moments when Supreme Court decisions and broader issues of judicial power interjected themselves into presidential elections in a significant way. Stephenson holds that in those cases—1800, 1832, 1860, 1896, 1912, 1924, 1936, 1968, and 1980–84—the court drew a democratic rebuke that usually affected the Court's jurisprudence.[15] A handful of other scholars have also approached the interface between the Supreme Court and elections, including partisan realignments.[16] This research provides interesting insights into one corner of the broader issue, but not much else has been done to explore that issue, especially by means of focusing on constitutional rhetoric.

At this point, it is important to clarify what is meant by campaign *rhetoric*. In modern parlance, *rhetoric* is often a term meant as a belittling pejorative, as in, "His statement was mere rhetoric" or, "She was more interested in rhetoric than action." In this study, *rhetoric* retains its loftier (or at least neutral) classical usage, meaning public argumentation used to persuade. Ancients like Aristotle put a high premium on the significance of rhetoric, thinking it an integral component of politics rather than a peripheral, or even disreputable, one. As William Raymond Smith puts it, "it is rhetoric that forms a link between principles and actions."[17] In the view of presidential scholar Jeffrey Tulis, "Rhetorical practice is not merely a variable, it is also an amplification or vulgarization of the ideas that produce it. Political rhetoric is, simultaneously, a practical result of basic doctrines of governance, and an avenue to the meaning of alternative constitutional understandings."[18]

Study of the role of the Constitution in campaigns can shed important light on—and might even be essential to understanding—the broader question of where constitutionalism stands in modern American political life. Such campaign rhetoric might be both a cause and an effect, both a barometer of the vitality of constitutionalism and a contributing factor helping to determine that vitality. The health of constitutionalism in government may thus be intertwined with the vibrancy of constitutionalism as a factor in campaigns.

As Sidney Milkis argues,

"The vitality of the American Constitution has come from its alliance with democratic debate about its meaning. Critical elections have been, so to speak, surrogate constitutional conventions, in which the American people have been drawn into partisan disputes about the proper understanding of their fundamental principles and institutional arrangements."[19]

Yet, Milkis laments, this power of each generation to define the Constitution electorally has been supplanted by a politics dominated by petty claims of rights and entitlements.

There are several specific ways in which the conversation about the Constitution in campaigns is intimately connected with the broader health of constitutionalism and, consequently, several reasons that we should care a great deal whether, how, and how much constitutional issues actually do become part of campaign rhetoric. First, attention to this question can help place deconstitutionalization and judicialism in a broader context. If the elected branches really do accept little responsibility for the interpretation and application of the Constitution, then one would expect negligible discussion of constitutional issues in political campaigns, though an issue might burst through from time to time just because of its symbolic importance to Americans. A great deal of campaign discussion would conversely indicate that the elected branches see a greater role for themselves.

Second, a variety of factors contribute to voter decision making, including partisanship, retrospective assessments of performance, and assessments of candidates' personality, character, temperament, and experience. However, issues and how they are discussed are a factor in voter choice both directly (when candidates' views on issues drive a vote) and indirectly (when party drives a vote and partisan identification is driven by the parties' issue stands over time). Indeed, some scholars argue that fundamental shifts in long-term voter loyalties are driven by the issue environment. James Sundquist, for example, argues that partisan realignments take place when the parties create new cleavages in the electorate by taking clearly opposing stands on a particularly salient and cross-cutting issue of the day, such as slavery in the 1850s, currency in the 1890s, and the New Deal in the 1930s.[20] David Mayhew, who has challenged the notion of electoral realignments, nevertheless points out the importance of issues like war in disrupting and reforming party coalitions.[21] Needless to say, if constitutional issues are not raised in campaigns they will likely not contribute to the choices of voters.

Third, campaign rhetoric also affects the approach and conduct of officeholders. There is substantial evidence that campaign promises and issue presentation subsequently serve as a meaningful guide to governing. Jeff Fishel and Gerald Pomper have shown that winning presidential candidates take their promises seriously. Therefore, campaign communications—including party platforms, though seldom read by voters today—must be considered a useful predictor of what that party's officeholders will at least attempt to do once in power. In this context, candidates who pay heed to constitutional concerns while campaigning may be more likely to pay them heed while governing.

Not least, campaigns, aside from their chief objective of persuading and mobilizing voters, arguably have an additional effect. They can educate voters, as well, by focusing on a particular set of issues or ideas. If a set of issues rarely finds its way into campaign rhetoric, another sort of education also takes place: the message is sent that the subject is relatively unimportant. Beyond the atmospheric cues established by discussion or nondiscussion of certain issues, an extensive literature exists indicating that political campaigns, despite their numerous flaws, succeed in adding to the stock of political information held by a significant proportion of voters (although political scientists are far from unanimous on which forms of communication are most important to the process of voter learning or which voters make the biggest gains through the course of the campaign).[22] Most of these studies measure growth in knowledge of the attributes or issue stands of the candidates, but there is no reason in principle that campaign rhetoric would not also lead to some learning about the issues themselves.

Indeed, Michael Delli Carpini and Scott Keeter argue in their book *What Americans Know About Politics and Why It Matters* that "[t]he political parties are critical actors in determining what citizens know and don't know about politics."[23] To Delli Carpini and Keeter, political learning by citizens requires cognitive ability, motivation, and opportunity (that is, access to information); of course, political campaigns provide opportunity and stimulate motivation. Of the twenty-one factors they tested, the five most important predictors of political knowledge were (in order) following politics and interest in campaigns, education, feelings of internal efficacy, propensity to discuss politics with others, and income. Two of the five, following politics (the top predictor) and propensity to discuss politics, were items promoted and stimulated by campaigns. Delli Carpini and Keeter also contend that political knowledge fosters both awareness and acceptance of democratic values, demonstrating specifically that relatively high levels of knowledge about civil liberties and the Supreme Court were strongly correlated with greater political tolerance.[24]

More broadly, the Constitution, as Edward S. Corwin argues in a 1936 seminal essay, is not only an instrument of governmental power but also a potent symbol. Corwin, Lerner, and others contend that it is a symbol, created by "the mass mind," of private liberty against government and, in a related vein, of the protection of the minority against tyranny of the majority; of national unity; of prosperity; of assimilation; of political rootedness and stability; in sum, "a visible symbol of the things men hold dear."[25] Lerner famously acknowledges that "Every tribe needs its totem and its fetish, and the Constitution is ours."[26] This assessment of the Constitution was grounded in no small measure of skeptical disdain, but the point remains: the Constitution has served as a critical and perhaps irreplaceable symbol of the American political order. Yet like any symbol, the constitutional symbol must be invoked to remain potent.

If campaigns can influence public sentiment, the reverse is also true. Because most candidates are in the business of trying to win, and because communication between candidates and voters is not a one-way street, campaign rhetoric can also serve as a barometer of public sentiment. At the very least, the prominence of particular issues tells us something about what the campaigns think the public is thinking about. Consequently, by tracing the degree to which constitutional issues are visible in electoral campaigns, we can also roughly trace the degree to which Americans have already made a place for those issues on their political agenda.

Altogether, there are a great many reasons why we should prefer more robust campaign dialogue on constitutional issues, and why we should likewise consider it an empirical test of the health of constitutionalism in the polity. The nature of the issues brought before the public in the course of electoral campaigns is important—contributing to voter choice, guiding officeholders to a course of action, serving as a gauge of public sentiment, and educating voters. The degree of prominence of constitutional issues in electoral campaigns can serve as a barometer of the vibrancy of the Constitution in public life and of the vigor of the elected branches in asserting some role in constitutional interpretation. The survival of the Constitution as a potent political symbol may well depend upon its use. Thus the stakes are high.

The Study

This study hence begins with the premise that the strength of constitutionalism in American politics can be gauged at least partly by the vigor of campaign conversation about the Constitution. The vigor of that conversation can itself be measured in a number of ways. Four general propositions that will define a vigorous constitutional rhetoric, and the measurable questions that flow from them, will form the basis of the study:

1. *All other things being equal, more constitutional rhetoric is better than less.* Although it might be possible to imagine some upper limit beyond which the quantity of constitutional rhetoric becomes irrelevant or even counterproductive, the undesirability of such rhetoric dwindling to zero is more obvious. This proposition leads to the question of how the number and rate of total constitutional references have changed over time, beginning with a raw count of constitutional references. However, given great variations over time in the length of party platforms and other campaign communications, the raw number of constitutional references is not a sufficient measure. To see what relative weight they have held in campaign rhetoric, this study will also use an index of constitutional references per thousand words.

2. *More open discussion of the Constitution is better than veiled or opaque discussion.* The key question here is how much constitutional rhetoric in American elections is explicit in character, and whether the balance between explicit and implicit mentions of the Constitution has shifted over time.[27] This will be measured primarily in terms of what proportion of all references were explicit and occasionally in terms of explicit references per thousand words.

r and more varied is better than consti-
cused. Questions flowing from this
ontent of constitutional rhetoric and
ow much rhetoric falls into varying
be measured in terms both of "con-
is mentioned across years) and of
cussed in the years it does appear).
t least half of the election years will
that represent at least 20 percent of
st half of the years they are men-
he threshold for depth. References
fifteen categories of constitutional

- constitutional amendments
- appointment and confirmation for constitutionally sensitive positions
- individual rights
- enumeration of powers
- federalism
- impeachment
- contraction or expansion of judicial power
- some presidential vetoes
- utilization of executive powers
- executive enforcement and administration of the law
- interbranch struggles relating to separation of powers
- assessment of specific federal court decisions or more general judicial trends
- support for a particular mode of constitutional interpretation
- issues of the constitutional sovereignty of the United States vis-à-vis international organizations or treaties, and
- substantively meaningless "perfunctory" references to the Constitution, such as "We pledge our fidelity to the Constitution."

As well as looking at the fifteen categories of constitutional rhetoric, categories will be collapsed into broader groupings of rights, structure, and constitutional interpretation. A detailed description of the fifteen categories can be found in appendix A.

4. *It is better for campaigns and candidates to engage one another on constitutional issues than to talk past each other.* The key question here is how much actual constitutional dialogue occurs during campaigns. In other

words, how often do candidates or parties engage in exchanges on constitutional issues? Those exchanges might take the form of either a "policy dispute," in which the two parties stake out opposing positions on the same constitutional issue, or a "performance dispute," in which the first party attacks the second for an alleged constitutional failing and the second attempts to refute the criticism.

To answer these questions, this study examines references to the Constitution and constitutional issues in a variety of political communications from 1840 through 2006. Those campaign communications include major-party platforms and direct messages (usually nomination acceptance letters or speeches) from the presidential candidates from 1840 to 2004, major-party television advertisements from 1952 to 2004, and presidential debates from 1960 to 2004. It will also examine campaign communications from minor parties or independent candidates receiving more than 5 percent of the nationally aggregated popular vote. Two types of governing documents—inaugural addresses and State of the Union messages from 1841 to 2006—offer an opportunity to test whether constitutional tendencies apparent in campaign rhetoric carry over into governing, and they are also included in the analysis. The use of a variety of modes of communication over a long period of time will make it possible to assess whether modern means of campaign communications have made it easier or harder to discuss the Constitution in campaigns. Appendix A details my methodology; appendix B details the sources used.

There are a number of limitations to this study that should be acknowledged forthrightly. First, the study examines campaign rhetoric—that is, appeals made by the campaigns directly to the voters—but not coverage of the campaigns in newspapers, newsmagazines, or television or radio news. Thus, it is a better gauge of what the candidates are saying than it is of what the voters are hearing. Second, it focuses only on national general election campaigns; it excludes primaries or nomination campaigns, as well as state and local campaigns. Congressional campaigns are included to the degree that party platforms cover them, but congressional candidates are not examined individually; hence the study is tilted toward presidential campaigns. While all platforms and presidential debates and a very large number of television advertisements were coded, only a small fraction of personal communications by the candidates were coded; each nomination acceptance letter or speech serves as a proxy for a great many speeches. Reasonable people might not code the same communication identically, especially when the reference is implicit or on the borderline between two complementary categories.

Finally, I make no effort to offer a normative evaluation of the plausibility, morality, or constitutional correctness of the constitutional arguments offered by candidates and their campaigns. As Jeffrey Tulis notes in his book *The Rhetorical Presidency*, one cannot "assume intelligent constitutional positions by virtue of the mere invocation of the word."[28] The reader will have to sort out the intelligent from the unintelligent references. The key object of this study is to do something more basic: test whether there are enough, open enough, broad enough, and responsive enough references to even make possible an intelligent constitutional conversation.

Decline and Resurgence

Ultimately, the story of constitutional rhetoric in American campaigns is one of a long and broad decline, and of a limited but real resurgence. Both parts of the story are surprising in their own way, and both are worth telling.

It is clear from this study that constitutional conversation has indeed suffered as a vibrant force in American elections. Insofar as that conversation tells us something important about the broader issue of constitutionalism in political life, constitutionalism has suffered. Furthermore, the decline in constitutional rhetoric in campaigns has paralleled a similar decline in key governing communications. Given the putative centrality of the Constitution to American politics, and the many ways the elected branches can participate in constitutional controversies, this decline will strike some as surprising, and many as troubling.

At the same time, it is too much to say that the Constitution is withering from rhetorical neglect. The picture is much more complicated than a simple decline of constitutional rhetoric, and there are even some contrary signs. Those hoping for the survival—or better yet, revival—of constitutionalism both in and out of campaigns can find much to confirm their worst fears, but more than they might expect to nourish hope. For pessimists, the real surprise may be that constitutional rhetoric has actually enjoyed a bit of a comeback.

Chapter 1 will establish in greater detail why constitutional issues should form a part of federal election campaigns despite the pretensions of judicialism. There is broad evidence that the framers of the Constitution themselves expected that the elected branches would play an important role in the defense and application of the Constitution. Additionally, there are numerous specific constitutional powers held by the elected branches (such as appointment and confirmation to the Supreme Court) that ensure them a place in the constitutional conversation. The fifteen categories of constitutional references that are used in coding are derived directly from this discussion.

The heart of the evidence and the argument is found in chapters 2 through 5, which work in turn through the constitutional rhetoric found in major-party platforms, candidate messages, TV ads, and presidential debates. The overall tendency is clear—less weight is given to constitutional rhetoric over time. References to the Constitution in key campaign messages have declined considerably since the mid-1800s, and references have become increasingly implicit and skewed toward individual rights. However, in most modes of communication, there has been an uptick in constitutional rhetoric in recent decades by a variety of measures. The last four decades have seen a modest revival of constitutional rhetoric in campaigns from a trough in the 1950s and 1960s, including new importance for issues such as court appointments and renewed importance for traditional issues such as federalism.

Furthermore, there is a significant difference between levels of constitutional rhetoric depending upon the mode of communication. Platforms are consistently the most constitution-oriented. Television advertising—the mode of campaign communication most prominent in the modern age—is also the mode that is consistently most barren of constitutional rhetoric. In contrast, presidential debates, another type of television campaigning, have sometimes featured a high level of constitutional content.

Chapter 6 takes a closer look at the role of third parties in promoting constitutional issues, finding that when third parties appear throughout American history, they often add significantly to the constitutional content of the campaign. Third parties, like major parties, talk less about the Constitution than they used to, but almost every such party from Free-Soilers in 1848 to the Reform Party in 1996 has engaged in a level of constitutional discourse exceeding that of at least one of its major-party opponents.

On the grounds that examination of the constitutional character of inaugural and State of the Union messages can illuminate the connections between campaigning and governing, chapter 7 focuses on them. Inaugurals and State of the Union addresses are a form of communication similar to nomination acceptance speeches. They have suffered a similar decline in rates of constitutional rhetoric and typically offer similar rates of constitutional rhetoric to those acceptance speeches. Despite their ceremonial status, they have not been immune from the general trend of a deconstitutionalization of political communication.

Chapter 8 will summarize and assess where the Constitution stands in modern American electoral politics and why. As we look to the future, conflicting signs are visible. Some evidence from 2000 and 2004 may indicate that the resurgence of constitutional rhetoric has reached a plateau, or has even begun receding, largely a victim of George W. Bush's disinterest in constitutional issues such as federalism or enumeration of powers. There is a strong ongoing base in public opinion, media, and interest groups for some kinds of constitutional rhetoric in campaigns, especially that dealing with rights, but not for other kinds.

The deconstitutionalization of campaign rhetoric in American elections has been real. The resurgence of that rhetoric in recent decades, though limited, is also real, and intriguing. It is an open question, with enormous implications for American political life, whether that resurgence can be sustained and broadened, or whether the place of the Constitution in campaigns will resume its downward spiral.

CHAPTER ONE

~

The Constitution
and Electoral Politics

Before one can assess how much of a place constitutional issues hold in our electoral politics, one must first establish in greater detail why the Constitution should be expected to hold a place there at all. To the eighteenth-century statesmen who wrote the Constitution, such a question would be inane. The Constitution belonged to the people, and the duty of defending it was shared by them and their representatives. Since the early to mid-twentieth century, however, the predominant conception of constitutional interpretation and enforcement in America has held that the U.S. Supreme Court is the proper repository of ultimate power in that realm. In this view, cases are "handed down" (as if from Mt. Sinai) and it is neither the duty nor the right of the elected branches to inquire too deeply into constitutional questions. The furthest reach of that conception has held that the highest federal tribunal is not only the decisive but also the sole legitimate actor in constitutional definition. The Supreme Court itself has asserted this position of judicialism, which has also arguably come to dominate the nation's law schools and legal profession.[1] This conflation of the Supreme Court with the Constitution has been noted by numerous astute observers, one of whom held that "it is not too much to say that the function of constitutional symbolism became auxiliary to the cult of the judicial power."[2]

The case for judicial power is relatively straightforward. The principle of constitutionalism which stands at the heart of the American system holds that the Constitution is the fundamental law, the enduring and supreme will of the American people with respect to the structure of the federal government and the rights of citizens. Consequently, no statute, federal or state, is valid if it conflicts with the Constitution. For this principle to be enforced, some entity of government must be charged with the task of determining when such a conflict has arisen, so resolution can be made in favor of the supreme law. To lodge such power in Congress would be to allow the lawmakers to pass judgment on their own handiwork. The difficulties inherent in such a scheme are obvious. In a sense, it would restore the inconveniences of the state of nature arising from (in Locke's words) "every man being a judge in his own case." As Congressman William Drayton of South Carolina argued in the House in 1832:

> Had [the framers] devolved upon Congress the right of deciding these controversies, they would have exonerated the Federal Legislature from the limitations which had been imposed upon it, and converted it into a despotic assembly, uncontrolled excepting by its discretion. Had they vested this right in the parties differing, they would have organized a system of confusion and anarchy, which would soon have resolved society into its original elements.[3]

Instead, the framers devised a federal judiciary, and lodged in its hands power extending "to all Cases, in Law and Equity, arising under this Constitution, the Laws of the United States, and Treaties made, or which shall be made, under their Authority. . . ."[4] As a neutral body, whose independence was assured by lifetime terms, the Supreme Court could decide constitutional controversies, thus averting tyranny or anarchy. While the Constitution does not explicitly mention judicial review, the concept seems to have been familiar to Americans of the founding era. In the pre-Revolutionary disputes with Great Britain, some leading Americans called on the British courts to invalidate what they considered to be improper acts of Parliament (though their primary efforts were aimed at persuading Parliament to reverse itself).[5] At the state level, the courts established after independence sometimes applied judicial review against state legislatures. Arguably, however, there were only two clear precedents of judicial review by state courts prior to the Federal Convention, one in New Hampshire and the other in North Carolina, and they provoked a firestorm of protest, including attempted impeachment and disciplinary hearings.[6]

The framers of the Constitution made a point of instituting an independent Supreme Court—something that had not existed before under the Articles of Confederation—as a check on the elected branches. (They left open the question of instituting a national judicial system of lower courts, an issue that was not settled until the Judiciary Act of 1789.) In the Federalist papers, Alexander Hamilton himself argued that an independent judiciary is, in a republic, an "excellent barrier to the encroachments and oppressions of the representative body. . . . Limitations [on legislative authority] can be preserved in practice no other way than through the medium of courts of justice, whose duty it must be to declare all acts contrary to the manifest tenor of the Constitution void."[7]

While textbooks often point to the 1803 case *Marbury v. Madison* as "establishing" judicial review of federal acts by the Supreme Court, many historians argue that the principle was already established by then in pension cases that came before circuit courts (e.g., *Hayburn's Case*, 1792), the case of *Hylton v. U.S.* in 1796, and the Judiciary Act of 1802. Many also argue that the Supreme Court's authority to invalidate unconstitutional *state* laws was understood from 1787 on.[8] In *Federalist* 80, Hamilton contended that the supremacy of the federal constitution was to be preserved by judicial review of state law by the Supreme Court. The only alternative was a congressional veto over state laws, a mechanism Hamilton assumed states would rather avoid (although it had been proposed at the Federal Convention in the Virginia Plan). The celebrated *McCullough v. Maryland*, as well as less well-known cases such as *Martin v. Hunter's Lessee* and *Cohens v. Virginia*, established this principle in practice from a relatively early date.[9]

The importance of the judiciary was transformed in the twentieth century into the doctrine of judicialism, or the view that decision of constitutional issues is, or should be, exclusively the responsibility of the Supreme Court. While advocates of judicialism agree that the Supreme Court is the decisive venue for constitutional interpretation, they do not always agree on what this means for the obligations of the elected branches. From within Congress and the executive branch, the view that constitutional interpretation is solely the province of the courts has sometimes led to lawmakers simply excusing themselves from any considerations of constitutionality. In this model of judicialism—what one might call irresponsible judicialism—Congress should pass and the president should sign whatever they prefer on policy grounds and leave it to the courts to sort out whether the action was consistent with the Constitution.[10] Another view, also based on judicialism—perhaps one could call it responsible judicialism—holds that Congress and the president do have a constitutional obligation. However, that responsibility is passive, limited to ensuring that legislation is consistent with prior judicial decisions.[11]

The Limits of Judicialism

Yet not only was judicialism not the sole view at the time of the founding and for the first 150 years of the American Republic but also for most of that time it was not even the most common view.[12] As one scholar noted, "[I]n the

early Congress occasional speakers suggested that questions as to the constitutionality of proposed legislation should be left to the courts, but they were
quickly shouted down."[13] Even today, judicialism is not universally acclaimed.
The doctrine of departmentalism, holding that each of the coequal branches
must contribute coequally to definition of the Constitution, retains defenders.[14]
And, regardless of theoretical assertions about which institution *should* decide
what the Constitution means, it remains true as a practical fact that the federal
judiciary does not possess a monopoly on constitutional interpretation. In particular, both the president of the United States and the United States Congress
are called upon regularly to understand and enforce the Constitution.

While it can be plausibly argued that the Supreme Court was meant from
the beginning to void clearly unconstitutional acts, that is not the same
thing as saying that it has the sole and unchallenged authority in the realm
of constitutional understanding. There are numerous reasons, grounded in
the constitutional design of the founders and in the nature of republican government, that would argue against such a monopoly view of the role of federal judicial power. Not least, members of Congress and the president, like
members of the Supreme Court, swear an oath of faithfulness to the Constitution, strongly implying that they have a positive and active duty that goes
well beyond merely providing obeisance to the Supreme Court.[15] The president's oath is actually specified in the text of the Constitution itself, and
pledges the chief executive to "preserve, protect, and defend the Constitution of the United States."[16] The congressional oath requires members to
"support and defend the Constitution of the United States against all enemies, foreign and domestic" and to "bear true faith and allegiance to the
same."[17] This oath was established by Congress itself through statute, as is the
oath administered to Supreme Court justices, which binds them to "faithfully
and impartially discharge and perform all the duties incumbent . . . under the
Constitution and laws of the United States." Thus, written into the Constitution itself was an oath pledging the president to defend the Constitution,
something that the framers did not even require of the Supreme Court.
Should anyone be tempted to think the presidential oath of office merely
symbolic and incapable of inferring duties or powers, recall that Abraham
Lincoln offered his presidential oath of office as a justification for emergency
measures taken at the onset of the Civil War. Likewise, Andrew Jackson justified his veto of the National Bank bill in 1832 by saying,

> It is maintained by advocates of the bank that its constitutionality in all its fea-
> tures ought to be considered as settled by precedent and by the decision of the
> Supreme Court. To this conclusion I cannot assent. . . . The Congress, the Ex-

ecutive, and the Court must each for itself be guided by its own opinion of the Constitution. Each public officer who takes an oath to support the Constitution swears that he will support it as he understands it, and not as it is understood by others.[18]

As always, insight into the thinking of the framers can be gained by examining the *Federalist*. Hamilton explicitly laid out the principle of judicial review in *Federalist* 78; altogether, only papers 78–82 were devoted primarily to the judiciary (out of eighty-five papers altogether)—not what one might expect if their purpose was to assert the centrality of the Supreme Court in the American constitutional system. In a few earlier papers, Publius refers to the judicial power in passing. In number 22, for example, Hamilton discusses the disadvantage for treaty enforcement of the lack of a judicial power in the Articles of Confederation; in 44, Madison refers to the judiciary as one of the institutions that would interpret legislation, but in *Federalist* 48 he reassures readers that the judiciary is safe because it is circumscribed by relatively certain "landmarks" in the constitution. In *Federalist* 73, Hamilton explains why the convention rejected an executive revisionary council including judges, saying that "the judges, who are to be interpreters of the law, might receive an improper bias from having given a previous opinion in their revisionary capacities" and that "by being often associated with the executive, they might be induced to embark too far in the political views of the magistrate, and thus a dangerous combination might arise between the executive and judiciary departments." This was the full extent of discussion of the judiciary in Federalist papers 1 through 77.

Yet the many papers before the judiciary series and the few after it were filled with discussion of constitutional interpretation, positing Congress, the executive, the states, and the people themselves as the primary players in defending the Constitution. For example, a number of papers pointed to other branches of the federal government as defenders of the Constitution and even as checks on the judiciary:

- *One of the most famous of the Federalist papers, Madison's number 51,* holds that the greatest security against constitutional usurpation and concentration of power "consists in giving to those who administer each department the necessary constitutional means and personal motives to resist the encroachments of the others."
- *Hamilton in* Federalist 66 *defends the impeachment and removal power of Congress* as "an essential check in the hands of that body upon the encroachments of the executive."

- *In number 71, Hamilton decries legislative usurpation,* and declares it "very difficult [though imperative] for the other members of the government to maintain the balance of the Constitution." Two papers later, Hamilton says the executive should not "be left to the mercy of the [legislature] but ought to possess a constitutional and effectual power of self-defense." To Hamilton, the executive veto was that power, and was meant to prevent encroachment "upon the rights of other members of the government . . . an institution calculated to restrain the excesses of lawmaking" chiefly designed to defeat "an immediate attack upon the constitutional rights of the executive." However, Hamilton in number 77 reminds readers that abuse of executive authority would likewise be "subjected to control by a branch of the legislative body."
- *In Federalist 79, Hamilton points out that* "the precautions for [judicial] responsibility are comprised in the article respecting impeachments," meaning that judicial "malconduct"—presumably including constitutional usurpation, as in the case of the president—is subject to check by Congress. In number 81, Hamilton elaborates on the "important constitutional check" on the judiciary of the congressional power of impeachment and removal, which gives to Congress "the means of punishing their presumption by degrading them from their stations." In Hamilton's view, this power was so formidable as to make a "phantom" of the "supposed danger of judiciary encroachments on the legislative authority."
- *In Federalist 80, another check upon the Supreme Court is extolled:* The "exceptions clause" allowing Congress to delineate exceptions to the appellate jurisdiction of the Court. Hamilton declares that "If some partial inconveniences should appear" regarding the powers of the judiciary, "it ought to be recollected that the national legislature will have ample authority to make such *exceptions* and to prescribe such regulations as will be calculated to avoid general mischiefs and to obtain general advantages."
- In another set of papers, Publius calls attention to the capacity and responsibility of the states to guard against violations of the Constitution. In this view, the states served an active balancing role against the danger of overcentralization of power:
- *In Federalist 17,* Hamilton argues that the states "will be able effectually to oppose all encroachments of the federal government."
- "I am unable to conceive," Madison reports in *Federalist 55,* "that the State legislatures, which must feel so many motives to watch and which

possess so many means of counteracting the federal legislature, would fail either to detect or to defeat a conspiracy against the liberties of their common constituents."

- The final paper in the series, number 85, addresses the amendment process. Hamilton avers that "We may safely rely on the disposition of the State legislatures to erect barriers against the encroachments of the national authority."

As the final authority on the Constitution, the people as a whole were expected to actively support it and block usurpations, even by force if necessary. Notably absent were expectations that ordinary citizens would simply leave defense of the Constitution up to assorted experts, judicial or otherwise:

- In Federalist 33, Hamilton contends that

  [T]he national government, like every other, must judge, in the first instance, of the proper exercise of its powers, and its constituents in the
  last. If the federal government should overpass the just bounds of its authority and make a tyrannical use of its powers, the people, whose creature it is, must appeal to the standard they have formed, and take such
  measures to redress the injury done to the Constitution as the exigency
  may suggest and prudence justify.

- In Federalist 49, Madison refers to Jefferson's argument that "The several departments being perfectly co-ordinate by the terms of their common commission, neither of them, it is evident, can pretend to an exclusive or superior right of settling the boundaries between them." He is un-willing to follow Jefferson's advice to frequently refer constitutional is-sues to the people themselves, but he does say that "a constitutional road to the decision of the people ought to be marked out and kept open, for certain great and extraordinary occasions." (Notably, Madi-son does not deny Jefferson's assessment of the coordinate nature of the branches.)

- In number 70, Hamilton argues that the constitutional safety of the execu-tive is advanced by both undiluted responsibility and

  a due dependence on the people . . . [T]he plurality of the executive
  tends to deprive the people of the two greatest securities they can have
  for the faithful exercise of any delegated power, first, the restraints of
  public opinion . . . and second, the opportunity of discovering with fa-
  cility and clearness the misconduct of the persons they trust, in order

either to their removal from office or to their actual punishment in cases which admit of it.

- In Federalist 84, *Hamilton explains the absence of a Bill of Rights* in the original Constitution by, among other things, pointing to the centrality of the people in the maintenance of rights, whether constitutionally specified or not: The security of liberty, "whatever fine declarations may be inserted in any constitution respecting it, must altogether depend on public opinion, and on the general spirit of the people and of the government." In an October 1788 letter to Thomas Jefferson, Madison conceded the possible utility of a Bill of Rights, not for the power it would give to courts to uphold the rights of the people but rather, primarily, for the educational effect it would have on the people. "The political truths declared in that solemn manner," Madison contended, "acquire by degrees the character of fundamental maxims of free government, and as they become incorporated with the national sentiment, counteract the impulses of interest and passion."[19]

Not infrequently, Publius combines discussion of two or more of the nonjudicial actors whose vigilance is necessary for the preservation of the Constitution. For example, Madison, in number 44, proclaims that the success of any constitutional usurpation by Congress "will depend on the executive and judiciary departments, which are to expound and give effect to the legislative acts; and in the last resort, a remedy must be obtained from the people, who can, by the election of more faithful representatives, annul the acts of the usurpers."

Two papers later, Madison posits the people and the states together as a crucial barrier to tyranny:

Let a regular army, fully equal to the resources of the country, be formed; and let it be entirely at the devotion of the federal government: still it would not be going too far to say that the State governments with the people on their side would be able to repel the danger. . . . Besides the advantage of being armed, which the Americans possess over the people of almost every other nation, the existence of subordinate governments, to which the people are attached and by which the militia officers are appointed, forms a barrier against the enterprises of ambition, more insurmountable than any which a simple government of any form can admit.

Likewise, a tyranny established by the Senate—a fear of the antifederalists—is dismissed in *Federalist* 63 when Madison holds that such a revolution could not take place unless the Senate corrupted in turn the state legislatures, the House of Representatives, and the people at large, who would instead likely defend the Constitution and their liberty.

Altogether, in instance after instance, Publius places a significant measure of responsibility for the maintenance of the Constitution in the hands of the elected branches of the federal government, in the state governments, and ultimately in the people. The supposition that the Supreme Court possesses that field of action solely—or even predominantly—is not consistent with this body of work. Other Federalists, writing or speaking in other venues, concurred. "A Citizen of New Haven," writing in support of ratification, argued that, "The judiciary department is perhaps the most difficult to be precisely limited by the constitution, but congress have full power to regulate it by law. . . ."[20] James Wilson, speaking in Pennsylvania, similarly contended that "the proceedings of the supreme court are to be regulated by the congress, which is a faithful representation of the people."[21]

Even Hamilton's exposition on judicial review in *Federalist* 78 contained numerous implicit caveats. First, judicial power was only legitimate when it was not fused with executive or legislative power. While his primary concern was that a feeble judiciary would be subsumed in practice under another branch, the reverse would be equally troubling. Further, Hamilton argues, judicial power lost legitimacy whenever it began to reflect "WILL, not JUDGEMENT." The ability of courts to strike down statutes that violate the Constitution does not "suppose a superiority of the judicial to the legislative power. It only supposes that the power of the people [and their Constitution] is superior to both." In the end, the judicial branch was the weakest of the three, Hamilton argued, because it lacked the power of the purse possessed by Congress and the power of the sword held by the executive. In other words, it cannot enforce its own decisions. Such a situation only constitutes weakness, however, if Congress and the executive are willing to consider not enforcing court decisions. The relative weakness of courts alleged by Hamilton is only an accurate appraisal if the other branches maintain their own capacity to interpret the Constitution and maintain the option of defending their own interpretations over those of the court.

Indeed, Hamilton's discussion, far from representing a bold assertion of judicialism, should be read in the context of antifederalist arguments against the federal judicial power. The antifederalist "Brutus," for example, complains that the federal courts

> will give the sense of every article of the constitution, that may from time to time come before them. And in their decisions they will not confine themselves

to any fixed or established rules, but will determine, according to what appears to them, the reason and spirit of the constitution. The opinions of the supreme court, whatever they may be, will have the force of law; because there is no power provided in the constitution, that can correct their errors, or control their adjudications. From this court there is no appeal . . . there is no power above them, to control any of their decisions. There is no authority that can remove them, and they cannot be controlled by the laws of the legislature. In short, they are independent of the people, of the legislature, and of every power under heaven. Men placed in this situation will generally soon feel themselves independent of heaven itself.[22]

Hamilton's rejoinder was hence both an explanation of the necessity of an independent judiciary in a constitutional republic and an attempt to assure readers that such a judiciary was not dangerous because it was hemmed in by other institutions and by the norms of restrained conduct that would guide it. Thus it might be said that the antifederalists anticipated judicialism but deplored it, while the Federalists denied that their system would produce it. Neither side embraced it.

Evidence for this proposition can be further inferred by the history of judicial review for many years after the founding. Indeed, from 1789 through 1864, only two congressional enactments and thirty-nine state laws were struck down through the agency of this mechanism. During the debate over the Alien and Sedition Acts in the late 1790s, five state legislatures held that the federal judiciary had exclusive authority to decide on the constitutionality of congressional acts.[23] However, Thomas Jefferson and James Madison asserted the right of states to declare federal acts null and void (in the Kentucky and Virginia Resolutions). While the Kentucky and Virginia Resolutions are usually viewed preeminently as documents advancing states' rights, they can as easily be seen as a refutation of judicialism. Jefferson relied on the states—not the Supreme Court—to vindicate the Constitution.[24] Madison's declaration, which states that "The General Assembly of Virginia doth unequivocally express a firm resolution to maintain and defend the Constitution of the United States,"[25] similarly declined to depend on the judiciary for the defense of rights. In 1800, in this national argument, it was Jefferson and Madison who won the day. Over the next quarter of a century, numerous states, mostly from the North, echoed the interpretation of Kentucky and Virginia. For example, the Ohio Resolve of 1820–21 declared that:

The committee are aware of the doctrine, that the Federal courts are exclusively vested with jurisdiction to declare, in the last resort, the true interpretation of the Constitution of the United States. To this doctrine, in the latitude contended for, they [Ohio legislators] never can give their assent . . . in great questions of political rights and political powers, a decision by the Supreme Court of the United States is not conclusive of the rights decided by it . . . this General Assembly do protest against the doctrine that the political rights of the separate States that compose the American Union, and their powers as sovereign states, may be settled and determined in the Supreme Court of the United States. . . .[26]

A decade later, a nullification crisis with South Carolina nearly brought civil war, while Andrew Jackson and Congress flatly ignored a Supreme Court ruling on Indian resettlement (with Jackson, perhaps apocryphally, reported as saying "[Chief Justice] Marshall has made his decision, now let him enforce it"). In the wake of the strong Jacksonian presidency, including vigorous use of the veto, the Whig Party derived much of its energy from a denunciation of that presidency as not only unwise but unconstitutional. In the aftermath of the *Dred Scott* decision, Abraham Lincoln argued that Supreme Court decisions were binding upon the parties in that particular case but not necessarily in any other similar case. He further argued that, since the court could err, citizens and their elected representatives must retain the right to work for a reversal. Otherwise, Lincoln argued in his first inaugural address, "the people will have ceased to be their own rulers, having to that extent practically resigned their government into the hands of that eminent tribunal."[27] Altogether, the period immediately following the founding, and in which political actors were most conversant with the mandates of the founding, saw courts reluctant to assert primacy in constitutional interpretation and elected officials equally reluctant to concede that primacy.

Aside from the ambivalence toward judicial power evident at the founding, two difficulties can be raised more abstractly to call into question the wisdom of allowing the federal courts a monopoly on constitutional interpretation. First, it is plainly contrary to the spirit of republicanism to place a claim of infallibility in any political institution devised and operated by human beings.[28] Indeed, the history of the Court itself is replete with demonstrations of its fallibility: *Plessy v. Ferguson* and *Brown v. Board* cannot both be correct in their holdings regarding segregation, the court could not be error-free in its interpretations of what constituted legitimate federal power both before and after the 1937 "switch in time that saved nine," and the views of *Bowers v. Hardwick* and *Lawrence v. Texas* on state antisodomy laws cannot be reconciled. Few would argue against the duty of the Court to check obvious legislative assaults on the Constitution, but in the doctrine of judicialism no one is assigned the task of checking the Court when it goes astray. This proposition is incompatible with the genius of the American system, which seeks to avoid the unchecked concentration of power in any hands in "a government which is to be administered by men over men" rather than by angels.[29] The aftermath of the 2000 presidential election forced Americans on both the left and the right to reexamine, at least for a brief moment, the assumptions of judicial infallibility underlying judicialism. On the right, calls were heard for the Florida legislature to override the pro-Gore decisions of the Florida Supreme Court, while laments were widely heard on the left about the U.S. Supreme Court's two decisions upholding George W. Bush's position.

The second scenario is not judicial usurpation but judicial neglect. Just as judicialism gives the political system no means to deal with courts that are consistently and aggressively in error—indeed, its most radical presumption is that the courts by definition cannot err because the Constitution is simply whatever the courts say it is—it gives members of the elected branches no resources with which to fill the breach if the federal courts are insufficiently active and simply refuse to exercise their power to enforce the Constitution. May Congress or the president simply disregard the constitutional implications of their actions because the courts have lost interest in defending a particular aspect of the Constitution? Judicialism would imply that the answer is yes, but the oath of office sworn by members of the legislative and executive branches—that they will positively defend the Constitution—would seem to say no. Chief Justice Earl Warren, who left a legacy that did much to bolster judicialism, nevertheless noted that the fact that the Supreme Court holds that a governmental activity is constitutional "does not necessarily answer the question of whether, in a broader sense, it actually is."[30] Furthermore, there are certain areas of constitutional dispute—particularly, but not exclusively, those having to do with relations between coequal branches—in which the federal courts have refused to intervene, not as a matter of neglect but as a matter of well-considered and deliberate self-restraint, utilizing the so-called "political questions" doctrine. It is hardly sufficient in those disputes to hold that the elected branches should stay out of the job of constitutional interpretation.

Interpreting and Enforcing the Constitution: Congress and President

There are also practical reasons to doubt the efficacy of judicialism as a theory of constitutional interpretation. Most importantly, there are a variety of ways that Congress and the president, due to their constitutional powers, can and often do engage in constitutional definition.[31]

There are at least six broad areas in which the action or inaction of Congress can define the Constitution independently, or largely independently, of judicial activity, and hence have the potential to bring the Constitution into electoral campaigns.

1. *Initiation of constitutional amendments.* Such amendments typically have one of four objectives: to structurally change the institutions or powers of American government; to add to the rights guaranteed individuals under the federal Constitution; to write particular policy preferences into the Constitution; and to undo Supreme Court decisions and restore the constitutional status quo ante. Only rarely does Congress succeed in the latter, but it often tries; and both the Sixteenth Amendment allowing the income tax and the Twenty-sixth Amendment mandating the eighteen-year-old vote are the result of such efforts.

2. *Appointment confirmation by the Senate.* Most commonly, this means hearings, debate, and votes in the United States Senate on presidential appointments to the federal bench, with obvious constitutional implications. The Senate must also confirm presidential appointments to executive branch positions such as attorney general and other high-ranking officers in the Department of Justice, civil rights deputies in several other departments, and, occasionally, a handful of other officials who are brought into the constitutional spotlight due to peculiar circumstances of the moment.[32]

3. *Congressional legislative action regarding individual rights, such as issues involving police powers, civil rights, and property rights.* As scholar John Dinan has demonstrated, throughout the 1800s the legislative branch (even at the state level) was considered the primary venue for the defense and advancement of rights.[33] The First Amendment of the Bill of Rights opens with the phrase "Congress shall make no law," and other amendments imply the prohibition. While courts may ultimately rule on whether Congress has overstepped those bounds, Congress itself faces that question first. In recent years, important legislation requiring an interpretation of individual rights has included the Religious Freedom Restoration Act, passed in response to a Supreme Court decision the congressional majority found disagreeable, the PATRIOT antiterrorism act of 2001, and the ban on partial-birth abortions passed in 2003.

4. *Congressional legislative action regarding the scope of federal authority.*
Specifically, this means Congress choosing how to read the enumerated
powers of Article I, Section 8. Almost always, the issue of federalism is
part of this debate, since an expansion of the boundaries of federal authority nearly always results in shrinking the residual powers held by
the states. The essential question is whether the enumerated powers
and the Tenth Amendment should be read as significantly limiting the
legislative authority of Congress, or whether the necessary and proper
clause and the general welfare clause give Congress something approaching carte blanche. (Some advocates of activist government even
argue that those clauses are irrelevant, as expansive federal powers are
inherent and residual.) The record indicates that the framers as a collective group did not share the latter reading.[34] Nevertheless, even at
the beginning, the precise boundaries laid out in the enumeration of
powers were subject to reasonable debate (with Hamilton, for example,
promoting a broader view of the necessary and proper clause, the general welfare clause, and more generally, the implied and inherent powers of the government). Even though the doctrine of enumerated powers fell on hard times in the mid-twentieth century, there has been in
recent years both a political revival (observable in elections in 1980,
1984, and 1994) and a limited judicial revival (seen in cases like *Lopez*
and *Morrison*) of enumerated powers as a principle possessing some
force. On the other side of the equation, the meaning and requirements of federalism have likewise remained a consistent source of debate since the 1790s. For the most part, "After the New Deal, the
Court generally let Congress define the boundaries of its own authority by refusing to read constitutional grants of power as limits on legislative power,"[35] thus putting these questions of constitutional definition almost wholly in the hands of the elected branches. More
generally, as regards both rights and federal authority, Congressman
Theodore Sedgwick of Massachusetts contended that "the whole business of legislation is a practical construction of the Constitution."[36]

5. *Impeachment and removal.* Congress wields the impeachment and removal power against members of the executive and judicial branches.
Exercise of this power requires one form of constitutional debate and
can involve, but does not necessarily require, a second form. First,
Congress is entirely on its own in coming to terms with the constitutionally correct grounds and procedures for use of this power. When
Bill Clinton faced impeachment, much of the debate centered on the
question of whether his actions met the constitutional standard of im-

peachment and removal. Second, because purported abuse of constitutional authority by members of the executive or judicial branches can serve as one justification for impeachment, Congress might engage in debate over the proper extent of that authority. In 1867, Andrew Johnson's impeachment and trial featured a debate over whether the president inherently possessed the power of removing executive branch appointees.

6. *Attempts by Congress to limit the power of the federal judiciary by statutory means*. This can include legislation defining judicial process, like restricting the use of court injunctions. More controversially, it can take the form of congressional refusal to appropriate funds for the executive enforcement of Supreme Court decisions (Jimmy Carter vetoed an appropriations bill in 1980 that prohibited spending money to enforce school busing) or legislation limiting the appellate jurisdiction of the Supreme Court in accordance with Article III, Section 2. This latter device has been considered by Congress in recent years on subjects such as busing, school prayer, same-sex marriage, and the pledge of allegiance. Between 1953 and 1968, in the era of Warren Court activism, over sixty "court-stripping" bills were introduced in Congress.[37]

In practice, a current line of thinking holds that Congress is usually deferential to the courts, that it does not possess all the intellectual resources it needs to challenge the courts regularly, but that it possesses the resources to challenge the courts selectively and will do so. As scholars have shown, a bill's opponents are more likely to use constitutional arguments than its supporters, and the chances of such arguments being raised in Congress are increased when committees or individual members take a strong interest in some constitutional question, when debate is wrapped around highly salient Supreme Court cases, or when the underlying politics push in that direction. Activism by the Supreme Court is a stronger prod to congressional action than perceived neglect.[38]

Several studies have been done of congressional attitudes toward the Constitution over the last four decades. These have generally found that a two-to-one majority of members of Congress do not believe, as an abstract proposition, that Congress should simply defer to the courts. Most believe that when constitutional arguments are raised in Congress, they are bona fide issues rather than a political ploy. Interestingly, these percentages have gone up in recent years, not down.[39]

There are also numerous areas in which presidents might contribute to interpretation of the Constitution.

1. *The executive veto was granted explicitly* as a means of defending the presidency from constitutional incursions by Congress, as well as to aid in the defense of the rights of the people. For the first decades of the Republic, presidents were much more likely to use their veto for constitutional reasons than for any other purpose. From George Washington through Andrew Jackson, roughly three out of every four vetoes were issued for constitutional reasons. Indeed, one of the great party divisions in American history was driven in large part by Jackson's veto of the national bank bill largely on constitutional grounds—even after the Supreme Court had ruled the bank constitutionally permissible. From Jackson through the Civil War, a solid majority of vetoes continued to be wielded on constitutional grounds, and much debate swirled around the question of whether it was even legitimate for presidents to veto bills on grounds of mere policy disagreement. After Andrew Johnson, the constitutional motivation for vetoes fell off dramatically, and from 1889 to recent times, only one in twenty vetoes were justified by reference to a constitutional reason.[40] (Even when presidents do not veto bills because of constitutional objections, though, they can insert such concerns into their signing messages, thus making those concerns part of the official record.)

2. *Like the Senate's role in appointment confirmation*, the president's role in appointments often carries constitutional freight. This is obviously true in federal court appointments. Some executive branch appointments also give the president the opportunity to advance a particular constitutional view.

3. *Presidents must, on frequent occasions, choose how they are going to interpret their own powers* when those powers are either vaguely worded or "exist" only in the wide spaces between things explicitly allowed and things explicitly prohibited. Presidents have dramatically changed their status in the American system by pushing these powers to their outer limits.[41]

4. *Presidents can take account of constitutional issues* as they exercise their executive function of enforcing the law, a function central to their office and grounded in the "Take Care" clause. It is this power of enforcement held by the executive branch that is largely responsible for Hamilton's assessment in *Federalist* 78 that the judiciary was the weakest branch of the federal government. Andrew Jackson's refusal to enforce the Supreme Court's Cherokee resettlement decision is a classic example of the use (or nonuse) of this power to check the judiciary and advance an alternative constitutional interpretation. While Jackson's

action is more often than not condemned today, the willingness of presidents to take that step is arguably essential to maintaining balance among the branches. In less dramatic ways, presidential administrations must choose how and with what vigor to enforce statutes and judicial decisions that may leave room for alternative constitutional interpretations. Presidents Eisenhower, Kennedy, and Johnson exercised considerable discretion in the vigor with which they attempted to enforce the famed *Brown v. Board of Education* desegregation decision, and Bill Clinton was noticeably lax in enforcing *Beck v. Communications Workers of America*, a 1992 ruling that ordered unions to publicize to their members that they could opt out of the portion of their dues used for political purposes.

There are, finally, a number of other ways in which both of the elected branches, either jointly or separately, can influence constitutional understanding and application.

Constitutional interpretation can come to the fore of both congressional and presidential action when the two elected branches are engaged in disputes over the proper location of the boundary between their powers. In those cases, the first constitutional debate takes place outside of the Supreme Court chambers; in most cases, it is the only debate. Such separation of powers questions, which attend issues as far-ranging as war powers, regulatory delegation, spending impoundment, the legislative veto, and executive privilege, can be extremely heated. Furthermore, the Supreme Court, appealing to the "political questions" doctrine, has frequently left these sorts of questions to the combat of the branches directly involved. This has meant not only that the elected branches are *allowed* to sort out these issues for themselves, but also that they usually have little choice. When the two elected branches come into sustained conflict, Congress has historically held the upper hand, though the president can also serve to initiate debate over constitutional change.[42] Even when the courts intervene, the elected branches can conspire to ignore them. When the Supreme Court ruled the legislative veto unconstitutional in 1983 in *Chadha v. INS*, Congress and the executive soon had passed another two hundred-plus bills with legislative veto provisions.[43]

Supreme Court decisions can be attacked or supported by either of the elected branches, and these views can affect the use of their powers. For example, as noted, Congress can use its position in the constitutional amendment process to try to reverse court decisions it does not like, or it can use its power to limit judicial power for the same end. Presidents can use their appointment power to try to change the composition of the Court in hopes that a new Court will either solidify or overturn past precedents. Both may use rhetorical criticism or support of Court decisions as a means of building electoral coalitions and putting pressure on the court.

The conduct of foreign policy by both the president and Congress (especially the Senate) helps to define the limits of U.S. sovereignty. This is particularly true in relation to the negotiation and ratification of treaties, economic agreements, and agreements to place the United States under one sort of international regime or another, whether legal or organizational. In each of these cases, the potential exists for the elected branches to voluntarily cede some portion of what might be considered U.S. sovereignty under the Constitution, especially in the modern system of collective security, important international organizations, and further development of international law.

In the course of resolving these issues, the president and members of Congress may rely upon—and may even participate in developing—a more general theory of the proper manner of interpreting the Constitution, though they do not have to. Typically, these theories call for either a strict or broad interpretation of the Constitution, and they can be applied to virtually any of the more specific issues cited above. Indeed, the legislative and executive powers listed above can be brought to bear to actively advance such principles. At varying points in American history, it has been not uncommon for the political parties to define themselves at least partly by reference to these general theories.

Least substantively, the very place of the elected branches in the constitutional system invites the president and members of Congress to stress their devotion to the Constitution. In particular, the president's oath of office gives him the opportunity (and, some might say, the duty) to stake out a role as a rhetorical spokesman for and defender of the Constitution.

Altogether, there are strong reasons, both theoretical and practical, why the elected branches of the federal government are and should be integral to the interpretation, application, and defense of the Constitution. Because the elected branches can exert control or influence over wide areas of constitutional development and interpretation, candidates for federal office frequently have the opportunity to bring these issues to the fore in electoral politics.

Indeed, in several early elections constitutional questions were central. In 1800, the Jeffersonian Republicans gained power in an election characterized by deep divisions over the proper interpretation of the young Constitution. Key issues included the constitutionality of the Alien and Sedition Acts, the proper constitutional bounds of executive authority, the breadth of the enumerated powers, and the role of the states in the federal system. As Max Lerner notes, "Both parties showed an amazing unanimity in pointing out the perfections of the Constitution; they delighted in honoring it, and they measured their distance from each other by reciprocal charges of violating it and departing from its spirit."[44] Elections in the Jacksonian era likewise revolved around questions of the constitutionality of the second national bank and the proper role of the executive in the constitutional system.

The very first paragraph of the very first national party platform—the Democratic platform of 1840—staked out a constitutional position, holding, "That the federal government is one of limited powers, derived solely from the constitution, and the grants of power shown therein, ought to be strictly construed by all the departments and agents of the government, and that it is inexpedient and dangerous to exercise doubtful constitutional powers."[45] Indeed, eight of the nine paragraphs of that first platform focused on constitutional issues of one sort or another. Fast-forwarding to 2004, the presidential candidates sparred over future Supreme Court appointments, the constitutional status of abortion, a proposed constitutional amendment banning same-sex marriage, and the civil liberties implications of the antiterrorism PATRIOT Act.

What has happened to constitutional rhetoric from internal improvements to same-sex marriage will occupy the remainder of the book. The fact that the elected branches can, and even should, take an ongoing interest in constitutional matters does not tell us how often they do or in what manner. As we will see, starting with party platforms, the answers point toward a polity that has been gradually but substantially deconstitutionalized. But it is not so simple.

CHAPTER TWO

~

The Constitution
in the Party Platforms

The major parties have been issuing platforms extolling their principles, proposals, and accomplishments since 1840, when the Democratic National Convention submitted to the public a nine-paragraph statement of party views. In a certain respect, the platform serves as the baseline of presidential campaigning. Among the campaign communications studied here, it is the only one that retained a consistent form throughout the period studied. The platform began as a written appeal and is still a written appeal.

Despite the longevity of the platform as a campaign tool and the long maintenance of its basic form, its character has changed significantly since 1840. Platforms have grown much longer, reaching more than 41,000 words in the 2004 Republican platform. In substance, they have become progressively less concerned with principles and more concerned with specific policy issues and proposals. And, where once they served as a statement of party direction that both preceded the selection of the presidential nominee and bound him, they are now largely dictated by the presumptive presidential nominee, in negotiation with varying factions of the party. (Though it should be noted that the very earliest platforms were often written after the nomination was determined, with the nominee in mind.[1]) As the platforms have grown longer and more tedious, they have played a less central role in campaigns. Indeed, in 1996, Republican nominee Bob Dole confessed that even he had not read his party's platform in its entirety. It may well be that what distinguished Dole from the bulk of contemporary party nominees was not his negligence but his candor.

Nevertheless, the platforms provide a strong indication of the issues of the day, the political tenor of the times, and the views of the party elites (including the presidential candidates and their close circle) whose negotiations produce them. For example, a study of the platform-writing process in 1992 concluded that platform committee appointments "were highly sought and bitterly fought over," and that the two key criteria during platform drafting were that the presidential candidate was comfortable with the result and that the platform give special attention to groups deemed essential to the formation of a winning coalition in November.[2]

Furthermore, there is much evidence that presidential candidates take their promises seriously, and that platforms remain a credible guide to what parties will do (or try to do) once they gain office. For those reasons alone, they remain an important indicator of what is or is not on the public agenda. In an extensive study of major-party platforms from 1944 to 1964, Gerald C. Pomper concludes that no more than one-quarter of platform text was devoted to "rhetoric." Only four of the twelve platforms had a majority of "nonrational" statements, including (according to Pomper's definition) mere rhetoric and vague pledges, approbation, or criticism.[3] The remainder—a majority in eight of twelve cases and a total of 52 percent of all platform statements in that period—consisted of fairly specific statements of policy approval or disapproval, pledges of continuity or action, and expression of goals or concerns.[4] Jeff Fishel, after undertaking a review of presidential promises in the years 1960–1984, reached the conclusion that those promises are a reasonably good guide to how presidents and their parties will act when in power, not only because the promises are often specific but also because there is a high level of performance by winning candidates.[5] A variety of other studies demonstrate the same thing. Looking at functional categories of the platform like defense, labor, and agriculture, winners made a good-faith effort to carry out up to 91 percent of their specific promises and no fewer than 54 percent.[6]

Even if the platforms as a whole are now read by few citizens, they still are summarized, excerpted, and analyzed by the media and by the campaigns themselves as they seek to sway specialized groups. Altogether, L. Sandy Maisel declares the party platform, despite its low readership, to be "the most important document that a political party produces";[7] to Gerald Pomper, it "most fully represents the party's intentions. . . . If platforms are indeed meaningless, it seems odd that they should occasion, as they have, severe intra-party disagreement, as well as the attention of interest groups, mass media and practical politicians."[8] A total of eighty-three of these major-party documents from 1840 to 2004 were read and coded for this analysis.[9]

What Platforms Said about the Constitution

Historically, there has been a significant amount of constitutional rhetoric in party platforms, spread widely across several categories. Clearly, the parties have not shied away from making constitutional arguments or discussing constitutional issues in their election-year summary of principles and programs. The capacity of the elected branches to influence constitutional questions has indeed led to the frequent interjection of those questions into campaigns. However, the content of that rhetoric has varied considerably from one election to the next depending upon the issues of the day and the constitutional ethos of the age, and rhetoric has been far from evenly spread; some constitutional issues have generally been neglected. Each category of constitutional rhetoric is examined below, in descending order of consistency (or the frequency with which it appears across years).

Individual Rights

From beginning to end, no topic was mentioned more consistently, or at greater depth. References to individual rights found their way into 95 percent of Democratic platforms and 90 percent of Republican platforms. Furthermore, in thirty of forty-two Democratic platforms and twenty-nine of forty-one Republican platforms, those references accounted for 30 percent or more of all constitutional references. Individual rights was actually the single biggest category in thirty Democratic and twenty-six Republican platforms.

In the earliest years of this study, such references tended to focus on "equality of rights" and generic dangers to "the liberties of the people" or "the rights of the people." This general call for the defense of the people's rights was seldom completely absent from the constitutional rhetoric of party platforms for the next century and a half. The 1852 Democrats amplified this theme by pledging to "sustain and advance among us constitutional liberty, by continuing to resist all monopolies and exclusive legislation for the benefit of the few at the expense of the many."[10]

In the next phase, which overlapped the first, major-party platforms began extolling specific rights like "entire freedom in matters of religious concernment"[11] (an 1856 Democratic response to the rise of the "Know-Nothings"). As the Republican Party supplanted the Whigs, its platforms were filled with appeals to the natural rights proclaimed in the Declaration of Independence and secured by the Constitution. Republicans, too, appealed to specific constitutional rights, like the right to keep and bear arms, rights to due process and impartial jury trial, freedom of speech and press, and security of individuals in their persons and property, all of which 1856 Republicans claimed had been violated in Kansas by federal authority. Both Democrats and Republicans came out for full protection of the constitutional rights of immigrants.

These themes endured, with Democrats accusing Republicans in 1864 and during Reconstruction of doing what Republicans had accused Democrats of doing to Kansas in 1856. Post–Civil War Republicans vowed to enforce the Thirteenth, Fourteenth, and Fifteenth Amendments and to ensure equality of rights under the law regardless of race. Interpretation or refinement of the Establishment Clause of the First Amendment became an issue in the late 1800s, with Republicans backing a national version of the so-called Blaine Amendments prohibiting government funding of sectarian education. Democrats, for their part, called freedom of education "an essential of civil and religious liberty" and "opposed state interference with parental rights and rights of conscience."[12] In the same period both parties gave some attention to the "freedom of the suffrage" (1880 Republicans) and the "right to a free ballot"[13] (1880 Democrats).

With the rise of industrial capitalism, late nineteenth-century platforms reemphasized older themes like equality of rights under the law. They also reaffirmed the right of property and, for the first time, endorsed the "strict enforcement of individual rights against corporate abuses."[14] The protection of the constitutional rights of labor became a theme of both parties' platforms around the turn of the century.

In the twentieth century, platforms took up individual rights issues like extension of the franchise to women, blacks, and citizens between eighteen and twenty-one. In the aftermath of World War I, as in the aftermath of the Civil War, the party out of power devoted considerable space in its platform to attacking the incumbent administration for curtailing individual rights. The party in power responded to these charges by defending its conduct and asserting its fidelity to the great principles of free speech and a free press. The 1920 Republican platform laid down a marker in its first paragraph: "The Republican Party, assembled in representative national convention, reaffirms its unyielding devotion to the Constitution of the United States, and to the guaranties of civil, political, and religious liberty therein contained."[15] Democrats responded by saying, "We resent the unfounded reproaches directed against the Democratic administration for alleged interference with the freedom of the press and freedom of speech."[16]

Democrats continued emphasizing equality under the law as opposed to special economic privilege, Republicans equality under the law as opposed to special racial privilege. Both declared for women's political equality, a stand that culminated in both parties' endorsement of an Equal Rights Amendment in the 1940s. Both regularly declared fealty to fundamental civil liberties found in the Bill of Rights. In 1928, Democrats demanded freedom of speech for the new medium of radio, reflecting a concern about government control of the airwaves that was repeated in both parties' platforms from time to time over the next three-quarters of a century.

These themes could be seen both before and after the onset of the New Deal. At the height of New Deal activism, however, the Republican platforms of 1936 and 1940 painted a broader picture, warning the nation of a threat to its fundamental liberties from an administration grown too powerful. "Instead of the Blessings of Liberty," the Republican platform held in 1940, "the Administration has imposed upon us a Regime of Regimentation which has deprived the individual of his freedom and has made of America a shackled giant."[17] These Republican charges reappeared in 1952.

As war once again loomed in 1940, the maintenance of civil liberties during moments of national peril drew renewed comment in the party platforms. This concern would not fully abate until the end of the Cold War some five decades later, and resurfaced with vigor in the 2004 election. At the same time, in the 1940s Democratic platforms began to call for equality of rights for blacks in a more than perfunctory way. Although their 1948 platform fight over Harry Truman's civil rights plank is legendary, Democrats used language that moved in that direction beginning in 1940, when their platform declared that "We pledge to uphold due process and the equal protection of the laws for every citizen, regardless of race, creed, or color."[18]

Civil rights increasingly took center stage as *Brown v. Board* and the burgeoning civil rights movement demanded a response. Both parties in 1956 and 1960 called for stiffer federal protection of black voting rights, obedience to court-ordered desegregation, and greater moves toward equality under the law. Democrats took pride in the Civil Rights Act of 1964, while Republicans pledged its "full implementation and faithful execution,"[19] despite Barry Goldwater's "no" vote on the floor of the Senate. Clearly, parties can use constitutional language to appeal to different constituencies, and Republicans here may have been trying to hold out something for both the Southern vote and their own Northern liberals (though Goldwater may also have simply voted against the Civil Rights Act on principle but been intent on enforcing it once it passed, also on principle).

Republicans in 1964 also began homing in on difficult, newly emergent social issues with implications for individual rights, calling for a constitutional amendment to overturn the Supreme Court's 1962 anti-school-prayer decisions and for legislation to curb the flow of obscene materials through the mail. These planks were a sign of things to come. In 1968, exploding crime and gun control joined the list of hot social issues, and both parties addressed the question of how to fight crime without unduly impinging on civil liberties. At the same time, Democratic platforms undertook a subtle shift away from "equality of rights under the law" to "equal justice under the law," a rubric which called forth greater protection of the rights of minority defendants, including stronger guarantees of public counsel. From 1968 through the 1970s, both parties expressed concern over threats to individual privacy posed by governmental or even private computerized databases, a concern that ultimately led in the 1990s to restrictions on the sharing of consumer data.

The Nixon years and their aftermath also called forth increasing Democratic attacks on wiretapping, harassment, and other government abuses against dissenters. The 1972 McGovern platform was filled with admonitions for prisoners' rights, dissenters' rights, and the rights of the accused. Civil rights questions shifted from basic civil rights guarantees to subsidiary policies like quotas and forced busing. For the remainder of the century, much of the platforms' discussion of individual rights revolved around the parties' reactions to novel judicial interpretations of the First Amendment (religion, flag-burning, obscenity), the Eighth Amendment (death penalty), the Fourteenth Amendment (affirmative action), and assorted penumbras (abortion, gay rights).

As important as the new issues were, and as much as they mobilized party activists, they never completely supplanted a number of longstanding themes, including pro forma affirmation of support for the Bill of Rights and other procedural safeguards, protection of civil liberties during war or crisis, and endorsement of some concept of equal rights.

From the beginning, individual rights were about as likely to be discussed in implicit as in explicit terms. Indeed, in the late nineteenth century, explicit references accounted for three of ten individual rights references, or fewer. However, in the twentieth century, there was some movement back in the direction of openly constitutional discussion of individual rights. Despite declining rates of explicit references overall, twelve party platforms since 1936 saw more explicit than implicit mentions of rights. In another two, explicit references were either tied with or only slightly behind implicit references.[20] On balance, discussion of individual rights in major-party platforms has been consistent, deep, and relatively open.

Federalism

The second most consistently referenced category of constitutional rhetoric was federalism, which found its way into 91 percent of Democratic and 78 percent of Republican platforms. Since 1936, 100 percent of Republican platforms and 94 percent of Democratic platforms have mentioned federalism. Early platforms often expounded general theories of federalism or declared for states' rights in the abstract. Democrats proclaimed that "states are the sole and proper judges of everything appertaining to their own affairs, not prohibited by the constitution."[21] Republicans in 1860, doubtless responding to criticism on this score, declared that "the Federal Constitution, the rights of the states, and the union of the states, must be preserved."[22] Post–Civil War Republicans also advanced a broad constitutional theory of federalism in their platforms, urging that "The United States of America is a nation, not a league,"[23] while their Democratic opponents decried centralization and favored local self-government and "the reserved rights of the States."[24]

These sorts of broad principles have remained common features of party platforms, though not uniformly across time. As late as 1924 and 1928, Democrats devoted a section of their platform to "The Rights of the States," demanding that "the constitutional rights and powers of the states shall be preserved in their full vigor and virtue. These constitute a bulwark against centralization and the destructive tendencies of the Republican Party. . . . [W]e demand a revival of the spirit of local self-government, without which free institutions cannot be preserved."[25] Republicans echoed those principles in 1928, arguing extensively in a section titled "Home Rule" that the federal government should zealously "respect and maintain the rights of the States and territories and . . . uphold the vigor and balance of our dual system of government. . . . [Efforts] to have the Federal Government move into the field of state activities, has never had, and never will have the support of the Republican Party."[26]

By 1936, the Republicans had become the party most likely to make broad statements of principle or to claim its opponents were trampling on the federal system. In that year, the GOP accused "the New Deal Administration" of constantly seeking to "usurp the rights reserved to the states and to the people,"[27] a theme it would repeat frequently over the next seven decades. In 1996, for instance, the Republican platform, which was arguably the most profederalism platform in either major party since the onset of the New Deal, bemoaned that the Tenth Amendment and other "constitutional tools given to the States to protect their role in the system have now been either eroded away, given away, or rendered impossible to use."[28] The proposed remedy—decentralization of power—took many forms, but from 1968 on consistently included proposals for block grants and devolution of programs back to the states.

Though Democrats deemphasized such notions, offering on occasion an alternative vision of federalism in which "state and local governments are strengthened—not weakened—by financial assistance from the Federal

Government"[29] (1960), as late as the 1950s they appealed to Jefferson and Jackson to "expressly recognize the vital importance of the respective States in our Federal Union."[30] Such broad sentiments did not recur after 1956. Clearly, the residual Jeffersonianism of the Democratic Party on this question took some time—nearly three decades—to dissolve, but it was finally completely supplanted by the imperative (as Democrats saw it) of national activism on economic questions and social questions like civil rights.

As the nineteenth century waned, another type of federalism reference gained ground: An increasing number of references crept into platforms assessing specific policy questions in terms of federalism. While proposing federal aid, the GOP acknowledged that "the work of popular education is one left to the care of the states."[31] Democrats assailed the Republicans' "usurpation of despotic control over elections in all the states" through the Force Bills of 1870 and 1871, which authorized the president to use federal troops to enforce Fifteenth Amendment black voting rights.[32] As the Progressive Era dawned, platforms addressed the federalism issues inherent in federal regulation of commerce, and in the question of whether federal rules should substitute for or complement state rules. Platforms became increasingly likely to affirm the congruence of new federal programs with the constitutional requirements of federalism. Both parties' platforms of 1912 proposed for the first time that, as Democrats put it, "control of the Mississippi River is a national problem" requiring a federal solution, and Republicans in 1916 argued the whole transportation system of the country "has become essentially national" and should be put under federal control, by constitutional amendment if necessary.[33]

Starting in 1932, varying platforms argued for or against federal responsibility for relief and other social programs, insurance regulation, pollution control, and voter registration procedures, as well as the state option for "right-to-work" laws built into the Taft-Hartley Act. They also gave a nod to federalism by urging greater federal activism in resource management and reclamation, nuclear waste disposal, education, mass transit, regional development, health care, urban renewal, and law enforcement, with stipulations that such activism be in keeping with the Constitution or subject to approval by state legislatures. Democrats in 1952 argued that they had designed numerous programs, including Selective Service, Social Security, the Agricultural Adjustment Administration, low-rent housing, and hospital programs, that "placed major responsibilities in States and counties."[34] In the mid-twentieth century, Republican platforms gave some consideration to the problem of taking care to avoid federal preemption of state revenue sources. For a couple of decades, civil rights became once again a question that was entangled in federalism concerns, though this was no longer obviously evident by 1964.

In the most recent years, there was a partial convergence of Democratic and Republican platforms regarding federalism. Democrats have not copied Republicans' sweeping pronouncements favoring principles of decentralization and states' rights, but they have called more modestly for state and local input and for restraint on unfunded mandates. Indeed, when Republicans gained control of all federal elected branches, 2004 Democrats vigorously condemned the unfunded mandates of the No Child Left Behind Act and defended the tradition of states' rights regarding family law (as they declared opposition to the federal marriage amendment). For their part, Republicans in 2004 toned down their abstract defense of federalism principles, and dramatically reduced the number of their federalism references.

Discussion of this constitutional principle is clearly influenced by the question of which party has the upper hand in the national government. As a cynic might expect, when Democrats lost their foothold at the national level, their appreciation for federalism grew; as Republicans gained in the corridors of central power, their concern for decentralization faltered. However, such an analysis is incomplete. The change in party power altered but did not reverse the parties' core values on federalism; even in 2004, Republicans were more likely to cite federalism than were Democrats.

Altogether, no category of constitutional rhetoric has been more thoroughly transformed into a predominantly implicit object of discussion. Since 1936, only one platform (1956 Democratic) contained more explicit than implicit federalism references, and only one other (1952 Democratic) had the same number of both kinds. All other major-party platforms since 1936 had more implicit than explicit references. Thus, while both individual rights and federalism are frequently mentioned, one cannot consider them equally prominent as constitutional issues in platforms. Federalism, which is inarguably central to the American constitutional structure and policymaking process and (if the founders were right) essential to the maintenance of American liberty, has been substantially relegated to a status as the constitutional principle that dare not speak its name. The fact that parties continue to discuss it, but generally in implicit terms, might be a clue that it is an issue more important to party activists (especially on the Republican side) than to the broader group of voters.

Constitutional Amendments

Constitutional amendments were mentioned in two-thirds of Republican platforms and three-quarters of Democratic platforms. However, in contrast to individual rights and, to a lesser degree, federalism, it was not a category discussed in depth. In only three platforms (Whigs in 1844, Democrats and Republicans in 1932) did this category represent 20 percent or more of the constitutional references. In 1932, it was actually the single most frequently mentioned constitutional category in both parties owing to the heated debate over Prohibition. Otherwise, in nineteen of the thirty-two Democratic platforms that mentioned constitutional amendments, those references were less than 10 percent of the total, as was the case in thirteen of twenty-seven Republican platforms that had such a mention.

In most cases, references to constitutional amendments were prospective in nature, either endorsing or criticizing proposed amendments. However, especially in 1920–1932 and the post–Civil War years, recently enacted amendments were also the subject of affirmations or criticism. Paradoxically, given the intense controversy surrounding enforcement of Prohibition nationally and the Civil War amendments in the South, platform language from both major parties would lead one to believe there was little controversy at all. Once amendments became part of the Constitution, both parties vowed support and enforcement.

In a few cases, platforms argued for making it easier to amend the Constitution or otherwise discussed the amendment process. In 1980, the Republican platform assailed federal interference in the Equal Rights Amendment ratification process. Most references, however, were to specific amendments. Major-party platforms discussed a dizzying array of constitutional amendments. Since 1900, Democrats or Republicans (sometimes both) commented on proposals including direct election of senators, limiting presidents to one or two terms, women's and eighteen-year-old suffrage, restrictions on child labor, banning the poll tax, increased electoral involvement for the District of Columbia, and term limits for the U.S. Congress. Aside from political reforms, many recent platforms proposed constitutional revisions to regulate the federal budgetary process, such as amendments to require a balanced budget, give a line-item veto to the president, and prohibit the retroactive levying of taxes. Some appeared in only one or two platforms and then disappeared, due either to success or ignominious failure. Others returned time and again, although as years passed they turned from real proposals into symbolic totems. Perhaps the best example is the Equal Rights Amendment, first endorsed in the Republican platform of 1940, followed by Democrats in 1944. Republicans dropped their endorsement in 1980. Democrats still call for an Equal Rights Amendment, though it was defeated in 1982.

Two interesting patterns should be noted. First, almost all platform references to constitutional amendments endorsed rather than opposed those amendments. Apparently, when party sentiment strongly favored an amendment, it was included in the platform; otherwise, silence spoke for the party. In only a handful of cases did parties openly declare against an amendment.

These included recent Republican opposition to an amendment making the District of Columbia eligible for statehood and Democratic opposition to a proposed balanced budget amendment, antiabortion amendment, and, in 2004, an amendment banning same-sex marriage. It would seem that parties' willingness to come out against proposed constitutional amendments has increased, especially when those amendments affect individual rights or promise to tilt the playing field against the party in either electoral or policy terms.

Second, the incidence of proposed amendments seeking to reverse particular judicial decisions has increased over time. Before 1964, two were discussed in party platforms: the measure that became the Sixteenth Amendment, reversing the Supreme Court's 1895 *Pollock* decision overturning the federal income tax, and the proposed but never adopted child labor amendment. From 1964 on, the number of such proposals in platforms has multiplied, including proposals to reverse Supreme Court decisions banning school prayer, requiring equal population districts for state legislatures, mandating school busing, declaring abortion on demand a constitutional right, and giving First Amendment protection to flag burning. The federal marriage amendment touted by the GOP in 2004 also represented an attempt to turn back certain state court decisions and to preempt similar decisions in the federal judiciary. Support for these court-checking amendments was uniformly found in Republican platforms. Not quite of the same character, one other amendment, proposed by both parties in the 1990s, sought to counter a variety of court decisions that expanded defendants' rights by guaranteeing "victims' rights" throughout court proceedings.

In contrast with the general direction of constitutional rhetoric over the last fifty years, discussion of constitutional amendments has not faded into a predominantly implicit dialogue. To the contrary, it is disproportionately explicit, with references since 1976 usually running a ratio of three to one—and not infrequently seven, eight, or more to one—in favor of explicit references. Altogether, in no twenty-year increment since 1912 have fewer than 76 percent of these references been explicit. This might be expected given the nature of the category, which is more difficult than most to discuss without explicit reference to its constitutional character.

Executive Power

References to executive power appeared in about two-thirds of the platforms of both parties. Like constitutional amendments, discussion of executive power was not highly concentrated within platforms. On only eight occasions did executive power represent 20 percent or more of the constitutional references in a major-party platform, and in only four platforms was it the highest-ranked category. It represented 20 percent or more of all references in moments one would expect: 1844 Whigs; both parties in 1864 and Democrats in 1868 (owing to the Civil War and its aftermath); Democrats in 1904 (reacting to Theodore Roosevelt's strong presidency); and Republicans in 1920 and 1964 (reacting to Wilson's wartime presidency and Johnson's aggressive use of executive power). Democrats in 1972 came close, as Nixon sought reelection. Otherwise, this category consisted of a broad but not deep scattering of concerns about civilian supremacy and military power, accusations of executive abuses or defenses against such accusations, or in some cases a perceived need for enhanced executive power.

For example, the 1844 Whigs called for "a reform of executive usurpations," while 1844 Democrats were "decidedly opposed to taking from the President the qualified veto power."[35] In 1864, Democrats attacked "the administrative usurpation of extraordinary and dangerous powers not granted by the Constitution" including "subversion of the civil by the military law in States not in insurrection." Republicans countered by declaring that "we approve and indorse, as demanded by the emergency and essential to the preservation of the nation and as within the provisions of the Constitution, the measures and acts which [President Lincoln] has adopted to defend the nation against its open and secret foes."[36] Democrats in 1904 and 1960 and Republicans in 1920, 1936, and 1968 openly attacked usurpations of executive authority, sometimes even referring to "tyrants" or "despots." Platforms in 1904 (Democratic), 1940 (Republican), 1972 (Democratic), and 1984 (Democratic) emphasized the importance of limits on the president's war-making authority. In 1984, for example, Democrats attacked Reagan for his "cavalier approach to the use of military force around the world," then affirmed their own "commitment to the selective, judicious use of American military power in consonance with Constitutional principles."[37] Several post–World War II platforms across party lines criticized, more mildly, executive secrecy, arbitrary conduct by regulatory agencies, or abuse of executive privilege. Democrats in 1972 attacked both secrecy and executive impoundment of congressionally appropriated funds. However, at varying points from the 1980s through 2004, both parties endorsed adding a line-item veto to executive powers.

As in constitutional rhetoric generally, there has been a marked decline of explicit rhetoric related to executive powers. Not since 1920 has there been a major-party platform that had more explicit than implicit references in that category. It is also interesting that platforms have included virtually no discussion of a general theory of executive power (in contrast, for example, to federalism, which was often discussed in terms of general principles). Rather, the parties confined themselves to more specific issues, and were considerably more likely to complain about executive abuse (as the out-party) than to defend or propose expansions of executive power. It is not hard to imagine that this tendency reflects the suspicion of executive power deeply ingrained in American history; and that it reflects as well the natural tendency of those not in possession of the executive power to be the most suspicious of it. The suspicions themselves are aroused in an ad hoc manner as the result of specific presidential actions; in contrast, federalism is fundamentally about the role of the federal government in American life, an unavoidable topic that calls forth both broad theories and specific prescriptions.

Enumerated Powers

Both parties referenced enumerated powers in roughly three out of every five platforms. Enumerated powers, which was once discussed quite openly in platforms, is still discussed explicitly more often than not, though there were few mentions of any kind in the 1960s and 1970s. Many references took the form of platform declarations that particular federal actions or proposed actions were outside of the scope permitted by the enumeration of powers. The earliest Democratic platforms, for example, held the national bank and internal improvements to be unsupported by constitutional authorization. Those issues formed the basis of the party division between Democrats and Whigs on economic policy. Indeed, other platforms identified specific federal activities as constitutionally permitted. Whigs in 1852, for example, argued that "The Constitution vests in Congress the power to open and repair harbors, and remove obstructions from navigable rivers" if needed for defense or interstate commerce.[38] A third type of reference to enumerated powers has consisted of a more abstract statement affirming that federal authority is limited to "the exercise of powers expressly granted by the Constitution."[39]

All three were relatively common in the nineteenth century, though they tailed off after the Civil War. Even in the twentieth century, such arguments were occasionally heard. In 1936, Republicans argued that the New Deal Democrats had exceeded the bounds of the Constitution. In 1964, they argued more abstractly that "Within our Republic the Federal Government should act only in areas where it has Constitutional authority to act."[40] In 1996, Republicans supported a requirement that the original sponsor of legislation "cite specific constitutional authority for the measure," and declared that "the federal government has no constitutional authority to be involved in school curricula or to control jobs in the workplace."[41]

However, from the onset of the New Deal up to the present day, a newer mode of discussing the issue became quite common: referring to the concept of enumerated powers sideways, if you will, by promising to pursue a novel federal action "in keeping with the Constitution." This phrasing makes the question of constitutionality secondary to the policy question at hand, but it also acknowledges that some constitutional limits still obtain. For example, Democrats claimed in 1936 that their program sought to meet the problems of the Depression "through legislation within the Constitution."[42] Another newer form of this discussion consisted of claims that the enumerated powers not only constitutionally permitted a course of federal action but also actually mandated it. The 1956 Democratic platform, for instance, referred to "the unique legal and moral responsibility for Indians which is imposed by the Constitution," and held that civil defense was "essentially a federal responsibility."[43]

The doctrine of enumeration of powers must be considered an essential element of constitutionalism, whether one chooses to interpret those powers narrowly or relatively broadly. The enumeration is, in theory, what gives Washington its power—and what limits its power. Without some notion of enumeration of powers, the federal authority is without bounds except those prescribed in the Bill of Rights. Yet discussion of this subject has declined steeply in frequency and rigor since 1840. Strongly conservative platforms such as those of the Republicans in 1964 and 1996 retained the earlier flavor of commentary, but are now the exceptions rather than the rule. In this respect, the fate of enumeration of powers as a topic of campaign discussion is significant evidence that deconstitutionalization has been real.

Properly understood, enumeration of federal powers can also be seen as the mirror image of states' rights, and it is undoubtedly significant that the latter has received so much more—but so much less explicit—attention than the former. This is confirmation, if any were necessary, that Americans prefer to hear about rights (even states' rights) than about limits, and that much of the discussion about federalism has represented a form of limited government on the cheap—an overwhelmingly implicit nod to decentralization unaccompanied by the hard commitment to enumerated federal powers that would be necessary to protect that decentralization.

Perfunctory Mentions

These nonsubstantive references were found in around half of the platforms. Whigs and Republicans were a bit more consistent in the year-to-year frequency of perfunctory references; 54 percent of their platforms contained at least one perfunctory reference, as did 45 percent of Democratic platforms. The former were also more likely to rely heavily on perfunctory references in selected years. In four Whig/Republican platforms, perfunctory mentions broke the 20 percent mark; in three of those, it was the highest category.

There were no Democratic platforms that shared that distinction. In particular, the Whigs were disproportionately fond of perfunctory references, undoubtedly owing to their party's ideological ambiguity on many substantive issues. In recent years, the consistency of perfunctory references has fallen off, but only slightly, and only among Democrats: eight of fourteen Republican platforms since 1952 (or 57 percent) had such references, while only five of fourteen Democratic platforms did (36 percent).

To cite just a few examples of this genre, the Whig platform of 1852 appealed to the people's "devotion to the Constitution."[44] Democrats in 1884 extolled "the liberal principles embodied by Jefferson in the Declaration of Independence, and sanctioned in the Constitution."[45] In more recent times, Democrats in 1980 praised "the spirit of liberty which imbues our Constitution,"[46] and Republicans in 1992 alleged that "Democrats have transformed what the Framers of the Constitution intended as the people's House into a pathological institution."[47]

In general, perfunctory references in platforms tell us nothing about the substance of constitutional issues but may tell us quite a bit about the degree to which parties view general appeals to the Constitution as successful vote-getting devices, and the degree to which their activists and officeholders view veneration of the Constitution qua Constitution as a value worth promoting.

Supreme Court Decisions and Judicial Power
These two categories, closely related in content, were also closely matched in frequency across time. Judicial power was referenced by 38 percent of Democratic and 34 percent of Republican platforms. Supreme Court or other federal court decisions were mentioned in 43 percent of Democratic and 32 percent of Republican platforms. The vast majority of those platforms contained relatively few such references, below 10 percent of the total. Judicial power accounted for 20 percent or more of only four Democratic and two Republican platforms, and was the biggest category in three—the 1912 Democratic and Republican platforms, and 1916 Democrats. Consideration of this issue was deep only between 1900 and 1916, as Progressive Era political figures grappled with issues like the proper role of the judiciary and how best to restrain judicial injunctions issued against labor.

The issue, however, enjoyed a recent comeback by both parties; every Democratic platform but one between 1956 and 1984 addressed it, while every Republican platform but one between 1972 and 2004 did so. The attitude of the two parties was very different. Democrats tended to uphold the importance of judicial power, sometimes even (as in 1972) advocating its extension through the empowering of class-action lawsuits. Republicans called for judicial power to be reined in. In 1972 they endorsed the Student Transportation Moratorium Act which aimed to halt all further court-ordered busing, while more generally arguing that Congress rather than unelected judges should play a greater role in defining and enforcing the Fourteenth Amendment. In 2000, they referred positively to the options of limiting judicial terms and limiting the appellate jurisdiction of the Supreme Court. In 2004, they went further, actually urging Congress to remove jurisdiction from the federal courts over the 1996 Defense of Marriage Act. Overall, Republicans argued that "We believe that the self-proclaimed supremacy of these judicial activists is antithetical to the democratic ideals on which our nation was founded."[48]

Likewise, the category of Supreme Court decisions was seldom discussed in depth. Only two major-party platforms—Democrats and Republicans in 1860—contained Supreme Court references representing 20 percent or more of the total, and only one (Democrats in that year) saw it as the biggest category. In that year, Democrats heralded the "final determination" by the Supreme Court of the powers held by Congress over slavery in the territories, while Republicans decried the "new dogma" and "dangerous heresy" of the *Dred Scott* decision and other "perversions of judicial power."[49] Otherwise, only a smattering of earlier platforms (like the Democrats in 1936 and both parties in 1956–1960) mentioned Supreme Court decisions like the anti–New Deal rulings or *Brown v. Board*. Unlike *Dred Scott*, *Brown* elicited support from both party platforms.

As with judicial power, commentary on Supreme Court decisions was not a regular feature of platforms until the late twentieth century. It found its way into every Republican platform from 1972 to 2004 and all but one Democratic platform in the same period. The decisions that were addressed concerned forced busing, equalization of school expenditures, abortion, the exclusionary rule and other defendants' rights cases, free press and obscenity decisions, the right of union members to opt out of that portion of their dues going to political expenditures, and drug testing in schools, as well as same-sex marriage in state courts. Sometimes the references endorsed the court decision at issue, but more often they rejected it.

Sometimes, as well, the parties staked out a position on broader tendencies and patterns of court decisions. Republicans particularly adopted this approach, frequently asserting that recent judicial decisions added up to a pattern of judicial usurpation. In 1984, for example, they declared that "We share the public's dissatisfaction with an elitist and unresponsive federal judiciary."[50] Even more bluntly, in 1996 the Republicans held that "The federal judiciary, including the U.S. Supreme Court, has overstepped its authority under the Constitution."[51] Democrats typically have not countered this argument head-on, but they have most consistently and most vigorously endorsed *Roe v. Wade*, the abortion case that conservatives often point to as a prime example of the judiciary run amok. More generally, the 1984 Democratic platform referred to the Supreme Court as "our most vigorous defender of the rule of law."[52]

The consistency with which judicial power issues and Supreme Court decisions are found in modern platforms—and the relative paucity of references in earlier years—is powerful evidence of the increased activism and politicization of the judiciary. It is also evidence that political actors have been unwilling to simply delegate consideration of such issues to the courts, even in an era characterized by the apparent ascendancy of judicialism.

Appointments

About one-fifth of all platforms in both parties (19 percent of Democratic and 22 percent of Republican) addressed the issue of appointments. In no single platform did those references reach 20 percent of the total. Such references have multiplied in recent years. Every one of the eighteen major-party platforms discussing appointments came after 1956. For most of the period since 1960, implicit references have held the upper hand, though since 1984 the advantage has diminished. In 2000 and 2004, the conversation was actually more explicit than implicit. Since 1960, a few platforms have made promises regarding the attorney general (Democrats in 1960, Republicans in 1968 and 1972). Most have addressed court appointments. While both parties have at various times discussed judicial appointments in terms of how many women and/or minorities were appointed to federal judgeships during their administrations, serious substantive issues have divided them.

Democrats have consistently promised to appoint judges who will uphold *Roe v. Wade*, and have often expressed concern that Republicans will appoint judges who will roll back not only *Roe* but also a raft of decisions that discovered new rights since the 1960s. In 1984, Democrats argued that a Reagan court "could be lost to the cause of equal justice for another generation;"[53] twenty years later, they similarly contended that George W. Bush had appointed "judges more interested in rolling back rights than protecting them. . . . We support the appointment of judges who will uphold our laws and constitutional rights, not their own narrow agendas."[54]

Republicans since 1972 have promised judicial appointments with "fidelity to the Constitution."[55] As years passed, they became more precise about what that means to them: In 1996, the Republicans vowed to select judicial nominees "who understand that their task is first and foremost to be faithful to the Constitution and to the intent of those who framed it."[56] Since 1980, Republican platforms have also supported "the appointment of judges who respect traditional family values and the sanctity of innocent human life."[57] They also frequently called for judges who paid as much respect to the rights of crime victims as to the "rights of criminals." In 2004, Republicans took Democrats to task for "obstructing" Bush's judicial nominees.

As in the case of Supreme Court decisions and judicial power, the rise of appointments as a topic of discussion signals an obvious willingness by the parties to engage in discussion about the Constitution by focusing on judicial matters. Again, the courts are not simply assumed to be beyond political control. To that degree, the constitutional rhetoric of campaigns in these areas raises an important conceptual question: If a major increase in constitutional rhetoric is traceable to political responses to controversial judicial action, does that represent a blow against judicialism or a confirmation of its power?

Mode of Constitutional Interpretation

Republicans made an argument about the proper mode of constitutional interpretation in one in ten platforms, the Democrats in a bit more than one in ten. However, most Democratic references came in the first five Democratic platforms (1840–1856) and none came after 1888. All four Republican references to the mode of constitutional interpretation appeared after 1980. Both parties declared for a mode of interpretation only when they were advancing a strict, limited, or original understanding of the Constitution. For example, Democrats in their earliest platforms repeated the phrase that "the grants of power shown therein [in the Constitution] ought to be strictly construed by all the departments and agents of the government."[58] Republicans in 1984 called for judges "who share our commitment to judicial restraint," a call echoed in 1988; in 1996 and 2000 they called for "original intent" as a guiding philosophy. None openly advocated a loose interpretation as such, though parties often adopted positions on enumerated powers and federalism that were more consistent with a loose than a narrow construction.

This disjunction highlights in a novel way the longstanding claim of some political analysts that Americans are "philosophically conservative and operationally liberal." That is to say, while the parties have not hesitated to offer programs that would seem at odds with some basic constitutional values, neither party has deemed it expedient to openly embrace an abstract theory of loose constitutional interpretation. This is a constitutional topic that has belonged exclusively to the more constitutionally conservative party of each era.

Impeachment

About one in ten Republican platforms (12 percent) and about one in twenty Democratic platforms (5 percent) mentioned impeachment. In no platform did such references break the 10 percent mark. Given the relative paucity of actual impeachments in American history, it is perhaps surprising that any party saw impeachment references in as many as one in ten plat- forms. Some references focused on actual impeachment actions and others put forward prospective theoretical arguments for how impeachment should be used.

Not surprisingly, both parties addressed President Johnson's impeachment in their 1868 platforms, with Republicans lauding the process and Democrats decrying it. It came up again in both parties' platforms in 1876, when they openly or subtly referred to the recent impeachment of the Secretary of War. The 1912 Republicans advocated an easier impeachment process as an alter- native to the popular recall of judges, a progressive proposal of the time. Eighty years later, in response to a controversial school-funding case decided by a federal court in Kansas City, Republicans urged that "When federal judges dare to seize the power of the purse, by ordering the imposition of taxes, they should be removed from office by the procedures provided by the Constitution."[59] Looking back to the Clinton impeachment, the 2000 Re- publican platform applauded "Members who did their duty to conscience and the Constitution."[60] These recent examples of impeachment references, cov- ering both the prospective principle and actual operation of impeachment, show that these constitutional concerns can still animate platform-writers on occasion.

Veto

Only in 1912 and 1996 did either party's platform mention the use of the presidential veto in a constitutional context, although the executive power category includes some references to the veto power more generally. The 1912 Democrats condemned William Howard Taft for vetoing a tariff reduc- tion just after contending that a protective tariff was unconstitutional. In 1996, the Republicans attacked Bill Clinton for "subordinating American national interests to the United Nations"—a matter of constitutional sover- eignty—"in vetoing bipartisan legislation that would have lifted the U.S. arms embargo [in Bosnia] and rendered the deployment of U.S. forces un- necessary."[61] The lack of veto references is understandable given the sharp decline in presidential vetoes rendered for constitutional reasons. In this sense, the paucity of references is a perfect barometer of the deconstitution- alization of the veto itself.

In addition, three categories saw such dramatic variations between the parties that it makes sense to discuss them separately:

Enforcement

Republican platforms discussed executive or general enforcement of constitutional provisions or statutes with constitutional implications 56 percent of the time. Democratic platforms lagged far behind at 33 percent. Overall, such references are scattered throughout the 164 years in question, and called for effective enforcement of provisions including the fugitive-slave clause, voting rights, the constitutional rights of blacks in the postbellum South, the Eighteenth Amendment (Prohibition), and the Civil Rights Act of 1964 and Voting Rights Act of 1965 (or civil rights as a whole). Some platforms also pledged more generally that the presidential candidate would take seriously his constitutional obligation to see that the laws be faithfully executed. In some periods, like the earliest period and the Prohibition era, enforcement references were mostly explicit. However, since 1932, about three-quarters of such references have been implicit. In other words, a function that is arguably the most basic constitutional obligation of the president remains a significant topic of conversation in platforms, but typically in language that severs the open link between the duty and the Constitution.

Separation of Powers

Republicans interjected separation of powers issues into their platforms 39 percent of the time, Democrats only 14 percent of the time. The issue was often raised by way of reaffirming the theoretical importance of separation of powers. It was also frequently raised through accusations that opponents were trampling on that framework, either with or without offering specific examples. Most often, these concerns took the form of allegations that the executive branch had invaded the prerogatives of the legislative branch. Democrats in 1868, 1872, and 1880 followed that pattern, and again in 1972–76; so did Republicans in 1936–1952, 1968, and 1996. In 1940, for example, Republicans argued that "Our greatest protection against totalitarian government is our American system of checks and balances. The constitutional distribution of legislative, executive, and judicial functions is essential to the preservation of this system."[62] Interestingly, these allegations were often made when the other party controlled Congress as well as the presidency; even under circumstances of unified party government by its foes, the opposition party preferred for that unified government to be subject to the cross-pressures of separation of powers rather than be a monolithic tool in the hands of the executive.

Conversely, separation of powers was sometimes a rallying cry for the party in the White House when it believed an assertive opposition Congress was interfering excessively with executive prerogatives. Republicans in 1976, promoting an incumbent president (Gerald Ford) who often complained of congressional interference in the conduct of foreign policy, held that "The branches of government can and should work together as the necessary pre-requisite of a sound foreign policy. We lament the reckless intrusion of one branch into the clear constitutional prerogatives of another."[63] As well, Re-publican platforms since 1968 have often held that judicial aggrandizement has threatened separation of powers.

Following a period overlapping the New Deal, during which 60 percent of separation-of-powers references were explicitly framed, the discussion of this topic has been overwhelmingly implicit in character. The most recent period experienced a comeback of explicit rhetoric on separation of powers, but it still accounts for only a little more than one-third of the total references in the category. Thus, like federalism, another key structural component of the American constitutional system, separation of powers is now not usually dis-cussed as an explicitly constitutional matter.

Constitutional Sovereignty

This issue was nearly nonexistent in major-party platforms until 1920. Since then it has appeared in seven Democratic platforms and twelve Republican platforms. This works out to a total from 1840 to 2004 of 17 percent of Dem-ocratic and 29 percent of Republican platforms—but a bit more than one-third of Democratic and one-half of Republican platforms since 1920. From that be-ginning, this category has been significantly more likely to receive implicit than explicit consideration. In almost every case, these references have reaf-firmed the party's fealty to American sovereignty, though most of the time Re-publicans were on the offensive and Democrats on the defensive. That is to say, Republicans contrasted their affirmation of constitutional sovereignty with the alleged willingness of Democrats to subordinate sovereignty to the dictates of international organizations, while Democrats sought to deny such charges.

In 1920, for instance, Republicans argued that a just and fair peace could be won "without the compromise of national independence, without depriving the people of the United States in advance of the right to determine for them-selves what is just and fair when the occasion arises" and called Woodrow Wil-son's scheme "intolerable for an independent people."[64] Democrats rejected

> as utterly vain, if not vicious, the Republican assumption that ratification of the [Versailles] treaty and membership in the League of Nations would in any

wise impair the integrity or independence of our country. . . . The President repeatedly has declared, and this Convention reaffirms, that all our duties and
obligations as a member of the league must be fulfilled in strict conformity with
the Constitution of the United States. . . . [65]

This issue recurred frequently, as both American global power and international interconnectedness grew, and was an important part of the foreign
policy debate of the 2004 election. In 1956, Republicans proclaimed that
"We maintain that no treaty or international agreement can deprive any of
our citizens of Constitutional rights."[66] In echoes of 1920, Republicans declared in 2004 that international organizations "can never serve as a substitute for, or exercise a veto over, principled American leadership."[67] Democrats, for their part, contended that "With John Kerry as Commander-
in-Chief, we will never wait for a green light from abroad when our safety is
at stake."[68]

Although this interplay dominated discussions of constitutional sovereignty, there were a handful of occasions on which a party platform would declare for a policy that unambiguously reduced sovereignty. In 1960, for instance, Democrats proposed repealing the "self-judging reservation" that
allowed the United States to remove itself from any World Court case in
which it was involved, a position they repeated in 1972.

The rise of constitutional sovereignty as an issue shows that new constitutional issues, unforeseen by the framers, can even today complement or
supplant issues of greater pedigree. As with many other issues, however, the
manner in which it is discussed downplays the constitutional character of the
question.

Overall Quantity of Constitutional Rhetoric

The introduction established four key tests for the health of constitutional
rhetoric. The first and most obvious question was "how much?"

When controlling for the wide variations that have occurred in platform
length over time, a clear picture emerges of a long and steady decline in the
weight given to constitutional rhetoric in major-party platforms. The first
platform in 1840 saw more than twenty constitutional references per thousand words. Twenty years after the Civil War ended, that figure fell consistently below ten mentions per thousand words. By 1900, it had fallen in half
again, and after 1948 it was again halved to three or fewer. Altogether, from
1840 to the present, constitutional references per thousand words have been
cut by a factor of nearly seven (see chart 2.1).

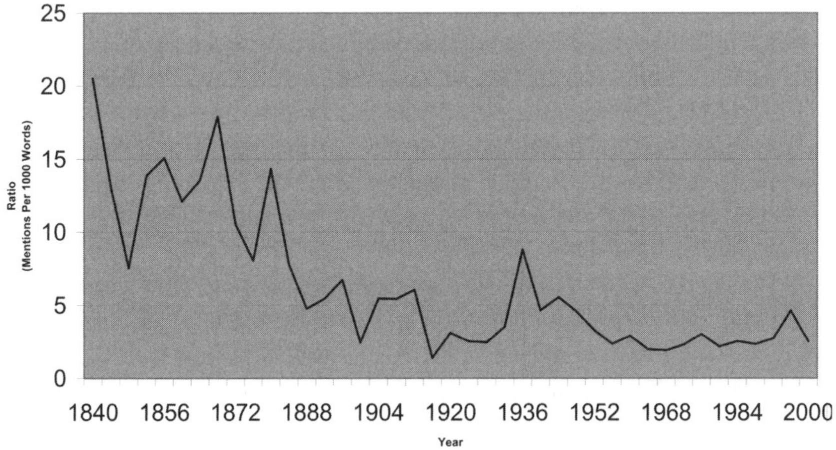

Chart 2.1. **Total constitutional references per one thousand words in major-party platforms 1840–2004**

One potential explanation for the overall twentieth-century decline in relative weight accorded to the Constitution in platforms is that foreign policy, which affords fewer avenues for constitutional rhetoric, became a larger proportion of the whole with the onset of American global power and entanglement. Of course, foreign policy can involve issues of executive power, separation of powers, and constitutional sovereignty, but touches on other constitutional questions only rarely. Upon examination, however, this explanation falls short. A quick study of the foreign policy and national security components of selected platforms shows that those concerns typically comprised less than 10 percent of party platforms until 1900, when the Spanish-American War and America's holdings abroad abruptly became a major issue. From then on, those concerns have consistently comprised roughly one-quarter to one-third of platforms. Yet the decline in the rate of constitutional references set in well before 1900, and continued despite an apparent stabilization in the discussion of foreign policy through most of the twentieth century.[69] Consequently, it seems clear instead that domestic issues that might once have been framed in constitutional terms were either not discussed in those terms any longer or were not discussed at all.

Despite the sharp decline in constitutional references per thousand words, however, it is striking that the major parties have often made constitutional issues a significant theme in party platforms from 1840 through 2004. In absolute terms, not controlled for platform size, the number of references to constitutional issues has gone up significantly in those 164 years, and especially in the last 50 years, reaching a peak in 1996 before receding (chart 2.2). Not only do elected officials have the opportunity to address constitutional issues, they have frequently taken advantage of that opportunity. In that respect, constitutional rhetoric in the parties remains healthy.

Furthermore, despite the overall decline in the weight of constitutional rhetoric, there have been several moments of revival. It is interesting to note the peaks after 1840: the buildup to the Civil War (1856–1860); the end of Reconstruction (1876); the Progressive Era (1912 and adjacent); the New Deal (1936); the changing of the guard in 1960; and the two-stage conservative counterrevolution (1976–1984 and 1996). Only a peak in 1888 seems rather incongruous. Clearly, at moments of political transition and turmoil, constitutional rhetoric makes a comeback, at least within the limits prescribed by the trends of the era—as a cause of the turmoil, as its effect, or (most likely) as a bit of both. Indeed, almost every case can be considered a moment defined by constitutional crisis or disputation. At the least, constitutional issues have been closely intertwined with these moments of political conflict. The timing of these peaks might also raise a question about the narrative explaining deconstitutionalization, which sees the Civil War, Progressive Era, and New Deal as key junctures of deconstitutionalization. The chart and the narrative can be reconciled if the junctures are seen as leading to sharper deconstitutionalization rather than being themselves characterized by it.

In addition, it is notable that overall rates of constitutional references have stabilized and indeed shown a slight uptick since reaching their lows in

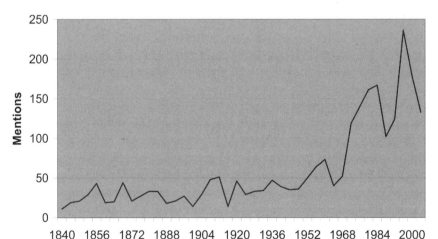

Chart 2.2   Total constitutional references in major party platforms, 1840–2004

the 1960s. After averaging only 1.9 references per thousand words in 1964 and 1968, at the bottom of the downward slope, platforms have since averaged 2.7, half again higher. Decline of constitutional rhetoric may be the picture painted most brightly by the rate of constitutional references since 1840, but elements of resurgence can also be seen by those who look closely.

In partisan terms, Republicans and Democrats occasionally switched places but were within a narrow range until the mid-1970s. Throughout most of the nineteenth century, Democrats used slightly more constitutional rhetoric than did Republicans, as measured by the absolute number of constitutional references. Starting in the 1920s, and more consistently after 1928, Republicans made more such references than Democrats, except for a brief time coinciding with the Nixon years. (This finding is consistent with a study of party ideology by John Gerring, who noted that Republican ideology began to emphasize decentralization and limited government in the 1920s in response to the Wilson presidency.)[70] Starting in 1976, a much bigger gap opened up than had ever previously been seen, with the raw number of Democratic constitutional references falling and the number of Republican references jumping dramatically. At its peak in 1996, the Republican platform contained 179 constitutional references, the Democratic platform 34. However, even the collapsed Democratic numbers in the 1980s and 1990s were a bit higher than was typical in the nineteenth and early twentieth centuries (chart 2.3).

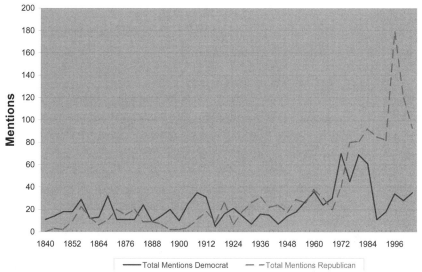

Chart 2.3. Total constitutional references in platforms by party, 1840–2004

While each party displays a distinct pattern of data, there is more difference between them when counting raw references than when it comes to the relative weight given to the Constitution measured by references per thousand words. Both parties peaked around the Civil War and gradually fell—the Republicans a bit faster than the Democrats—until reaching a low in the 1920s. The New Deal controversies brought a bump in both parties—the Republicans more than the Democrats—followed by another decline reaching another low point around 1968 (for Democrats) or 1972 (for Republicans). Subsequently, both parties' frequency of constitutional rhetoric climbed very modestly—Republicans more than Democrats—but never regained even the level of the 1930s and 1940s. (chart 2.4) Thus, the yawning gap in the 1990s between Republican and Democratic platforms in the raw number of references largely reflected shorter Democratic platforms after 1984, and much of the gap disappears when controlled for platform size. Nevertheless, from 1952 to 2004 Republicans had a higher rate of constitutional references than Democrats in thirteen of fourteen elections. Sometimes the gap was negligible, but sometimes it was substantial, and the average Republican rate outpaced the average Democratic rate by a three-to-two margin. The biggest gap in references per thousand words came in 1996, when Republicans—in the midst of the 104[71] Congress with its limited-government constitutional ferment—had more than three times as many references per thousand words as Democrats.

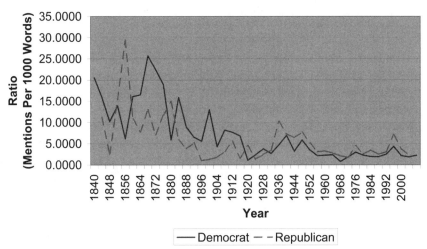

Chart 2.4a. Total constitutional references per one thousand words in platforms, 1840–2004

Explicit vs. Implicit Rhetoric

A second key question is how much of the constitutional rhetoric of American campaigns is explicitly framed and how much is implicitly framed. The earliest platforms depended heavily on explicit language when discussing constitutional concerns. In no year from 1840 to 1872 did explicit references fall below 50 percent of the total. From 1872 to 1948, explicit and implicit references vied for the upper hand, as the two lines crossed paths several times. Of the twenty elections in that period, eleven saw more implicit references, seven saw more explicit references, and two had an equal number of each. From 1952 through 2004, however, in no election did explicit constitutional references in platforms outnumber implicit references. A consistent and substantial gap has opened up, in which implicit discussion of the Constitution has never fallen below 60 percent of the total and has more typically been in the 65–75 percent range. Like overall levels of constitutional rhetoric, explicit rhetoric has experienced a modest recovery since 1968, moving from around 10 percent to around 30–35 percent of all references (chart 2.5).

Neither major party deviated significantly from this overall pattern. As a percentage of references, Democratic platforms since 1948 have actually been somewhat more likely than Republican platforms to frame constitutional questions explicitly.

A review of the fifteen categories of constitutional rhetoric across time shows a more complicated picture (table 2.1). Some categories have consistently

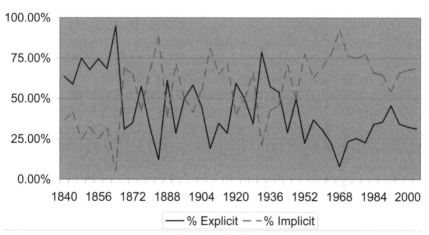

Chart 2.5. Percentage of explicit and implicit constitutional references in major-party platforms, 1840–2004

Table 2.1 Percentage of explicit platform constitutional references by category, 1840–2004

Category	1840–1860 (%)	1864–1884 (%)	1888–1908 (%)	1912–1932 (%)	1936–1956 (%)	1960–1980 (%)	1984–2004 (%)
CA	0	88	40	93	76	85	79
APP	N/A	N/A	N/A	N/A	N/A	5	38
IR	51	30	36	47	49	36	40
EP	89	79	93	60	88	10	56
FED	67	29	22	14	12	3	15
IMP	N/A	0	N/A	0	N/A	N/A	75
VETO	N/A	N/A	N/A	0	N/A	N/A	0
EXEC	0	40	43	50	23	6	26
ENF	67	22	50	93	25	21	27
SOP	N/A	17	N/A	0	60	7	37
SCD	60	0	75	0	0	33	28
JP	N/A	100	0	14	57	6	45
MODE	100	N/A	100	100	100	100	100
CONSOV	N/A	N/A	N/A	20	38	0	5
PERF	100	100	100	100	100	100	100

Note: N/A=not available.

retained a high level of explicit rhetoric (constitutional amendments, for example). Some, like individual rights, have remained moderately explicit across time. Some drifted from high to moderate levels (enumerated powers, Supreme Court decisions) or from moderate to low levels (executive powers). Federalism went from a high level to a low level. A number of categories like appointments and constitutional sovereignty, which appeared only in the twentieth century, have always had relatively low levels of explicit rhetoric. A few have bounced around, showing no predominant pattern. However, no category showed a systematic movement toward a more explicit rhetoric over the course of the study.

As in the aggregated data, the categorical data show a significant trough in explicit rhetoric in the 1960–1980 period. In categories as diverse as individual rights, enumerated powers, federalism, executive powers, enforcement, separation of powers, and judicial power, references in that period were less likely to be explicit than references either before or after. In some cases, like enumeration of powers, executive powers, and separation of powers, the drop and subsequent recovery were extreme. Appointments were not discussed prior to 1960, but were rarely discussed explicitly in 1960–1980 and much more so after that; the degree to which constitutional sovereignty was discussed explicitly fell dramatically in 1960–1980 and did not recover.

Breadth of Constitutional Rhetoric

The third key question defining the health of constitutional rhetoric is whether that rhetoric is broad, covering a gamut of constitutional issues, or narrow. The very first platform, the Democratic platform of 1840, devoted the bulk of its attention to a balanced consideration of enumerated powers (45 percent of all references) and individual rights (36 percent). The first paragraph resolved "That the federal government is one of limited powers, derived solely from the constitution, and the grants of power shown therein, ought to be strictly construed by all the departments and agents of the government, and that it is inexpedient and dangerous to exercise doubtful constitutional powers."[72] The platform went on to criticize internal improvements, federal assumption of state debts, chartering of a national bank, and federal interference with "the domestic institutions of the several states" as outside the constitutional limits of federal legislative authority. Individual rights were framed as a matter of equal rights for all and special privileges for none. The nine paragraphs of the 1840 Democratic platform, suffused as they were with constitutional themes, were repeated more or less verbatim and incorporated into Democratic platforms from 1844 through 1856.

Despite all of the twists and turns of constitutional rhetoric in party platforms over the next 164 years, individual rights and the issue of federal authority (framed either as an issue of enumerated powers or federalism) have remained the most frequent subjects of that rhetoric over time, along with the subject of constitutional amendments.

At the opposite extreme, a number of subjects were rarely touched upon. For example, only two platforms contained a reference to the presidential veto within its constitutional context. Only a handful included any references to impeachment or mode of constitutional interpretation. At least two subjects—constitutional sovereignty and appointments—were not discussed in the nineteenth century but increasingly found their way into twentieth and twenty-first century platforms. Other than one anomalous reference in the Democratic platform of 1900, constitutional sovereignty became a concern starting in 1920, in the aftermath of the League of Nations debate. The issue of appointments, focusing on judicial appointments but occasionally including the U.S. attorney general, surged starting in 1968, as Warren Court activism invited concern by both parties over the makeup of the Supreme Court.

All in all, five of fifteen categories of constitutional rhetoric appeared in more than half of the platforms in both major parties from 1840 to 2004. Those were individual rights, federalism, constitutional amendments, executive powers, and enumeration of powers. Another two, references about enforcement and perfunctory references, appeared in more than half of the Republican platforms but fewer than half of the Democratic platforms. Appointments, impeachment, veto, separation of powers, Supreme Court decisions, judicial power, mode of constitutional interpretation, and constitutional sovereignty all appeared in fewer than half of both parties' platforms (table 2.2).

Of course, merely appearing in a platform is not enough to gauge the importance of an issue to a campaign. Depth can be measured by testing in how many of the years that it appeared as a category it represented 20 percent or more of all of that platform's constitutional references. Only two categories—individual rights in both parties and federalism in Republican platforms—passed that threshold most of the time. All other categories were discussed in a less concentrated fashion.

Thus, only two categories of constitutional rhetoric appeared in platforms both highly consistently and at considerable depth: individual rights and federalism, and the latter only in Republican platforms. At the opposite extreme, three categories appeared rarely for both parties and were rarely discussed in depth when they did appear (impeachment, veto, and mode), and another four fit that description only among Democrats (enumerated powers,

Table 2.2.   Consistency of constitutional reference categories, 1840–2004

Category	% Dem. Platforms	% Rep. Platforms
Individual rights	95.2	90.2
Federalism	90.5	78.0
Const. amendments	76.2	65.9
Executive powers	64.3	68.3
Enum. of powers	59.5	58.5
Perfunctory	45.2	53.7
Enforcement	33.3	56.1
Supreme Court decisions	42.9	31.7
Judicial powers	38.1	34.1
Separation of powers	14.3	39.0
Const. sovereignty	16.7	29.3
Appointments	19.0	22.0
Mode of const. interp.	14.3	9.8
Impeachment	4.8	12.2
Veto	2.4	2.4

separation of powers, constitutional sovereignty, and perfunctory). The rest were found either often but not deeply or deeply but not often.

If one looks only at the modern era—say, since 1952—the picture changes a bit, entirely by moving up to the group of highly consistent though shallow references, categories including appointments, Supreme Court decisions, and judicial power, as well as enforcement for Democrats and constitutional sovereignty and separation of powers for Republicans. In short, the distribution of categories has moved up since 1952 because the consistency of those categories has improved. (See appendix C, table C1 for a breakdown of categories along the continuum of consistency and depth in platforms from 1952 to 2004.)

To get a better sense of the general tendencies, it is useful to group the fourteen nonperfunctory categories of rhetoric into three broader groupings: rights, consisting of the individual rights category; structure, including federalism, enumeration of powers, separation of powers, executive powers, and veto; and constitutional interpretation and application, including constitutional amendments, appointments, mode of interpretation, impeachment, enforcement, constitutional sovereignty, Supreme Court decisions, and judicial power.

In general, the three groupings have tracked each other fairly closely in terms of total references. The third grouping—constitutional interpretation—has generally lagged below the other two, except during the 1920s when the Eighteenth Amendment (Prohibition) was a pressing concern and during the late 1930s as the Supreme Court's response to the New Deal became the center of attention. The only times either rights or structure have burst significantly ahead of the other were in the first platforms, which featured a much heavier emphasis on structure; the Progressive Era, which likewise saw structural concerns dominate; and 2004, when consideration of rights dominated and both structure and interpretation fell dramatically (chart 2.6).

Both Democrats and Republicans have generally hewed to the pattern of all three groupings rising or falling more or less together. However, in the last quarter century, both parties experienced exceptions to that rule. In the late 1970s and early 1980s, Republicans devoted substantially greater attention to structural categories than to other types of constitutional concerns. From 1984 through 2004, Democratic platforms were dominated by rights at the expense of structure and interpretation, a tendency that was copied by the Republicans in 2004. These disparities reflected quite well the fundamental realities at the heart of each party's governing philosophy. Republicans under the influence of Reagan and Reaganism viewed the constitutional structure of limited government, particularly federalism and enumerated powers, as the bedrock of liberty. Likewise, Democrats, under the influence of both rights-oriented legal doctrines and interest groups that defined their agenda in terms of preserving or discovering rights, placed their conception of individual rights above other considerations. The sudden decline of structural concerns in the Republican platforms of 2000 and 2004 undoubtedly reflected the con

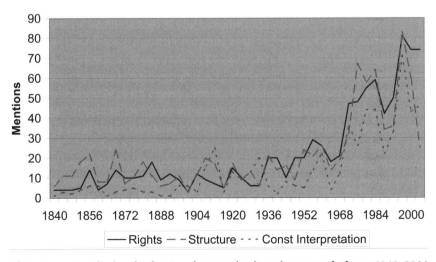

Chart 2.6.   Constitutional references by grouping in major-party platforms 1840–2004

ascendancy of George W. Bush's big government "compassionate conservatism." It also meant that the nation's constitutional rhetoric, as reflected in platforms, became somewhat unbalanced, no longer enjoying the combination of Democratic rights talk and Republican talk about structure.

If this trend continues, it will represent a blow to the cause of constitutionalism in campaigns, and will reflect a decline in an important component of constitutionalism in governing. Perhaps it was anomalous that each party should for a time carve out a niche for itself on either the field of rights or the field of structure, but such a situation was superior to the new type of anomaly in evidence in 2000 and 2004, in which both parties disproportionately emphasize rhetoric in the same field. From a standpoint of partisan politics, this development also raises the interesting question whether the Bush presidency will be seen as the moment when Republicans gave up fighting on their preferred constitutional ground and began playing on the Democrats' home field.

Constitutional Exchanges

The final test of healthy constitutional rhetoric in campaigns is whether parties and candidates engage in some sort of dialogue on constitutional issues rather than talking past each other. Here, the constitutional rhetoric of party platforms, as voluminous as it has become in absolute terms in the last quarter century, often does not do a good job of conveying constitutional debates of the moment to the public. On some issues—in early platforms, the question of whether internal improvements were a constitutional expenditure of federal funds, or more recently, what to do about abortion—the parties stake out coherent and opposing positions. However, on a raft of other questions, either the parties express greater agreement with each other than is warranted given the degree of controversy surrounding the issue, or else one side speaks while the other is silent. Support for constitutional amendments is voiced much more often than opposition; aggressive use of executive powers is often criticized but seldom defended; controversial Supreme Court decisions are more often assailed than supported; strict construction of the Constitution is sometimes endorsed, but loose construction never is; the constitutional sovereignty of the nation is often upheld, but rare is the platform that calls for curtailing it.

This is not to say that opposing platforms have featured no constitutional exchanges. Indeed, there were sixty-two such exchanges in twenty-four of forty-one elections, an average of roughly one and a half per election since 1844. Moreover, the pace of these exchanges is quickening: since 1972, every election has seen platform exchanges—forty in all, or an average of four and a half per election. Appendix C, table C2 catalog these exchanges. The balance between policy disputes (when the two parties stake out opposing positions on the same constitutional issue) and performance disputes (when one party attacks the other for an alleged constitutional failing and the other attempts to refute the criticism) clearly favors the former over the latter. About two-thirds of constitutional exchanges in platforms have been over policy disputes. A good example of a policy dispute would be the conflict over abortion. Good examples of performance disputes would include Democratic criticisms in 2004 that George Bush was not vigorously enforcing civil rights laws or protecting civil liberties and the subsequent Republican claim that Bush was actually performing those tasks well. While position taking is useful to voters and important for party activists, performance disputes are arguably more central to the task of holding public officials accountable for their constitutional conduct. It is, however, not possible to delineate an ideal balance between the two types of constitutional exchanges.

Conclusion

Major-party platforms provide a useful baseline for assessing constitutional rhetoric in American election campaigns. On balance, the picture that emerges is of a less powerful constitutional conversation over time. It is clear that platforms fall short of the standard that was laid out in the introduction—that, generally speaking, more constitutional rhetoric is better than less; explicit rhetoric is better than implicit; a balanced rhetoric is better than an unbalanced one; and a constitutional dialogue is better than a monologue. In fact, in many important respects, trends in party platforms are moving in the wrong direction. The state of constitutional rhetoric in major-party platforms offers much support to fears of the deconstitutionalization of American politics.

In proportion to the size of the platforms, constitutional issues have receded dramatically since 1840. If discussion of constitutional issues has grown, discussion of other issues has grown much more, having the effect of largely swamping the constitutional rhetoric. To the degree that the platforms serve as an educational device for voters, this is problematic. It is also problematic insofar as it reflects a governing fact: the size and scope of government may have grown tremendously (hence also the programmatic pronouncements of platforms), but concern with constitutional propriety has not come close to growing proportionately.

In addition, constitutional rhetoric in platforms has become heavily weighted to the implicit since 1840. The proportion of constitutional references that are explicit in character has shrunk dramatically. This trend may impose little cost to party activists and other highly informed voters, many of whom undoubtedly recognize the constitutional meaning with which such references are pregnant, but it imposes a heavier cost on the general public, in two ways. Voters are not provided the full context of the issues, and an opportunity is lost to provide them a broader education in the Constitution. In some areas of rhetoric, this trend is quite dramatic. From 1840 to 1860, 67 percent of all federalism references were explicit; from 1984 to 2004, only 15 percent were.

While platforms have featured a nontrivial number of exchanges between the parties on constitutional issues, they have often failed to provide exchanges when one might have expected them. This means that many of the most important constitutional issues in American politics are discussed sideways rather than debated frontally.

The three broad groupings of rights, structure, and constitutional interpretation were generally well balanced, until recently. This was true within the major parties, neither of which broke this mold very often. It was also true between parties; in the late twentieth century, for example, a Democratic lean toward individual rights was balanced by a Republican lean toward structure. A recent deemphasis on structure by George W. Bush–era Republicans has left this interparty balance in question.

When broken down into the fifteen categories, only a couple of categories appeared on a basis that was both broad and deep. There was a certain zero-sum quality to this assessment in regard to depth (though not consistency), so it was not possible for all categories to be discussed deeply, but it is still notable that so few were—and also that relatively few were highly consistent.[73] The more detailed breakdown exposes a shortcoming in the apparent balance seen when grouping categories: most of the weight of structure is carried by federalism, while few other crucial structural issues receive deep or sustained attention. Overall, while constitutional rhetoric in platforms over time was distributed among a broad range of topics, there are only a handful that have appeared regularly and at any significant depth.

However, not all of the fifteen categories have risen or fallen together. Under the ongoing influence of the New Deal, discussions of issues like federalism, enumeration of powers, and separation of powers have declined in frequency and/or openness since 1936. On the other hand, with the rise of an activist judiciary, references to Supreme Court decisions, judicial power (and its control), and judicial appointments have become much more common since 1960, as has the issue of constitutional sovereignty since 1920 with the rise of American power in the world.

Indeed, more generally, platforms have hardly been—and are not now—devoid of constitutional argument. Indeed, the absolute number of constitutional references in platforms has gone up considerably. By raw numbers, the Constitution and constitutional issues have been the source of substantial and growing commentary.

Constitutional rhetoric in party platforms reached a nadir in the 1960s and 1970s in terms both of constitutional references per thousand words and the proportion of references that were explicit. There has been a subsequent, though generally modest, recovery since then in those measures. There has also been a rise in the number of constitutional exchanges in platforms in recent decades. On balance, the result has left constitutional rhetoric short of the position that it held prior to the 1950s or 1960s. Nevertheless, the recovery is an indication that constitutional conversation in campaigns is not dead. It is also an indication that judicialism is not simply triumphant, insofar as much of the recovery has been fueled by increased "talking back" of political actors through criticism of court cases and proposals for constitutional amendments and restrictions on judicial power.

Both parties have contributed to this modest recovery. Democrats, for example, are more likely than Republicans to address constitutional questions explicitly, and references by both parties are necessary to produce an exchange. Five categories for Republicans went from inconsistently appearing before 1952 to consistently appearing after 1952, as did four categories for Democrats. However, on balance, Republicans have carried more of the weight. They produced most of the enormous increase in raw references since 1980, have almost always outperformed Democrats in references per thousand words in recent years, and have done more to broaden the rhetoric beyond rights into areas like federalism, enumeration of powers, and mode of constitutional interpretation. The decline of Republican concern with constitutional structure under George W. Bush consequently signals an important change in the character of the party, and it may also signal trouble for the general recovery of constitutional rhetoric in American elections, such as it has been.

The party platforms may be the long-term baseline of electoral rhetoric in America, but they are also unique in some ways. They are written documents, meant to be read. They have evolved into comprehensive documents, espousing principles and policies relating to a wide range of issues. They have also become campaign statements aimed perhaps first and foremost at party activists and the party-in-government. How will their constitutional rhetoric stack up against other modes of campaign communication, which in modern times tend to be audiovisual in character, more selective in the themes they emphasize, and aimed for a general audience of citizens and voters?

CHAPTER THREE

~

The Constitution
in Candidate Messages

Of the key forms of campaign communication included in this study, none has changed as fundamentally as the nomination acceptance message. For more than a century, that message has been delivered in the form of a speech, though the speech was not delivered at the national convention itself until Franklin Roosevelt did so in 1932. In that speech, Roosevelt initiated a long tradition of candidates turning a phrase that helped define their campaigns, when he declared "I pledge to you, I pledge to the American people, a new deal." Indeed, for much of this time, especially in the television age, the nomination acceptance speech has been considered by strategists to be the candidate's best unmediated opportunity to introduce himself and his ideas to the general public. As one television pundit said prior to John Kerry's 2004 acceptance speech, that form of campaign communication "operates on two planes. It has to be a speech that will energize the party . . . but it also has to connect the candidate to the national audience."[1] That audience is substantial: There can be no question that many more Americans now watch the candidates' acceptance speeches than read the parties' platforms in their entirety. About one in four Americans say that the conventions help them make their voting decision, a number roughly equal to those who say political advertising contributes to their decision. Furthermore, the acceptance speech often serves a broader function, as a guide that directs a campaign's subsequent communications strategy, including its paid advertising.[2]

Prior to the acceptance speech, candidates wrote nomination acceptance letters, which were subsequently reprinted and became part of the public campaign. Nomination acceptance messages underwent a fundamental transformation when they were delivered in person at the convention attended by radio and then television coverage. At that point, most Americans stopped experiencing these messages as written communications and began experiencing them as primarily audio or audio/visual communications, a very different kind of medium.

A number of content analyses have been performed on nomination acceptance speeches, but none have focused on constitutional rhetoric.[3] In this study, a total of eighty-seven of these letters and speeches from major-party candidates were coded. In some cases between 1840 and 1876, the letters were so pro forma as to give little or no information about the campaign message, and in those cases an alternate was selected for examination—sometimes another widely publicized letter by the candidate and sometimes another speech either by the candidate or by a surrogate. In all cases, a direct message was selected that could be expected to receive wide public and press attention and to summarize what the candidate considered key points of his campaign message.

This assessment of candidate messages is also different from the analysis of other campaign communications in another way. The study of major-party platforms and presidential debates looks at all of those communications, and the sample of television advertisements is quite large, and in some years probably comes close to capturing the candidates' entire television spot ad campaign. In this chapter, one or two letters or speeches are used as a proxy for that mode of communication, although each campaign used literally hundreds of such communications by the candidate and/or surrogates over a period of weeks or months. Thus, some greater caution should be used in drawing conclusions from them.

Nevertheless, the evidence from these messages generally confirms the picture drawn by an examination of party platforms. Constitutional rhetoric has been, and at times continues to be, an important part of candidate messages. If anything, however, deconstitutionalization is advanced further in candidate messages than it is in platforms. The weight of constitutional rhetoric in messages has declined over time, as has the openness with which it is expounded. Furthermore, fewer constitutional subjects are addressed consistently in candidate messages than in platforms, and very few constitutional exchanges occur between candidates in modern times.

What Candidate Messages Say about the Constitution

At least some references can be found for each of the fifteen topics in candidate messages since 1840. As in platforms, the capacity of the elected branches to affect constitutional interpretation and development has frequently been translated into actual appeals on constitutional issues during presidential campaigns. However, the field of references has clearly narrowed over time. Individual rights and federalism are the most consistently cited issues in this venue, as well, although the overall volume of references to constitutional topics is significantly lower in candidate messages than platforms.

Individual Rights
Discussion of rights was both voluminous and varied, finding its way into 88 percent of Republican and 81 percent of Democratic candidate messages, by far the most consistently mentioned topic in either party. Furthermore, the topic was by far the most salient category of rhetoric, as references to rights represented 30 percent or more of all references in twenty-five of forty-two years for Democrats and twenty-four of forty-two years for Republicans. It was the most-mentioned category twenty-six times for Democrats and twenty-one times for the Republicans. No other category came close.

Discussion of individual rights, however, became increasingly implicit after the Civil War. Since 1936, only about one-quarter of rights references in candidate messages have been explicit, a record considerably worse than in platforms.

The rhetoric of rights found in nineteenth-century messages largely mirrors that found in platforms. Prior to the Civil War, rights were discussed in general terms such as a commitment to equal rights under the law or general threats to the rights and liberties of the people as a whole. In the era of the Know-Nothings, discussion included consideration of the rights of immigrants. Henry Clay spent considerable effort attempting to rebut the Democratic claim that a national bank would threaten the liberties of the people and spoke in favor of the constitutional privileges of naturalized citizens. Winfield Scott's acceptance letter in 1852 also extolled "equal rights" and proposed to allow "the right of citizenship" for immigrants who served one year in the army or navy.[4] Even John Fremont, running as the first Republican candidate in 1856, made reference only to the general rights and liberties of the people endangered by the power of the slaveholders. Likewise, on the Democratic side, Martin van Buren in 1840 referenced the Alien and Sedition Acts of four decades before and ended with an expression of confidence that no one would succeed in misleading or intimidating the people "into a surrender of their Constitution and their liberties."[5]

Starting in 1860, the Civil War and post–Civil War themes emerged, dominated by questions of whether slavery was a right as defined in the *Dred*

Scott decision and by questions of how to ensure the rights of civilians during the war, and freedmen and white Southerners after the war. Lincoln's 1860 Cooper Union speech went on at length denying that possession of slaves was a distinctly and expressly affirmed right in the Constitution, and condemned Democrats for seeking to stifle freedom of speech by suppressing antislavery declarations. At the same time, Stephen Douglas attacked the Republican view that slavery violated the rights of slaves and that it called into question the justice of the Constitution.[6]

George B. McClellan reverted to an earlier form in 1864, simply calling for protection of the "rights and liberties" of the people. This spare formulation was in contrast with the Democratic platform, which was much more animated in its denunciation of alleged administration threats to a long list of basic rights. In 1868, the Democratic nominee was more specific: Horatio Seymour attacked congressional Republicans for establishing an arbitrary military government in the South and depriving Southerners of the vote, then listed key rights which were allegedly under assault, like security of the home against search and seizure, and freedom of speech, the press, and religion. He summarized the call of the Democratic convention as demanding "the restoration of the rights and liberties of the American people."[7] Horatio Greeley, when accepting both the Liberal Republican and Democratic nominations four years later, emphasized the restoration of rights to the white South, especially restoration of the elective franchise.

Republicans' version of rights centered on "equal rights" in 1868,[8] an explicit defense of "the rights of the colored men of the country" in 1872,[9] and a lengthy demand by Rutherford B. Hayes in 1876 for "the complete protection for all [American] citizens in the free enjoyment of all their constitutional rights." "There can be no enduring peace," Hayes warned, "if the constitutional rights of any portion of the people are habitually disregarded. The moral and national prosperity of the Southern States can be most effectually advanced by a hearty and generous recognition of the rights of all, by all. . . ."[10] Hayes's opponent, Democratic nominee Samuel Tilden, also called for "equality before the law" and the protection of all citizens, "whatever their former condition, in every political and personal right,"[11] despite his strong appeal to Southern whites.

From the end of Reconstruction after the 1876 election, the discussion of rights fell off dramatically. When the subject was raised, it was in the form of occasional admonitions about the importance of preserving a free ballot. The chief exception came in 1884, when Republican James G. Blaine canvassed a wide array of rights issues, including the need for security in personal and civil rights regardless of race, the importance and complexities of religious liberty, and the need for a ballot untainted by either fraud or coercion. "To deposit a fraudulent vote is no worse a crime against Constitutional liberty than to obstruct the deposit of an honest vote."[12]

In his first election campaign in 1884, when he defeated Blaine, Grover Cleveland argued that "the curtailment of the absolute rights of the individual should only be such as is essential to the peace and good order of the community."[13] In his reelection campaign of 1888, Cleveland espoused the "guarantee to our colored citizens of their rights of citizenship,"[14] as did his opponent, Benjamin Harrison. Running yet again in 1892, Cleveland pointed to the tariff as an infringement of property rights; Harrison's renomination brought a letter with no references to rights at all. In keeping with Cleveland's and Harrison's commercial orientation, William McKinley made no mention of rights in his lengthy acceptance address of 1896 and only one mention in 1900.

It was William Jennings Bryan, McKinley's Democratic opponent, who turned presidential campaign rhetoric in a different direction by revitalizing the conversation about rights. In the course of his 1896 Madison Square Garden acceptance address, Bryan affirmed his support for property rights, expressed support for equality under the law, and cautioned against the danger of "great aggregations of wealth . . . trespassing upon the rights of individuals." He concluded with a paean to "freedom of conscience, freedom of thought and freedom of speech."[15] Four years later, during his rematch against McKinley, Bryan reiterated the doctrine of "equal rights for all, special privileges for none," amplified his earlier theme by arguing that "Property rights are most secure when human rights are most respected," and concluded with a vision of an American Republic in which "civil and religious liberty stimulate all to earnest endeavor."[16]

In the early twentieth century, key themes by candidates included (1) a general commendation of the constitutional rights of Americans, (2) a commendation of specific rights, (3) a general commitment to equality under the law, (4) a specific commitment to the equal rights of blacks, and (5) endorsement of women's suffrage.

The first theme was voiced by a number of candidates who called for the preservation of liberties (Taft 1912) and of the "constitutional rights" and "democratic liberties" of Americans (Hughes 1916), or warned against the curtailment of liberties (Hoover 1932). Specific rights mentioned in candidate messages included "life, liberty, and property" (Parker 1904), property rights (Taft 1912), religious freedom (Davis 1924 and Hoover 1932), and rights of speech, press, and assembly (Harding and Cox 1920, Smith 1928).

References to equality under the law or equal rights were also made by a number of candidates in both parties, including Theodore Roosevelt (1904),

Taft and Bryan (1908), Harding and Cox (1920), Davis (1924), and Hoover (1928). Taft devoted a section of his 1908 address to the rights and progress of the Negro, and proclaimed his endorsement of his party's platform calling for the protection of Negro rights. Harding echoed these sentiments, as did Coolidge at great length. Women's suffrage received favorable mentions from Hughes, Harding, and Cox, then ended as the novelty of the Nineteenth Amendment wore off. Neither of Woodrow Wilson's acceptance speeches, in 1912 and 1916, contained any references to individual rights.

The candidate messages of 1920 captured most of these themes, and were perhaps the best examples in that era of messages devoted to rights. At particular issue was the disposition of rights in the aftermath of the Great War. Warren Harding condemned the continuation of wartime regimentation and the suppression of rights in the late Wilson administration, saying the pro-Bolshevik movement "is not to be halted in throttled liberties. We must not abridge the freedom of speech, the freedom of press, or the freedom of assembly, because there is no promise in repression. These liberties are as sacred as the freedom of religious belief, as inviolable as the rights of life and the pursuit of happiness."[17] His Democratic opponent, James Cox, undoubtedly stung by Republican criticism, averred that "The necessity for the drastic laws of war days is not present now, and we should return at the earliest opportunity, to the statutory provisions passed in time of peace for the general welfare. There is no condition now that warrants any infringement on the right of free speech and assembly nor on the liberty of the press."[18]

As the New Deal matured, battle lines were shaped that endured in some form for the rest of the century. On one hand, Alf Landon made the argument that economic liberty and political liberty were closely connected. "Crushing debts and taxes," Landon argued, "invariably retard prosperity and they sometimes lead to situations in which the rights of the people are destroyed. . . . Neither political nor civil liberty long survive the loss of economic liberty. Each and all of these liberties, with the precious human rights which they involve, must be preserved intact and inviolate."[19] Franklin Roosevelt made another kind of connection between economic and political liberty: "the political equality we once had won was meaningless in the face of economic inequality." The "economic royalists" opposing him favored protection of the right to vote "but denied that the government could do anything to protect the citizen in his right to work and his right to live."[20]

This new framework recurred in several speeches over the following decades. Barry Goldwater revived Landon's argument in 1964, holding that "We see in the sanctity of private property the only durable foundation for constitutional government in a free society."[21] Bob Dole followed suit, arguing in 1996 that "The freedom of the marketplace is not merely the best guarantor of our prosperity. It is the chief guarantor of our rights, and a government that seizes control of the economy for the good of the people ends up seizing control of the people for the good of the economy."[22]

Otherwise, the old themes remained vibrant. A large number of candidates extolled rights or liberties in general. Franklin Roosevelt praised our liberties, which were "placed into glorious operation" under the Constitution and the Bill of Rights. Eisenhower's first message contained the observation that Americans must "guard and extend their rights." Humphrey promised no compromise on "securing human rights."

Specific rights also continued to be the object of consistent attention, with candidates professing fear for civil liberties in wartime (Willkie 1940) and fealty to religious liberty or separation of church and state (Kennedy 1960, Clinton 1996, Bush 2004); supporting the right to dissent and freedom of speech (Nixon 1968 and Clinton 1996), as well as the right to keep and bear arms (Gore 2000); and touting rights to "life, liberty, and pursuit of happiness" (Carter 1976, Reagan 1984). Controversial social issues relating to rights occasioned expressions of support for voluntary school prayer by Reagan (1984) and Bush (1988 and 1992), as well as varying views on abortion. Reagan, Bush the elder, Dole, and Bush the younger expressed opposition to abortion rights (or support of the rights of unborn children, depending on one's point of view), while Clinton and Gore defended abortion rights (or opposed fetal rights). Clinton and Gore both endorsed an amendment to secure "victims' rights," and Jimmy Carter proclaimed in 1976—in the aftermath of recent revelations about government spying—that "We can have an American government that does not oppress or spy on its own people but respects our dignity and our privacy and our right to be left alone."[23]

The general principle of equality under the law, equal rights, or equal justice claimed support from a wide array of candidates, including Wendell Willkie, Dwight Eisenhower, Richard Nixon, Lyndon Johnson, Gerald Ford, Bill Clinton, Bob Dole, and Al Gore. In comparison to the first half of the twentieth century, specific concern for civil rights for blacks veritably exploded starting with Harry Truman's acceptance speech in 1948. Both parties' candidates explicitly made such expressions in 1956, the Republican in 1960, the Democrat in 1964, the Republican in 1968 and 1972, both parties' nominees in 1976, the Democrat in 1980 and 1984, both parties' nominees in 2000, and the Democrat in 2004. After fundamental civil rights were secured in the 1960s, however, candidates (in the same way as party platforms) began to dispute peripheral and less morally obvious innovations advanced by civil rights activists. Consequently, Gerald Ford condemned forced busing in 1976 and George Bush attacked "quotas" in 1992, while Al Gore defended "affirmative action" in 2000. However, these forays into controversial civil rights questions were not as common in messages as in platforms. Similarly, the Equal Rights Amendment for women drew favorable comment from Carter and Mondale in successive elections, but has not been discussed by Democratic candidates since, in contrast with the Democratic platform.

This latter point indicates that, while there is considerable overlap, candidate messages treat a somewhat different class of individual rights questions than do platforms. To the extent that they diverge, modern platforms fix on controversial symbolic issues with appeal to base activists while messages focus on live issues of interest to the swing voters who are watching by the millions on television.

Federalism

The question of states' rights and federalism was raised by candidates or their surrogates in 52 percent of election years by Republicans and 41 percent of election years for Democrats, making it the second most consistently cited category over time. Federalism has suffered a dramatic decline in explicit discussion. Through 1888, nearly half of all federalism references were open. Yet from 1936 to 1956, only about one of every seven federalism references was explicit; from 1960 on, there have been no explicitly constitutional federalism references in nomination acceptance speeches.

While the Democratic platform prior to the Civil War consistently touted federalism and states' rights—indeed, often in identical language transferred from one platform to the next—candidate messages were much more variable. Martin Van Buren made a single, generic reference to the rights of the states; James Polk made no mention of the topic in the two brief messages selected for the sample; Lewis Cass wrote extensively on states' rights, but almost exclusively as the topic related to the preservation and extension of slavery; James Buchanan, speaking for Franklin Pierce in 1852, gave but one nod to states' rights but, like Cass, tied the principle to permitting "the Southern States to manage their own domestic affairs, in their own way, without interference."[24] By 1856, when speaking for himself, Buchanan reiterated the same point extensively. On the eve of disunion, Stephen Douglas spoke often of states' rights, but always in the context of slavery and the legal status of the Negroes. Hence, where the party's platforms tended to emphasize states' rights as an abstract principle, its candidates or their spokesmen tended to emphasize the application of the principle to the specific issue of slavery.

On the Whig and Republican side in these years, it is clear that the parties' candidates were cognizant of criticisms that they favored some form of "consolidation" (a term commonly used to denote extreme centralization destroying the distinctive character of the states). William Henry Harrison conceded that "There is truth" in the proposition that "one of the great dangers in our government is, the powers vested in the general government would overshadow the government of the States." He turned this fear against his opponents by alleging that the Democratic patronage machine was "urging 100,000 office holders to meddle in the State elections," a signal threat to the liberty of the states.[25] Henry Clay barely touched upon the topic, Zachary Taylor touched on it not at all, nor did Winfield Scott. Again we see a difference between the party and the party's candidates. Though mainstream Whigs had fairly well-developed ideas about the relationship of the federal government to the states, Whig candidates rarely expressed them.

As the Republican Party arose to fill the void left by the decay of the Whigs, their candidates proved less reticent. John C. Fremont focused on individual rights, but Abraham Lincoln devoted a large portion of his Cooper Union speech to the question of the role of the federal government in establishing rules regarding slavery in the territories and new states.

Once the Civil War was underway, rhetoric on federalism shifted. Democrats starting with George McClellan reverted to rhetorical commitments to the constitutional rights of the states in the abstract, a theme he mentioned thrice in a relatively short acceptance letter. Horace Greeley, as the fusion candidate of the Democrats and Liberal Republicans in 1872, committed himself to "aim at local self-government and not at centralization" and pledged that "there shall be no Federal subversion of the internal polity of the several States and municipalities."[26] While Samuel Tilden took a swipe at the "centralism" of the Republicans, Winfield Hancock in 1880 articulated a coherent theory of the federal system, citing the Tenth Amendment verbatim and saying:

> The General and State Governments, each acting in its own sphere, without trenching upon the lawful jurisdiction of the other, constitute the Union. This Union, comprising a General Government with general powers, and State Governments with State powers for purposes local to the States, is a polity, the foundations of which were laid in the profoundest wisdom.[27]

Grover Cleveland, whose letters represented a marked decline of constitutional rhetoric in general, finally brought forward a federalism issue in 1892, in his third consecutive nomination acceptance letter: an objection to

Republican efforts to "control the suffrage of the States through Federal agencies." Cleveland was followed by William Jennings Bryan, who revived constitutional rhetoric in general but continued Cleveland's neglect of federalism issues. Bryan mentioned no such issues in 1896, 1900, or 1908. Likewise, Judge Alton Parker in 1904 refrained from making any federalism references. While Democratic platforms throughout this period retained a discussion of the party's views on federalism, both of the main factions of the party—the conservative, business-oriented, and progold wing represented by Cleveland and Parker and the agrarian, populist wing represented by Bryan—nominated men who were not inclined to bring those issues to public attention in their most important campaign communications.

Republican discussion of federalism in this period was also limited. Party spokesmen fashioned a nationalist interpretation of the institutions of the federal government in 1864, and asserted the rightful authority of the federal government to enforce civil rights against the states in the Reconstruction South in 1872.[28] James Garfield in 1880 made an extended argument for national supremacy, while vowing to protect the rights properly reserved to the states. He went on to argue that "all the people and all the States are members of one body, and no member can suffer without injury to all." Garfield also pointed to education as an area of policy which was "entrusted to the States and to the voluntary action of the people."[29] In 1892, Benjamin Harrison attacked Democrats for giving new authority to states in banking issues. Otherwise, in this era, Republicans in 1868, Hayes in 1876, Blaine in 1884, Harrison in 1888, and McKinley in both 1896 and 1900 had nothing to say about federalism. After the Civil War, only Garfield made an argument parallel to arguments often found in Republican platforms.

In the first third of the twentieth century, William Howard Taft reflected on the role of the states relative to the federal government in antitrust law (1908) and banking regulation (1912). Republican Charles Evans Hughes in 1916 and Democrat John Davis in 1924 remarked upon the character and importance of the federal system. Hughes called for an America "maintaining a well-ordered constitutional system adapted to local self-government without the sacrifice of essential national authority,"[30] while Davis called for the preservation of "local self-government as against a centralized bureaucracy."[31] In 1928, Al Smith called for a constitutional revision of the Eighteenth Amendment allowing for state choice regarding prohibition, a call echoed by Herbert Hoover four years later.

The 1932 candidate messages offered a distinct difference of emphasis, though Hoover and Roosevelt literally said the same thing. Their argument was that depression relief was primarily a local responsibility, but that the federal government had a role to play. However, Hoover focused on state responsibility and the limits of the federal role, and Roosevelt focused on the federal responsibility for the general welfare and the limits of state and local capacities. Hoover's embrace of states' rights anticipated the tone of Republican messages on federalism for the next seven decades, though it is interesting to note that Republican platforms had taken this stance beginning in the 1920s. Roosevelt's embrace of national action and skepticism of the states stood in some contrast to the Democratic platform of 1932, but it was Roosevelt's speech, not the 1932 platform, that set the pace for future Democratic messages. From 1936 to 2004, ten of eighteen Republican candidate messages included a mention of federalism, and those mentions were uniformly critical of centralization and supportive of stronger states and local governments. In that same period, only two of eighteen Democratic messages included a reference to federalism, and those did not come until 1996 and 2000.

Republican promotion of decentralized government in the new environment fostered by the New Deal was first evident in Alf Landon's acceptance speech of 1936. Landon decried centralization, referred to the reserved powers of the states, and pledged that "We propose to maintain the constitutional balance of power between the States and the Federal Government."[32] Several Republican nominees followed Landon's lead. Eisenhower devoted an extended portion of his 1956 speech to the hazards of centralization, boasting that his administration had "stemmed the heedless stampede to Washington."[33] Goldwater called attention to the "land of liberty built by decentralized power" and pledged to revitalize the "beauty of this Federal system of ours [which] is in its reconciliation of diversity with unity."[34] Nixon promised to send power back to the states, as did Reagan in 1980. (In 1984, Reagan talked of how he had succeeded in restoring authority to the states.)

In some cases, candidates related federalism to specific issues. Willkie complained about the centralization of power against farmers, while Ford and Bush the younger claimed to support local control of education. In recent years, Democratic candidates have haltingly returned to this theme after six decades of absence. Running for reelection, Clinton took credit for congressional action to stop unfunded federal mandates against state and local governments. And in 2000, Gore joined Bush in acknowledging local responsibility for education. In this sense, recent acceptance speeches have paralleled platforms.

The long-term drop-off of federalism references in candidate messages, especially among Democrats, was consistent with that found in platforms but more extreme. Constitutionalism in campaign rhetoric has suffered correspondingly.

Executive Power

The powers of the president were a topic of discussion in candidate messages about two-fifths of the time for both parties. Democrats were slightly more likely to raise the issue, though Whigs and Republicans were more likely to make the issue a highly salient part of their constitutional rhetoric. More than half of executive power references were explicit through the turn of the century, a figure that fell to one-third from 1960 to 1980 and was cut in half again after 1980.

As one might expect, Whigs particularly assailed abuse of executive power. In what at least one political historian has considered the first example of face-to-face appeal to voters by a presidential candidate,[35] William Henry Harrison told a Dayton, Ohio audience in 1840 that "He who declared that the seeds of monarchy were sown in the soil of the Constitution, was a leader in my school of politics."[36] A significant portion of his long address was dedicated to that theme. Henry Clay took the Democrats to task for the memory of Andrew Jackson's veto of the bank bill, complaining that "Unfortunately, our chief magistrate possesses more powers, in some respects, than a King or Queen of England."[37] In 1848, Zachary Taylor blasted the excessive use of the president's veto, which he held put the American system "in danger of undergoing a great change from its true theory."[38] Four years later, Winfield Scott agreed that resort to the veto power should always be "most cautiously exercised and under the strictest restraints and necessities."[39]

In the meantime, Democrats paid little heed to the Whigs' concerns about executive powers. James Buchanan, speaking on behalf of Franklin Pierce in 1852, complained that the natural order between the commander in chief and military subordinates had been inverted by Scott's nomination over incumbent Millard Fillmore. When speaking for himself in 1856, Buchanan pledged "that all the power and influence Constitutionally possessed by the Executive shall be exerted, in a firm but conciliatory spirit," to restore the harmony of the states.[40] (This pledge can, of course, be viewed somewhat ironically given Buchanan's paralysis when the secession crisis arrived in full force in late 1860.)

In 1864, in the midst of the Civil War, the Whig fears about executive usurpation reappeared, this time as part of the Democratic campaign. Eight years later, Horace Greeley called for a constitutional amendment limiting presidents to one term, a proposal repeated by Samuel Tilden and Grover Cleveland. (Somewhat incongruously, Horatio Seymour attacked the Republicans in 1868, in the wake of the Andrew Johnson impeachment, for "shackling the executive."[41])

Republicans made rare reference to executive powers in these days, defending the president against charges of arbitrary action in the Reconstruction South in 1872. The issue of executive appointments was raised as a matter of executive powers in 1876 and again in 1880, as civil service agitation picked up strength; additionally, Rutherford B. Hayes neither endorsed nor condemned the one-term proposal, but said as a matter of personal preference that he would abide by its limits. Issues of executive power then receded from candidate messages for the remainder of the nineteenth century. Twentieth-century references to executive powers generally fell into three types. In one, challengers complained about executive usurpation. In 1916, for example, Charles Evans Hughes objected that Woodrow Wilson had not received congressional authorization before seizing Veracruz; Al Smith made the same complaint about Calvin Coolidge's dispatch of Marines to Nicaragua.

Sometimes those concerns were much broader, alleging a pattern of executive abuse, and were related in much starker language. In 1920, Warren Harding spoke out against Wilson's "autocracy," confessing alarm "over the failure to restore the constitutional methods when the war emergency ended."[42] In 1936 Alf Landon argued that Franklin Roosevelt had engaged in "a substitution of personal for constitutional government," and condemned a "new and dangerous impulse . . . to take away and lodge in the Chief Executive, without the people's consent, the powers which they have kept in their State governments or which they have reserved in themselves."[43] As Roosevelt sought a fourth term in 1944, Thomas Dewey continued the thrust, promising that "This election will bring an end to one-man government in America."[44] Dewey also attacked "petty tyrannies" in the regimented wartime economy and contended that Roosevelt had proven that the founders had been right when they held three terms to be too many. Interestingly, despite numerous accusations in the broader political arena of abuse of constitutional powers by the executive since 1944, including charges directed at Presidents Johnson, Nixon, Reagan, Clinton, and Bush the younger, this theme has not recurred openly in acceptance speeches.

A second theme of candidate message rhetoric on executive powers consisted of a positive exposition of presidential powers. Sometimes this exposition was not terribly substantial, as in several cases in which candidates referred to the performance of their duty under the Constitution, a reference by John Davis to the president's power to appoint, and a reference by Franklin Roosevelt to his duties as commander in chief. Sometimes candidates were more expansive in their declarations. Perhaps the most forward and articulate of these expressions was offered by Theodore Roosevelt, who defended himself against charges that he had overstepped his bounds in Panama by saying:

> The decisive action which brought about this beneficent result was the exercise by the President of the powers vested in him, and in him alone, by the Constitution . . . But the Constitution must be observed positively as well as negatively. The President's duty is to serve the country in accordance with the Constitution; and I should be derelict in my duty if I used a false construction of the Constitution as a shield for weakness and timidity or as an excuse for governmental impotence.[45]

Similar sentiments were articulated by Ronald Reagan in 1980, noting the responsibility of the president for the security of the American people, and Al Gore in 2000, who contended that the presidency was "the only job in the Constitution that is charged with responsibility of fighting for all the people."[46]

The third major theme of the twentieth century, and a theme distinguishing modern messages from their nineteenth-century antecedents, was a discussion of the limits of presidential power that defined those limits as unfortunate, often accompanied by calls to expand executive powers accordingly. In 1924, John Davis accused congressional Republicans of going too far in their goal of reversing the "executive autocracy" of the Wilson years. Herbert Hoover in 1932 sadly conceded that the president has no constitutional role in the process of constitutional amendment. In the most colorful example, Gerald Ford declared in his acceptance speech that "the President of the United States is not a magician who can wave a wand or sign a paper that will instantly end a war, cure a recession, or make a bureaucracy disappear. A President has immense powers under the Constitution, but all of them ultimately come from the American people and their mandate to him."[47] A number of speeches, including Reagan's in 1984, Bush's in 1992, and Clinton's in 1996, included a call for a line-item veto. Finally, the presidential oath of office was held up in several speeches as either a limitation on presidential power (Landon, in particular, used it this way) or a means of empowering the president.

Constitutional Amendments

References to constitutional amendments found their way into a little more than one-third of candidate messages in each party. As in platforms, references to constitutional amendments in candidate messages were and have remained predominantly explicit rather than implicit in character.

In some cases, these were references made to already-enacted amendments like the Thirteenth, Fourteenth, and Fifteenth Amendments after the Civil War, which a series of Democrats called "inviolable." Winfield Scott proposed allowing citizenship for immigrants who served a year in the army or navy, a proposal that would have required a constitutional amendment to effect. Horace Greeley, Samuel Tilden, and Grover Cleveland endorsed a one-term limit for the president, and Rutherford B. Hayes called for an amendment to prohibit tax aid to sectarian schools.

Twentieth- and twenty-first-century references to constitutional amendments took three basic forms. Throughout, numerous candidates have called for passage (or opposition to) specific proposed amendments. William Howard Taft opposed as unnecessary an amendment expressly permitting a federal income tax. William Jennings Bryan (1908) and Woodrow Wilson (1912) demanded direct election of U.S. Senators, while William Howard Taft offered lukewarm support to that revision in 1908. Jimmy Carter and Walter Mondale called for passage of the Equal Rights Amendment (1980–1984); Ronald Reagan, George H. W. Bush, and Bob Dole called for a balanced budget amendment (1984, 1992, and 1996); Reagan and Bush endorsed an amendment permitting voluntary school prayer (1984, 1988, and 1992); and Bill Clinton and Al Gore expressed support for a "victims' rights amendment" (1996 and 2000). In 2004, George W. Bush endorsed a federal marriage amendment to prohibit same-sex marriage, while John Kerry attacked the president for proposing it. In Bush's view, "Because the union of a man and a woman deserves an honored place in our society, I support the protection of marriage against activist judges."[48] In Kerry's speech, the Democratic nominee accused Bush of opportunism and divisiveness, saying, "[L]et's never misuse for political purposes the most precious document in American history, the Constitution of the United States."[49]

A second type of reference came when candidates praised or otherwise commented upon recently ratified amendments. The easier of these cases was the Nineteenth Amendment, guaranteeing to women the right to vote in federal elections, which was heartily endorsed by both 1920 candidates. The harder case was the Eighteenth Amendment—the Prohibition amendment—which was given substantial attention by both parties' candidates through the 1920s, as they grappled with difficult questions of enforcement and revision.

Finally, a handful of candidates eschewed discussion of specific amendments in favor of reflection on the process and uses of amendment in general. Bryan in 1900 reminded the people of their right to amend the Constitution, while Taft in 1912 criticized progressive proposals to change the amendment process. Alf Landon, in the midst of a great political and policy upheaval, argued that momentous changes in the powers of government should be effected by amendment rather than fiat:

> The people have the right, by the means they have prescribed, to change their form of government to fit their wishes. If they could not do this, they would not be free. But change must come by and through the people and not by usurpation. Changes should come openly, after full and free discussion, and after full opportunity for the people to express their will.[50]

Altogether, as in platforms, candidates have been more likely to support than oppose an amendment. Unlike many other topics in candidate messages, references to amendments have not fallen off dramatically.

Enumeration of Powers

References to enumeration of powers appeared in about one in three messages of both parties overall. However, as with platforms, these figures disguise a drastic decline in the twentieth century. Of the fourteen Republican messages including a mention of enumeration of powers, only one came after 1936—Barry Goldwater's nomination acceptance speech in 1964. On the Democratic side, there were fifteen candidate messages that included a reference to enumeration of powers, not one of which came after 1924.

In keeping with the pattern found in the discussion of federalism, some early Democrats like Martin Van Buren stressed the strict limits of congressional authority in general, while others like Lewis Cass applied the principle of limited congressional authority to the right of Congress to regulate slavery in the territories. Buchanan applied the principle to Winfield Scott's proposed changes in naturalization law (holding them unconstitutional) and to the fugitive-slave laws (holding them within Congress's power).

In the antebellum era, the Democrats' Whig opponents promoted the constitutionality of congressional acts to charter a national bank (1840) and distribute to the states funds from the sale of public lands (1844). In 1860, Lincoln denied that the power of emancipation lay with the federal government, but insisted that it "has the power of restraining the extension of the institution" of slavery.[51]

As the nineteenth century was drawing to a close, Republicans like James Garfield proclaimed the constitutional authority of Congress to expend funds for river and harbor improvements, "provided that the expenditures for that purpose are strictly limited to works of National importance."[52] Garfield also proposed that the federal government use "all its constitutional authority" to end abuses of rights in the states.[53] Two elections later, Benjamin Harrison rejected the Democrats' contention that the protective tariff was unconstitutional, a position repeated in 1904 by Theodore Roosevelt. Roosevelt also included in his nomination acceptance letter a long passage acknowledging the limits on national power regarding economic regulation but pledging to act forcefully "[w]ithin the limits defined by the national Constitution."[54]

As Winfield Hancock laid out a theory of federalism in his acceptance letter, so he addressed the question of enumerated powers, saying that the powers granted in the Constitution "define and limit the authority of the General Government."[55] Grover Cleveland, in his first election, contended that improvement of waterways was acceptable within the limits of the Constitution, a formulation that became increasingly common in candidate messages as in platforms. In 1892, Cleveland explicated the Democratic Party's position, found in its platforms and refuted by Republican nominees, that a protective tariff exceeded the bounds of Congress's lawful authority.

Democratic candidates in the early 1900s brought the notion of enumerated powers into their acceptance messages in a variety of ways. These included Bryan's 1900 attack on imperialism as having "no warrant in our Constitution;"[56] Alton B. Parker's discussion of the tariff and more general exposition on the importance of observing strict constitutional limits; Bryan's 1908 call for campaign finance laws as "constitutionally within the control of Congress;"[57] and Woodrow Wilson's 1912 call for promotion by the federal government of agricultural, industrial, and vocational education "in every way possible within its constitutional powers."[58] In 1920, James Cox pointed to the Constitution as the "license and limitation given to and placed upon the law making body," and addressed regulation of food in light of the responsibility of the federal government to oversee "interstate commerce."[59] The final Democratic reference to enumeration of powers came in 1924 when the nominee pledged action on behalf of farmers to the constitutional limits of federal power.

Meanwhile, just as Democrats were losing their interest in enumerated powers, Republicans were obtaining theirs. At first, this interest was exerted on behalf of a broader conception of constitutional limits, as William Howard Taft exulted that "The power of the federal government to tax and expend for the general welfare has long been exercised, and the admiration one feels for our Constitution is increased when we perceive how readily that instrument lends itself to wider Governmental functions in the promotion of the comfort of the people."[60] He then cited examples of the use of the interstate commerce clause to advance the position of the worker. Taft, as well as Charles Evans Hughes four years later, carried on the old argument in defense of the constitutionality of the protective tariff.

In 1920, 1928, 1932, and 1936, Republicans shifted to emphasizing the limits that enumeration of powers placed on federal legislation. "The laws of Congress must harmonize with the Constitution," Warren Harding held in 1920, "else they soon are adjudged to be void."[61] Herbert Hoover emphasized the broad functions of federal authority in 1928. When in 1932 he again held that "The function of the Federal Government in these times is to use its reserve powers and its strength for the protection of citizens and local governments by supporting our institutions against forces beyond their control," he coupled this sentiment with an admonition that federal authority was not to supplant the responsibilities of states, localities, or individuals.[62] When Alf Landon drew the unenviable task of facing Franklin Roosevelt in 1936, he applauded the progress made against economic abuses through use of the interstate commerce power and pledged to use the full powers of the federal government to break up monopoly, but also asked whether Americans would continue to recognize "that certain functions"—and here he clearly meant only certain functions—"are delegated to the federal government."[63]

Though Republican platforms would frequently return to that theme over the next sixty-eight years, the only Republican candidate to include it in his nomination acceptance speech was Barry Goldwater in 1964. Goldwater called for strong action in areas of clear governmental responsibility, but promised "government performing only those needed and constitutionally sanctioned tasks which cannot otherwise be performed."[64] Enumeration of powers may consequently be the topic that most clearly illustrates that candidate messages have suffered a greater degree of deconstitutionalization than platforms. If candidate messages are aimed more to a general audience and platforms to activists, this disparity also provides an important indication that voters find enumeration of powers a less compelling component of constitutionalism than do party activists (especially in the Republican Party).

Perfunctory Rhetoric

Perfunctory constitutional rhetoric was used in four of ten Democratic messages and in three of ten Republican messages. Moreover, almost the entire bulk of these references were made prior to 1940. Since that time, only three candidates made such a reference—Barry Goldwater in 1964, Jimmy Carter in 1976, and Bill Clinton in 1996. What was once rhetorical commonplace in candidate messages has withered into near-complete disuse. Thus, not only have candidates increasingly shied away from discussion of a variety of substantive constitutional issues, they have also surrendered the rhetorical flourish of purely symbolic constitutionalism. Goldwater held that "We Republicans see in our constitutional form of government the great framework which assures the orderly but dynamic fulfillment of the whole man."[65] Carter called for "An America that lives up to the majesty of its Constitution."[66] Clinton professed his belief in the Constitution and said, "If you believe in the values of the Constitution, the Bill of Rights, the Declaration of Independence . . . you are part of our family and we're proud to be with you."[67] Otherwise, recent candidates have maintained silence.

In Clinton's, Carter's, and Goldwater's references one could hear the echoes of common forms of the perfunctory reference in years past: vague praise of the Constitution and American constitutionalism, forms that were frequently used in candidate messages from 1840 to 1936. Fremont, for example, referred to "constitutional freedom,"[68] and Parker referred to constitutionalism, arguing that our republic was "based on law and a written Constitution."[69]

A variation stressed loyalty to the Constitution. Candidates like William Henry Harrison, Van Buren, Buchanan, Douglas, McClellan, Taft, Harding, Davis, and Coolidge touted this concept. Buchanan and Douglas made numerous references to rebuffing threats to "Union and Constitution." McClellan avowed "love and reverence for the Union, Constitution, Laws and Flag of our country."[70] In similar fashion, Taft in 1912 declared that "The Republican Party stands for the Constitution as it is" and called for "true constitutional and representative rule by the people."[71] In 1936, Franklin Roosevelt and Alf Landon exchanged barbed comments, with Landon pledging to "restore our government to an efficient as well as constitutional basis"[72] and Roosevelt complaining that his opponents "seek to hide behind the flag and the Constitution."[73] References like these tested the line between the truly perfunctory and the substantive.

Several candidates referred to the framers of the Constitution and several referred to events or the passage of time since the formation of the Constitution. Finally, in a number of instances, messages used "constitutional" as a modifier referring to obligations, manner of election, and such. Winfield Hancock put forth the truism that "The Constitution forms the basis of the Government of the United States."[74]

Enforcement

Each party's candidate messages referred to constitutional enforcement in roughly one of every four election years. This category appeared a bit less consistently in Democratic candidate messages than in Democratic platforms, and much less consistently (by about one-half) in Republicans' messages than in their platforms. There were only four enforcement references from 1932 to 2004. Until 1980, enforcement references were more often explicit than implicit, perhaps because of the frequency with which candidates discussed enforcement of constitutional amendments.

These references typically took one of two forms. In many cases, candidates simply expressed their intention to do their constitutional duty to take care that the laws be faithfully executed. For example, James Garfield proclaimed that "If elected it will be my purpose to enforce strict obedience to the Constitution and the laws."[75] Perhaps the most intense such declaration was made by James Cox, who argued in 1920 that

> The public official who fails to enforce the law is an enemy both to the constitution and to the American principle of majority rule. It would seem quite unnecessary for any candidate for the presidency to say that he does not intend to violate his oath of office. Anyone who is false to that oath is more unworthy than the violator himself.[76]

Seven more candidates' messages included similar appeals, including Clay (1844), Hancock (1880), Cleveland (1884), Roosevelt (1904), Bryan (1908), Davis (1924), Ford (1976), and Bush (2000).

The second type of enforcement reference focused on the enforcement of a particular provision of the Constitution or statute with constitutional significance. In 1860, Stephen Douglas, for instance, devoted no small portion of his selected speech to the question of enforcement of the laws passed under the fugitive-slave clause of the Constitution. Another issue drawing significant enforcement attention was individual rights. While Alton B. Parker called for the enforcement of rights more generally, civil rights for blacks was a more common theme. In 1876, both parties' candidates pledged themselves to use executive power to protect the constitutional rights of citizens regardless of color, a pledge repeated by William Howard Taft in 1908. Both Richard Nixon in 1968 and Al Gore in 2000 included a reference to the enforcement of civil rights. (It is probable that some of the late-nineteenth-century commitments to general enforcement of the Constitution were actually aimed at this issue as well.) Taft, in particular, made an unusually detailed and forthright statement:

> The Republican platform, adopted at Chicago, explicitly demands justice for all men without regard to race and color, and just as explicitly declares for the enforcement, and without reservation, of the Thirteenth, Fourteenth, and Fifteenth Amendments to the Constitution. It is needless to state that I stand with my party squarely on that plank in the platform, and believe that equal justice to all men, and the fair and impartial enforcement of these amendments is in keeping with the real American spirit of fair play.[77]

Candidate messages from 1920 to 1932 were deeply concerned with enforcement of another constitutional provision: the recently ratified Eighteenth Amendment, or Prohibition. Every Republican message in those four elections contained references, often voluminous, to this issue. Without mentioning Prohibition, Cox's 1920 blast may also have been intended to address it, and the next two Democratic messages did so openly. Indeed, enforcement was the most frequently mentioned category in Alfred Smith's speech in 1928. As suddenly as that theme had arisen, it disappeared after repeal of the Eighteenth Amendment in 1933.

Supreme Court Decisions and Judicial Power

As in platforms, candidate messages dealt with these directly judicial topics with about equal consistency, and with sufficient consistency to place them around the middle of the pack of fifteen categories. However, as with almost every other category in candidate messages, the actual frequency with which these references appeared across time was much lower than in platforms. Altogether, both parties' candidate messages reference Supreme Court decisions one-sixth of the time and judicial power between one-fifth and one-quarter of the time. While there was not a clear pattern of judicial power references, references to Supreme Court decisions have been uniformly implicit since 1912.

Interestingly, references to Supreme Court decisions were actually spread more evenly across time in candidate messages than in platforms, where they were concentrated in recent years. In 1840, Martin Van Buren cursed the (by then four decades past) Federalist use of the judiciary before the election of Jefferson, and both Lincoln and Douglas devoted large portions of their selected addresses in 1860 debating the recent *Dred Scott* decision. Other decisions receiving attention from candidates include the *Pollock* decision invalidating the federal income tax (decried by Bryan in 1896); precedents establishing congressional authority over U.S. territories (McKinley 1900); cases regarding monopolies (Parker 1904, Taft 1908 and 1912) and labor rights (Taft 1908 and Wilson 1916); and *United States v. Butler*, which overturned the New Deal Agricultural Adjustment Act (Landon 1936).

In more recent times, Richard Nixon used his 1968 acceptance speech to criticize court decisions that "have gone too far in weakening the peace forces as against the criminal forces in this country."[78] Bill Clinton in 1992 and Al Gore in 2000 included praise to *Roe v. Wade* in their acceptance remarks. Otherwise, recent candidates have shied away from frontally praising or attacking court decisions that are often vigorously dissected in party platforms.

Discussions of judicial power have likewise been less heavily loaded onto recent messages. Horatio Seymour accused 1868 Republicans of trammeling the judiciary, and six messages between 1908 and 1928 included calls for restricting the use of judicial injunctions against labor—Taft in 1912, Wilson in 1916, Cox in 1920, Davis in 1924, and both Smith and Hoover in 1928. In 1976, Gerald Ford called for restrictions on court-ordered busing, while in 1992 George H. W. Bush called for "judicial restraint."

Two candidates used their messages to expound a broader theory of judicial power—and one that envisioned more rather than less powerful courts. William Howard Taft in both 1908 and 1912 assailed a "dangerous attack upon the power of the courts" waged by his opponents,[79] and specifically expressed opposition to the recall of judges and other populist/progressive devices to reduce the independence of the judiciary. In the same line, Calvin Coolidge declared in 1924 that "We believe that our liberties and our rights are best preserved, not through political, but through judicial action."[80] One might consider Coolidge's statement an early example of the acceptance of judicialism by the elected branches.

In three elections, the candidates tussled over the authority of the courts. In 1860, Lincoln complained that some sought to maintain slavery in the territories through use of the judiciary, while Douglas accused Republicans of not sufficiently acceding to the courts. In 1896, McKinley accused Democrats and Populists of fomenting a "dangerous and revolutionary assault on law and order"[81] by seeking to undermine the authority of the courts; while criticizing the *Pollock* decision, Bryan disclaimed any desire to "dispute the authority of the Supreme Court." Bryan went on to say, however, "I shall also refuse to apologize for the exercise by [the National Convention] of the right to dissent from a decision of the Supreme Court."[82] Finally, in 1968, Richard Nixon attacked recent court decisions but averred that he respected the court's authority; not sure whether to believe him, Hubert Humphrey argued that the answer to burgeoning civil disorder "does not lie in an attack on our courts."[83] As with references to Supreme Court decisions, candidates in recent years have been noticeably more reticent than party platforms to call for (or even debate) restrictions on the power of the judiciary. Whatever their positions on particular cases, candidates of both parties have clearly considered it disadvantageous to appear hostile to the independent judiciary itself.

Constitutional Sovereignty

The issue of American sovereignty vis-à-vis international organizations or treaties, was, in messages as in platforms, virtually unheard before 1920, although there were a couple of Democratic mentions prior to that. In 1848 the Democratic Party's nominee assailed the Wilmot Proviso for offering Mexico a veto over American slaveholding, and in 1896 attacked the gold standard for giving power over American finances to foreign bankers. Aside from these two cases, the other ten messages in which issues of constitutional sovereignty appeared came in 1920 or after, with the greater entanglement of the United States with world affairs and international organizations. Altogether, Democratic candidates raised the issue in one of eight of their messages and Republicans in about one in six of their messages, a number about one-third lower than found in their platforms. Well below 50 percent of these references have been explicit.

As in platforms, the issue came to a head in 1920 as the nation continued the debate over the Treaty of Versailles and U.S. participation in the League of Nations. Warren Harding's nomination acceptance speech was heavily laced with references to constitutional sovereignty and to accusations that Wilson and the Democrats had sought to surrender that sovereignty. James Cox's speech contained an extended rebuttal and proposals for how to preserve sovereignty while yet joining the League.

These same arguments continued in 1924 and, on the Republican side, 1928. In 1932 Hoover called for joining the World Court "under proper reservations preserving our freedom of action," and vowed that "We shall enter no agreements committing us to any future course of action or which call for use of force to preserve peace."[84] As late as 1936, Alf Landon repudiated any "plan that would take from us that independence of judgment that has made the United States a power for good in the world."[85]

By 1944, Thomas Dewey was taking a more balanced approach, decrying both those who would stand aloof from the world and those few "who believe it would be practical for America or her allies to renounce all sovereignty and join a Super-state."[86] A half century later, Bob Dole promised not to allow national sovereignty to be infringed by the World Trade Organization or any other international body, adding that "when I am president every man and every woman in our armed forces will know that the president is commander in chief, not Boutros Boutros-Ghali or any other UN Secretary General."[87] Finally, under attack by Republicans for alleged willingness to subordinate U.S. interests to the United Nations or foreign allies, John Kerry pledged in 2004 that "I will never give any nation or international institution a veto over our national security."[88] Although the subject grew considerably in importance beginning in 1920, candidate references were still rather sporadic— certainly in comparison to platforms—and typically arose in response to specific international situations. Dole, for example, was obliquely referencing an incident in which an American soldier on peacekeeping duty was reprimanded for wearing a U.S. flag on his uniform while on a UN mission. Criticism of Kerry was related to specific diplomatic circumstances surrounding the 2003 invasion of Iraq by U.S. forces.

Separation of Powers

A key structural question of American government, separation of powers has nevertheless fallen out of favor as a topic of discussion by presidential nominees. No Democrat has raised the issue since 1940, and no Republican since 1964. Overall, separation of powers has appeared in about one in seven Democratic messages and one in five Republican messages.

Early messages emphasized the need to prevent the executive from infringing on the lawmaking or judicial authority (Harrison 1840, Scott 1852, Greeley 1872). Carl Schurz, speaking for Republicans in 1868, decried the bitter struggles between the branches that had taken place under Andrew Johnson. Rutherford B. Hayes pointed in 1876 to the patronage system as destroying the independence of the branches, while Grover Cleveland's 1884 acceptance letter demarcated the lawmaking function from the executive function within government.

In Alton Parker's 1904 message, the Democratic candidate offered voters a civics lesson reminding them of the importance of the three coordinate branches and the duty of each branch to refrain from undermining the others' powers. William Howard Taft in 1912 referred four distinct times to the importance of the independence of the judiciary. Like Parker, Warren Harding reminded voters of the essence of separation of powers, and extolled the Senate's role in checking presidential authority, declaring, "Its members are the designated sentinels on the towers of constitutional government."[89] Democratic nominee James Cox retorted that the Senate had improperly obstructed the president's peacemaking power. Four years later, Calvin Coolidge expressed pro forma endorsement of our three branches of government, and in 1928 Alfred Smith acknowledged the Senate's role in treaty ratification.

The final two references to separation of powers in candidate messages came in 1940 and 1964. In the former instance, Franklin Roosevelt extolled "the coordination of the executive, the legislative, and the judicial branches" and referred to recent defensive measures taken "with due congressional approval."[90] Twenty-four years later, Barry Goldwater proclaimed that "we must have balance between the branches of government at every level."[91] Forty years after that, the topic had not been heard again in acceptance speeches, despite its obvious importance to American government and despite a number of controversies testing the boundaries of each branch's authority. The eclipse of discussion about separation of powers must be considered to be both a quantitative and qualitative decline in constitutional rhetoric.

Appointments

Constitutionally relevant appointments were mentioned by candidates of both parties in about one out of ten election years, a figure half that found in platforms. As in the platforms, though, references to appointments in candidate messages have been heavily loaded onto recent times. Fewer than one-third of appointment references have been explicitly constitutional. Except for a 1924 promise by John Davis to refrain from applying any (unconstitutional) religious test to his appointments, no one mentioned this topic until 1968.

Starting in that year, appointments were discussed by Nixon in 1968 and 1972, Mondale in 1984, Dukakis in 1988, George H. W. Bush in 1992, Dole in 1996, and both George W. Bush and John Kerry in 2004. Nixon promised a new attorney general and judges who would be tougher on criminal defendants; Mondale promised a Supreme Court dedicated to justice; Dukakis called for a high-quality Justice Department and federal judges who understood the Constitution. Bush the elder warned that "Clinton and Congress will stock the judiciary with liberal judges who write laws they can't get approved by the voters."[92] Dole attacked Bill Clinton's liberal judicial appointees and promised judges who would interpret the Constitution rather than amend it. Bush the younger and Kerry sparred, with Bush promising judges "who know the difference between personal opinion and the strict interpretation of the law"[93] and Kerry promising an attorney general who "actually upholds the Constitution."[94] This category of references offers another way in which candidates have responded to judicialism in the last half of the twentieth century. Their rhetorical efforts, however, have not matched those found in the party platforms.

Mode of Constitutional Interpretation

This subject was mentioned in only two Democratic and three Republican messages, only one of which came after 1860. Despite being a persistent topic of early Democratic platforms, the mode of interpretation was only raised by James Buchanan in 1852 (as a surrogate) and by Stephen Douglas in 1860. Buchanan accused the Whig candidate, Winfield Scott, of planning to make the Constitution "a mere nose of wax, to be twisted, and turned, and bent in any direction which the opinion or caprice of the moment might dictate."[95] Douglas proclaimed in 1860 that "we stand by the Constitution as our fathers made it, and by the decisions of the constituted authorities as they are pronounced in obedience to the Constitution."[96]

Henry Clay expounded on this question, saying "In early life, on deliberate consideration, I adopted the principles of interpreting the federal Constitution, which have been so ably developed and enforced by Mr. Madison, in his memorable report to the Virginia Legislature. . . ."[97] In 1860, Lincoln complained to the Southerners that they were threatening to destroy the government "unless you be allowed to construe and force the Constitution as you please."[98] Not until 2004 did another Republican candidate address this question, when George W. Bush called for judges who would "know the difference between personal opinion and the strict interpretation of the law."[99]

Discussion of the mode of constitutional interpretation is perhaps the most highly abstract of the fifteen categories of rhetoric. Its nearly total absence from candidate messages for more than a century until its recent reappearance is an indication of the difficulty of presenting such abstract intellectual arguments in direct campaigning, all the more so in the age of modern media. Thus, another key feature of constitutionalism has nearly evaporated from the rhetoric of presidential candidates speaking directly to the American people. That a reference was made as recently as 2004 shows that the potential still exists for such a discourse to enter campaigns.

Veto

This constitutional category appeared in a mere one message per party. Whig Zachary Taylor proposed, in keeping with his party's philosophy, that the veto power should never be used "except in cases of clear violation of the Constitution, or manifest haste and want of due consideration by Congress."[100] More concretely, Alfred Smith in 1928 pointed to Woodrow Wilson's veto of the Volstead Act—the implementing legislation for the Prohibition amendment—as a defense of liberty.

Impeachment

Only two Democratic and no Republican messages raised this issue. One Democratic candidate made critical reference to the failed Andrew Johnson impeachment (1868); the other pointed out that a key difference between being a senator and a president was that the latter was subject to impeachment for malfeasance (1920). Both the veto and impeachment are subjects that have not declined so much as they have simply remained consistently at a very low level of discussion throughout the long period in question.

Frequency of Constitutional References in Candidate Messages

As seen in the dramatic year-to-year ups and downs of constitutional rhetoric, candidate messages have a more idiosyncratic character than party platforms. As one set of analysts pointed out when discussing nomination acceptance speeches, "It is not surprising that the personality of a candidate for the office of President of the United States should produce a distinctive stamp on the candidate's nomination acceptance speech."[101] Every election or two, a new candidate emerges with a new style and a new set of priorities. Parties, on the other hand, usually change more slowly.

It is nevertheless possible to see that the decline of constitutional rhetoric in campaigns has proceeded farther in candidate messages than in platforms. Only four major party candidates completely avoided constitutional questions in their messages: Polk in 1844, Dewey in 1948, Stevenson in 1952, and McGovern in 1972. The overall number of constitutional references in candidate messages saw frequent ups and downs. The absolute peaks came in 1860 and on either side of the Wilson era, 1908 and 1920. Other major peaks came in 1928, 1936, 1968, and 1992–1996. In general, however, one sees a rough plateau from 1840 until the 1880s broken only by the spike of the Civil War; a considerable bulge around the turn of the century; a precipitous decline after 1936; and a new, lower plateau for the next seven decades. This pattern is in considerable contrast to party platforms, which have seen an increase in the total number of references. Platforms have grown much longer, and accommodate more references. Candidate messages have lengthened, but not as drastically, and that lengthening has not brought an increase of constitutional references in its train (chart 3.1).

Also unlike platforms, which have seen a major divergence between the parties in terms of the number of references, Democratic and Republican references have tracked each other closely except for a gap that opened up during the Progressive Era, when Democrats largely discontinued use of constitutional rhetoric in their acceptance speeches. To the extent that a difference can be seen otherwise, Republican candidates used slightly more

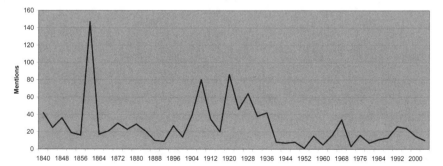

Chart 3.1.   Constitutional references in major-party candidate messages, 1840–2004

constitutional rhetoric than Democrats between 1952 and 2000, when they surrendered their advantage.

When references are adjusted for constitutional mentions per thousand words, three distinct eras emerge, each one with lower typical ratios than before.[102] The first lasted from 1840 to 1880; the second from 1884 to 1936; the third from 1940 through 2004. In the first period, messages ranged from about four to about ten constitutional mentions per thousand words. By the last period, messages ranged from 0.4 to 2.9 mentions per thousand words, with ten of seventeen years below 2.0 mentions per thousand words (chart 3.2).

Both parties experienced this three-stage decline, though since 1920 Republican peaks have consistently been about half again higher than Democratic peaks. The first inflection point where one stage seemed to move into another coincided roughly with an abrupt lengthening of candidate messages as candidates moved first into longer acceptance letters and then into long acceptance speeches. The second inflection point came roughly as candidates began to accept their nominations in person, and had their speeches covered on radio.

Because there are so many dramatic ups and downs in the trend line, it is more difficult to identify a clear trough of attention to constitutional issues. However, there is some slight evidence of a revival in rates of constitutional references in candidate messages. From 1952 through 1972, acceptance speeches averaged 1.5 references per thousand words; after 1972 they averaged 1.7 references per thousand words. The three years with the lowest rates all came in the first period (1952, 1960, and 1972). However, after some

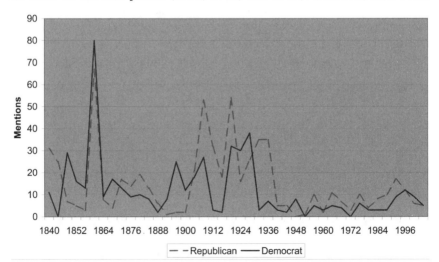

Chart 3.2. Constitutional references in candidate messages by party, 1840–2004

resurgence in messages, the rate of constitutional references fell back below one per thousand words in 2004.

Explicit vs. Implicit Rhetoric

As with platforms, there is a fairly clear trend of declining explicit constitutional rhetoric relative to implicit rhetoric once the peaks and valleys are brushed away. Explicit constitutional rhetoric was common in messages through the 1924 election, representing more than half of the total in twelve of twenty-two elections from 1840 to 1924. From 1928 through 2004, explicit rhetoric was a majority of references once. It reached the low 40 percent range twice, and was mostly found in the 30 percent range and below. This means that the eclipse of explicit rhetoric in candidate messages predated that in platforms by two decades or more, and was more severe (chart 3.3).

Neither party has significantly outperformed the other on this score. Democrats have had only one year since 1940 when a majority of their constitutional rhetoric was explicit; Republicans have only had two such years in that time. Both parties have experienced many years since 1924 when 100 percent of the constitutional content of their candidates' messages was implicit. Altogether, twenty-three major-party candidates since 1840 (out of a total of eighty-four) have offered messages with no explicit constitutional references at all, sixteen of them since 1932.[103]

When looking at the fifteen categories individually over time, it becomes clear that the deterioration of explicit constitutional rhetoric in messages has been quite broadly based (table 3.1). Constitutional amendments is the only category that started off as predominantly explicit and has remained so, though at a reduced rate in the most recent period. Enforcement has come close to this record, but in the most recent period fell off dramatically. Enumerated powers began as a topic that was almost always discussed explicitly, but from the New Deal onward was discussed much less explicitly, when it

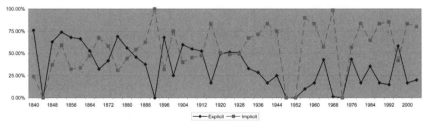

Chart 3.3. Percentage of references explicit and implicit constitutional in major-party candidate messages. 1840–2004

Table 3.1. Percentage of explicit candidate message references by category, 1840–2004

	1840–1860 (%)	1864–1884 (%)	1888–1908 (%)	1912–1932 (%)	1936–1956 (%)	1960–1980 (%)	1984–2004 (%)
CA	80	91	96	82	0	100	59
APP	N/A	N/A	N/A	0	N/A	0	29
IR	42	53	22	32	26	22	25
EP	90	57	80	67	0	50	0
FED	48	45	25	23	14	0	0
IMP	N/A	0	N/A	0	N/A	N/A	N/A
VETO	100	N/A	N/A	0	N/A	N/A	N/A
EXEC	62	54	63	37	43	33	17
ENF	100	67	60	74	N/A	67	0
SOP	50	0	50	92	0	0	N/A
SCD	58	N/A	45	0	0	0	0
JP	33	0	8	35	N/A	67	0
MODE	100	N/A	100	N/A	N/A	N/A	100
CONSOV	100	N/A	0	26	0	N/A	0
PERF	100	100	100	100	100	100	100

Note: N/A=not available.

was discussed at all. Both federalism and individual rights were originally discussed explicitly a bit more or a bit less than 50 percent of the time, and then in the late nineteenth century experienced a decline by roughly half. Ever since then, only about one in four rights references have been explicit. The same was true of federalism until the New Deal era, when it began experiencing another sharp decline. Since 1960, 100 percent of federalism references in candidate messages have been implicit.

Unlike platforms, in which the percentage of explicit references in several categories of constitutional rhetoric experienced a broad recovery over the last quarter century, candidate messages have enjoyed no such recovery. The only category showing a significant increase in the proportion of explicit references in the 1984–2004 period was appointments; individual rights showed a slight upward tick. The proportion of references that were explicit in other categories remained stagnant or continued experiencing declines. From 1984 to 2004, acceptance speeches had a smaller percentage of explicit references than did platforms in every one of the ten categories in which both had at least one reference, by a margin that averaged 23 percent.[104]

Breadth of Constitutional Content

Generally speaking, candidate messages dealt with fewer issues, and with fewer issues in depth, than did platforms. If platforms have fallen victim to deconstitutionalization by way of a narrowing of campaign rhetoric, candidate messages have fared worse. Individual rights is the only category that appeared in more than half of each party's messages and that represented at least 20 percent of the references in those messages where it appeared. Federalism was the only other category that was highly consistent, and then only in Republican messages, but it did not meet the threshold for depth, since it did not represent at least 20 percent of the constitutional mentions in at least half of the messages where it appeared. In Democratic candidate messages, federalism appeared neither consistently nor deeply.

A handful of categories—appointments for both parties and executive powers, perfunctory, and vetoes for Republicans—were discussed in depth but appeared in fewer than half of the messages. All other categories—nine of fifteen for both parties and another three for Democrats—failed in both consistency and depth. These included constitutional amendments, enumerated powers, impeachment, enforcement, separation of powers, Supreme Court decisions, judicial powers, mode of constitutional interpretation, constitutional sovereignty, and, for Democrats, perfunctory references and those relating to executive powers and veto. Several categories appeared very infrequently indeed, most notably mode of interpretation, veto, and impeachment, none of which were discussed in more than three messages in either party. These were also the least frequently cited topics in party platforms.

As with platforms, since 1952 a number of categories in candidate messages have improved their position on the continuum of consistency and depth. However, in contrast with platforms, no categories moved from low consistency to high consistency. Instead, constitutional amendments, constitutional sovereignty, judicial power, and mode of constitutional interpretation went from shallow to deep, meaning that most of the time when they appeared, they constituted at least 20 percent of the constitutional references in that message. (The veto category for Republicans moved the other direction.) (Appendix C places each category along the continuum in messages from 1952 to 2004.)

While the overall ordering of the categories was similar in both platforms and candidate messages, there were two significant differences. One was that there was no really big difference between the parties' candidate messages in terms of the frequency with which some topics were raised, as there was in a few platform categories. Second, the absolute frequency with which topics were mentioned across time was considerably lower in messages. Every category but two very low frequency categories (impeachment and separation of powers) was cited more consistently by both parties in platforms than in candidate messages. In most cases, the discrepancy was rather large. For example, constitutional amendments were discussed in three-quarters of Democratic and two-thirds of Republican platforms, but only a bit more than one-third of candidate messages; federalism appeared in nine of ten Democratic and eight of ten Republican platforms, but barely more than half of Republican messages and only four of ten Democratic messages; executive powers were mentioned in two-thirds of each party's platforms, but only two-fifths of each party's candidate messages (table 3.2).

When grouped into the three areas of rights, structure, and constitutional interpretation, the references in candidate messages bore a striking similarity to the trends found in platforms. An analysis of the combined messages shows that the three groupings have followed each other closely, except for the earliest messages, which were disproportionately influenced by issues of structure, and for two peaks of constitutional interpretation rhetoric corresponding to early twentieth-century debates over judicial power and constitutional amendments and then, a bit later, the Prohibition amendment (chart 3.4).

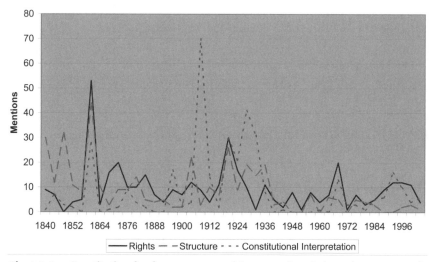

Chart 3.4. Constitutional references grouped by general topic in major-party candidate messages, 1840–2004

Table 3.2. Consistency of references to constitutional categories in platforms and candidate messages, 1840–2004

	Platforms		Messages	
Category	D	R	D	R
Const. amendments	76.2	65.9	35.7	38.1
Appointments	19.0	22.0	9.5	11.9
Individual rights	95.2	90.2	81.0	88.1
Enum. of powers	59.5	58.5	35.7	33.3
Federalism	90.5	78.0	40.5	52.4
Impeachment	4.8	12.2	4.8	0.0
Veto	2.4	2.4	2.4	2.4
Executive powers	64.3	68.3	40.5	40.5
Enforcement	33.3	56.1	26.2	28.6
Separation of powers	14.3	39.0	14.3	19.0
Supreme Court decisions	42.9	31.7	16.7	16.7
Judicial powers	38.1	34.1	19.0	23.8
Mode of const. interp.	14.3	9.8	4.8	7.1
Const. sovereignty	16.7	29.3	11.9	16.7
Perfunctory	45.2	53.7	40.5	31.0

Candidate messages also saw a pattern similar to that found in platforms when looking at the parties separately. One interesting deviation from the norm came in 1860. Contrary to what many might expect, it was the Republican candidate (Lincoln) whose message produced a spike in structural references, while the Democratic candidate (Douglas) produced a spike in references about rights. Douglas spoke at length about the rights of slaveholders postulated in the *Dred Scott* decision, while Lincoln's address focused on a federalism question—the role of the federal government in regulating slavery in the territories. More recently, Democratic candidates since 1948 have put rights well ahead of other concerns. Republican candidates in the same time period have issued messages less heavily weighted to a single theme. In several elections, the Republican candidate's message leaned toward structure or interpretation, though the bulge in structural references was not as pronounced as in Republican platforms.

Constitutional Exchanges in Candidate Messages

Finally, constitutional exchanges in candidate messages fell well short of even the modest baseline set in platforms. In the forty-two presidential elections held during the time frame of this study, candidate messages saw twenty-two constitutional exchanges (about one-third the number in platforms) in which both candidates or their surrogates mentioned the same constitutional issue and disagreed about it or criticized each other over it.[105] Exchanges in candidate messages can be found in Appendix C, table C3.

On the one hand, this averages more than one exchange in every other election cycle. On the other hand, the twenty-two exchanges were concentrated in fourteen elections, meaning exchanges actually took place in one of every three elections. More to the point, only three of the exchanges occurred after 1936. From 1840 to 2004, slightly over half of the exchanges—twelve of twenty-two—represented head-to-head policy disputes, as opposed to around two-thirds of platform exchanges. Clearly, candidates are both less interested in engaging each other over constitutional issues than they once were, and less interested in engaging each other than are the parties as institutions. When they talk about the Constitution in their nomination acceptance messages at all, most of the time they are talking past each other.

Conclusion

Key messages by candidates or their surrogates from 1840 to 2004 contained a wide array of constitutional issues, indicating that often not only party platform-writers but also the candidates themselves, in more or less direct communications with American voters, were concerned with those issues. However, if platforms left something to be desired in terms of constitutional rhetoric, candidate messages suffered the same problems to a greater degree. By the standards established in the introduction, constitutional rhetoric in messages is far from healthy.

The messages revealed the same problems as the platforms—a decline in the weight given to constitutional issues over time, a decline in the proportion of references that were explicitly constitutional in nature, and a narrowing of the rhetoric over time, with topics like enumeration of powers, federalism, executive powers, separation of powers, and even perfunctory references falling off dramatically in one or both parties in the twentieth century. Republicans, who had held a bit of an edge in constitutional rhetoric in candidate messages, surrendered that edge in the Bush years, as they did in platforms. Almost every constitutional category in both parties was mentioned more consistently in platforms than in candidate messages, usually by wide margins. In contrast with platforms, candidate messages have also featured a decline even in absolute references, and exchanges have declined dramatically rather than increased in recent years. Overall, except that references per thousand words edged ever so slightly upward after 1972 (before falling again in 2004), messages have not enjoyed the modest recovery of constitutional rhetoric that platforms have.

The deconstitutionalization of candidate messages is highly meaningful for assessing the state of constitutionalism in electoral politics in general. Comparing acceptance speeches and platforms, the campaign communication that is more widely accessible and the one that is now more aligned with modern technology—the acceptance speech—features considerably less vibrant constitutional rhetoric. It is also tantalizing to note that the steep dropoff of constitutional rhetoric in candidate messages in the twentieth century roughly coincided with the transformation of the nomination acceptance message into a mass media event. Perhaps the most thoroughgoing transformation of campaign communications, however, arrived with the advent of broadcast television advertisements, the subject of the next chapter.

CHAPTER FOUR

~

The Constitution
in Television Advertising

Political television ads appeared nationwide for the first time in 1952.[1] Since that first Eisenhower-Stevenson race, presidential campaign ads have become increasingly sophisticated technically and have played a bigger and bigger role in election strategy and campaign dynamics. Indeed, it is no exaggeration to say that television advertising is the essence of the modern campaign's mass appeal. It is also no exaggeration to say that disregard for constitutional issues has generally characterized that essence.

By a variety of measures, major-party presidential campaign television advertising has offered a considerably narrower and shallower version of the constitutional rhetoric found in party platforms or even candidate messages. While some patterns found in platforms are repeated in ads, campaign ads are consistently much less likely to contain constitutional references, explicit constitutional references, or a broad range of constitutional issues than are platforms. This phenomenon has been true across parties and across elections, and shows little sign of abating.

According to Kathleen Hall Jameison, "Political advertising is now the major means by which candidates for the presidency communicate their messages to voters. As a conduit of this advertising, television attracts both more candidate dollars and more audience attention than radio or print. Unsurprisingly, the spot ad is the most used and most viewed of all available forms of advertising."[2] Modern presidential and U.S. Senate campaigns spend the bulk of their money purchasing airtime for television ads, about 60 percent of fall expenditures in recent presidential races.[3] When asked directly, few voters (5 percent in one poll) report learning "a lot" about candidates from such ads, but a number of studies indicate that ads can actually have a much greater impact than that, especially in a synergistic combination with other sources like news and debates and especially in races with candidates who are less well known.[4] All in all, about one-quarter of voters report that political advertising helps them make their vote decisions.[5] Indeed, whatever voters tell pollsters, analysts purported to show that voters in the 1972 election actually received more usable information from television advertisements than they did from the television news, findings that have since been confirmed in the 1990s.[6] Some evidence points to the possibility that television ads are more effective at "reinforcement" and "activation" than "conversion"—that is, they are more likely to strengthen and mobilize one's supporters than they are to turn opponents into supporters.[7]

Undoubtedly, many more citizens are exposed to the cacophony of thirty-second spots than to any other form of campaign communication on a daily basis, at least in states that are targeted by campaigns for major media buys. Presidential debates exceed television ads in exposure at one moment in time, but they are few in number. At any rate, ads offer a better gauge of what campaigns want to emphasize, since the journalists and private citizens who ask the questions have considerable independent influence over the content of debates. Indeed, presidential election campaigns are now largely defined in the public memory by the most noteworthy ads, such as Lyndon Johnson's Daisy Girl, Ronald Reagan's Morning in America and Bear in the Woods, George H. W. Bush's Willie Horton, and George W. Bush's Windsurfing ads. At any rate, the professionals who run campaigns seem to believe that ads can make a big difference, under the right conditions.[8]

While party platforms have grown increasingly long, television ads have gotten shorter, now typically airing for thirty seconds and using fewer than one hundred words. While television ads usually use a narrator and often include written messages on the screen, they are fundamentally visual and emotive in character, focusing on action, setting, and other images complemented by mood-setting audio devices like music and varying voiceovers.[9] Most often, ad campaigns form a combination of fluffy personal features, positive issue expositions, and fast-paced attack-and-response exchanges. Voter surveys have indicated that "People believed that ads were the most effective in influencing general feelings about the candidates, and least effective in the communication of substantive information."[10] Some earlier studies, however, showed that the elections of 1972 and 1980 contained more issue advertising than generally thought.[11] A recent study by Darrell West demonstrates that, from 1952 to 2004, specific domestic and foreign policy ads (a combined 25 percent of the total) have lagged behind ads emphasizing personal qualities (33 percent) and domestic performance (30 percent). However, according to West, specific policy appeals are generally on the upswing since the 1970s. (West shows negative advertising in presidential races to have likewise risen, as issue ads are the most likely type of ad to be negative.)[12]

The question germane to our study is how many of those policy appeals have constitutional content. West's study delineates specific policy areas, several of which were potentially overlapping with constitutional concerns, but he did not devote a distinct category to those concerns. Furthermore, while most constitutional references take the form of specific policy appeals or appraisals, not all do. Some fall into areas labeled in West's study as domestic performance or international affairs, and the category of perfunctory constitutional references used in this study is fundamentally unsubstantive.

There are a number of reasons that one must be cautious in trying to discern the impact of a set of television advertisements by looking at ad transcripts. Prior to the 1990s, it was extremely difficult to tell how many times each ad was run, nor can one say exactly how many people watched each ad. Consequently, it is impossible to weight the importance of each ad. Furthermore, while every effort was made here to review the largest possible number of ads, the ads reviewed for 2000 and 2004 were but a sample of the hundreds of spots that were run by presidential campaigns in those years. Holes in other years probably exist as well.

Nevertheless, 1,155 major-party ads were examined and coded for constitutional content. The largest source of television ad text was the Annenberg Center CD-ROM "The Annenberg/Pew Archive of Presidential Campaign Rhetoric" (2000), which contained a large number of general election ads run by major-party candidates between 1952 and 1996, with the exception of Goldwater in 1964. To supplement the Annenberg collection and to fill in the gaps of 1964, 2000, and 2004, the following sources were used: (1) the American Museum of the Moving Image (AMMI), located in New York, whose online exhibit "The Living Room Candidate" included (as of summer 2006) a sample of 238 ads from every major-party general election campaign from 1952 to 2004; (2) The Spot: The Rise of Political Advertising on Television (revised edition), published in 1984, which contained the transcripts of a number of television ads from 1952 to 1980; (3) The Center for Political Communication at the University of Oklahoma, which provided the bulk of the 1964 Goldwater ads; and (4) Stanford University's political communications projects, "In Their Own Words," featuring collected ads from 2000 and 2004.[13]

While a platform is a single document written once every campaign, each ad can be seen as an individual document. This examination of ads will hence include a measure of the percentage of ads in each year or each campaign containing at least some constitutional rhetoric. Further, because different campaigns used wildly varying numbers of ads, it does not make sense to compare aggregate references for each year or campaign; for comparison across years, only the ratio of references per thousand words will be used.

What Does Television Advertising Say about the Constitution?

The constitutional content of television ads between 1952 and 2004 is notable primarily for its sparseness and relatively narrow focus. As in other venues, the category of individual rights predominates, but television ads are less likely to refer to the secondary issues. Categories of rhetoric are examined below in order from most to least consistent across years.

Individual Rights

Ads referencing individual rights appeared in 71 percent of Democratic campaigns and 50 percent of Republican campaigns since 1952. A slightly higher proportion of ads with a constitutional reference mentioned rights. Only about one out of five individual rights references were explicitly framed. Individual rights was the constitutional topic receiving the greatest mention in ten Democratic campaigns and five Republican campaigns. No other topic held that distinction as often.

For the first quarter century of presidential television advertising, civil rights issues were a common theme. In 1952, Adlai Stevenson's only constitutional ad pointed out that he had made a statement in the South "for civil liberties and full equality."[14] In 1960, both Kennedy and Nixon likewise emphasized civil rights. Nixon talked about "civil rights, equal rights for all our citizens . . . the record shows there's been more progress in civil rights in the past eight years than in the preceding eighty years."[15] Kennedy likewise proclaimed that "I'm not satisfied until every American enjoys his full constitutional rights," and defended school desegregation. On his behalf, Eleanor Roosevelt contended that Kennedy was committed to "human rights" and "equal opportunity under law," and urged viewers to "read again our Bill of Rights." At the same time, Kennedy devoted a lengthy ad to broadcasting a portion of his famous speech before Protestant ministers in Houston, Texas. The excerpted clip was introduced by a narration reminding viewers that "Article VI of the Constitution provides that there shall be no religious test of a man's right to hold public office" and contending that the election of

1960 would determine whether "the Constitution as written shall prevail." Kennedy himself declared in favor of "an America where the separation of church and state is absolute."[16]

In 1964, civil rights appeared again, as a Johnson ad pointed to the president's success in carrying out Kennedy's civil rights promise. Texas Senator John Tower recorded a message on behalf of Barry Goldwater assailing the Civil Rights Act of 1964 as a "coldly calculated and shrewdly drawn measure . . . [that is] whittling away your rights slowly so you won't notice until it hits you personally." Offering a completely different tone, Goldwater also ran an ad in which he proclaimed that "I was fighting for civil rights long before it became popular. Laws are not the whole answer. The real answer is in the hearts of men." (These contrasting Goldwater ads show how ads can present different arguments to targeted audiences, unlike platforms that make a single national argument.) Like Kennedy in 1960, Goldwater also made broader arguments regarding individual rights. In one ad, Ronald Reagan, speaking for Goldwater, complained that "Our natural unalienable rights are now considered to be a dispensation of government." Goldwater himself appealed to voters to "join me in helping restore the individual freedoms and initiatives this nation once knew."[17]

Like Johnson's, Hubert Humphrey's campaign boasted of the 1964 Civil Rights Act and showed Humphrey in his nomination acceptance speech obliquely referring to Nixon's quest for George Wallace voters, saying "Winning the presidency for me is not worth the price of silence or evasion on the issue of human rights."[18] Humphrey also ran a number of other ads extolling his civil rights record. Four years later, George McGovern halfheartedly defended school busing, while Richard Nixon vigorously attacked it. To a lesser extent, Nixon also used advertising to support extension of the right to vote to eighteen-year-olds. Another Nixon ad, looking back on the sense of impending anarchy prevalent when Nixon ran four years before, articulated that mob rule was not fertile ground for civil rights.

Following in Nixon's footsteps, Gerald Ford's 1976 campaign assailed busing. However, Ford's discussion of individual rights was quite broad, and showed the growing influence of both social and economic conservatives in the Republican Party. Ford's campaign came out against gun registration, saying, "President Ford doesn't think it makes sense to increase controls over the rights of individuals." A second ad extolled the importance of property rights, and a third noted that the Republican platform "supports the efforts of those who seek a constitutional amendment to end abortion on demand."[19]

From then on, civil rights rapidly receded and other rights issues came to the fore. In 1980, Jimmy Carter ran two ads extolling "equal rights" for women, and three of his ads emphasized the theme of separation of church and state, which surrogates like Sen. Abraham Ribicoff and Leonard Bernstein claimed was threatened by Ronald Reagan and the Moral Majority. These themes were picked up four years later by Walter Mondale, who attacked the Republicans' stand on equal rights and abortion and argued that some of their best friends are "Jerry Falwell and radical conservatives who want to impose their beliefs on everyone." Mondale called on Americans to "fight to protect personal and religious freedom."[20] For his part, Reagan joined in the religious freedom debate, pointing out that he supported "an equal access bill permitting religious student groups the same freedom to meet in public high schools during nonschool hours as right now other student groups are allowed to do."[21]

After a hiatus of two election cycles, individual rights reappeared in campaign ads in 1996. Bill Clinton's campaign warned in several ads that with a Bob Dole–Newt Gingrich team in power, a "woman's right to choose" could be "gone."[22] Clinton also touted his support of the Religious Freedom Restoration Act. Dole ran one ad supporting "our Second Amendment rights" and opposing "racial quotas and preferences."[23] In 2000, Al Gore argued for a "crime victims' bill of rights," secured by a constitutional amendment, while a Bush ad referred in passing to the Fifth Amendment in the process of discussing the Clinton-Gore fundraising scandal. John Kerry's 2004 campaign called for a defense of privacy and abortion rights.

Although individual rights represented the most-frequently discussed constitutional topic in television ads, as in other forms of communication, references were relatively meager in number and applied to a relatively narrow band of rights issues. Even this most consistent of categories in television ads has not delivered a broad foray into constitutionalism most of the time.

Constitutional Amendments

Discussed in 29 percent of Republican and 21 percent of Democratic campaigns, constitutional amendments were the second most consistently appearing constitutional topic in television ads. Democrats called for the Equal Rights Amendment (1984) and a victims' rights amendment (2000), while assailing Republican support for a human life amendment (1996). Republicans supported for an amendment to guarantee the eighteen-year-old vote (1972), called for human life amendment (1976), and called twice for an amendment requiring a balanced federal budget (1984 and 1992). Accentuating the dominance of individual rights among constitutional references in presidential television ads, four of the six constitutional amendments that were discussed had to do with rights.

About 6 percent of Democratic ads and 13 percent of Republican ads with constitutional content mentioned amendments. In party platforms, most constitutional amendment references were explicit rather than implicit; likewise, in television ads, 100 percent of such references were explicit. Also, as in platforms, there was very little dialogue taking place. On only one subject—a human life amendment restricting abortion—did the parties run opposing advertisements, and they appeared twenty years apart. Instead, both parties generally adhered to the pattern of expressing support for amendments they liked rather than attacking amendments they disliked.

Federalism

The third most consistently discussed category, federalism, appeared in television ads in 29 percent of Republican campaigns and 14 percent of Democratic campaigns, though a smaller proportion of each party's ads. The lack of constitutional seriousness of television ads can be seen in their treatment of this topic, among others. There were no explicit references to federalism of the sixteen references overall. Ads referencing federalism appeared in only one election after 1976.

Republican ads on federalism uniformly advocated decentralization of power and respect for the prerogatives of state and local governments. In 1956, an Eisenhower ad framed the choice between Ike and Stevenson as a choice between "states' rights" and "centralization of government."[24] Nixon in 1968 called for a return to the efforts of communities. Ronald Reagan, speaking for Gerald Ford in 1976, pointed out that the Republican platform promised to "turn authority and education back to the states and the local school districts where it belongs."[25] In the same way, George W. Bush's 2000 campaign ads repeatedly called for respecting local control of schools, even as he proposed federally based accountability standards.

Democratic ads referring to federalism were more mixed in their messages. John F. Kennedy used several advertisements to advocate federal aid to education, saying of education that "This is not 50 separate states. This is a national problem. . . . I think that it is, as well as a state responsibility, it is a federal responsibility." At the same time, he said "the responsibility remains with the state and with the local community. And I would be completely opposed to the federal government having the responsibility." Addressing a broader question of public philosophy and the role of government, Kennedy was shown debating Nixon and proclaiming, "I know that there are those who say that we want to turn everything over to the government. I don't at all. I want the individuals to meet their responsibility. And I want the states to meet their responsibility. But I think there is also a national responsibility."

A Kennedy ad also attacked Nixon on civil rights by showing a clip of Barry Goldwater proclaiming to a Southern audience that the 1960 Republican platform on civil rights had gone "too far away from states' rights" in order to win votes in New York.[26] In 2000, Al Gore attacked Bush for proposing that states be allowed to set a lower minimum wage than the federal standard.

Altogether, in recent years TV ads have virtually ignored this crucial structural question of American constitutionalism, despite the fact that a large number of issues in any election year could conceivably be framed in terms of federalism. When the subject does come forth, its appearance is veiled by implicit language.

Perfunctory References

Ads with perfunctory references to the Constitution appeared in 29 percent of Democratic and 7 percent of Republican campaigns (and a much smaller proportions of ads). Those campaigns included Kennedy, Johnson, Carter in 1976, Mondale, and Reagan in 1980. Kennedy referred to men who fought for "the Constitution, the Bill of Rights," and to the constitutional oath of office.[27] Reagan likewise cited his gubernatorial oath of office, which included a promise to support and defend the U.S. Constitution. Johnson's ad made passing reference to the constitutional qualifications for office. Carter was quoted as calling for "an America that lives up to the majesty of its Constitution and the simple decency of its people."[28] Mondale cited the phrase "We the People," drawn from the Constitution's preamble.[29]

No perfunctory reference was noted after 1984. As in the other modes of communication, the perfunctory reference to the Constitution, once a staple of political rhetoric at all levels of American government, has virtually disappeared in television ads.

Supreme Court Decisions and Judicial Power

Criticism or affirmation of Supreme Court decisions showed up in 28 percent of Democratic and 14 percent of Republican campaigns, most in the 1960s and 1970s. Only one out of every four such references was explicitly framed. In the first instance, John F. Kennedy ran two ads in 1960 endorsing the Supreme Court's school desegregation decisions; in one of the two, he also criticized President Dwight Eisenhower for failing to endorse *Brown*. In 1968, Hubert Humphrey defended the courts against attacks that they were too permissive on crime. In the three later cases—the Nixon and McGovern campaigns of 1972, and the Ford campaign of 1976—the topic was court-ordered busing. As discussed above, both Nixon and Ford attacked busing. Indeed, Nixon had more references to busing than to any other constitutional subject in 1972. McGovern responded by saying "You may not like busing, I may not like it. That's not the issue . . . The Supreme Court—and I didn't appoint Warren Burger as Chief Justice of the Supreme Court—Richard Nixon did—and he wrote the decision that a certain amount of busing was required as an instrument of improving the schools."[30]

In the same ad, McGovern launched into an exploration of judicial power, undoubtedly in response to Republican efforts to legislatively curtail court jurisdiction over busing, saying, "The question is whether we're going to have a court that rules on constitutional questions of that kind or whether everybody's going to be his own judge. . . . If we're gonna run a democracy we've gotta respect the Court. . . . You don't always agree with the decisions of the Court, but you kill this court system and you'll kill liberty in this country."[31] For its part, the Nixon campaign attacked McGovern for an apparent flip-flop on the antibusing legislation. This discussion in two competing ads contained the only examples from 1952 to 2004 of any reference for or against attempts to curtail the power of the courts by legislative action. Thus, that category appeared in 7 percent of both Democratic and Republican campaigns, and a miniscule percentage of the two parties' ads. In 2004, John Kerry returned to the issue of Supreme Court decisions by warning that "The Supreme Court is only one vote away from outlawing a woman's right to choose."[32]

Altogether, though such ads have appeared, the degree of controversy around judicialism that has animated platforms has been absent from television ads. While discussion of these issues has intensified in other venues, the peak of references to them in television ads came in the 1960–1980 period and has declined since then. Thus, ads have contributed to deconstitutionalization not only by neglecting a bevy of crucial constitutional questions but also by failing to offer a significant debate over judicialism.

Executive Powers

Republicans addressed executive powers in only three campaigns (21 percent), Democrats in only two campaigns (14 percent). The Democratic campaigns were 1960 and 1988. In the former, Kennedy touted the president's power to sign executive orders ending housing discrimination. In the latter, Michael Dukakis, attempting to gain points from the negative public perception of Dan Quayle, ran an ad reminding Americans that one in five vice presidents have "had to rise to the duties of commander in chief . . . [and] take on the responsibilities of the most powerful office in the world."[33]

In the aftermath of Vietnam and Watergate, Gerald Ford proclaimed that he had created "a nonimperial presidency."[34] In 1984, Republicans touted in two ads the restoration of presidential authority under Reagan, asking, "Isn't it interesting that no one anywhere is saying the job of president is too big for one person?"[35] Finally, Bob Dole made an implicit argument about the character of the commander in chief position when his campaign attacked Bill Clinton for using his status as commander in chief to claim the protection against lawsuits offered by the Soldiers and Sailors Relief Act of 1940.

In all of these cases, the executive powers reference was implicit; in many it was also highly attenuated or peripheral, offering little to the constitutional understanding of citizens.

Appointments

Republicans used television ads referring to appointments in two of fourteen campaigns, or 14 percent of the time; Democrats in three campaigns, or 21 percent of the time. In no cases were appointment references explicitly constitutional. As in platforms, this issue did not appear in television advertising until 1968, when Richard Nixon was endorsed by Sen. John Tower on the grounds that "I think he would appoint to the court judges who are as interested in protecting the law-abiding citizen as the criminal."[36]

In 1980, Jimmy Carter's campaign boasted of Carter's record in appointing "more U.S. attorneys or federal judges from minorities or women."[37] Four years later, Carter's vice president, Walter Mondale, ran no fewer than three ads touting the danger of Reagan appointing justices to the Supreme Court with the aid of the Moral Majority. In one, Mondale himself declared that "This election is about Jerry Falwell picking justices to the Supreme Court," as an announcer called on voters to leave the future a legacy of "a Supreme Court free to judge for liberty." In a second, a man on the street admitted, "I kind of like" Reagan, but then had second thoughts: "But Jerry Falwell picking Supreme Court judges?" In the third ad, an announcer declared that all one must do to join Reagan's and Falwell's party is to believe that "All new Supreme Court justices must rule abortion a crime even in cases of rape and incest."[38] Bob Dole's 1996 campaign held in one ad that Dole would "support conservative federal judges, not liberal ones."[39] Finally, John Kerry in 2004 ran two advertisements referring to George W. Bush's appointment of "far right judges determined to take away our privacy" and claiming that if reelected "Bush will appoint antichoice, antiprivacy justices."[40]

Clearly, appointments have become an increasingly notable topic. However, even as the subject has drawn more references, ad-makers have avoided using language that directly connects appointments to the Constitution.

Constitutional Sovereignty

Ads addressing this topic were found in 14 percent of Republican campaigns (and in only 5 percent of their constitutional ads) and 7 percent of Democratic campaigns (and 4 percent of their constitutional ads). The first instance came in a 1964 Barry Goldwater ad in which Texas Senator John Tower attacked Lyndon Johnson's running mate Hubert Humphrey. Humphrey, Tower pointed out, was a founding member of Americans for Democratic Action, a liberal group advocating, among other things, "the surrender of much of America's national sovereignty."[41] The theme next appeared in 2004, when George W. Bush's campaign assailed John Kerry for famously suggesting in a debate that U.S. action abroad should first pass a "global test." Viewers were assured that "President Bush believes decisions about protecting America should be made in the Oval Office, not foreign capitals."[42] In response, Kerry ran an advertisement reminding voters that he had agreed that the U.S., acting through the president, had the right to act abroad preemptively. In another ad, Kerry said, "I will never cede America's security to any institution or to any other country."[43]

While the profile of this issue was raised in 2004 television ads, as in platforms and messages, the subject was addressed in an entirely implicit manner. In this respect, ads were no worse than other forms of communication; campaigns were generally reluctant to point out that these questions were fundamentally constitutional at heart.

Enumerated Powers

John F. Kennedy's 1960 call for "a government which acts, which exercises its full powers, and its full responsibilities" and his declaration that education was also "a national responsibility" were the sole examples of even the most oblique reference to enumeration of powers contained in any campaign's advertising.[44] This meant that 7 percent of Democratic campaigns made such a reference, while no Republican campaigns did so. This record represents a remarkable display of the generally a-constitutional character of television advertisements. A subject that was long at the center of constitutional argument has been entirely unheard in television spot advertising for nearly five decades.

Enforcement

Again, Kennedy's campaign offered the only example from this category, when in one of his ads defending *Brown v. Board* he declared that "We're going to have to make progress towards implementing the Supreme Court decision."[45] Having argued that educational equality was "in the Constitution," this call for enforcement must be considered explicitly constitutional. No other enforcement references appeared in either party.

Other categories, including separation of powers, mode of constitutional interpretation, impeachment, and veto, were not represented in any major-party campaign's television ads between 1952 and 2004. While the last two were rarely seen even in platforms, the first two must be considered important components of any serious conversation about American constitutionalism. Their complete absence provides even further evidence of the shortcomings of television ads as a medium for transmitting constitutional arguments.

Overall Frequency of Constitutional References in Television Ads

Television ads first appeared after most of the decline in constitutional rhetoric in platforms and candidate messages had already occurred. In a narrow sense, television ads have actually contributed to the resurgence of constitutional rhetoric in campaigns. The lowest point in television rhetoric came in the first two television ad elections, 1952 and 1956, when campaigns made constitutional references at an average rate of 0.16 per thousand words. Those ratios have since gone up, including two periods of considerably greater constitutional rhetoric from 1960 to 1972 and 1996 to 2004. As in other venues, references to categories such as appointments and constitutional sovereignty have grown more frequent with time.

In a larger sense, however, television advertising has been a major contributor to the deconstitutionalization of electoral politics, because of its low absolute level of constitutional rhetoric. It is remarkable how consistently presidential campaigns since 1952 have eschewed constitutional rhetoric in their television advertising. Of the twenty-eight major-party campaigns in that period, in only seven did 10 percent or more of the ads contain any sort of constitutional rhetoric—Eisenhower in 1956, Kennedy in 1960, Goldwater in 1964, Humphrey in 1968, Nixon in 1972, Carter in 1976, and Bush in 2000. Of those seven, three discussed the Constitution in at least two of ten ads. Bush made constitutional references in about one in five of his ads, Humphrey in about one in four, and Nixon in about one in three. At the other extreme, four candidates did not have a single advertisement containing any sort of constitutional rhetoric—Dwight Eisenhower in 1952, Adlai Stevenson in 1956, George H. W. Bush in 1988, and Bill Clinton in 1992. Altogether, only 92 of 1,155 major-party ads contained any kind of constitutional reference—8.0 percent. A total of 8.6 percent of Democratic ads and 7.2 percent of Republican ads contained some kind of constitutional reference.

Even candidates widely regarded as possessing a political philosophy grounded in a strict constitutionalism did not break out of this mold. Only 10 percent of Barry Goldwater's television ads touched on constitutional questions in any way, while only 4 percent of Ronald Reagan's in 1980 and 6 percent of Reagan's in 1984 did. In 1996, when Republicans put a record number of constitutional references into their platform, only 6 percent of Bob Dole's television advertisements had any sort of constitutional content.

It is possible to isolate the most influential or noteworthy ads by using selective samples chosen by students of presidential television advertising. For instance, the AMMI electronic database of 238 television spots is a modest subset of the larger group under study here, but it is a significant sample and one that is presumably selected on the basis of the contemporary importance of the ads as well as the degree to which they were reflective of the general ad campaign. When coded for constitutional references, only 18 of these 238 ads—or 7.6 percent—contained any constitutional references at all, a slightly lower proportion than that found in the larger set. Of the fourteen election years surveyed in the AMMI ad sample, four had no ads with constitutional content from any campaign. In only four years were there constitutional references in ads from both sides, and in only one case was there a real dialogue taking place. In two years the competing ads were on different subjects: in 1960, Kennedy tackled religious freedom while Nixon discussed civil rights, and in 1976 Carter's perfunctory reference was matched against Ford's promise of a nonimperial presidency. In one other year, the subject was the same but both candidates agreed: in 2000, Bush and Gore both pledged themselves to local control of schools. Only in 2004 was there a real exchange—between Bush and Kerry on constitutional sovereignty.

Another, even more selective, sample can be found in *The Spot: The Rise of Political Advertising on Television*, a book written by Edwin Diamond and Stephen Bates examining the history of television ads from the elections of 1952 through 1984. *The Spot* offers the full text of forty-four major-party general election ads the authors considered especially notable or significant. Of those forty-four ads, none contained any sort of constitutional mention.[46] This sample excludes selections from campaigns after 1984, but is nevertheless illuminating.

Measured as a ratio of constitutional references per thousand words, there is a great deal of variability. On balance, however, major-party platforms have contained significantly greater constitutional rhetoric than corresponding television advertising campaigns. Since 1952, only six of fourteen Democratic campaigns and five of fourteen Republican campaigns produced ads with a ratio of greater than one reference per thousand words; every single platform in this period exceeded that standard. In every campaign but three—Humphrey in 1968, Nixon in 1972, and Gore in 2000—platforms had higher ratios than ads, usually by a wide margin. Altogether, both Democratic and Republican platforms averaged more than twice as many constitutional references per thousand words than their ads. (See table 4.1.)

From 1956 through 1976, Republican ads consistently had higher ratios than Democratic ads by varying margins. From 1980 through 2004, the parties have repeatedly switched places. Democratic ads had their highest constitutional content in 1960, 1968, 1984, 1996, 2000, and 2004; Republicans in 1960, 1964, 1972, 1992 and 2000. The highest ratio for either party came in 1972, when Richard Nixon's ads focused on the topics of forced busing and the eighteen-year-old vote. Only in two years—1960 and 2000—did both parties enjoy a relatively high level of constitutional content in their television advertising at the same time. Overall, although the Republican Party has a slightly higher average rate of references, each party has held the advantage in seven elections during that period.

Table 4.1. Total constitutional references per thousand words, ads vs. platforms, 1952–2004

Year	Democrats		Republicans	
	Ads	Platforms	Ads	Platforms
1952	.29	2.03	.00	5.18
1956	.00	2.10	.31	2.63
1960	1.77	2.24	3.01	3.93
1964	.30	1.24	3.28	3.66
1968	**2.52**	1.85	.65	2.00
1972	.80	2.77	**3.42**	1.80
1976	.26	2.17	.83	3.90
1980	.69	2.02	.31	2.34
1984	1.11	1.93	.62	3.35
1988	.40	2.27	.00	2.34
1992	.00	2.28	1.09	2.87
1996	1.22	1.88	.98	6.43
2000	**1.98**	1.16	2.95	3.46
2004	1.44	2.01	.47	2.29
Average	**.91**	**2.00**	**1.28**	**3.30**

Note: **Bold** indicates instances in which the rate for ads exceeded the rate for platforms.

Explicit vs. Implicit Rhetoric

The content of constitutional rhetoric in television ads is overwhelmingly implicit. In two of fourteen elections from 1952 to 2004 the number of ads with explicit constitutional references reached or exceeded 50 percent of the total—1976 and 1992. (This is, recall, 50 percent of the roughly 8 percent of ads that contained some type of constitutional reference.) Looking at individual campaigns, candidates reached the 50 percent mark in five of twenty-eight campaigns. In this one respect, television ads compare favorably with platforms since 1952, however, only in 1992 were more than half of references expictit (chart 4.1).

However, half of the campaigns in both parties ran not even one explicitly constitutional ad. In the AMMI sample, of the eighteen ads containing a constitutional reference, only four mentioned the Constitution explicitly—and two of those mentions were perfunctory. Similarly, in the larger universe of ads, only one-quarter of constitutional ads had an explicit reference and only one-quarter of all constitutional references were explicit, compared with about one-third of all such references in recent platforms. (Twenty-nine percent of Democratic and 22 percent of Republican constitutional ads had an explicit reference.) Furthermore, in thirteen of fourteen Republican campaigns and twelve of fourteen Democratic campaigns, explicit references per thousand words in television ads were exceeded by the same in platforms. Only the Johnson, Gore, and 1972 Nixon campaigns broke this pattern, and the explanation in the first two cases lay in unusually

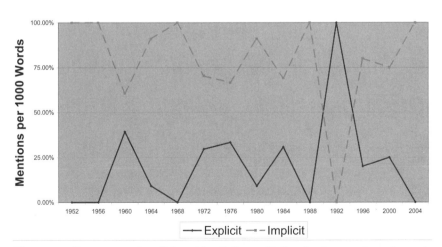

Chart 4.1. Percentage of explicit and implicit constitutional references in major-party TV ads, 1952–2004

low ratios in platforms rather than higher ratios in ads. In the campaigns from 1952 to 2004, Democrats' explicit ratios in platforms averaged three times higher than those ratios in ads while Republicans' platforms outdid their ads by more than a factor of four. (table 4.2.)

When broken down, of the thirteen categories other than perfunctory or mode of constitutional interpretation, only references to constitutional amendments were consistently more likely to be explicit than implicit; indeed, all amendment references were explicit. (As well, the one enforcement reference was explicit.) Every federalism, appointment, enumeration of powers, executive powers, and constitutional sovereignty reference from 1952 to 2004 was implicit. The only positive trend was seen in the individual rights category, which went from 18 percent explicit in 1960–1980 to 28 percent explicit in 1984–2004. Since rights was by far the most commonly referenced category in television ads, this gain was significant. Nevertheless, it stands out as a solitary exception to the norm (See table 4.3). Overall, the percentage of constitutional references in television ads that were explicitly framed fell modestly from 29 percent in the 1960–1980 period to 25 percent in the 1984–2004 period.

Table 4.2. Explicit constitutional references per thousand words, ads vs. platforms, 1952–2004

| Year | Democrats | | Republicans | |
	Ads	Platforms	Ads	Platforms
1952	.00	.79	.00	.67
1956	.00	.86	.00	.88
1960	.81	.99	.00	.75
1964	**.30**	.25	.00	.92
1968	.00	.18	.00	.10
1972	.54	.70	**.38**	.37
1976	.26	.75	.08	.78
1980	.00	.60	.31	.38
1984	.37	.38	.15	1.53
1988	.00	1.03	.00	.80
1992	.00	1.32	1.09	1.22
1996	.20	.77	.24	2.12
2000	**.79**	.58	.42	.98
2004	.00	.61	.00	.72
Average	**.23**	**.70**	**.19**	**.87**

Note: **Bold** indicates instances in which the rate for ads exceeded the rate for platforms.

Table 4.3. Percentage of explicit constitutional references in television ads by category, 1952–2004

Category	1952–1956	1960–1980	1984–2004
CA	N/A	100	100
APP	N/A	0	0
IR	0	18	28
EP	N/A	0	N/A
FED	0	0	0
IMP	N/A	N/A	N/A
VETO	N/A	N/A	N/A
EXEC	N/A	0	0
ENF	N/A	100	N/A
SOP	N/A	N/A	N/A
SCD	N/A	26	0
JP	N/A	20	N/A
MODE	N/A	N/A	N/A
CONSOV	N/A	0	0
PERF	N/A	100	100

Note: N/A=not available.

Breadth of Constitutional Rhetoric

Just as constitutional references and explicit constitutional rhetoric point to ads as a relatively deconstitutionalized medium, the range of issues discussed in ads is narrow compared with other venues. In the broadest set of 1,155 major-party ads, there was only a single category that appeared in at least half of the campaigns between 1952 and 2004: individual rights. Democrats ran ads discussing rights in ten of fourteen elections, Republicans in seven of fourteen. It was by far the most consistently mentioned category in ads by both parties.

At the other extreme, four categories—separation of powers, impeachment, veto, and mode of constitutional interpretation—did not appear in either party's ads in a single election. Another two categories were mentioned by one party in least one election but never by the other party: enumeration of powers and enforcement did not appear in any Republican campaign. Furthermore, the range of discussion continues to narrow: Three categories that appeared in 1960–1980 did not recur in 1984–2004, including enumeration of powers, enforcement, and judicial power. Altogether, only seven categories made it into as many as two Republican ad campaigns since 1952, and only seven appeared in as many as two Democratic campaigns (table 4.4.). By far the broadest constitutional rhetoric was found in John F. Kennedy's 1960 advertising campaign. Kennedy ran ads that mentioned six different constitutional categories. Indeed, without Kennedy's campaign, there would be another two categories in which Democrats would have no references.

Table 4.4. Percentage of campaigns with constitutional references in television ads, 1952–2004

Category	% of Dem. campaigns (N=14)	% of Dem. ads (N=56)	% of Rep. campaigns (N=14)	% of Rep. ads (N=36)
Individual rights	71.4	67.8	50.0	55.6
Const. amendments	21.4	5.4	28.6	13.9
Federalism	14.3	7.1	28.6	25.0
Perfunctory	28.6	12.5	7.1	2.8
Supreme. Court. decisions	28.6	8.9	14.3	16.7
Appointments	21.4	12.5	14.3	5.6
Executive power	14.3	3.6	21.4	11.1
Const. sovereignty	7.1	3.6	14.3	5.6
Judicial power	7.1	1.8	7.1	2.8
Enum of powers	7.1	3.6	0.0	0.0
Enforcement	7.1	1.8	0.0	0.0
Separation of powers	0.0	0.0	0.0	0.0
Impeachment	0.0	0.0	0.0	0.0
Veto	0.0	0.0	0.0	0.0
Mode of const. interp.	0.0	0.0	0.0	0.0

Only one category was discussed in television ads with both high consistency and significant depth: individual rights. It was not only the most consistently referenced category, but in fifteen of the sixteen campaigns in which the rights category appeared, it represented 20 percent or more of the references. In contrast with party platforms, but like candidate messages, many categories appeared in fewer than half of the campaigns but were at least 20 percent of all constitutional mentions in most of the years when they did appear. For example, judicial power appeared in only one Democratic campaign but represented 40 percent of the references in that campaign. Most of the categories in ads featured campaign discussion that failed the tests for both consistency and depth, including (among others) constitutional amendments, enumeration of powers, enforcement, and those categories with no references. These categories constituted seven of fifteen categories for both parties, one for Republicans only, and two for Democrats only (see appendix C). Altogether, a massive gap exists between ads and platforms in the frequency of discussion of most constitutional issues from election to election (table 4.5).

When consolidating the fourteen substantive categories of constitutional rhetoric into three broader groupings of rights, structure, and constitutional interpretation, the rights grouping in television ads has towered over the other two groupings with only a few exceptions. Platforms saw structure in a close

Table 4.5. Percentage of campaigns with platforms and television ads containing constitutional references, 1952–2004

Category	% Dem. campaigns (N=14)		% Rep. campaigns (N=14)	
	Ads	Platforms	Ads	Platforms
Individual rights	71.4	100.0	50.0	100.0
Const. amendments	21.4	100.0	28.6	92.9
Federalism	14.3	92.9	28.6	100.0
Perfunctory	28.6	35.7	7.1	50.0
Appointments	21.4	64.3	14.3	64.3
Supreme Court decisions	28.6	71.4	14.3	78.6
Const. sovereignty	7.1	28.6	14.3	57.1
Executive power	14.3	78.6	21.4	92.9
Judicicial power	7.1	64.3	7.1	78.6
Enum. of powers	7.1	35.7	0.0	64.3
Enforcement	7.1	78.6	0.0	78.6
Separation of powers	0.0	14.3	0.0	71.4
Impeachment	0.0	0.0	0.0	14.3
Veto	0.0	0.0	0.0	7.1
Mode of const. interp.	0.0	0.0	0.0	8.6

second to rights and interpretation usually lagging far behind. In contrast, after 1968, television advertising saw interpretation—issues like court decisions and appointments, judicial power, and constitutional amendments—typically in second place and occasionally even surpassing rights. Here, it is structure that has usually been the poor last-place finisher, except in 2000, when it came out ahead of all because of the candidates' repeated claims of support for federalism by way of local control of education (chart 4.2).

Examining the much narrower AMMI sample, seven of eighteen constitutional ads were devoted to individual rights, and six dealt with structural issues. Two were perfunctory, two dealt with constitutional sovereignty, and one referred to past court decisions. Thus, the AMMI sample was more balanced—that is, not as heavily skewed toward rights—as was the larger sample.

In recent years Democrats have more consistently given rights the pride of place. Since 1980, by contrast, Republicans have frequently placed either structure or interpretation ahead of rights. To this extent, whatever their other differences, the ads repeat and confirm a pattern found in the platforms.

Constitutional Exchanges in Television Advertising

On the occasions when constitutional issues are raised by a campaign, they are much more likely to be ignored than engaged by the opposing campaign.

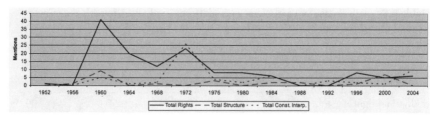

Chart 4.2. Constitutional references grouped by general topic. Major-party TV ads, 1952–2004

From 1952 to 2004, it is possible to identify only five clear constitutional exchanges, cases in which the campaigns ran ads on conflicting sides of the same constitutional topic in the same year: civil rights in 1960 and 1964, busing and legislative attempts to limit judicial power in 1972, and constitutional sovereignty in 2004.[4] (Constitutional exchanges in television ads are found in appendix C, table C4). In terms discussed in earlier chapters, three were "policy disagreements" and two were "performance disputes."

This shortage of exchanges is notable, given the degree to which attack and rapid response now characterize television advertising by campaigns. While platforms have seen an increase in constitutional exchanges—demonstrating that a large number of issues exist on which parties or candidates might form exchanges—ads have mostly avoided them. They have remained, with very few exceptions, an arena of monologue, when the campaigns have anything to say at all.

Conclusions

Television advertising has firmly established itself as the primary means of delivering campaign messages in the world of presidential campaigns. It is consequently of great importance to gauge what messages campaigns choose to convey through that medium. If platforms are the language of activists, advocacy groups, and political elites, television ads may be the idiom of the ordinary voter. If that is so, there is cause for considerable concern. Indeed, it would seem that deconstitutionalization of electoral rhetoric is a linear chronological process, in which parties and campaigns talk less about the Constitution as time goes on, overlaid by the increasingly a-constitutional character of new forms of media.

There are some commonalities between platforms and campaign advertising. In both, individual rights is by far the most consistently discussed constitutional topic, followed in rough order by federalism, constitutional amendments, and perfunctory references. In both, Supreme Court decisions, appointments, or judicial power, to the degree that they are discussed at all, have appeared as a relatively recent consequence of the rise of the politicized judiciary. Television ads have contained a periodical sprinkling of constitutional issues and language, and that sprinkling has generally worked in the direction of encouraging Americans to be more jealous of their rights. Furthermore, when television advertising for presidential campaigns began in the 1950s, constitutional issues barely registered at all; in relation to 1952 or 1956, their prominence has grown. It is not inaccurate to say that, like other forms of campaign communication, television ads have experienced a modest upsurge in constitutional discussion in recent decades.

On the other hand, in comparison to platforms, the constitutional rhetoric of which has itself deteriorated over time by a number of standards, the constitutional rhetoric in presidential campaign ads is impoverished. On average, television advertising displays the following characteristics:

- A significantly lower level of constitutional references per thousand words than platforms, by a factor of two over time;
- A significantly lower level of explicit constitutional references than platforms, by a factor of three or four over time;
- A more unbalanced constitutional rhetoric among broad areas, with rights dominating more fully on television than in platforms at the expense of constitutional interpretation and (especially) structural questions;
- A narrower range of rhetoric than that offered by platforms, with a much larger number of constitutional categories that enjoy no or very few references. Important categories which were fairly consistently referenced in platforms, such as separation of powers, enumeration of powers, executive power, Supreme Court decisions, and judicial power, barely registered or did not register at all in television ad campaigns. Even federalism, the third most consistent category in television ads, has appeared only once in each party's campaigns since 1976.
- A noticeably lower propensity for engaging in constitutional dialogue through rhetorical exchanges.

All in all, campaigns have been at best cautious, and often positively averse, to raising constitutional issues or using constitutional arguments on television, even when such issues are crying out to be addressed and even when the parties themselves are quite happy to address those issues extensively in their platforms. One is struck by the paucity of advertising for or against Goldwater's constitutionalism as outlined in *Conscience of a Conservative*, Nixon's or Reagan's New Federalism initiatives, a number of controversial assertions of executive power, or the fundamentally opposed constitutional visions of Bill Clinton and the 1996 Republicans who produced a platform arguing extensively for a reinvigoration of federalism and the concept of enumerated powers.

To the extent that voters are educated through campaign advertising, the constitutional education they receive every four years is poor indeed. In their book on television campaign advertising, *The Spot*, Edwin Diamond and Stephen Bates express the fear that "the prevalence of high-gloss, high-tech media campaigns may be trivializing electoral politics."[48] Diamond and Bates are relatively sanguine about the danger, but insofar as electoral politics has been and can be about serious constitutional matters, trivialization—or, one might say, an alarming deconstitutionalization—has indeed occurred.

That this phenomenon is connected to the nature of the medium, not just the nature of the times, can be inferred from the fact that television ads have been relatively a-constitutional from their beginning and have mostly remained so even when platforms experienced a limited reconstitutionalization. Of course, there is no reason in principle why candidates cannot use television ads to advance constitutional arguments; yet clearly campaigns have calculated that it is usually not profitable to do so. Perhaps ads depend too heavily on images, and offer too few words, to provide fertile ground for the exposition of constitutional abstractions. The Constitution does not fit easily on a bumper sticker, or on the thirty-second ads that serve as the televised equivalent. As a consequence, the medium most responsible for conveying campaign messages on a day-to-day basis is largely stripped of constitutional rhetoric. Whether television can redeem itself in another context is the subject of the next chapter.

CHAPTER FIVE

The Constitution
in Presidential Debates

If television ads as a whole represent the low point of constitutional rhetoric in campaigns and a sullen confirmation of the fears of those who see a deconstitutionalized polity, presidential debates offer a different view. While debates, too, fall short of the standards outlined in the introduction, they do a better job of promoting constitutional conversation than ads, or even modern candidate messages, in almost every measure. Indeed, they offer some hope that deconstitutionalization is not inexorable, and that modern communications methods are not inherently inimical to constitutional dialogue. All in all, debates stand in significant contrast to television advertising in terms of constitutional rhetoric. The Constitution is discussed more often, more openly, and more broadly in debates than in ads, and debates occasion many more constitutional exchanges between candidates.

The first presidential debates were held between John F. Kennedy and Richard M. Nixon during the 1960 campaign. After a sixteen-year hiatus, debates resumed in 1976 and have been held in every presidential election year through 2004. In all, major-party presidential nominees participated in twenty-four presidential debates from 1960 to 2004 (although one of these did not include both major-party candidates).[1] All twenty-four debate transcripts from 1960 to 2004 have been coded.

Along with the nomination acceptance speeches at the conventions, the debates are now the most important media events of the campaigns for the candidates. Audiences have reached 80 million, and as many as 80 or 90 percent of Americans have watched at least one debate per election. As a result, the debates themselves have arguably contributed to key shifts of momentum in the campaigns of 1960, 1976, 1980, 2000, and 2004. While the immediate and direct effects of debates on voter choice are usually found to be modest, they can have a profound effect on election outcomes in the end, especially in close races.[2]

Like campaign ads and unlike platforms, presidential debates are fully a creature of the television age. Like both campaign ads and platforms, the effect of debates on voters is amplified by subsequent news coverage and analysis.[3] Unlike both platforms and campaign ads, debates are not easily amenable to scripting by the campaigns. Candidates spend hours studying briefing books and rehearsing with advisors, but they cannot know (much less dictate) what questions will be asked of them or what their opponent will say or do. Nevertheless, studies have shown that candidates have been able to retain control over at least one-third and sometimes more than two-thirds of the debate rhetoric through the time-honored technique of answering the question they wish had been asked.[4]

Confident appearance and quality of argument is not always decisive, and the "winner" of a debate as judged by instant polls and trained debate scorers is not always the real winner strategically, once the media, the public, and the campaigns themselves fasten on to some aspect of the debate as the "most important." A number of studies have confirmed that debates raise the profile of some issues, help to clarify candidate issue positions, and help set the candidates apart on those issues. Some scholars also suggest that debates activate the electorate, make it easier for candidates to be held accountable for their campaigns, increase the public's acceptance of the candidates, give voters a chance to test the "presidentialness" of the candidates under pressure, and possibly even strengthen faith in democracy among voters and political socialization among young people.[5] (Concerns are also sometimes raised that the question-and-answer format is not conducive to an optimum exchange of ideas, that candidates can too easily evade issues, or that the voters most likely to get new information are not the voters most in need of information.) Altogether, more voters (in one poll, 45 percent) report receiving a lot of information about candidates from debates than from any other source.[6] They are thus always high-stakes affairs.

Because of the role of journalists in structuring the events, debates can be a window into both the rhetoric of the candidates and the priorities of the elite media. Consequently, this chapter will examine both candidate rhetoric and the pattern of questioning by debate moderators.

What Do Candidates Say about the Constitution in Presidential Debates?

In contrast with television ads, debates have featured a more extensive, deeper, and somewhat broader constitutional discourse. Constitutional arguments raised in debates are often more richly textured than in ads, sometimes surprisingly so. However, the subjects that have dominated discussion are largely the same, with rights, as always, leading off.

Individual Rights

Democrats and Republicans both referred to individual rights in three-quarters of their debates. Half of all constitutional references in debates were about rights. Debate discussions about rights began with a focus on civil rights, then broadened to include, most commonly in recent years, abortion and variations on the question of church-state relations.

In 1960, discussion of individual rights centered around civil rights. In his opening statement in the very first televised debate, John F. Kennedy said "I'm not satisfied until every American enjoys his full constitutional rights."[7] Kennedy and Richard Nixon had two back-to-back exchanges in the second debate about how to promote school desegregation in particular and civil rights in general. Both candidates in 1960 pointed out the foreign policy implications of guaranteeing constitutional rights at home, Nixon in the first and fourth debates and Kennedy in the fourth ("so that people will believe that we practice what we preach"[8]).

In 1976, Jimmy Carter and Gerald Ford shared an exchange over wiretapping, and in two debates Carter expressed fear that government secrecy made it possible for the government "to depart from the principles of our Constitution and Bill of Rights."[9] The two also had an exchange in their last debate about implementation of the Voting Rights Act, another over a number of proposed constitutional amendments impacting individual rights, and a third on Supreme Court appointments that largely turned on their assessment of recent court decisions on individual rights issues (such as criminal defendant rights).

Four years later, Ronald Reagan and John Anderson exchanged views on the interplay of church-state relations, abortion, and court appointments. Then, Reagan and Carter contested over the proposed Equal Rights Amendment. In 1984, Reagan and Mondale repeated these same debates with intensity. Mondale also called for respect for individual liberties in the context of immigration reform. In the 1988 Bush-Dukakis debates, Bush criticized the American Civil Liberties Union and its view of individual rights, while the two candidates had an exchange on abortion in each of their two debates.

The 1992 debates saw a number of old and new individual rights issues. Clinton acknowledged "the right to keep and bear arms," a sentiment Bush echoed.[10] Bush called for habeas corpus reform to keep criminals from being let off on technicalities, as did Perot. The incumbent also criticized racial quotas. Four years later, Clinton and Dole had an extensive exchange on quotas and affirmative action, and another on religious freedom and church-state questions. Dole also mentioned property rights, and introduced discussion of two constitutional amendments related to rights, one that would allow school prayer and one that would allow prohibition of flag-burning.

The 2000 and 2004 debates contained numerous exchanges on abortion. In the first Bush-Gore debate, extended sparring on abortion was occasioned by a question on Food and Drug Administration approval of the RU-486 abortion drug, but wandered into a related discussion on abortion more generally, the *Roe v. Wade* decision, and Supreme Court nominations. Gore also offered his view that a "right to privacy" exists within the Fourth Amendment.

As the discussion turned to homosexual rights for the first time in a presidential debate, Bush averred that he supported "equal rights but not special rights."[11] Gore vowed to protect the "rights of hunters or sportsmen" and the "right [of homeowners] to have a gun if they wish to."[12] He also promised to crack down on the marketing of "garbage" to kids by entertainment companies but to "respect the First Amendment."[13] In the final debate, an intense Bush-Gore exchange took place over quotas and affirmative action. Previously, the two also discussed racial profiling in law enforcement as a civil rights issue.

In the midst of the war on terror, Bush and Kerry sparred over whether the PATRIOT Act endangered civil liberties. Responding to a citizen question, Bush said, "I don't think the PATRIOT Act abridges your rights at all."[14] Kerry, on the other hand, maintained that "People's rights have been abused . . . what we also need to do as Americans is never let the terrorists change the Constitution of the United States in a way that disadvantages our rights."[15] Bush and Kerry also twice sparred over abortion, which Kerry explicitly called a "constitutional right." This issue, as in past debates, was quickly caught up in the question of court appointments.

In the final 2004 debate, the two men clashed over same-sex marriage, which Kerry framed primarily as an individual rights issue. Bush framed the question in a different way, as we will see below. They discussed affirmative action, with Kerry criticizing Bush but Bush merely agreeing with Kerry that "we shouldn't have quotas."[16] Before attacking Bush for allowing the assault weapons ban to expire, Kerry made sure to report that "I respect the Second Amendment and I will not tamper with the Second Amendment."[17] Both candidates also made clear their devotion to freedom of religious belief and practice.

All in all, this perennial leader among constitutional subjects was often interjected into debates, and there can be no doubt that the depth of the conversation was significantly superior to that found in television ads (though not necessarily that found in platforms).

Constitutional Amendments

Constitutional amendment references appeared in more than half of the years in which debates were held. Amendments were the subject of 13 percent of constitutional references in debates, making it the second most frequent category. Three-quarters of these references were explicit. In presidential debates, discussion of constitutional amendments began to appear in 1976, when an extensive exchange occurred between Carter and Ford in their last debate over several proposed constitutional amendments. Carter expressed disapproval of a human life amendment, school prayer amendment, and amendment to ban school busing; Ford declared support for a human life amendment and a voluntary school prayer amendment.

In 1980, the human life amendment and school prayer amendment entered the discussion again, as did the Equal Rights Amendment in the second debate. In 1984, the Equal Rights Amendment, school prayer, and abortion amendments were likewise topics of controversy. When Bush and Dukakis debated, Bush twice advocated a balanced budget amendment. As the incumbent, Bush thrice repeated this call in 1992. He also demanded a constitutional amendment to limit congressional terms, leading to an exchange in the first debate with Clinton, who opposed a term limits amendment, and Perot, who supported it. Bush came back to this proposal in the final debate.

In the Clinton-Dole debates, Dole brought back the topic of the balanced budget amendment at several junctures in both debates, and brought back the school prayer amendment in the second debate. Clinton came out against the latter. Dole also advocated the anti-flag-burning amendment. In 2004, Bush and Kerry fought over the proposed marriage amendment defining marriage as between one man and one woman. The president supported it; the challenger opposed it as writing discrimination into the Constitution.

Thus, amendments regarding rights dominated the earlier and most recent debates, while more structural concerns like the balanced budget amendment, line-item veto, and term limits were well represented in the middle years. The most recent shift reflects a more general shift in recent elections away from a discourse more balanced between rights and structure and toward a discourse disproportionately emphasizing rights.

Appointments

The question of appointments, almost all focusing on Supreme Court and other federal court nominations, was the third most frequently cited constitutional issue, accounting for a bit more than one in ten references. These references appeared in two-thirds of debate years. Until recently, almost all such references were implicit. However, in 2000 about one-quarter of appointment references were explicit, a figure which grew to three-fifths in 2004.

As in other modes of campaign discourse, this issue was absent in 1960 but appeared in force starting in 1976, and was often connected with specific issues like abortion or philosophy of constitutional interpretation. In their final debate, the exchange between Carter and Ford on Supreme Court decisions was tied up in a broader discussion of what qualities they would look for in Supreme Court nominees. In the Reagan-Anderson meeting of 1980, the candidates debated the Republican platform's call for the appointment of judges who respected "the sanctity of human life." Weeks later, in the Reagan-Carter debate, the incumbent president boasted of the number of women and minorities appointed to federal judgeships.

As Anderson had done in 1980, Walter Mondale attacked what he called the Republican platform's "religious test for judges" and the alleged influence of Jerry Falwell on court appointments.[18] Reagan responded, leading to two extensive exchanges between the candidates. Bush and Dukakis had a similar exchange in their second debate, with Bush calling for judges who would exercise restraint and Dukakis assailing Bush for having supported the ill-fated nomination of Robert Bork. The two returned to this issue at the close of the debate.

In 2000, a discussion on abortion turned into a conversation on appointments when Gore pointed out that "Governor Bush has declared to the anti-choice group that he will appoint justices in the mold of Scalia and Clarence Thomas, who are known for being the most vigorous opponents of a woman's right to choose."[19] Bush answered that judges "ought to look at the Constitution as sacred. They shouldn't misuse their bench. I don't believe in liberal activist judges. I believe in strict constructionists. Those are the kind of judges I will appoint."[20] For the first time in a presidential debate, one of the candidates (Bush) also made a point of promising to appoint "an attorney general that enforces the law."[21]

Four years later, Bush and Kerry had two exchanges on court appointments, with Bush again denying a litmus test but promising strict interpretation of the Constitution and Kerry, like Gore, attacking Bush for promising judges like Scalia and Thomas. Kerry alleged that Bush's lower court appointments showed he would appoint people to the Supreme Court determined to overturn *Roe*. More generally, Kerry said he would not "appoint a judge to the Court who's going to undo a constitutional right, whether it's the First Amendment, or the Fifth Amendment, or some other right that's given under our courts today" (including abortion).[22]

Thus in debates, as in other forms of campaign communication, candidates have spent increasing effort staking out their positions on court appointments. Indeed, it is a subject that has attracted a higher ranking among the fifteen categories in debates than in other venues, at least partially because of the high level of interest by the journalists asking the questions.

Federalism

Federalism has been the fourth most cited category of constitutional discourse in debates, and the last of only four categories to garner at least one in ten references (10.1 percent). Indeed, each debate year since 1960 has seen at least one reference to federalism. Virtually all such references have been implicit, and most have been about specific issues rather than general theories about the proper ordering of the federal system. The first debate in 1960 featured an exchange between Kennedy and Nixon on the federalism implications of federal aid to education. Nixon argued, "When the federal government gets the power to pay teachers, inevitably in my opinion, it will acquire the power to set standards and to tell the teachers what to teach. . . . My objection here is the potential cost in controls and eventual freedom for the American people by giving the federal government power over education."[23] Kennedy contended in response that aid could be given "without any chance of federal control."[24] At other points, Kennedy stressed a mix of state and federal responsibility for the nation's progress, as did Nixon.

In the final Carter-Ford debate, the candidates had an exchange in which they both argued for greater flexibility in federal aid to subnational governments, with Carter emphasizing local government and Ford insisting on including state governments. Ford also voiced support for a human life amendment that would restore decision making on abortion to the states.

Federalism as a topic recurred in 1980, when Reagan advocated in his debate against Anderson "turning back tax sources to state and local governments, as well as the responsibilities for those programs."[25] Later in the same debate, Anderson called states' rights "anachronistic" (as of 1860, no less).[26] In the Reagan-Carter debate, Reagan argued again that "I happen to believe that the federal government has usurped powers of autonomy and authority that belong back at the state and local level."[27] After four years in office, Reagan spoke of his administration's program of "returning authority and autonomy to the local and state governments that has been unjustly seized by

the federal government" and accused Democrats of pursuing a "path of centralizing authority in the federal government, lacking trust in the American
people."[28] In the 1988 debates, Bush sought the mantle of Reagan by saying
that "my fundamental philosophy is to give local and state government as
much control as possible."[29] He also attacked "the liberals" for thinking "it
should all be turned over . . . to Washington, D.C."[30] Four years later, running for reelection, Bush reiterated his call for federalism in education. Perot
agreed, saying "the more local, the better."[31]

In 1996, Dole referred to the Tenth Amendment and said "Where possible, I want to give power back to the states and back to the people."[32] Clinton responded that his administration had already "given more authority to
the states" than the previous two (Republican) presidents.[33] He also de-
flected Dole's calls for school vouchers by arguing that any such programs
ought to be reserved to action at the state level. Throughout the two 1996
debates, Dole frequently interjected the broad theme of "returning power to
the states and the people."

After 1996, discussion of federalism returned to a less abstract frame. Education was again the focal point in the first debate of 2000, when Gore and
Bush both repeatedly claimed fidelity to the principle of "local control." Saying, "I don't believe in command and control out of Washington, D.C.,"[34]
and "I believe in local control of governments,"[35] Bush also expressed concern about the potential federalization of the police.

In 2004, both candidates referred to federalism in the debate over same-
sex marriage. Kerry used a federalism argument to oppose the federal marriage amendment and to explain his vote against the 1996 Defense of Marriage Act (DOMA), arguing that "the states have always been able to
manage those laws."[36] For his part, Bush pointed to DOMA, which prevented states from being forced to recognize same-sex marriages granted in
other states, as itself a defense of federalism, and attacked Kerry for having
voted against it.

What is perhaps most interesting about the use of federalism in debates is
that candidates actually use it often here in a way that they could use it in
ads but almost never do—both as a form of attack against opponents who are
claimed to be transgressing the limits of federalism or as a defense or an explanation for their own positions. This is the sort of argument, connecting
broader constitutional principles to specific policy issues, that would enrich
the national conversation were it more generally applied.

Supreme Court Decisions

Discussion of Supreme Court decisions, accounting for a bit more than one
in twenty constitutional references in debates, appeared in five of nine years.

In contrast with platforms, many such references were supportive of specific judicial decisions rather than overwhelmingly critical. Kennedy, in the second 1960 debate, went on at length endorsing and calling for execution of *Brown v. Board*. In 1976, Carter and Ford went back and forth about a number of Supreme Court decisions. Carter endorsed recent civil rights cases, the one-man-one-vote decisions, the judicially imposed right of poor criminal defendants to state funded counsel, and other protections for the accused; Ford attacked the *Miranda* ruling.

In the Reagan-Mondale debates, Reagan criticized court decisions removing religion from the public square. He also attacked *Roe v. Wade*, drawing a defense of the court's decision from Mondale. The same decision was defended by name by Gore in 2000, and by Kerry repeatedly in 2004. In the final Bush-Gore meeting, Gore also asked Bush if he supported the Supreme Court's decisions regarding affirmative action (in keeping with debate rules, Bush did not answer). Against Kerry, Bush assailed lower court rulings that held unconstitutional the phrase "under God" in the Pledge of Allegiance and state court rulings against traditional marriage. Bush also used the *Dred Scott* decision as an example of an activist judiciary and the kind of judging he hoped to avoid, drawing heated objections from liberal commentators.

While the number of references is small, the references that occur are again more interesting, more varied, and of greater educational value than those found in ads or, for the most part, other venues. For example, Bush's use of *Dred Scott* ignited a short-lived but serious national debate over judicial power and whether his interpretation of that case was the correct one. No reference to a Supreme Court decision in any other venue in recent memory produced such a discussion.

Executive Powers

This category represented about one in twenty references and showed up in more than half of the debate years. Discussion of executive powers was sometimes quite openly constitutional in character, and sometimes only obliquely so. As with federalism, that discussion tended to revolve around specific issues rather than theories of executive power. In the third Kennedy-Nixon debate in 1960, Kennedy proposed expanded presidential powers to deal with strikes during time of national emergency; in the next and final debate of that year, Kennedy reminded viewers twice of the president's constitutional responsibility for the conduct of foreign affairs. In the next debate—the first Ford-Carter debate sixteen years later—Carter called for an extension of presidential powers by making the appointment of the chairman of the Federal Reserve Board coterminous with the president's entry into office, an innovation that Ford strongly opposed.

George H. W. Bush repeatedly proposed a line-item veto for the president in both 1988 and 1992. In 1992, the Federal Reserve question reappeared, with Bush (like Ford before) decrying suggestions that it be put under greater executive control. Both 1996 debates featured accusations by Dole that Clinton was abusing the pardon power, a charge Clinton denied. In a more theoretical vein, four years later, Clinton's vice president (Gore) elucidated Theodore Roosevelt's "stewardship" theory of the presidency, arguing that the president was "the only position in our Constitution that is filled by an individual who is given the responsibility to fight not just for one state or one district or the well-connected or wealthy, but to fight for all of the people."[37] This was the sort of theoretical argument about executive power generally absent from the other forms of communication in modern times, although Gore himself made this same argument in his nomination acceptance speech.

Constitutional Sovereignty

Altogether, only 4.4 percent of references from 1960 to 2004 pertained to constitutional sovereignty. These arguments were made in one-third of all debate years. However, that low figure masks the degree to which the subject has grown in importance in recent years. George H.W. Bush initiated discussion of this topic in 1988 when he averred that America could not turn over defense decisions to the United Nations. After that moment, constitutional sovereignty became an increasingly frequent object of conversation, culminating in the 2004 debates, when one in six references fell in that category. Bush's view was repeated by Dole in 1996 when he complained that "we have to determine when our interests are involved, not the United Nations' interests"[38] and that Clinton had turned important decisions over to the UN. Clinton defended himself later, saying in reference to events in Kurdish Iraq that his own view was that "sometimes we cannot let other countries have a veto on our foreign policy."[39]

The issue fully came into its own in 2004, swirling around the debate over the Iraq war. In the first debate, devoted to foreign policy, Kerry said, "No president, through all of American history, has ever ceded, and nor would I, the right to preempt in any way necessary to protect the United States of America." He then went on to argue that such action should pass "the global test" before proceeding.[40] Bush responded immediately with a criticism of the "global test," and then went on to attack Kerry's support of the International Criminal Court as not in America's interest and not consistent with American sovereignty. Bush reiterated this argument against the International Criminal Court in the second debate. Undoubtedly attempting to undo the damage of his "global test" comment, Kerry concluded the second debate by saying "I will never cede the authority of our country or our security to any other nation. I'll never give a veto over American security to any other entity."[41] In the third Bush-Kerry debate, constitutional sovereignty was again prominent. Bush pressed the point, reminding viewers that Kerry "proposed America pass a global test. In order to defend ourselves, we'd have to get international approval. . . . I will never turn over our national security decisions to leaders of other countries."[42] Kerry remained on the defensive, holding that "I have never suggested a test where we turn over our security to any nation. . . . No nation will ever have a veto over us."[43] As in the second debate, Kerry concluded the third by reiterating that "I will never allow any country to have a veto over our security."[44] The question at the center of these exchanges was not whether national sovereignty was good, but who would do a better job of preserving it. The exchanges also helped define the 2004 presidential contest; Kerry's "global test" comment, in particular, became fodder for Bush advertisements portraying Kerry as too beholden to foreign opinion.

Enforcement

The remaining eight categories, starting with enforcement, have seen activity representing fewer than 2 percent of references. Nevertheless, more than half of debate years saw at least one enforcement reference. In the second Kennedy-Nixon debate, Kennedy called for greater executive vigor in enforcement of *Brown v. Board*. In 1976, Ford claimed to be enforcing the Voting Rights Act vigorously, while Carter said minorities needed more than "minimum enforcement of the law" when it came to civil rights.[45] In 1984, Mondale referred to the president's oath to "take care, to faithfully execute the laws of the land," and called for strict enforcement of civil rights laws. In 2000, no doubt referring obliquely to Clinton and Gore's legal troubles, Bush closed the third debate by swearing to "uphold the laws of the land" as well as the dignity of the office.[46] For his part, Gore repeatedly called for civil rights enforcement, a concern echoed in 2004 when Kerry posed the question whether America would have a Justice Department that would enforce civil rights laws. In these cases, enforcement was very much tied to rights. As with sovereignty, the prime question addressed in the debates was whether the incumbent party was doing a good enough job of enforcement.

Perfunctory References

The relatively few perfunctory references were broadly spread out, being heard in 44 percent of Democratic debate years, 22 percent of Republican debate years, and seven of nine years altogether. For example, Carter in 1976 referred to "what our Constitution stands for," "the meaning of the Constitution," and "the vision of the Constitution."[47] Reagan referred to "our most sacred documents—the Constitution and the Declaration of Independence,"[48] Perot to "the framers of the Constitution."[49] Bill Clinton referred perfunctorily to "the Constitution, the Bill of Rights, and the Declaration of Independence."[50] Gore pointed to the oath he had taken to the Constitution nine times in his political career.

Mode of Constitutional Interpretation

This topic, largely ignored in other fora, was mentioned in one-third of debate years by each party. Furthermore, the comments that came forth were often unusually illuminating. In a discussion not seen in campaign advertising in any year, Carter in 1976 laid out the philosophy that the courts should "interpret the uh—the Constitution and the laws uh—equally between property protection and personal protection. But when there's uh—a very narrow decision . . . I think the choice should be with human rights."[51] In 1988, Bush called for judges who "will not legislate from the bench, who will interpret the Constitution."[52] In 2000, in perhaps the single best example of a head-to-head conflict on this question, his son called for "strict construction," while Gore declared that "the Constitution ought to be interpreted as a document that grows with our country and our history."[53] Again in 2004 the younger Bush, then running for reelection, called for "strict construction."[54]

If the loss of perfunctory references and references to mode of constitutional interpretation in candidate messages and TV ads must be counted a loss for constitutionalism, then their relative vigor in debates must be counted as a hopeful sign for it. Debates were far from devoid of such references, and one can see again that several of the arguments made when discussing the mode of interpretation were considerably more sophisticated than those raised in the other televised venues.

Judicial Powers

This category appeared in six presidential debates, and in all but one case (Carter in 1976) the speaker hoped to restrain judicial power. Republican candidates in five of the six elections between 1980 and 2004 brought up the issue at least once in a debate. Reagan assailed Carter's 1980 support of the Equal Rights Amendment on grounds that the amendment would put the issue "in the hands of unelected judges,"[55] and then four years later expressed opposition to the abuse of judicial power to quash free exercise of religion. In 1988, 2000, and 2004, Bush and son called on judges to not "misuse their bench" by engaging in activism.[56]

Nevertheless, these references were fairly vague, and failed to offer support for specific measures to rein in the judiciary. Candidates are simply not anxious to embrace positions that might allow their opponents to label them enemies of an independent judiciary. This feature of recent candidate messages, ads, and debates would seem to reinforce the pretensions of judicialism. While candidates are willing to address the issue indirectly, by discussing appointments and Supreme Court decisions at length, they (though not the parties) are generally cautious about attacking judicial power frontally.

Separation of Powers
This crucial element of the constitutional structure was raised as an issue in four debate years. In the first debate of 1976, Ford responded to Carter's criticisms of his vetoes of Democratic spending bills by implying that unified party control of government was contrary to the spirit of the Constitution: "I think it [unified Democratic government] would be contrary to one of the basic concepts in our system of government—a system of checks and balances."[57] In the second debate of 1976, Carter attacked the exclusion of Congress from foreign policy during the Nixon-Ford years.

In his homespun manner, Perot reminded viewers in 1992 that "The president can't order Congress around. Congress can't order the president around."[58] In 2000, Bush argued that activist judges "ought not to take the place of the legislative branch of government,"[59] an argument he repeated in 2004 against Kerry.

Enumerated Powers
Two candidates implied some notion of enumerated powers. Kennedy elucidated the "national responsibility,"[60] and Reagan in 1984 contended that "there are tasks that government legitimately should enforce and tasks government performs well."[61] In other cases, candidates proposed that action be taken "within the Constitution of the United States."[62]

Separation of powers and enumeration of powers are both examples of how debate rhetoric on the Constitution sometimes falls into the shortcomings suffered in other venues. In neither case does the subject at hand receive the attention it deserves, given its place in the American system. In approaching these structural issues, the platform is the only mode of communication that is reasonably adept. Here, debates have not escaped deconstitutionalization.

Two categories—impeachment and veto—had no activity. This result was consistent with very low levels of references in platforms, candidate messages, and TV ads.

Overall Frequency of Constitutional References in Debates

Debates entered the world of presidential campaigns even later than television advertisements, long after the decline suffered by platforms and candidate messages had set in. Nevertheless, just as ads can be said on balance to have contributed to the deconstitutionalization of campaign rhetoric, debates can be said to have been part of the resurgence of constitutional rhetoric.

Overall, debates offer much more consistent consideration of constitutional issues than do ads. Democratic and Republican candidates each made at least one constitutional reference in 91 percent of their debates. Nor has there been any slackening in recent years. All eight presidential debates held in the three election cycles of 1996–2004 saw at least one constitutional reference per candidate.

Since the first debates in 1960, the number of total constitutional references and references per thousand words has increased. Between them, Kennedy and Nixon made forty-nine constitutional references in their four debates. For the next three decades, that figure remained roughly the same, with the exception of a spike in 1976, when Jimmy Carter and Gerald Ford made sixty-seven such references between them. In the three elections from 1996 to 2004, however, there were 65, 88, and 120 combined constitutional references by the competing candidates.

When adjusted for the fact that the number of debates varies from year to year, the increase in references since 1960 is even more striking, and appears sooner. Of the whole period 1960 to 2004, the 1960 debates were the low point. In 1976, when debates resumed, references per debate nearly doubled, to a level where they remained for the most part until the next sharp rise in 1996–2004. Only 1992 saw a brief decline (see table 5.1).

The number of constitutional references per thousand words has likewise shown an increase. The two lowest years were 1960 and 1992. The three highest years were 1996–2004, with 1984 in a close fourth place (see chart 5.1). It is notable, and curious, that constitutional rhetoric in debates continued rising even in 2004 when platforms, acceptance speeches, and television ads all experienced a fall in the rate of constitutional references. Indeed, in 2004 debates outpaced each of the other modes of communication, including platforms.

For the most part, the parties' rates of constitutional references per thousand words have not strayed far from each other. The comment-and-response format of debates probably contributes to this phenomenon. However, Republicans have held a slight edge. Republican candidates had the higher rate of references in fourteen of twenty-three major-party debates, and had a

Table 5.1. Constitutional references and references per debate, 1960–2004

Year	Constitutional references	Constitutional references per debate
1960	48	12.0
1976	67	22.3
1980	39	19.5
1984	48	24.0
1988	45	22.5
1992	45	15.0
1996	65	32.5
2000	88	29.3
2004	120	40.0

higher per-debate reference average in six of nine debate years, including all five from 1988 to 2004. Both parties showed upward movement in their rates of constitutional references in recent years. However, Republicans have been on a general upward trajectory since 1960, while Democrats have shown more variability. Their low point came in 1992, followed by increasing rates in 1996–2004.

Explicit vs. Implicit Discourse

In four out of five debates there was at least one explicit constitutional reference by at least one of the candidates. Democratic candidates used at least

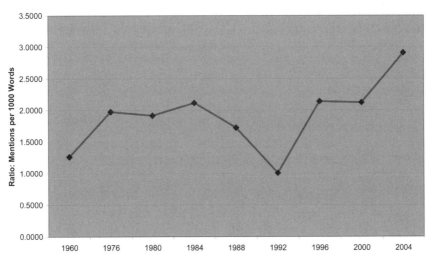

Chart 5.1. Constitutional references per one thousand words in debates, 1960–2004

one explicitly constitutional reference in 57 percent of their debates, Republicans in 54 percent. Nevertheless, the percentage of references that were explicitly constitutional was low, as it was with other forms of campaign communication.

In no year were a majority of references explicit. In four years—1976–1984 and 2004—more than 30 percent of references were explicit. In five years—1960 and 1988–2000—fewer than 30 percent were. The peak was in 1980, when 44 percent of the constitutional references were open rather than implicit. Otherwise, there has been great variability (chart 5.2).

Among the thirteen categories that can be coded either explicit or implicit, only three enjoyed explicit percentages of 50 percent or greater in the period of 1984–2004: constitutional amendments, enumeration of powers, and judicial power, and the latter two had few references. (Only amendments exceeded 50 percent explicit in 1960–1980.) During the most recent period, references to five categories became more explicit while references to another four categories, including individual rights and federalism, became less explicit. However, leaving aside the two categories that had no references at all (veto and impeachment), there was only one category that was 100 percent implicit in the 1984–2004 period. By way of contrast, there were four such categories in the previous period (1960–1980). On balance, not much changed. Debate references have not grown more explicit, as platforms, nor have they grown less so. A total of 36 percent of debate references from 1960 to 1980 were explicit, while 35 percent from 1984 to 2004 were. (See table 5.2).

On this question, Republicans have had a somewhat more consistent performance than Democrats. Six of nine Republican candidates fell between 20 and 50 percent, with none exceeding 50 percent. Democrats have ranged from 63 percent in 1980 to 0 percent twice (1988–1992).

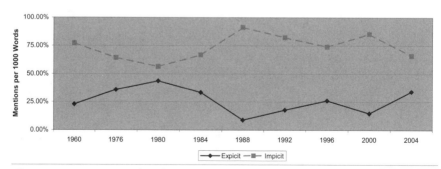

Chart 5.2. Percentage of explicit and implicit constitutional references in debates, 1960–2004

Table 5.2. Percentage of explicit debate constitutional references by category, 1960–2004

Category	1960–1980	1984–2004
CA	100	63
APP	0	35
IR	38	22
EP	0	50
FED	11	8
IMP	N/A	N/A
VETO	N/A	N/A
EXEC	20	5
ENF	29	40
SOP	0	33
SCD	0	32
JP	33	50
MODE	100	100
CONSOV	N/A	0
PERF	100	100

Note: N/A=not available.

Breadth of Constitutional Discourse

Although debates featured a broader array of constitutional issues than television ads, the dominant topic was individual rights, as in other modes of campaign communication. Just how dominant depends on how one looks at it. In the most basic sense, 49.3 percent of all constitutional references in debates were on that subject, making it far and away the most common category. When thinking about consistency and depth, though, there are two plausible ways of constructing the data. One could measure consistency using years as the key unit—that is, in how many elections did the topic receive at least one mention in a debate? This approach is consistent with the assessment of platforms, messages, and ads in previous chapters. It is also consistent with seeing the debates as cumulative exercises, and accommodates the fact that some individual debates historically have focused exclusively or almost exclusively on foreign policy, leaving a much smaller range of possible constitutional topics for consideration. Alternately, one could use individual debates as the unit of measurement—that is, in how many debates was there a reference to the subject? The latter offers more data points—twenty-four debates rather than nine years in which debates were held—and takes account of the fact that each debate largely stands on its own, with significantly varying viewership and distinct interpretation and analysis from the media.

When looking at individual debates as the unit of measurement, four of every five debates had some discussion of individual rights. Next came federalism, mentioned in nearly three in five debates by Republican candidates (though Democrats mentioned it in only about one in four debates). No other category was mentioned in as many as half of the debates by either party. Other categories that received substantial attention were appointments, executive powers, constitutional amendments, Supreme Court decisions, enforcement (among Democrats), and judicial power (among Republicans). Only two topics received no mentions in any debate—impeachment and veto.

As in television ads, candidate messages, and platforms, rights was also by far the topic discussed in greatest depth—that is, not only did it appear in the most debates but the attention afforded it in those debates was unsurpassed by any other category. In all of the seventeen debates in which Democratic candidates mentioned individual rights, those references represented 20 percent or more of all constitutional references. On the Republican side, that was true in thirteen of eighteen debates. The subject of rights was the most mentioned constitutional topic in thirteen debates by Democrats and eleven debates by Republicans. No other category came close.

When putting consistency and depth together, then, we find a familiar picture. As in platforms, only individual rights in both parties and federalism among Republicans passes both the consistency and depth tests. As among television ads, and in contrast to platforms, no categories appear that are highly consistent but shallow. All other categories are distributed between the low consistency, deep position and the low consistency, shallow position.

When we turn to years as the unit of measurement, we find that there is indeed an important cumulative effect, so that subjects that are mentioned in a modest percentage of debates are often mentioned in a much larger proportion of years. Looked at this way, there are four categories that received mentions in both parties in more than half the years when debates were held, and in another three that reached that level for one party but not the other. Rights still prevailed as the most consistently mentioned category, the only category to be discussed by both parties in 100 percent of the years when debates were held. Republicans also mentioned federalism in 100 percent of debate years, Democrats in 55 percent. Both constitutional amendments and appointments received attention in about two-thirds of debate years. Furthermore, Democrats mentioned enforcement in more than half the years, while Republicans brought up both executive power and judicial power more than half the time (table 5.3). Just as remarkable, a number of categories that get short shrift in other media and that are minimally represented from de-

Table 5.3. Consistency of constitutional category references
as a proportion of debates and years, 1960–2004

	% Democrats		% Republicans	
	Debates	Years	Debates	Years
Individual rights	73.9	100.0	75.0	100.0
Federalism	26.2	55.0	58.3	100.0
Appointments	30.4	66.0	41.7	66.0
Executive powers	26.1	44.0	37.5	55.0
Const. amendments	21.7	55.0	37.5	66.0
Enforcement	30.4	55.0	12.5	22.0
Supreme Court decisions	21.7	44.0	16.7	33.0
Const. sovereignty	17.4	22.0	20.8	33.0
Judicial powers	4.3	11.0	20.8	55.0
Perfunctory	17.4	44.0	8.3	22.0
Mode of const. interp.	13.0	33.0	12.5	33.0
Separation of powers	4.3	11.0	12.5	33.0
Enum. of powers	8.7	22.0	4.2	11.0
Impeachment	0.0	0.0	0.0	0.0
Veto	0.0	0.0	0.0	0.0

bate to debate appear in a significant number of years. For example, discussions regarding the mode of constitutional interpretation—perhaps the most fundamental of all categories of constitutional rhetoric—appear in about one of ten platforms and in no television advertisements, but appear in one-third of debate years.

When debates are aggregated yearly, references to individual rights remain highly consistent and deep, but federalism for Republicans (barely) drops away, as Republican federalism references reached 20 percent of the total in only four out of nine debate years. However, the category of constitutional amendments now joins individual rights, the only category other than federalism to do so in any of the four modes of campaign communication studied here. Democrats have four and Republicans three additional categories that appear in more than half the debate years but do not reach the threshold for depth. There are also ten Republican and nine Democratic categories that fail on both the consistency and depth fronts. If debates hold an advantage over ads and candidate messages, it is not at the bottom but at the top end of this continuum. (See appendix C, table C1 for a complete cataloguing of categories in terms of consistency and depth of discussion.)

What this frame of analysis does not capture, of course, is the absolute amount of constitutional discourse or the complexity and variety of arguments. In these respects, the debates are quite different from television ads, offering at times a sophistication of arguments that advertising does not match.

When consolidating categories into the three broad groupings of rights, structure, and constitutional interpretation, rights holds a clear advantage over time. In two out of three debate years, it is the most common category of discourse. Rights had the fewest references among the categories in only one election year (1992). Questions of structure are consistently left far behind, never finishing first and finishing as high as second only twice in nine elections (1960 and 1992). Questions of constitutional interpretation are sometimes a strong challenger to rights, attracting the largest number of references in one-third of elections and a respectable number in several others. In 2004 there were sixty-one rights references, sixty constitutional interpretation references, and three structural references (chart 5.3). In that sense, debates typically fall well short of the standard of balanced discourse. To the extent that consideration of structural issues is an essential component of constitutionalism, debates, like other televised campaign communications, are undermining it.

Constitutional Exchanges in Presidential Debates

While some topics were a quadrennial source of debate exchanges, such as the intersection of abortion and court appointments, exchanges covered a fairly wide range of issues, including affirmative action, wiretapping, con-

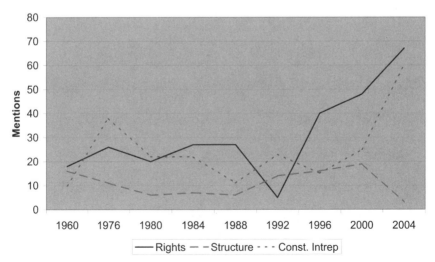

Chart 5.3. Constitutional debates references grouped by general topic, 1960–2004

gressional term limits, church-state relations, and the subordination of U.S. foreign policy to international bodies. Altogether, three-quarters of debates contained at least one constitutional exchange, defined as an instance in which the candidates have an exchange using either explicit or implicit constitutional language on the same or related constitutional issues. There were an average of three constitutional exchanges between candidates in every two debates, and the number of such exchanges has grown in recent years. Bill Clinton and Bob Dole had four constitutional exchanges in two debates in 1996, George W. Bush and Al Gore had another five in their three 2000 debates, and Bush and John Kerry had ten in three debates in 2004, more than in any previous election. Altogether, there were thirty-seven constitutional exchanges in debates from 1960 to 2004, of which about three-fifths were head-to-head disagreements on policy. In the remainder of the exchanges, candidates agreed on constitutional values but disagreed over whether a particular policy correctly reflected those values. As in platforms, a number of topics drew little head-on debate. Altogether, however, debates fostered a stronger and more supple constitutional dialogue than any other form of campaign communication. (Exchanges in presidential debates are found in appendix C, table C5)

Debate Questions

Candidates in debates are constrained by the questions posed to them. In all presidential debates from 1960 to 2004, candidates were asked a total of 496 questions.[63] Of those questions, 7.1 percent (thirty-five questions) had some constitutional content. However, only five questions in forty-four years—1 percent of the total—were explicitly framed constitutional questions.[64] There were constitutional questions in one form or another asked in fifteen of twenty-four debates, or 63 percent of the total (See appendix C, table C6).

Beginning in 1992, one debate every election year has featured a town-hall setting with questions asked by audience members rather than journalists (though moderators have retained substantial control over audience participation and selection of questions). Interestingly, in the debates of 1992–2004, citizen questioners in the town-hall debates have asked more constitutionally oriented questions than journalists did in the other debates. Indeed, in 1992 and 1996 the town-hall debates were the only debates to feature a constitutional question. In sum, from 1992 to 2004, about one in eight citizen questions had some constitutional content, while only one in thirty-three journalist questions did. While negligible in number, the only explicitly constitutional questions of the period were also asked by citizens.

Of the moderator, panelist, and citizen questions from 1960 to 2004 that had constitutional content, about two-thirds (twenty-five questions) were related to individual rights. About one-quarter (a total of nine) had to do with appointments. The remainder were a sprinkling of one to three questions each about constitutional amendments, Supreme Court decisions, executive powers, and federalism (see table 5.4). All in all, consistent with other modes of campaign discourse, debate questions were heavily tilted to rights and generally shortchanged questions of structure. There has, for example, not been a question focusing on federalism since one was asked in 1960. This has not stopped candidates from talking extensively in constitutional terms about some of these structural issues, although those discussions were more often than not implicit. It is therefore not difficult to discern that the low priority placed on structural issues in debates is largely due to the lack of sustained questioning on those topics by moderators, panelists, and ordinary citizens.

Conclusion

All in all, debates contained a much broader and richer discussion of constitutional questions than did television ads. There were more topics discussed, and they were discussed more often. Indeed, only two of the fifteen categories of constitutional discourse were without any debate references, and these were two—veto and impeachment—that barely registered even in the party platforms. A number of the constitutional themes aired in the debates were amplified by television ads, some of which even included debate footage. If there has been some recovery of constitutional discourse in American campaigns, debates have not only reflected but also helped to drive that recovery. In the sixteen-year gap between the first set of debates in 1960 and the

Table 5.4.   Categories of constitutional questions in debates, 1960–2004

Category	Number of questions	Percentage of all questions*	Percentage of const. questions*
Individual rights	25	5.0	71.4
Appointments	9	1.8	25.7
Const. amendments	3	.6	8.6
Supreme Court decisions	3	.6	8.6
Executive powers	2	.4	5.7
Federalism	1	.2	2.9

* Columns total more than 100 percent because some questions fall into more than one category.

second set in 1976, constitutional references per debate nearly doubled, before doubling again in 1996–2004. Furthermore, aided by the format, debates were much more likely to produce actual dialogue. While the issues were sometimes oversimplified or even distorted, they were present, and quite often both candidates addressed them.

Not only have debates contributed to the general resurgence of constitutional rhetoric in campaigns but also they seem to have acquired a constitutional momentum somewhat independent of what is going on in other venues of communication. While others were falling back in 2004, debates reached new highs of constitutional references, driven by repeated forays into constitutional sovereignty, court appointments, and issues like abortion and same-sex marriage.

Interestingly, the relatively high degree of constitutional rhetoric found in debates was mostly in spite of, rather than because of, the questions asked by journalist moderators. Indeed, even as the number of constitutional references by candidates in debates was rising, the percentage of questions asked about constitutional questions was reaching a new low in 1992, 1996, and 2000 (at 4.1, 4.8, and 4.2 percent respectively). To the extent that an extrapolation can be made, the selection of journalists' questions may provide a troubling insight into the degree to which the nation's top political journalists consider constitutional questions interesting and worth attending to.

When discussing the candidates' views of the Constitution, debates seem to live up to their billing as a medium that provides substantial information. Indeed, debates sometimes bring an intellectual level to the discussion of issues that is rarely seen on television otherwise, and their constitutional disputations can inspire national conversations in a way that platforms no longer do. They are, in that sense, more useful than platforms, because they are much more widely accessed by the voting public. Debates may also provide the most unvarnished view of what candidates really believe, despite the hours spent by the campaigns and candidates practicing and preparing for each debate.

Even after all of that, constitutional rhetoric in debates shares common weaknesses with that found in other venues: in a typical year, rights overshadow other constitutional topics pushed forward by the preferences and biases of the moderators. And an overwhelming proportion of constitutional references are only implicit. Open discussion of the Constitution is relatively unusual in debates, as in presidential campaigns generally.

CHAPTER SIX

~

The Constitution and Third Parties

Major parties have been the focus of the analysis thus far, but third parties have often played an important role in American politics and policy development. As scholars such as Steven J. Rosenfeld, Daniel A. Mazmanian, and James L. Sundquist have pointed out, third parties have often served the role of promoting change and filling a vacuum caused by the major parties' unwillingness to address rising but controversial issues. While rarely successful electorally, a number of third parties have forced their concerns onto the national agenda and lured one or both of the major parties to accommodate some of their views in an attempt to co-opt them.[1] As we will see, third-party campaigns have also tended to be more constitutionally oriented than major-party campaigns. While the frequency of their constitutional references has fallen over time, as in major-party campaigns, almost every significant third-party campaign from 1840 to the present has enriched the constitutional dialogue to some degree. On balance, third parties have mitigated the trend of deconstitutionalization in electoral politics.

This chapter will examine the fourteen third parties since 1840 that garnered at least 5 percent of the national popular vote. This cutoff, like all cutoffs, is somewhat arbitrary; some third parties, like Strom Thurmond's Dixiecrats and Henry Wallace's Progressives in 1948 or Ralph Nader's Green candidacy in 2000, were quite important historically even though they did not meet the 5 percent threshold. Nevertheless, a general threshold much below 5 percent seems too low. Since 1974, a 5 percent threshold to define significance has also found support in federal election law, which stipulates such a threshold to determine eligibility for federal election funds by third-party or independent candidates.

The fourteen cases that met the 5 percent standard included the Free-Soil Party in 1848; the American Party in 1856; the Constitutional Union Party and Southern Democratic breakaway faction in 1860; the Liberal Republicans, who ran a fusion ticket with the Democrats in 1872; the People's (or Populist) Party in 1892 and again in 1896, when they as well as Democrats nominated William Jennings Bryan; the Progressive ("Bull Moose") Party and the Socialist Party in 1912; Robert LaFollette's Progressive Party of 1924; George Wallace's American Independent candidacy in 1968; John Anderson's independent candidacy in 1980; and Ross Perot's independent and Reform Party candidacies in 1992 and 1996. The Republicans, often cited as the most successful third party in American history, present a special problem and are not counted. In their very first presidential campaign in 1856, they were already the second-place vote getters.

In the first nine decades of this study, third parties quite often put great emphasis on constitutional concerns. Of the ten third parties through 1924, several clearly stand out as highly constitutionally oriented in their rhetoric. At the end of the long forty-four-year gap between La Follette and George Wallace, non-major-party efforts emerged as much more personalist than before. Wallace wrote his party's platform and refused to allow anyone to run under his label for Congress or other lower offices. Anderson ran a campaign openly independent of party, as did Perot in 1992. When Perot formed a party for the 1996 election, it was built around him and he retained control over its machinery. Even some of these more personalist efforts gave considerable attention to constitutional concerns.

The Perot Exception

The great exception was Ross Perot's 1992 campaign, which was largely disinterested in constitutional questions. When Perot, a billionaire entrepreneur, threw his hat into the ring in 1992 as an independent candidate, he started down a road that made him a key figure in the politics of the 1990s. Running at a time of rising dissatisfaction with Washington, Perot presented himself as an outsider of the "radical center" tapping into concerns about the federal deficit, economic competitiveness, partisan gridlock, and the influence of special interests. Feared by some who saw him as authoritarian, paranoid, and mercurial, Perot nevertheless appealed to millions of Americans with his folksy manner, blunt style, and promises of "getting under the hood" to diagnose and decisively attack the nation's problems. For a time in June

1992 he was in a close second place behind George H. W. Bush in the polls. After a decline in the polls, he dropped out of the race, only to return on October 1. He participated in all three of the 1992 presidential debates, and was judged by television viewers to have "won" at least the first of the three. On election day, Perot won 19 percent of the vote, the most by a non-major-party candidate since Theodore Roosevelt in 1912. His vote was spread broadly, however, and he did not win any states.

Perot's 1992 campaign was one of the most constitutionally lacking third-party or independent campaigns of the entire period from 1840 to 2004. He made no constitutional references at all in his ads or his candidate message (the speech announcing his return to the race in October 1992). His "platform" (a campaign book entitled *United We Stand*) contained support for abortion on demand. It also contained support for some constitutional amendments, like abolition of the Electoral College and changing election day to a Saturday and Sunday, while criticizing the balanced budget amendment as "phony." The book addressed executive powers and federalism, calling for a line-item veto for the president, local control and accountability for schools, and more power for local officials, especially in law enforcement and health care. Finally, Perot's book included numerous perfunctory references to the Constitution, like "The first words of the Constitution are 'We, the People.' We created the Constitution . . . we have to restore the intent and meaning of the Constitution we created."[2] The raw number of constitutional references was not negligible, but they were buried in an approximately 24,000-word document.

Perot's use of constitutional rhetoric was actually more frequent in the first debate than the other candidates', but he lagged well behind Bush in the other two debates (tying Clinton in the basement). He made one perfunctory reference in the first debate: "That is the way the framers of our Constitution meant it to be, a government that comes from the people."[3] In the second debate he made an observation in relation to separation of powers ("The president can't order Congress around. Congress can't order the president around"[4]), a plea to pay more attention to victims' rights than criminals' rights, and statements supporting term limits and local control of education. The third debate saw no constitutional references by Perot.

Altogether, he had fewer constitutional references per thousand words than either of his opponents in his platform, his message, the sample of television ads used in this study, and the debates in the aggregate. His campaign could be entered as evidence of the deconstitutionalization of American electoral politics—as can the fact that his constitutionally challenged campaign won a larger percentage of the vote than any non-major-party candidate in half a century. Charles Kesler described Perot's run as "an ominous conjunction of disdain for political parties and barely suppressed impatience with the Constitution."[5]

However, Perot's campaign also stands out as an exception to the common course of third-party and independent campaigns. More typically, third-party or independent campaigns have raised the level of constitutional rhetoric. Indeed, no other third-party campaign between 1840 and 1996 had so little to say about the Constitution relative to their major-party competition.

These campaigns can be put into three ascending categories of constitutional rhetoric depending on how much they had to say about the Constitution relative to their competition. In the first level of constitutional contribution lie third parties that finished with a rate of constitutional references in between the two major parties in one or more modes of communication. In other words, while they were outdone by one of the major parties in every venue, there was at least one venue in which they outperformed the other party, hence raising the overall level of discussion of constitutional issues. This group was defined by modest but real constitutional contribution.

In the next level of constitutional rhetoric, a number of third parties outpaced both of their major-party rivals in at least one form of communication. That is to say, in at least one (but not all) of the venues, their constitutional arguments led the field quantitatively. This group can be said to have shared in constitutional leadership—though only shared.

In the highest category are third parties or independent candidates whose frequency of constitutional rhetoric outpaced both major-party opponents in all modes of communication (or, in the modern era, at least three of four). These were campaigns that consistently put more emphasis on the Constitution than any of their major-party rivals. Often, they were defined by the constitutional ground that they staked out. In some sense, they dominated the constitutional debate, at least quantitatively.

Constitutional Contribution

In the first level, third parties contributed significantly to the constitutional conversation by raising the average level of constitutional rhetoric in at least one mode of communication. These parties ranged from the Free-Soil Party aiming to stop the spread of slavery into the territories in 1848 to the 1912 Progressives led by Theodore Roosevelt. Other parties in this group included the American (or Know-Nothing) Party and the Populists in 1892, their first run for the presidency.

Free-Soil (1848)

The Free-Soil Party nominated Martin Van Buren, who had served as the eighth president of the United States as a Democrat. Van Buren had grown disaffected from the increasingly proslavery Democrats, and threw his lot in with the Free-Soilers. Van Buren ran on a party platform that acknowledged the lack of constitutional power to restrict slavery in states where it existed, but contended for the right of Congress to block its spread to the territories. Congress is denied the power, the Free-Soilers argued, to deprive anyone of life, liberty, or property without due process, meaning that Congress "has no more power to make a SLAVE than to make a KING." Consequently, the platform resolved "That it is the duty of the federal government to relieve itself from all responsibility for the existence or continuance of slavery wherever that government possess constitutional power to legislate on that subject."[6] Thus, the platform tread heavily in the regions of individual rights, enumerated powers, and federalism.

In his nomination acceptance letter, Van Buren reiterated and endorsed the platform, discussing rights, federalism, and enumerated powers, with the strongest emphasis on the last. He affirmed that the Constitution did not permit Congress to interfere with slavery in the states, but that the constitutionality of a congressional prohibition on slavery in the territories was "clear." He also made several perfunctory references to the Constitution, and pointed out that a bill restricting slavery in some of territories (the Oregon Bill) had "received the constitutional approval of the present executive—an approval which it was his sworn duty to withhold, if he had not been satisfied that all the provisions of the bill were in conformity to the Constitution."[7]

Altogether, the Free-Soilers raised the level of constitutional discussion in the election of 1848. Van Buren's message had more constitutional references per thousand words than Zachary Taylor's Whig messages, though fewer than Lewis Cass's Democratic message, and four of five of Van Buren's references were explicit, better than either major-party candidate. Likewise, although the Free-Soil platform was less heavily constitutional than the Democratic platform, it was considerably more so than the Whig platform. Van Buren won nearly 300,000 votes, or about 10 percent of the total, but no electoral votes.

American Party (1856)

The American Party selected another former president, Millard Fillmore, as its nominee. Otherwise known as the Know-Nothing Party, the American

Party offered a platform that was filled with constitutional references extolling freedom of religion and separation of church and state, calling for restrictions on the right to vote for immigrants, demanding a constitutional amendment lengthening the period required for immigrants to reside in the United States before becoming eligible for naturalization, and making passing positive references to judicial review and enforcement of the law. The party also tried to finesse the slavery question by calling for "The unequalled recognition and maintenance of the reserved rights of the several states" and "non-interference by Congress with questions appertaining solely to the individual states, and non-intervention by each state with the affairs of any other state."[8] Thus the platform touched on rights, federalism, enforcement, constitutional amendments, and judicial power.

By comparison, Fillmore's nomination acceptance letter was noticeably reticent about constitutional issues. He mentioned only his determination to "perform every duty confided by the Constitution and the laws to the Executive."[9] While his letter had a lower rate of constitutional references than his two major-party opponents, the American Party platform had nearly as many references per thousand words as the Republican platform and many more than the Democratic platform. Ultimately, Fillmore won 874,534 popular votes nationwide—21.6 percent of the votes cast—and eight electoral votes from the state of Maryland.

People's Party (1892)

Agrarian discontent revolving around currency deflation, protectionism, and perceived exploitation by banks and railroads led to a series of movements and third parties throughout the late 1800s. The culmination of these efforts took the form of the People's Party, or Populist Party, formed at a convention in Omaha in 1890.

The 1892 Populists were not particularly concerned with constitutional questions. Their platform made one reference to "equal rights and equal privileges," and proclaimed that "We assert our purposes to be identical with the purposes of the National Constitution, to form a more perfect union and establish justice, insure domestic tranquility, provide for the common defense, promote the general welfare, and secure the blessings of liberty for ourselves and our posterity."[10] In all, both major-party platforms gave greater weight to consideration of the Constitution than did the Populists. However, their presidential nominee, James Weaver, offered a message that was not far from the Democratic message and was considerably higher than the Republican candidate message in terms of constitutional references. Weaver won over one million votes (8.6 percent). He prevailed in four states outright and shaved off a handful of electors elsewhere for a total of twenty-two electoral votes.

Progressive Party ("Bull Moose," 1912)

The 1912 election saw two third parties that demonstrated considerable electoral strength and that affected the course of politics and policy in the nation for decades. The more powerful of the two was the Progressive Party, led by former President Theodore Roosevelt. Roosevelt had long been at loggerheads with the "Old Guard" faction of the Republican Party. Although he was distrusted by many Republican progressives, he gradually identified himself with the progressive wing of the Republican Party. In 1908, as he was leaving office, he endorsed William Howard Taft as his successor. By 1910, he became convinced that Taft had strayed from the progressive path and prepared to reenter politics. Ultimately, he challenged Taft unsuccessfully for the Republican presidential nomination in 1912. Certain that he had been unfairly denied nomination by a convention "steamroller," he bolted the Republican Party with his supporters and formed the Progressive Party. In November, Roosevelt finished second behind Democrat Woodrow Wilson, winning 27 percent of the vote and eighty-eight electoral votes.

The Progressive platform focused on supporting a number of constitutional amendments, including direct election of senators, an income tax amendment, amendments expanding federal economic power, and even an amendment making the amendment process itself easier. Federalism was a second key issue, with the Progressives calling in several places for a more nationalist understanding of the relationship between federal and state authority. A third theme was an attack on judicial power, including opposition to injunctions and advocacy of means to reverse court decisions: "The Progressive party demands such restriction of the power of the courts as shall leave to the people the ultimate authority to determine fundamental questions of social welfare and public policy."[11] Added was a sprinkling of references to enumeration of powers, and women's suffrage, as well as perfunctory references. The number and weight of constitutional references by the Progressives was actually high compared with major-party references in typical past years, but not in 1912. The Progressive platform was less interested in constitutional questions than any of the other three big vote-winning parties of 1912.

Roosevelt's speech had the second highest rate of constitutional references of the four addresses of 1912. The candidate spoke at length, elaborating well beyond the positions offered in the platform, about constitutional revision, the power of the courts, the federal system, specific Supreme Court decisions relating to trusts, and the constitutionality of the protective tariff.

He also endorsed equal rights and women's suffrage and contended that "We Progressives stand for the rights of the people. When these rights can best be secured by insistence upon States' rights, then we are for States' rights; when they can best be secured by insistence upon National rights, then we are for National rights."[12] After Teddy Roosevelt's defeat in 1912, he and most members of the Progressive Party gradually drifted back into the Republican fold.

Constitutional Leadership

A second group of third parties exerted more substantial constitutional leadership, using constitutional rhetoric at a rate that led the field in at least one (but not all) of the modes of campaign communication. These parties included the Constitutional Union Party, the Liberal Republicans, the 1896 Populists, the Socialists, and the 1996 version of the Perot phenomenon, the Reform Party.

Constitutional Union (1860)
The Constitutional Union Party was formed in 1860, largely by former Whigs and American Party activists determined to patch together the Union. It had its greatest strength in the border states and the moderate regions of the North and South. Its short platform outdid even the Southern Democrats for frequency of constitutional references. However, its references tended to be formulaic and heavily weighted to the perfunctory. The party vowed to recognize "no political principle other than THE CONSTITUTION OF THE COUNTRY, THE UNION OF THE STATES, AND THE ENFORCEMENT OF THE LAWS," and pledged to reestablish "the rights of the People and of the States."[13]

The Constitutional Union Party's presidential nominee was John Bell of Tennessee, and his nomination acceptance letter was quite sparse in terms of constitutional issues in comparison with both his party's platform and messages by other parties' candidates. The letter included three perfunctory references pledging Bell to "due observance in the conduct of the government of the Constitution" and vigorous action "for the maintenance of the Constitution and the Union."[14] The Constitutional Union ticket polled about 589,000 votes, or about 13 percent of the total, garnering thirty-nine electoral votes from Kentucky, Tennessee, and Virginia.

Liberal Republicans (1872)
Republicans dissatisfied with the corruption of the Grant administration, tough Reconstruction policies, and the protective tariff bolted and ran a Lib-

eral Republican ticket with Horace Greeley at its head. Still in postwar disarray, the Democrats opted to nominate Greeley as well. The two shared a common platform, though Greeley wrote separate nomination acceptance messages to each convention.[15]

Greeley's messages contained a bit less constitutional rhetoric than the speech delivered by the Republican surrogate for U.S. Grant (Senator Oliver Morton). Nevertheless, Greeley's messages gave greater weight to constitutional questions than had most of the messages delivered before 1860. Greeley called for protection of equal rights and suffrage for black and white Southerners alike; "subject to our solemn constitutional obligation to maintain the equal rights of all citizens, our policy should aim at self-government and not at centralization." He also called for the supremacy of civilian over military authority and protection of the writ of habeas corpus, and condemned "Federal subversion of the internal polity of the several States and municipalities." Finally, Greeley expressed a determination to bolster separation of powers and to support a constitutional amendment limiting presidents to one term.[16]

The joint Liberal Republican/Democratic platform was more thoroughly stacked with constitutional references, though its content closely paralleled Greeley's letters. All in all, the platform had more than twice as many constitutional references per thousand words than did the Republican platform. Greeley won over 2.8 million votes (44 percent) and six states against Grant, though he died before the electoral votes were cast.[17]

People's Party (1896)

In contrast with their campaign four years earlier, populists in 1896 more obviously raised the level of constitutional rhetoric in the campaign. The People's Party platform was significantly more concerned with constitutional questions than the Republican platform, while the Democratic platform, which itself was written by the populist-leaning wing of that party, had the greatest concern with such questions. William Jennings Bryan, who was the nominee of both Democrats and Populists, gave an acceptance speech that was significantly more concerned with constitutional questions than was the acceptance speech by Republican William McKinley.

The Populist platform ranged over questions including opposition to abuse of executive power, the Supreme Court's *Pollock* decision invalidating the federal income tax, an alleged breakdown of separation of powers, use of judicial power to impose injunctions against labor, wholesale restriction on the right to vote in certain states, and "the destruction of the political rights and personal liberties of the citizens" by the great railroad corporations. The Populists also put themselves on record as favoring direct election of the president, vice president, and senators, and establishment of a system of initiative and referendum, "under proper constitutional safeguards.[18] In many respects, the Populists presaged the Progressives and ultimately the New Deal.

Bryan's speech, delivered in Madison Square Garden, echoed many of the same themes, including equality under the law and a lengthy disquisition criticizing the *Pollock* decision as well as asserting the right and duty to object to faulty court decisions and attempt to have them reversed. He also touted basic civil liberties like freedom of conscience, thought, and speech, and brought arguments of constitutional sovereignty into the debate as they related to America's entanglement in the international gold standard: "We will not offend other nations when we declare the right of the American people to govern themselves, and, without let or hindrance from without, decide upon every question presented for their consideration."[19] Altogether, Bryan and the Populists pushed a series of constitutional issues that McKinley's Republicans had no interest in raising or addressing.

Socialists (1912)

The other relatively successful minor party in 1912 was the Socialist Party led by Eugene Debs. The Socialists had formed the party in 1901, had been convinced in 1908 that their time had come, and had elected over 1,200 candidates to local office between 1910 and 1912. It was a party dominated by a coalition of radical labor activists and radical intellectuals. The reformist mood of 1912 gave them their best opportunity to make an impact. In the end, Debs won about 6 percent of the vote, the peak electoral performance of any American socialist party.

The Socialist platform had the highest rate of constitutional references of the four key parties of 1912, providing more constitutional references per thousand words than Democrats, Republicans, or Progressives. The Socialists' chief constitutional concerns were judicial power and federal court decisions, individual civil liberties and voting rights, and a series of constitutional amendments. They also advocated a drastic change in executive powers in the form of abolition of the president's veto power.

In terms of judicial power, the Socialists demanded "The abolition of the power usurped by the Supreme Court of the United States to pass upon the constitutionality of the legislation enacted by Congress. National laws to be repealed only by an act of Congress or by a referendum vote of the whole people."[20] Other measures to tame judicial power included abolition of lower federal courts, the election of all judges for short terms, and curbing the power to issue injunctions. Like the Progressives, the Socialists were inflamed by a series of court decisions overturning child-labor and other worker-protection statutes. Constitutional amendments proposed by the Socialists included the establishment of a national system of initiative, referendum, and recall, abolition of the Senate and veto power of the president, direct election of the president and vice president, and easier rules for ratification of constitutional amendments. They also proposed immediately calling a new constitutional convention.

Interestingly, Debs's acceptance letter ignored almost all of these subjects. Instead, he briefly criticized the courts, briefly bemoaned the right to property, and called for equal individual rights. In contrast to the platform, Debs's letter was third out of four in the weight it gave constitutional concerns; only Woodrow Wilson's message was below Debs's. Perhaps Debs's real passion was in legislation to ameliorate working life rather than structural reform of government. Nevertheless, between the platform, which outdid all others, and the message, which outdid one of the two major-party candidates, the Socialists clearly enhanced the degree of constitutional discussion in the 1912 election.

Reform Party (Ross Perot, 1996)

The winner of the 1992 election, Bill Clinton, received only 43 percent of the vote, and George Bush won 38 percent, meaning that Ross Perot—or at any rate, his supporters—held the balance of power. The next four years saw both Democrats and Republicans angle hard to appeal to the Perot voters on issues such as deficit reduction (attempted in different forms by both parties), campaign-finance reform (sought by Democrats), and other reforms like term limits (pushed mostly by Republicans). Perot himself sought to institutionalize his influence by forming a third party, the Reform Party, around the principles he espoused in 1992. At first disavowing any intent to run again in 1996, Perot stepped in at the last minute to take the Reform nomination away from former Colorado Governor Richard Lamm. However, the intervening years had not been kind to Perot. Much of his previous support had ebbed away. Perot's own volatility, policy initiatives by Clinton and the Republican 104th Congress, and an improving economy had cut the ground out from under the Texan. Perot was never enough of a factor to win participation in the 1996 debates, which proceeded without him. This time, he won about 9 percent of the national vote—impressive for a third party but decidedly unimpressive in comparison to his 1992 showing.

Perot's second run, in 1996, was different than the first. His candidate message, a nomination acceptance speech at the Reform party convention, was, as in 1992, little concerned with the Constitution.[21] To the extent that he had such concerns, he focused on a proposed constitutional amendment to require voter approval for federal tax increases and made a mention of the need to "restore local control over the schools."[22]

The Reform Party platform, however, was wildly different from the 1992 Perot book, in two ways: It ran to 656 words, arranged completely in a series of bullet points, instead of approximately 24,000 words. And it had a much higher rate of constitutional references, by a factor of six—enough to significantly outpace both Democratic and Republican platforms, despite the fact that the Republican platform was more weighted to constitutional issues than any Republican platform since 1948. Parallel to Perot's speech, the spare Reform platform concentrated its constitutional attention exclusively on constitutional amendments. These included support for congressional term limits, the balanced budget amendment, holding national elections on a Saturday and a Sunday, abolition of the Electoral College, and the requirement for voter approval of tax increases.[22]

Constitutional Domination

At the highest level, a third group of third parties or independent candidates has fairly dominated its rivals in terms of constitutional references, finishing at the top of the field in not one but all modes of communication (or in modern times, three of four). This is not to say that they always dominated the constitutional agenda, much less that their concern with the Constitution dominated the overall campaign agenda. It is to say that in the numerical competition in rates of constitutional rhetoric, they were essentially unbeaten. The campaigns at this highest level included the Southern Democrats, the La Follette Progressives, the American Independent Party, and John Anderson.

Southern Democrats (1860)
As the nation veered toward civil war, its party system split asunder as well. Divided between supporters of "popular sovereignty" and an uncompromising proslavery position, the Democratic Party faced a deepening schism. When the national convention, held in Charleston, adopted a platform report that was insufficiently proslavery for the taste of the fire-breathers, the bulk of the Southern delegates bolted the convention. When it reconvened in Baltimore, what remained of the national Democratic Party nominated Stephen A. Douglas. The disaffected Southerners held their own convention and nominated John C. Breckenridge.

Those Southern Democrats adopted a platform committed to the "property right" of slavery, declaring that territories seeking entry into the union should be considered on an equal footing whether or not they wished to come in as slave states, and condemning state legislative actions interfering with fugitive-slave laws as "subversive of the Constitution." They also pledged themselves to "protect the naturalized citizen in all his rights" and to promote a transcontinental railroad "to the extent of the Constitutional authority of Congress."[23] The Southern Democratic platform had more constitutional references per thousand words than either the national Democratic or Republican platforms; it was outdone only by the other third party of 1860, the Constitutional Union party.

Breckenridge's letter of acceptance was even more heavily loaded with constitutional language, consisting of an extended discussion of the equal rights to property of citizens of all the states, a thorough exposition of his theory of the federal system, and a positive reference to the *Dred Scott* decision. Though Breckenridge's mention of *Dred Scott* was implicit, 85 percent of his abundant references were explicitly constitutional in character. His purpose was summarized, as he said, "By a little constitutional struggle, it is intended to assert and establish the equality of the States, as the only basis of union and peace. When this object, so national, so constitutional, so just, shall be accomplished, the last cloud will disappear from the American sky."[24] Altogether, in a message of only around 1,300 words, Breckenridge cited federalism seventeen times and individual rights eight times, while making one reference to a Supreme Court decision and one perfunctory reference. His acceptance letter contained more than twenty references per thousand words, far above any other candidate of that constitutionally contentious year. When the votes were counted, Breckenridge had received nearly 850,000 votes, slightly over 18 percent of the total. In the process, he won seventy-two electoral votes from nine soon-to-be-Confederate states, plus Delaware and Maryland.

Progressives (La Follette, 1924)

The old Republican split between the "old guard" and the "progressives," which had led to Theodore Roosevelt's third-party campaign in 1912, resurfaced in 1924. Republican Progressive Robert La Follette, who had served as governor and U.S. senator from Wisconsin, left the Republican Party in 1924 to run against Calvin Coolidge. In La Follette's view, Coolidge was too closely tied to the business interests of the party, and the corruption of the late Warren Harding's administration repelled him further. There was no repeat of 1912, however. Coolidge won in a landslide, and La Follette finished third, without even attaining leverage as the man holding the swing bloc of voters; the Progressives' and the Democrats' votes combined would not have defeated Coolidge. Nevertheless, La Follette did poll 17.2 percent of the vote, winning Wisconsin's thirteen electoral votes and serving, in the view of some scholars, as a way station for liberal and labor Republicans on their way to becoming New Deal Democrats.[25]

Both La Follette's Progressive platform and his nomination acceptance speech contained much more constitutional content than those of either of his major-party rivals. The platform, much like the Socialist platform of 1912, condemned the judicial "usurpation" of judicial review, quoted Abraham Lincoln's famous warning about the dangers of giving too much deference to judicial power, and proposed several means to bring the judicial branch under the control of the people. It also proposed a bevy of constitutional amendments, including a child labor amendment and amendments to provide for congressional override of judicial review, popular election of judges for terms not to exceed ten years, direct popular nomination and election of presidents, an initiative and referendum process at the federal level, and a popular referendum to determine war. The Progressives called for preservation of the political liberties of the people and condemned invasions of "the people's rights by unlawful arrests and unconstitutional searches and seizures."[26]

La Follette himself delivered one of the most constitutionally laden candidate messages of any in the sample, totaling eighty-eight constitutional references, 92 percent of which were explicit. In his address, La Follette devoted long passages to questions of individual rights and recapitulated the party's position on amendments, arguing against his opponents' unwillingness even to submit the amendments to the people for their consideration. La Follette then spent a little under one-third of his rather long speech expounding his views on the character of the federal judiciary, the proper scope of judicial power, the best means of controlling that power, and trends in judicial decisions, including complaints lodged against Supreme Court decisions on the income tax, child labor, the minimum wage, and antitrust law. In the process, he reiterated the platform's stand supporting a legislative or popular override of judicial review, and explaining why that was a preferable solution to impeachment of judges. In no other candidate message of any major or minor party did any candidate offer so thorough a discussion of the character of judicial power in the constitutional system, and only rarely so thorough a discussion of any other constitutional topic.[27] All in all, La Follette's Progressive campaign had the effect of raising much higher the profile of constitutional issues in the election of 1924.

American Independent Party (1968)

George Wallace served as the Democratic governor of Alabama from 1963 to 1967. During his tenure, he gained notoriety by resisting desegregation of Alabama's schools, famously vowing in 1963 to stand in the school doorway to prevent entrance by black students and the U.S. Marshals who accompanied them. As a result of that incident, he was one of the most well known (or notorious) of the Southern segregationists. At the same time, he honed a populist appeal on cultural matters and, later, foreign policy that could attract white blue-collar voters from industrial states. Presenting himself as a voice for law and order and traditional values amid the rising tide of the 1960s counterculture, and simultaneously serving as a magnet for racial "backlash" against civil rights agitation, Wallace had placed surprisingly well in the 1964 Democratic presidential primaries in Indiana, Wisconsin, and Maryland. By 1968, Wallace decided to make another run for the presidency, this time outside the two-party system. Forming what he called the American Independent Party around himself, Wallace fought court battles to ensure ballot access in all fifty states. More than a mere independent candidate, but less than the representative of a genuine grassroots movement or a vibrant third party in the mold of the Free-Soilers, the Populists, or the Progressives, Wallace waged a national campaign claiming there was "not a dime's worth of difference" between the two major parties. Though his greatest strength was in the deep South, Wallace polled significant votes in every region. It was never entirely clear whom he threatened more. He drew more support from the traditional Democratic base in the South and from among blue-collar ethnics in the North, but these were precisely the voters who might have been moving toward the Republicans already. On election day, Wallace received 13.5 percent of the national vote and forty-six Southern electoral votes. If La Follette's 1924 candidacy served as a way station for many voters moving from a Republican affiliation to a Democratic affiliation, Wallace clearly served the same role for a movement in the opposite direction.

Regardless of the mode of campaign communication, Wallace and the American Independent Party unambiguously showed more interest in constitutional issues than either the Democrats or Republicans of 1968. The American Independent Party platform had twice as many constitutional references per thousand words as either of its rivals; Wallace's selected speech contained more than three times as many references per thousand words as his rivals' candidate messages; and this study's sample of his television ads had two-and-a-half times the rate of references of Hubert Humphrey's ads and more than ten times the rate of Richard Nixon's.

The constitutional topics in which the American Independent Party platform was most heavily interested were federalism and enumeration of powers, judicial questions, individual rights, and constitutional amendments. The heart of the platform lay in an extensive argument, both abstract and directed to specific policy questions, about the proper nature of the federal system and the constitutional limits of Washington's authority. It called for "Reestablishment of the authority and responsibility of local government by returning to the states, counties, and cities those matters properly falling within their jurisdiction and responsibility." The American Independent Party proceeded to delineate federal from state authority, arguing that the founding fathers had "visualized the tyranny and despotism which would inevitably result from an omnipotent central government; and, they sought to avoid that peril by delegating to that central or federal government only those powers which could best be administered by a central or federal government" and reserving remaining powers to the states in the Tenth Amendment. The federal authorities were charged with violating this scheme in numerous particular areas, including education, voting eligibility, regimentation of farmers, housing, and state legislative reapportionment. Wallace offered instead block grants and restored authority for the states.

Likewise, federal courts were condemned at length for overstepping their bounds, going beyond what Congress would have legislated and showing excessive solicitude for the lawless element. Individual rights were discussed primarily in terms of property rights: "We feel that private property rights and human rights are inseparable and indivisible. Only in those nations that guarantee the right of ownership of private property as basic and sacred under their law is there any recognition of human rights." Equal treatment under the law was touted, but civil rights was only addressed specifically by way of attacking the "so-called 'Civil Rights Acts'" as divisive.

The platform also endorsed a number of constitutional amendments, either implicitly or explicitly. These included support for school prayer and amendments to require popular retention votes for federal district judges and periodical re-confirmation by the Senate of appellate court judges and Supreme Court justices. These references were concentrated in platform sections titled "Local Government," "The Federal Judiciary," "Private Property," "Crime and Disorder," and "Education." [28]

In Wallace's representative message, an address in Madison Square Garden on October 24, 1968, he returned several times to the theme of "local government." "We are going to turn back to you, the people of the states, the right to control our domestic institutions," Wallace promised. He applied this principle to school busing, saying "Not one dime of your federal money is going to be used to bus anybody any place that you don't want them to be bussed in New York or any other state."

Supreme Court decisions played a major part in Wallace's speech, as well. He complained that "The Supreme Court of our country has handcuffed the police," and criticized as well the Court's school prayer and obscenity cases and its ruling that communists could work in defense plants. Finally, the topic of individual rights was more prominent in Wallace's speech than in his platform. Property rights and busing occupied some attention, but in contrast to the platform much of Wallace's speech revolved around the question of the right of dissent in wartime. The candidate drew a distinction between legitimate dissent and treason, saying that if you disagree with the war, that is your right, but "if you arise and make a speech the next day and say I long for Communist victory, every average citizen in New York knows that one is dissent and the other is something else. . . . I'm going to have my attorney general seek an indictment against any professor calling for communist victory and stick him in a good jail somewhere."[29]

Of the three Wallace ads accessed at the American Museum of the Moving Image, one had constitutional content. In it, a narrator criticized school busing and Wallace himself pledged to "turn back absolute control of the public school system to the people of the respective states." These references produced a ratio of 6.3 constitutional references per thousand words, far in excess of Humphrey's 2.5 or Nixon's 0.6 references per thousand words. The Wallace ad sample is admittedly small, but the results are consistent with findings from his other modes of communication.

John Anderson (1980)

In 1980, Representative John Anderson, a Republican from Illinois, was one of seven serious contenders for the Republican nomination for president. By midway through the nomination campaign Anderson succeeded in becoming one of the three main candidates behind Ronald Reagan and George H. W. Bush. A representative of the much shrunken liberal wing of the Republican Party, Anderson espoused gun control, abortion on demand, a fifty-cent-a-gallon tax on gasoline, and hostility to the growing ascendancy of social conservatives in the party. Outgunned by Reagan and Bush, Anderson finally left the Republican contest at the end of April 1980. Instead of retiring to private life, however, Anderson jumped into the general election race as an independent candidate, bolstered by an admiring media and polls showing dissatisfaction with the major-party choices. Anderson polled as high as 20 percent over the summer, but his core appeal was limited to white, college-educated, affluent voters of the center-left. He debated Reagan before a televised audience in September, but was frozen out of the climactic debate between Reagan and Carter in October because his national poll support had dropped below 15 percent. In the end, Anderson won 6.6 percent of the national vote, but because his vote was relatively evenly distributed he won no states and hence no electoral votes.

The campaign brochure used as a proxy for Anderson's platform spent considerable attention on the issues of individual rights and constitutional amendments. He reiterated his support for the Equal Rights Amendment, his prochoice position on abortion, and his opposition to a constitutional amendment restricting abortion. Anderson also made clear his support for affirmative action programs and past civil rights legislation, and the brochure touted his "eloquent opposition to a constitutional amendment banning busing for school desegregation."[30]

Anderson's candidate message, announcing the launching of his independent candidacy, contained little constitutional content—only one reference to the "precious right of franchise." Even though his candidate message was at the bottom of the three candidates' messages in terms on constitutional mentions, it was clumped close to Carter's and Reagan's acceptance speeches. In his television ads, his one debate performance, and the campaign brochure used to represent his platform, Anderson made a higher rate of constitutional references than either Reagan or Carter.

His debate with Reagan produced a number of constitutional arguments by Anderson, generally focusing on the interplay of individual rights and controversial social issues. He stressed his prochoice position on abortion, criticized the drive for a constitutional amendment to restrict abortion, and attacked Republicans for advocating an antiabortion "litmus test" for the appointment of federal judges. He also addressed the broader question of church-state relations, arguing that religious leaders instructing their congregations on how to vote "violates the principle of church and state" and disavowing a constitutional amendment he had sponsored as a congressman in the 1960s declaring America to be a "Christian nation." In the same vein, Anderson pointed out that he had voted twice against proposed constitutional amendments restoring school prayer. Anderson's other constitutional reference during his 1980 debate disdained federalism sideways, calling nationalism today "as anachronistic as states' rights was in the days of Jefferson Davis."[31]

As with Wallace, the Anderson television ads available for study are limited. Nevertheless, his commitment to "equal rights" was sufficient to win him a far higher rate of references per thousand words than either Carter or Reagan.

Constitutional issues did not occupy a central place in Anderson's overall campaign in the way they did for Wallace, La Follette, or the 1860 Southern Democrats. Nevertheless, his discussion of those issues in most venues outpaced that of his opponents, including Reagan, who had devoted a large part of his political career to advancing a particular view of the Constitution but whose 1980 campaign was dominated by economic and foreign policy concerns.

Conclusion

As many scholars have previously demonstrated, third parties often serve an important creative role in American politics even though they face enormous obstacles and rarely attain even modest electoral success. They can highlight issues left dormant by the major parties, can mobilize new voters or get old voters to look at politics in a new way, and can even serve as a halfway house for voters moving from one major party to the other.

As a result, it must be considered significant that the most successful third parties or independent candidates since 1840 have overwhelmingly tended to enrich the constitutional discussion. Third-party efforts have not been free of the effects of deconstitutionalization—their rates of constitutional references per thousand words have declined over time, as have those of the major parties—but they have mitigated it. Overall, eleven of fourteen third-party or independent platforms matched or exceeded at least one of the major-party platforms in constitutional references per thousand words, as did eight of fourteen candidate messages (table 6.1.).

Of the fourteen who attained at least 5 percent of the vote, only one—Perot in 1992—made very little constitutional contribution to the campaign. In three of four forms of campaign communication, Perot was at the bottom of the pack in terms of constitutional references per thousand words; in the fourth (debates) he barely nosed out the last-place finisher.

Otherwise, there were three campaigns that had the highest rates of constitutional rhetoric across the board: the Southern Democrats of 1860, the Progressives of 1924, and the American Independent Party of 1968. Trailing closely was John Anderson in 1980, who enjoyed the highest rates in three of four modes of communication and nearly a tie in the fourth. These parties or candidates significantly raised the level of constitutional discussion. Furthermore, the third parties or independent campaigns that accomplished this ranged across time and across the ideological spectrum. Their large-scale use of constitutional rhetoric might be the only thing that John Breckenridge and Robert La Follette, George Wallace and John Anderson have in common. Of ideological tendencies, only the "radical center," in the form of Ross Perot's 1992 campaign, failed to make a serious constitutional contribution.

Another five third-party or independent campaigns employed higher rates of constitutional rhetoric than their major-party rivals in one category of communication: the Constitutional Union Party of 1860, the Liberal Republicans in 1872, the Populists of 1896, the 1912 Socialists, and Perot in 1996.

Finally, four campaigns placed between the major parties in at least one mode of communication, starting with the Free-Soilers (with lower rates

Table 6.1. Constitutional references per thousand words in third-party and major-party discourse, 1840–2004

Year	Party	Platform	Message	Ads	Debates
1848	Free Soil	6.7	3.8		
	Democrat	9.7	7.6		
	Whig	2.6	2.9		
1856	American	19.3	1.4		
	Democrat	11.9	8.7		
	Republican	23.1	2.8		
1860	Con. Union	23.7	3.0		
	S. Democrat	16.5	20.1		
	Democrat	16.1	10.2		
	Republican	10.9	8.5		
1872	Lib. Repub.	17.4	6.1		
	Republican	7.1	8.8		
1892	Populist	2.0	2.1		
	Democrat	5.6	3.0		
	Republican	5.2	.4		
1896	Populist	6.7	2.2		
	Democrat	0.4	2.2		
	Republican	1.0	.3		
1912	Progressive	4.0	2.8		
	Socialist	7.9	1.3		
	Democrat	6.6	.5		
	Republican	5.3	3.8		
1924	Progressive	9.5	11.5		
	Democrat	3.6	3.4		
	Republican	1.3	2.5		
1968	Amer. Indep.	4.0	5.1	6.3	
	Democrat	1.8	1.4	2.5	
	Republican	2.0	1.5	.6	
1980	Anderson	3.2	.5	6.3	3.3
	Democrat	2.0	.6	.7	.4
	Republican	2.3	.8	.3	1.6/1.6
1992	Perot	1.6	-0-	-0-	.4/1.0/0
	Democrat	2.3	2.0	-0-	0/1.0/0
	Republican	2.9	3.5	1.1	.2/3.7/2.9
1996	Perot	10.7	.8		
	Democrat	1.8	1.7		
	Republican	6.4	2.1		

than the Democrats but higher rates than the Whigs in both platform and message) and including the American Party of 1856, the 1892 version of the People's Party, and the 1912 Progressives (who finished in the middle position between the major parties in one of their two modes of communication while finishing in last place in the other mode). These parties did not dominate or even lead the constitutional discussion, but the constitutional discussion was enriched because of their campaigns.

The effect of these parties in raising constitutional questions varied—in the most striking instance, the American Party's second-place platform made over nineteen constitutional references per thousand words, much higher than many parties that placed first in other years—but in any case was nontrivial. In every case but Perot in 1992, third parties or independent candidates discussed the Constitution enough to raise the two-party average in at least one venue of campaign communication. All in all, third parties averaged considerably more references per thousand words in both platforms and candidate messages than either major party (see table 6.2).

Of course, it hardly bears pointing out that quantity should not be conflated with quality. Several of these parties used their voluminous constitutional rhetoric to advance constitutional notions that were dubious at best, ranging from nativism to a defense of slavery or segregationism to advocacy for the destruction of property rights, limited government, and an independent judiciary. The question that concerns us here is not whether the constitutional positions of the third parties were good or bad, but whether they took key constitutional issues of the day seriously and whether they contributed to causing Americans to think more often about the Constitution.

There is a less consistent answer to the question of how much of third parties' constitutional rhetoric was explicit rather than implicit. For three parties or candidates—Socialists in 1912 and Perot in both 1992 and 1996—references were less likely to be explicit than for either of the opposing major parties. There were another three parties that finished ahead of both of their major-party rivals on this dimension in all or most means of communication—Populist in 1892, Progressives in 1924, and American Independent in 1968. There was little clear correlation between the rankings

Table 6.2. Average constitutional references per thousand words in third-party election years

Party	Platform avg.	Cand. message avg.
Third party	9.5	4.3
Democrats	6.5	3.8
Whigs/Republicans	5.8	3.2

of third parties in terms of total constitutional references and percentage of references that were explicit, except that Perot (1992) was at the bottom of both lists and the American Independent Party was in the top group in both. Altogether, the third parties were a bit less likely to have explicit references in their platforms than were the major parties, and were more likely than Democrats but less likely than Republicans to have explicit references in their candidate messages.[32]

Finally, on balance, it is clear that third parties have been less driven by rights than have the major parties. Third parties have consistently employed constitutional rhetoric that is more balanced between areas of rhetoric—that is, they have shown greater concern for structural and interpretation questions—than have the major parties. Categories like federalism, constitutional amendments, Supreme Court decisions, and judicial powers have played a prominent part in many third-party campaigns. As Donald Grier Stephenson, Jr. noted, the Populists of 1896, the Progressives and Socialists of 1912, the La Follette Progressives of 1924, and George Wallace in 1968 were all at the center of key electoral disputes over the Court.[33] In only two years—1856 and 1980—did a third-party or independent campaign concentrate more of its attention on rights than on the other groupings of constitutional issues (see charts 6.1). On average, 30 percent of constitutional references in third-party platforms fell in the individual rights category; in the twelve third-party years, Democrats averaged 39 percent and Republicans 43 percent. Six of fourteen third parties had a lower rights percentage than both major parties; another five had a lower rights percentage than one of the ma-

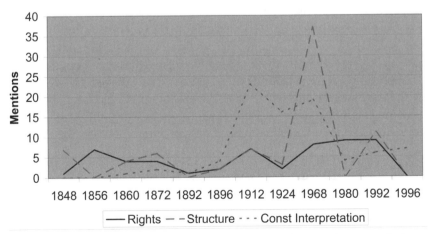

Chart 6.1. Constitutional references grouped by topic in non-major party platforms 1848–1996

Table 6.3. Constitutional references to individual rights as percentage of total platform references, 1840–1996

Year	Third-party platforms	Democratic platforms	Whig/Republican platforms
1848	13	22	0
1856	54	24	59
1860	20/50*	0	31
1872	36	36	67
1892	33	43	86
1896	22	29	100
1912	5/35**	3	33
1924	10	48	0
1968	14	61	25
1980	100	62	36
1992	23	89	45
1996	0	56	34
Average	**30**	**39**	**43**

Note: A lower rights percentage represents greater diversification of discourse.
* Constitutional Union/Southern Democrat
** Progressive/Socialist

jor parties. In other words, in only three cases—Southern Democrats in 1860, Socialists in 1912, and John Anderson in 1980—was a third-party or independent platform more heavily weighted toward rights than both major parties (table 6.3). Perhaps as outsiders third parties are more concerned with addressing the rules of American political life than are the more comfortably situated major parties.

None of the third parties discussed in this chapter won a presidential election. Some seriously affected the course of the campaign, while others were less influential. As a group, however, they embraced discussion of constitutional issues to an extent that both raised the level and broadened the range of constitutional rhetoric in those elections. To the extent that they moved the debate in America, more often than not they moved it in the direction of more consideration of the Constitution than the two-party system was inclined to offer. In keeping with their role of questioning the status quo, they also pushed to the forefront issues of constitutional change. This tendency of third parties can be counted as another one of their signal contributions to American electoral politics. It also means that as long as third-party activity remains possible, the onward march of deconstitutionalization cannot be taken for granted.

CHAPTER SEVEN

Constitutional Rhetoric
and Governing

When the campaign ends and the votes are counted, governing begins. A crucial question is whether the deconstitutionalization seen in campaign rhetoric has carried over into governing rhetoric. If not, then perhaps the trends in campaign rhetoric are of limited importance. Campaign rhetoric, in that case, might be notable in itself because of the way it educates voters, but it would serve as no broader barometer of the health of constitutionalism in government.

However, an examination of two crucial forms of presidential communication—inaugural addresses and State of the Union messages since 1841—indicate that constitutional rhetoric in a governing context has largely paralleled the trends found in campaign rhetoric. Constitutional rhetoric found in those two venues has been somewhat more likely to be explicit than most campaign rhetoric, and it tends to be less preoccupied with rights at the expense of other subjects. Nevertheless, the general pattern of content is quite similar. The course of constitutional rhetoric from era to era will be familiar.

Even more interesting, despite their highly formal and ceremonial character, these two forms of governing communication now have rates of constitutional references that put them in a league with candidate acceptance speeches and television ads, which represent the bottom of the constitutional barrel in campaigns. Not only does campaign communication serve as a barometer of governing rhetoric, but that governing rhetoric has actually surpassed campaigning in its degree of deconstitutionalization. Of course, inaugural addresses and State of the Union messages are only two forms of presidential communication; other television and radio speeches, news conferences, and news interviews are not included. However, of all the forms of presidential communication, one might expect these two to be most imbued with constitutional content and to represent the ceiling of presidential rhetoric on the Constitution, not the floor.

Inaugural Addresses

The inaugural address, given every four years as a president begins his term of office, represents simultaneously the endpoint of the campaign and the beginning of the process of governing. Consequently, presidents seek to tie together themes of their recent campaign and themes that they hope will dominate their administration. Traditionally, inaugural addresses have tended to be relatively short and to avoid detailed consideration of policy. As Karlyn Kohrs Campbell and Kathleen Hall Jameison recognize in their book on presidential rhetoric, *Deeds Done in Words*, inaugural addresses serve a variety of functions, including appealing to national unity, affirming traditional political values, expounding on the principles that will guide the new president, and demonstrating that the new president understands the character of the office, including its limitations.[1]

In a 1937 study, political scientist John McDiarmid observed that "Presidential inaugural addresses afford an interesting sample for the study of our 'official vocabulary.'" In a content analysis of inaugural addresses, McDiarmid found that the overwhelming majority of presidents included in their addresses a reference to the "Constitution" or "constitutional." "The fact that Presidents have contributed to a 'Constitution worship' . . . is indicated by the high praise which they have frequently bestowed upon that document."[2] A brief overview of inaugural addresses can help us assess that claim and its limits.

William Henry Harrison's inaugural address, the first in the period of the study, was highly constitutional in its content. It was also by far the longest, and was delivered in freezing rain that led to Harrison's untimely death from pneumonia. Harrison, the first Whig president, offered an extensive theory of constrained executive powers and veto usage contrasting with the Jacksonian view. Other antebellum inaugurals devoted considerable attention to federalism, enumeration of powers, and individual rights, as well as executive powers. James Buchanan's 1857 address included these themes, and added an extended discussion of the mode of constitutional interpretation, contending that "strict construction of the powers of the Government is the only true, as well as the only safe, theory of the Constitution."[3]

Abraham Lincoln's first inaugural, delivered on the cusp of civil war, was dominated by questions of federalism as well as enforcement of the fugitive-slave clause, an issue on which Lincoln wished to offer assurances to the South. Lincoln also addressed at some length issues of executive power (his constitutional duty to preserve the union), issued a measured warning against allowing Supreme Court decisions to supersede self-government, and offered constitutional amendment as an alternative to revolution. Lincoln's second inaugural was much shorter and much loftier than the first, addressing no constitutional issues but rather focusing on national healing and renewal.

Post–Civil War inaugurals became less constitutionally oriented. To the degree that they contained constitutional content, it was more likely than before to be aimed at individual rights, such as the rights of the freed slaves (including enforcement of the Fifteenth Amendment) and defense of religious freedom. James Garfield, for example, pledged that "So far as my lawful authority can extend [Negroes] shall enjoy the full and equal protection of the Constitution and the laws."[4] In this era, Garfield was most interested in constitutional issues, William McKinley least, though McKinley represented the culmination of a process of decline starting with Grant's second inaugural. In that process, Garfield offered a momentary spike. In his relatively few constitutional references, McKinley was almost exclusively interested in individual rights, with a sprinkling of enforcement and executive powers. Throughout this period, perfunctory references in inaugural addresses were quite common. For example, Garfield talked of the Civil War as "the supreme trial of the Constitution,"[5] Grover Cleveland called on Americans to "renew our pledge of devotion to the Constitution,"[6] and Benjamin Harrison referred to his presidential term as the "twenty-sixth under the Constitution."[7]

The Progressive Era saw little constitutional concern in inaugural addresses from Theodore Roosevelt or Woodrow Wilson. Only William Howard Taft included a large number of constitutional references in his 1909 inaugural address. Taft commented at great length on the question of Negro rights, and departed from the norm by devoting a major section of his address to a defense of judicial power: "The American people, if I understand them, insist that the authority of the courts shall be sustained, and are opposed to any change in the procedure by which the powers of a court may be weakened."[8] In this area, Taft joined the battle raging in campaign rhetoric over the power of the courts.

And, as in campaign rhetoric, Warren G. Harding emphasized the preservation of America's constitutional sovereignty in 1921, declaring that "a world supergovernment is contrary to everything we cherish and can have no sanction by our Republic."⁹ Such sentiments were repeated by Calvin Coolidge and Herbert Hoover, who also delivered substantial sections on judicial power and individual rights, including property rights. As the 1920s wore on, Hoover confronted in his inaugural the constitutional question of the Eighteenth Amendment and its enforcement. All three Republican presidents considered structural issues like federalism, enumeration of powers, and separation of powers.

As economic crisis struck and the New Deal was launched, Franklin Roosevelt's use of constitutional language steadily declined in quantity. In his first inaugural, he emphasized executive powers and separation of powers, as he discussed both his capacity and his intention to act against the emergency. In his second inaugural, Roosevelt defended the New Deal's conception of federalism by painting the Depression as beyond the ameliorative capacity of the states and his response as within a broad but legitimate conception of enumeration of powers: "A century and a half ago [our forefathers] established the federal government in order to promote the general welfare and secure the blessings of liberty to the American people. Today we invoke those same powers of government to achieve the same objectives."¹⁰

Then, within a few years of McDiarmid's observation, the Constitution passed out of usage in inaugurals for an extended period. Postwar inaugurals featured a dearth of constitutional references for three decades. Facing the onset of the Cold War against communist totalitarianism, Harry S. Truman's handful of references were devoted to a praise of individual rights such as freedom of speech and religion. Subsequent presidents Eisenhower, Kennedy, Johnson, and Nixon made no or virtually no constitutional references; deconstitutionalization not only reached but enveloped the inaugural address. In a foreshadowing of their parties' electoral directions for the next three decades or more, Johnson made a brief reference to the Bill of Rights, and Nixon in his second inaugural made only a pair of back-to-back references to federalism. Clearly, the content and quantity of constitutional rhetoric in this period was parallel to that found in campaigning; in comparison to previous periods, there was a shortage of such rhetoric both before and after election day.

As in campaigning, a slow turnaround occurred. Jimmy Carter made three references to individual rights, then Ronald Reagan in 1981 made half a dozen constitutional references ranging from individual rights to federalism to enumeration of powers to executive power. In keeping with sentiments he expressed in his nomination acceptance speech and the debates with John Anderson and Jimmy Carter, Reagan pledged "to demand recognition of the distinction between the powers granted to the federal government and those reserved to the states or to the people."[11] Reagan's first inaugural address thus contained more constitutional references than did all of the inaugural addresses from 1953 through 1973 combined. Likewise, Reagan's second inaugural was thick with references to federalism and the limits and responsibilities of the federal government found in the enumeration of powers. He also called for a constitutional amendment to balance the budget, and for protections for the rights of the unborn.

This upsurge in constitutional rhetoric was not matched by subsequent presidents except for Bill Clinton in his second inaugural, but every address since 1989 has contained at least one constitutional reference. In 1997, Clinton twice used the term "a more perfect union" (a form of perfunctory reference),[12] talked about equality under the law, pointed to the civil rights revolution, and pledged to use the powers of his office to the best effect. By standards of the nineteenth century, this was hardly a stellar record; in comparison to the drought of the 1950s and 1960s, it represented a distinct improvement.

Altogether, constitutional rhetoric in the forty-two inaugural addresses from 1841 to 2005 confirms the general outlines established in campaign platforms, speeches, ads, and debates. As one can see in chart 7.1, constitutional mentions in inaugural addresses have fallen off tremendously since 1841, especially coming down after 1929. Even taking into account that 1841 provides an inflated baseline, the trend was clearly downward.

Five inaugural addresses from 1841 to 2005 contained no constitutional references—Lincoln in 1865, Theodore Roosevelt in 1905, Wilson in 1917,

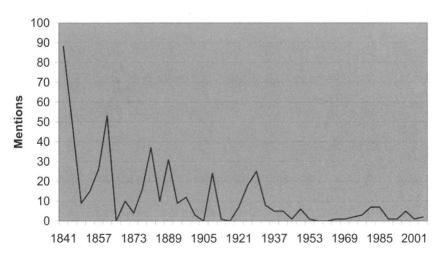

Chart 7.1. Constitutional references in inaugural addresses, 1841–2005

Eisenhower in 1957, and Kennedy in 1961.[13] Eight contained but a single reference: Wilson in 1913, Roosevelt in 1945, Eisenhower in 1953, Johnson in 1965, Nixon in 1969, George H. W. Bush in 1989, Clinton in 1993, and George W. Bush in 2001. At the other extreme, the largest number of references were recorded by William Henry Harrison (eighty-eight in 1841), Lincoln (fifty-three in 1861), Polk (forty-nine in 1845), and Garfield (thirty-eight in 1881). Twentieth-century highs were reached by Taft in 1909 (twenty-four) and Hoover in 1929 (twenty-five). At no time after 1929 has any inaugural address contained more than eight constitutional references; post-1929 highs were reached by Roosevelt in 1933 (eight), Truman in 1949 (six), and Reagan in 1985 (seven). Consistent with campaign rhetoric, constitutional references in inaugural addresses actually reached a low point in the 1950s and 1960s before making a bit of a comeback at the end of the century. Altogether, the most obvious extended trough came from Eisenhower's first inaugural through Nixon's first inaugural, when in succession addresses included one, zero, zero, one, and one references. Similarly, references per thousand words have shown a general downward trend with a low reached in the 1950s and 1960s before a modest recovery. From 1953 to 2005 they have averaged 1.06 references per thousand words, a level comparable to television ads, which were easily the weakest form of campaign communication studied here (chart 7.2).[14]

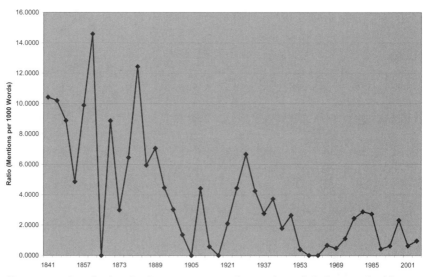

Chart 7.2.   Constitutional references per one thousand words in inaugural addresses, 1841–2005

From 1841 to 2005, Republican inaugural addresses produced modestly more constitutional references per thousand words than Democratic addresses. This overall lead masks a significant difference from one era to another. In fact, Democrats held a slight lead over Republicans from 1841 to 1901 and 1953 to 2005, but were outdone by nearly a two-to-one margin from 1905 to 1949. Interestingly, in all three eras, the party with the greater rate of references was the party that had a more difficult time winning the presidency, though that was not true when the data were aggregated (table 7.1).

Explicit vs. Implicit Rhetoric

As in campaign communications, inaugural addresses have experienced a decline in explicitly constitutional rhetoric. From 1841 to 1969, explicit references frequently outnumbered implicit references. Since 1969, implicit references have opened up a consistent and substantial lead, representing no less than 60 percent of constitutional references; in five of ten addresses in that period, there were no explicit references at all (chart 7.3). This decline in the percentage of references that are explicitly constitutional came considerably later than in platforms or candidate messages; perhaps the more formal, traditional, and ritualistic setting of the inaugurals provided support for a longer time for a higher proportion of explicit references. Indeed, even in the modern era, in inaugural addresses from 1953 to 2005, explicit references averaged 30 percent of the total, a figure slightly above the average in platforms and well above the average in candidate messages and television ads.

Content

In inaugural addresses, the three major groupings of rights, structure, and constitutional interpretation have clung close to each other most of the time since 1841. Structural issues predominated until the Civil War, since which time the rights category has held an advantage more often than not. Since World War II, as in campaign rhetoric, rights have been particularly emphasized by Democratic presidents, who went five inaugurations in a row

Table 7.1. Average constitutional references per thousand words in inaugural addresses, 1841–2005

Years	Whigs/Reps.	Democrats
1841–1901	6.55 (n=11)	6.95 (n=5)
1905–1949	4.34 (n=5)	2.25 (n=7)
1953–2005	.98 (n=9)	1.21 (n=5)
Average	**4.10 (N=25)**	**3.33 (N=17)**

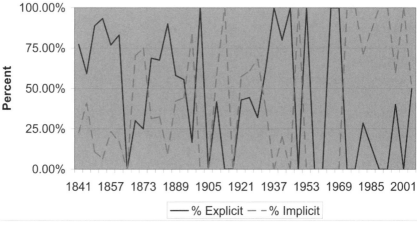

Figure 7.3. Percentage of explicit and implicit constitutional references in inaugural addresses, 1841–2005

without a mention of any other nonperfunctory constitutional topic until Bill Clinton broke the streak with a single mention of executive power in 1997. Since the late 1920s, Republicans have put interpretation and/or structure ahead of rights, until George H. W. Bush in 1989 and George W. Bush in 2001 and 2005 produced three Republican inaugurals in a row with naught but rights as a constitutional topic. Despite being by far the most frequently referenced topic, rights have averaged only 30 percent of all constitutional references in inaugurals, significantly below the prominence of that topic in the campaign communications, in which they averaged between 47 percent and 56 percent.

Of the fifteen categories of rhetoric, the general hierarchy of categories is roughly consistent with what one finds in campaigns. Individual rights is most consistently mentioned in inaugural addresses by both parties, followed by perfunctory references, federalism, executive powers, and enumeration of powers. Vetoes, impeachment, mode of constitutional interpretation, and the relatively new issue of constitutional sovereignty are at the bottom. There are a few significant departures from campaign rhetoric: appointments and Supreme Court decisions are at the bottom of the list, and perfunctory references are the second most consistent kind of reference, perhaps not surprisingly, given the ceremonial character of the occasion. Some differences found between the parties in platforms are replicated in inaugural addresses, for example the much higher propensity of Republicans to discuss enforcement and constitutional sovereignty; others are sui generis, like the Republican monopoly on discussion of constitutional amendments (table 7.2).

Table 7.2. Consistency of constitutional topics in inaugural addresses, 1841–2005

Category	Dem. inaugurals (N=17)	Rep./Whig inaugurals (N=25)
Individual rights	58.8	60.0
Perfunctory	52.9	44.0
Federalism	41.2	48.0
Executive powers	41.2	48.0
Enum. of powers	29.4	44.0
Enforcement	11.8	48.0
Judicial powers	11.8	24.0
Separation of powers	11.8	16.0
Mode of const. interp.	17.6	8.0
Const. amendments	0.0	28.0
Const. sovereignty	0.0	12.0
Veto	5.9	4.0
Supreme Court decisions	0.0	4.0
Appointments	0.0	0.0
Impeachment	0.0	0.0

Individual rights holds its familiar place as both highly consistent and deep, accompanied there by perfunctory references among Democrats. Among categories that are mentioned infrequently but with depth are found federalism, executive powers, enforcement, enumerated powers, and separation of powers among Democrats, and perfunctory references among Republicans. The remainder of the fifteen categories are mentioned neither consistently nor deeply. This means that the general pattern of inaugural addresses is more like candidate messages or television ads than platforms (see appendix C, table C7).

In sum, inaugural addresses, which one might expect to be heavily laden with constitutional language, are not in the modern era. Despite their ceremonial nature they have, like campaign rhetoric, manifested a clear trend of declining concern with constitutional subject matter.

State of the Union Messages

The State of the Union message is delivered annually by the president according to the Constitution's mandate that "the president shall, from time to time, provide to the Congress a report on the State of the Union." George Washington and John Adams delivered the earliest State of the Union reports as speeches, but Thomas Jefferson discontinued the practice as too monarchical and substituted a written report. Woodrow Wilson resumed speech-giving before a joint session of Congress. Thus, throughout the period relevant to this study, presidents produced annual State of the Union messages in the form of a written report to Congress (from 1841 through 1912) and a speech to Congress (from 1913 on, with a few exceptions). These messages are in normal times the most widely anticipated and broadly reported rhetorical efforts of a sitting president, and serve as a good measure of the public agenda facing the nation. Written messages tended to be much longer than inaugural addresses; since 1913, when presidents began again delivering the message as a speech, it has been shorter than before but remained considerably longer than inaugural addresses.

As Campbell and Jamieson argue, State of the Union messages typically involve an application of values to information, leading to specific policy recommendations, calling them "one symbolic moment in which the head of state has woven the cloth of common national history, character, and identity."[15] These scholars also pointed out the connection between the two types of addresses, noting that

> In a general sense, each annual [State of the Union] message is rooted in a president's most recent inaugural. The inaugural lays down the principles that will govern a presidency while demonstrating presidential commitment to the country's basic principles. In State of the Union addresses, presidents revive the principles to which they committed their presidencies and show how those principles will be reflected in their legislative programs.[16]

With 164 messages included in this study, it is not possible to examine them as deeply as other communications in previous chapters. However, the State of the Union messages of recent presidents are worth looking at in more detail.

Franklin Roosevelt's earliest State of the Union addresses concerned themselves relatively little with constitutional issues, but paid some attention to issues like executive powers and separation of powers, as a defense against charges that Roosevelt was autocratic, and federalism and enumeration of powers, as an argument for expanded federal authority. The 1937 State of the Union, at the beginning of Roosevelt's second term and at the onset of his court-packing effort, was unusually preoccupied with questions of judicial power and mode of constitutional interpretation. "The vital need is not an alteration of our fundamental law," Roosevelt argued, "but an increasingly enlightened view in reference to it."[17] As World War II loomed, the emphasis of Roosevelt's constitutional rhetoric shifted toward individual rights, with frequent references to the Bill of Rights and specific rights such as freedom of speech, freedom of religion, and freedom of the press. Throughout his presidency, Roosevelt also made frequent use of perfunctory constitutional references, such as "The Constitution wisely provides that the Chief Executive shall report to Congress on the state of the union."[18]

In Roosevelt's wake, Harry S. Truman produced a long, written report in 1946, but resumed delivery of an address in 1947. In that speech, he devoted a section to civil rights containing numerous individual rights references. He repeated extensive calls for civil rights protections in 1948, 1949, 1950, and 1953. A sentence or two covered the same ground in 1951 and 1952, when international events were more prominent. His final message (1953) included a long summary of the constitutional duties of the president. Altogether, though, Truman's messages represented a full-scale coming to dominance of individual rights as a subject in State of the Union messages.

Both Truman and Dwight D. Eisenhower included calls for the protection of civil liberties by those conducting congressional investigations. Eisenhower, like Truman, frequently included references to civil rights, with particular focus on voting rights, but he also paid much more attention to federalism than did his predecessor. He promised, for example, to attend to education "without impairing in any way the responsibilities of our states, localities, communities, or families"[19] and declared that "federal aid should in no way jeopardize the freedom of local school systems."[20] In his 1957 message, Eisenhower expressed a broader, more theoretical concern, that the future might hold "a dangerous degree of centralized control over our national life."[21] (He was also the first in modern times to call for a line-item veto for the president.) In his penultimate State of the Union message, Eisenhower gave about equal attention to rights and federalism, and also reintroduced the issue of constitutional sovereignty, when he advocated repeal of the United States' self-judging reservation in the World Court (the only instance in which a Republican president or presidential candidate supported a constriction of national sovereignty).

Civil rights remained the predominant (and sometimes exclusive) constitutional theme for John F. Kennedy and Lyndon Johnson in State of the Union addresses. Johnson also supported some constitutional changes, including an amendment to prohibit "faithless electors" in the Electoral College, an amendment to give U.S. House members a four-year term, and laws to clarify presidential succession. In 1966, Johnson took a turn toward structural issues, calling for a commission to examine the federal system and to "develop a creative federalism to best use the wonderful diversity of our institutions."[22] In his last few addresses, Johnson specifically emphasized the state and local responsibility for crime control. Nevertheless, rights clearly outshone federalism or other issues in the New Frontier/Great Society era.

A broader shift in the direction of federalism was seen in the Nixon administration. Indeed, Nixon's 1971 State of the Union message was built around extensive discussion of his "new federalism" proposal, and his messages generally spoke more about federalism than about individual rights (though rights references were not absent, and included increasing attention to privacy rights). In his final message, in 1974, Nixon fired a shot on behalf of beleaguered executive authority, vowing that he would never do anything that "weakens the office of the president of the United States or impairs the ability of the presidents of the future to make the great decisions that are so essential to this nation and the world."[23] While carrying on the promotion of federalism, Gerald Ford also consistently repeated Nixon's call for a strong presidency and criticized congressional micromanagement of the executive branch, especially in foreign affairs.

Jimmy Carter's State of the Union reports were generally a-constitutional in content. His few constitutional references were devoted to individual rights concerns and ratification of the proposed Equal Rights Amendment.

When Ronald Reagan attained the presidency, he did so on a platform extolling a return to decentralized government. Consequently he, like Nixon in 1971, offered an extensive plan to revitalize the federal system in his 1982 State of the Union address. "This administration has faith," Reagan explained, "in state and local governments and in the constitutional balance envisioned by the founding fathers."[24] (However, most of his federalism references in this address were implicit rather than explicit.) Reagan's messages also included numerous references to individual rights issues such as civil rights, criminal defendant rights, abortion, and rights of religious expression. Constitutional amendments were a favorite topic for Reagan, as he regularly advocated amendments to require a balanced federal budget, allow prayer in schools, and restrict abortion. He consistently proposed that the president be given a line-item veto, and frequently made an argument, at least implicitly, about enumeration of powers, among other things referring to defense as the prime responsibility of the federal government. In 1987—the bicentennial of the constitutional convention—Reagan's address was filled with constitutional references, including a large number of perfunctory references and a strong statement of enumerated powers as a doctrine of limited government: "In the Constitution, we the people tell the government what it can do and that it can only do those things listed in that document and no others."[25]

Reagan's successor, George H. W. Bush, was considerably less likely to use constitutional references than Reagan had been, but continued some of Reagan's themes. In particular, Bush made some mention of federalism and decentralized government and called for a line-item veto. With controversy swirling around proposed congressional civil rights legislation, Bush included a statement on civil rights in his 1991 address. Interestingly, Bill Clinton's addresses also included numerous federalism references—most by way of promoting state autonomy and innovation—interspersed with references to specific individual rights and to the general concept of rights as embodied in the Bill of Rights. Clinton, like his two predecessors, called for a line-item veto; however, he called on Congress to reject the balanced budget amendment. This record of constitutional rhetoric offers one powerful indication that Clinton was, as many have suggested, a "moon" to Reaganism's "sun." After 1997, however, Clinton's use of constitutional language nearly evaporated, except for perfunctory mentions at the beginning or end of each address and a couple of efforts to prod the Senate into confirming stalled judicial appointments.

This newest constitutional drought in State of the Union messages continued through the beginning of George W. Bush's presidency, which was occupied with questions of war and terrorism. Beginning in 2004, however, he began regularly including language calling for action on conservative judicial appointments, expressing concern about oversized judicial power, and advocating a constitutional amendment prohibiting same-sex marriage. Altogether, Bush demonstrated more concern for reining in an imperial judiciary than any president in a State of the Union address since Roosevelt in 1937. In 2006, Bush also renewed the call for a line-item veto for the executive, the fourth consecutive president to do so.

With 164 State of the Union messages from 1841 to 2006 and sometimes rapidly changing events in the nation and the world, the line representing total constitutional references in State of the Union messages presents more zigzags than inaugurals. Nevertheless, the same overall trend is observable, with a gradual decline until reaching a lower plateau in the 1930s. However, an interesting trend is apparent when examining the constitutional references per thousand words. The rate of references started relatively high, fell dramatically in the late nineteenth century, then made a substantial recovery in the twentieth century. One can easily reconcile the overall downward trend of total references with the somewhat "U-shaped" trend of references per thousand words by remembering that the total word count of State of the Union messages grew enormously in the late 1800s before shrinking just as enormously after 1913. References declined, but not as fast as the length of messages, leaving fewer references but higher ratios in the twentieth century. Nevertheless, in both numbers and ratios of references, the late 1990s and early twenty-first century showed another dip (charts 7.4 and 7.5).

In the years since the New Deal, Republican presidents consistently have used more constitutional rhetoric than have Democratic presidents. Overall,

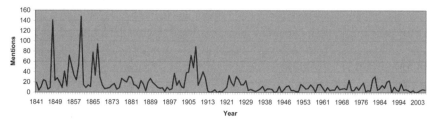

Chart 7.4. Total constitutional references in State of the Union messages, 1841–2006

Republicans averaged nearly twice as many references per thousand words as Democrats. Four of six Republican presidents in this period have averaged more than 1.5 references per thousand words, while only one Democrat—Franklin Roosevelt, at the very beginning of this period—has. The president with by far the highest average rate of constitutional rhetoric in his State of the Union messages was Ronald Reagan, and the only three to average over ten references per thousand words were Reagan, Ford, and Eisenhower (table 7.3). This phenomenon stands in some contrast with inaugural addresses, where Democrats have had a slight recent advantage, though it is consistent with party platforms and other forms of campaign communications where modern Republicans have held a lead. Reagan's case is an interesting one, for another reason. It is here, in governing, that Reagan was most likely to give voice to his concern with constitutional issues of limited government, often expressed in his many years of public argument. In contrast, most presidents in recent times have been less likely to use constitutional rhetoric in governing than in campaigning, especially if one includes platforms in the calculation.

Explicit vs. Implicit Rhetoric:

State of the Union messages, alone among the forms of communication examined in this study, have not suffered a dramatic deterioration in the pro-

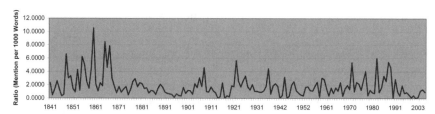

Chart 7.5. Total constitutional references per one thousand words ing State of Union messages, 1841–2006

Table 7.3. Average constitutional references in State of the Union addresses by administration and party, 1934–2006

	Avg. references	Avg. references/1000 words
George W. Bush	3.2	.72
Bill Clinton	5.7	.72
George H. W. Bush	5.3	1.29
Ronald Reagan	15.9	3.49
Jimmy Carter	8.8	.83
Gerald Ford	12.3	2.64
Richard Nixon	9.8	2.46
Lyndon Johnson	7.3	1.47
John Kennedy	5.3	.89
Dwight Eisenhower	10.3	1.75
Harry Truman	6.6	1.03
Franklin Roosevelt	5.6	1.67
Democratic average	**6.6**	**1.10**
Republican average	**9.5**	**2.06**

portion of constitutional references that are explicitly framed. Some deterioration has occurred at the lower end; not a single State of the Union message prior to 1895 was completely devoid of explicit constitutional references, while twenty-five since then have been. However, at the upper end, the references of a significant number of State of the Union addresses since 1948 (fourteen in all) have been at least 50 percent explicit—a fact true of combined platforms in no year and of nomination acceptance speeches in only one year in that time. There was no clear partisan pattern in terms of explicit percentage of constitutional references.

Content

Taken as a group, State of the Union messages have typically exhibited a rough balance among the groupings of rights, structure, and interpretation, especially after the Civil War. While rights has sometimes carried the greatest weight, it has never towered over the other broad subjects. Democratic presidents since World War II have usually afforded rights pride of place. The one exception was Bill Clinton; rights represented a plurality of references in only one of his seven State of the Union addresses. (Clinton thus offered a substantial contrast between his inaugural rhetoric and his State of the Union rhetoric—perhaps a contrast between what he wanted to do and what he was able to do.) Republican presidents have more often than not put structure or interpretation ahead of rights, sometimes by a wide margin. Only

Dwight D. Eisenhower and Ronald Reagan delivered addresses outside of that pattern; seven of Eisenhower's nine and four of Reagan's seven addresses gave rights a plurality of references, though it was often a narrow one.

As with other communications, State of the Union messages have most consistently addressed individual rights among the fifteen more specific categories of constitutional rhetoric. Rights were mentioned in 84 percent of Republican and 78 percent of Democratic State of the Union messages. However, State of the Union messages, like inaugural addresses, averaged only 31 percent of their references in the rights category. In a familiar pattern, among other categories, only federalism, enumerated powers, and executive powers were mentioned at least half the time, and those only by Republican presidents. The usual suspects were found at the bottom: veto, impeachment, and mode of constitutional interpretation. Appointments were also seldom mentioned, as was constitutional sovereignty, especially among Democrats. Of categories found in the broad middle of the spectrum, Republicans showed considerably more consistent interest in Supreme Court decisions, judicial powers, constitutional amendments, and enforcement than did Democrats; the latter particularly mirrors the pattern in other modes of communication. Both parties' presidents used perfunctory references in about one-third of the State of the Union messages (table 7.4). In general, most constitutional topics were mentioned much more consistently in State of the Union messages than in inaugurals.

Individual rights for both parties and federalism for Republicans appeared both consistently and with depth, a result utterly consistent with other modes of communication. Republican presidents mentioned both enumerated powers and executive powers in more than half their messages but the categories usually represented fewer than 20 percent of all constitutional references in those messages. Appointments for both parties, and constitutional amendments and enumerated powers for Democrats, were mentioned in fewer than half the messages but were usually more than 20 percent of references when they appeared. All other categories fell short of the thresholds for both consistency and depth (appendix C, table C7).

Conclusion

All in all, the deconstitutionalization of rhetoric found in campaigns since 1840 has been replicated in inaugural addresses and State of the Union messages. Likewise, the limited resurgence of constitutional rhetoric in the last three or four decades has appeared in this governing rhetoric as well.

Table 7.4. Consistency of constitutional categories in State of the Union messages, 1841–2006

Category	% Dem. messages	% Rep. messages
Individual rights	77.9	84.4
Federalism	45.6	69.8
Executive powers	48.5	59.4
Enum. of powers	36.8	59.2
Const. amendments	16.2	42.7
Enforcement	22.1	38.5
Perfunctory	38.2	34.4
Judicial powers	16.2	34.4
Supreme Court decisions	16.2	34.4
Separation of powers	17.6	15.6
Const. sovereignty	1.5	11.5
Mode of const. interp.	8.8	2.1
Appointments	4.4	5.2
Veto	2.9	4.2
Impeachment	0.0	2.1

Inaugural addresses generally fit the mold of campaign rhetoric, and are especially comparable to candidate messages and television ads, the two campaign outlets at the bottom of the scale, in terms of overall ratios and the general distribution of categories. They vary insofar as a higher percentage of inaugural references is explicit and a lower percentage is devoted purely to rights.

State of the Union messages tend to be more inclusive of a wider range of issues, with most topics appearing more consistently than in inaugurals. In this respect, they are more like party platforms or debates than candidate messages or ads, although their rate of constitutional references is usually considerably lower. On average, State of the Union messages also employ more constitutional references per thousand words than do inaugurals, although the two frequently switch places.

There are a larger number of categories showing a significant gap between the parties in State of the Unions than in inaugurals or campaign communications. Perhaps campaigning requires a response to the other side that promotes more similar levels of consistency in categories—certainly debates do—while inaugurals by their nature discourage discussion of particularly divisive topics. State of the Union messages might offer a more unvarnished exposition of what each party uniquely values and hopes to achieve.

Of course, both modes of presidential communication now take the form of a televised speech—essentially the same mode as a modern nomination acceptance speech. As with campaign communications, there is a noticeable correlation between deconstitutionalization and the shift to modern communications technology. Looking at each presidential campaign winner since 1932 in terms of platforms, nomination acceptance speeches, inaugural addresses, and State of the Union addresses yields some interesting findings. Platforms maintain the highest average rate of constitutional references. Acceptance speeches are roughly comparable on average to inaugurals and State of the Union messages, but are a shade higher. Despite the low rate of constitutional references in nomination acceptance speeches, about two-thirds of presidential winners made more references in their acceptance speeches than in their inaugural addresses (twelve of nineteen) or their average State of the Union addresses (eleven of nineteen). Although most presidents have had a more varied record, some have shown a consistent tendency to deliver a higher level of constitutional rhetoric either in

Table 7.5. Constitutional references per thousand words by winning presidential candidates, 1932–2006

Candidate/year	Platform	Cand. message	Inaugural	State of the Union avg.
F. Roosevelt/1932	4.70	.69	4.26	1.28
F. Roosevelt/1936	6.92	3.49	2.77	2.28
F. Roosevelt/1940	3.21	.85	3.72	1.36
F. Roosevelt/1944	5.12	3.90	1.79	0.00
H. Truman/1948	3.29	2.98	2.64	.89
D. Eisenhower/1952	5.18	.47	.41	1.46
D. Eisenhower/1956	2.63	2.30	0.0	1.99
J. Kennedy/1960	2.24	1.17	0.0	.89
L. Johnson/1964	1.24	2.12	.67	1.44
R. Nixon/1968	2.00	1.50	.47	2.58
R. Nixon/1972	1.80	.68	1.11	2.28
J. Carter/1976	2.17	2.05	2.44	.83
R. Reagan/1980	2.34	.86	2.05	2.83
R. Reagan/1984	3.35	1.57	2.73	3.98
G. H. W. Bush/1988	2.34	2.42	.43	1.29
B. Clinton/1992	2.87	2.05	.63	1.02
B. Clinton/1996	1.88	1.67	2.32	.49
G. W. Bush/2000	3.46	1.46	.63	.44
G. W. Bush/2004	2.29	.99	.96	1.13
Average	3.11	1.74	1.58	1.50

campaigning or in governing. Kennedy, Johnson, and George H. W. Bush used considerably greater constitutional rhetoric while campaigning than while governing; Reagan and Nixon (in his second term) were more constitutionally oriented in office than on the campaign trail. (See table 7.5.)

The connection between campaign rhetoric and governing rhetoric is made clear not only by the close approximation of the ordering of constitutional topics in them, but by the rough congruence of the trend lines over time. Constitutional references per thousand words in winning party platforms corresponds well with the rate of references in inaugural addresses and State of the Union messages. State of the Union messages have typically been at the low end of this comparison, platforms at the high end, and inaugurals in between, but their ups and downs have generally tracked each other well.

The degree to which campaigns drive governing, governing drives campaigns, and independent events drive both governing and campaigns is not easy to untangle, but clearly constitutional rhetoric in campaigns is not floating freely somewhere in the political ether. Whatever the mix of cause and effect, campaign rhetoric about the Constitution matters because it is tied to governing rhetoric. And, despite public cynicism to the contrary, governing rhetoric is important because it is not infrequently tied to governing itself.

~

CHAPTER EIGHT

Conclusion: Constitutional Rhetoric and Its Prospects

Constitutional rhetoric in election campaigns is an important component of the nation's political conversation for a number of reasons. Contrary to popular impression, political figures take their own political rhetoric seriously, making an effort to carry out their campaign promises most of the time. Voters themselves often base their vote, at least partially, on the candidates' or parties' governing ideologies or stands on key issues. The amount and character of constitutional rhetoric can serve as a barometer of the importance with which candidates and voters view constitutional questions. Since at least some voters learn at least something from the content of campaigns, the amount and character of constitutional rhetoric in campaigns will contribute to a greater or lesser degree to the constitutional literacy of the citizenry. And because judicialism is a doctrine that comports well with neither republican theory nor actual constitutional practice, the attitude and conduct of elected officeholders toward the Constitution is important. Altogether, if the Constitution is both substantively and symbolically crucial to the well-being of the American Republic, it matters a great deal whether it is discussed in campaigns much or little, well or poorly.

Consequently, it makes a great deal of difference whether and to what degree campaign rhetoric has truly become deconstitutionalized. That rhetoric is important in and of itself, to the degree that it sets the tone for and affects American elections, and it is important for what it says about the state of constitutionalism in the polity.

This study has assessed that question. It can offer only imperfect answers, not least because quantitative measures of campaign rhetoric cannot, in the end, distinguish between constitutional arguments that are sound and those that are not. Stephen Douglas's defense of *Dred Scott* is counted the same as Abraham Lincoln's criticism of it. To make an argument about the Constitution is not always to make an argument for constitutionalism—but such arguments are a necessary condition for the practice of constitutionalism.

Historical Overview of Constitutional Rhetoric

The earliest years of this study were characterized by a broad and balanced discussion of individual rights, enumeration of powers, federalism, and executive powers. Democrats argued for a Jeffersonian decentralization and limited federal government, Whigs for a Jeffersonian fear of unbridled executive power. Perfunctory references to the Constitution were common, as were extended constitutional arguments laying out broad theories of federal-state relations (especially among Democrats).

From the period immediately preceding the Civil War through the end of Reconstruction, rights and federalism dominated constitutional rhetoric, along with criticisms or defenses of the use of executive power. In 1860, *Dred Scott* and the broader topic of the proper bounds of judicial power were also topics of heated discussion. During the war and Reconstruction, Republicans defended a broad interpretation and aggressive use of the powers of the presidency, while Democrats decried executive usurpation. Both parties claimed fealty to the guarantees of individual rights contained in the Thirteenth, Fourteenth, and Fifteenth Amendments to the Constitution, though Republicans spent considerably more energy promising vigorous enforcement of those guarantees.

Exhausted by the Civil War and the contention following it, with some deep constitutional issues already settled and others unlikely to be settled anytime soon, Americans turned their attention toward expansion and commerce. This pragmatic commercialism affected both parties; at the end of this era, neither Cleveland's Democrats nor McKinley's Republicans expressed great interest in constitutional questions. When they did, those expressions tended to be true to form, with Republicans emphasizing rights and national union and Democrats calling for strong states and limits on Washington. Both hearkened to the old standard of equality under the law, though Republicans tended to address the issue in terms of civil rights and Democrats in terms of the rights of the common economic orders. The dominant trend, however, was of disengagement from constitutional disputes.

After an extended trough in such rhetoric, the Progressive Era brought an upsurge in discussion about constitutional amendments and the judiciary—

both retrospectively (by way of analysis of Supreme Court decisions) and prospectively (by way of assessing possible constraints on judicial power). This was true of the major parties, as well as the Progressive Party and the Socialist Party in 1912. William Howard Taft fought a rearguard action against what he saw as attempts to undermine the Constitution by undermining the judiciary.

Despite the burst of constitutional discussion by parties in 1912, Woodrow Wilson's presidency itself saw remarkably little constitutional rhetoric of any kind. The aftermath of his presidency, however, witnessed a new growth in debate in terms of executive power and individual rights, stimulated by Wilson's controversial use of presidential power during World War I. Two new issues quickly came to dominate the constitutional conversation. The aftermath of the Great War saw the substantial rise for the first time of the issue of constitutional sovereignty with debates over American entry into the League of Nations. Additionally, the Eighteenth Amendment (Prohibition) became a fixture of campaign rhetoric through 1932 as parties and candidates grappled with the increasingly problematic and unpopular amendment.

The New Deal era was, as one might predict, a time of considerable interest in questions having to do with the proper boundaries of federal power (federalism and enumerated powers) as well as executive power. When the Supreme Court declared many of Franklin Roosevelt's new programs unconstitutional, a new debate over the role of the Court flared for a time, though it was soon extinguished when the Court's resistance collapsed in 1937 and 1938. Roosevelt's foes made a constitutional argument that he had overstepped his bounds and was threatening to bring a form of centralized autocracy in his train. For his part, Roosevelt claimed that his opponents were hiding behind the Constitution. As World War II commenced, Roosevelt's own rhetoric shifted toward highlighting fundamental individual rights in contrast with the nation's totalitarian enemies.

In the midst of war, the overall rate of constitutional rhetoric resumed its long downward course, reaching a low point sometime around the 1960s (depending on the mode of communication). Issues like federalism, enumeration of powers, and separation of powers appeared less and less frequently. Perfunctory references fell off as well, reflecting a deconstitutionalization of rhetoric that went beyond reluctance to discuss the constitutional implications of specific policies.

After the bottom of this trough was reached, constitutional rhetoric in campaigns and in government experienced a modest resurgence. The rise of the civil rights issue and subsequent policy embellishments like forced busing and racial preferences meant that constitutional individual rights would receive enhanced attention. At the same time, a number of policy issues that had been drained of constitutional meaning were reinjected with some; conservatives succeeded in promoting greater discussion of federalism and what one might call traditional individual rights, such as property rights, religious expression, and Second Amendment gun rights. The Supreme Court made a number of decisions that turned a number of social questions that had rarely been constitutional before into constitutional issues—school prayer, pornography, the death penalty, abortion, flag burning, gay rights. Consequently, as in the Progressive Era, the modern era has seen judicial questions take a crucial place in the rhetoric, including much discussion about court decisions such as *Roe v. Wade*, judicial power, and (for the first time) judicial appointments. Finally, constitutional amendments, many designed to overturn court decisions, have played a major role in campaign rhetoric and electoral coalition-building, especially by Republicans, as have issues of constitutional sovereignty. The latter fundamentally revolved around the degree to which U.S. foreign policy should be constrained by international organizations such as the United Nations. In 2004, all of these issues could be seen operating in the presidential campaign rhetoric. Altogether, some issues that had been deconstitutionalized were reconstitutionalized and some other issues were constitutionalized for the first time. Government and events were simply generating more constitutional issues for campaigns to discuss.

Taking a long view, the weight of constitutional rhetoric in American politics is considerably lower than it once was. The rate of constitutional references per thousand words has substantially declined over time in both platforms and candidate messages. This decline is tempered by the fact that the absolute number of constitutional references in platforms has generally increased over time as platforms have grown longer.

The degree to which constitutional rhetoric is openly framed as such has likewise declined. The rate of explicit constitutional references per thousand words has fallen even faster than total references over time across a wide variety of modes of communication. The percentage of constitutional references that are explicitly framed has fallen considerably since 1840, and has typically been well below 50 percent regardless of the mode of communication for more than half a century.

On balance, the data of this study are consistent with the trend of a substantial "deconstitutionalization" of government since the mid-nineteenth century proposed in chapter 1. Deconstitutionalization has been real, and remains a part of the political landscape. The first broad drop in constitutional rhetoric came after Reconstruction. The early twentieth-century trough of constitutional rhetoric came during the years of ascendancy of Woodrow

Wilson, although 1912 saw a great deal of such rhetoric from other sources. Another key drop came after the controversies of the 1930s were decided in favor of the New Deal.

Furthermore, this drop has been apparent in governing communications like inaugural addresses and State of the Union messages. Indeed, rates of constitutional rhetoric have fallen further in those venues than in platforms. It is not only American electoral politics that has experienced a deconstitutionalized rhetoric, but American governance as well.

The modest resurgence since the 1960s can be seen both in constitutional rhetoric generally and in explicit constitutional rhetoric. The recovery has not regained most of the lost ground, but it has been noticeable in platforms, candidate messages, and debates, as well as inaugural addresses, which have in recent years grown more constitutional in their focus. All modes of communication have also seen an increase in the number of exchanges in recent years. Ads have taken the most varied course, but here too experienced their most constitutionally averse phase in the 1950s and have experienced moments of somewhat greater constitutional content since then.

Even though a broad range of constitutional topics was discussed in 2000 and 2004, there were signs that the partial recovery of constitutional rhetoric may have reached its limits and begun to recede. The presidential debates saw more constitutional references and exchanges than ever before and ads held their own, but platforms and candidate messages saw a significant decline in the rate of constitutional references. This decline was particularly tied to a significant reduction in Republican concern with structural issues during the George W. Bush ascendancy. It came after a sharp increase in 1996, however, and it is too early to know whether 2000–2004 represented a new downward trend or just a regression to the mean that will leave intact the higher baseline established since the 1950s and 1960s.

The Republican trends under Bush highlight the degree to which constitutional discussion has been increasingly dominated by rights. Of the three broad groupings—rights, government structure, and constitutional interpretation—rights have tended to lead, though structure and interpretation have often held their own in every venue. When broken down into the fifteen more specific categories, however, individual rights has been the most consistently and most deeply discussed constitutional topic by far. Topics like federalism and constitutional amendments have also been well represented, but a number of crucial topics have been less frequently mentioned in recent decades. Two topics in particular—constitutionally related vetoes and impeachment—have barely registered in either the recent or distant past. Only individual rights were established as being discussed with both high consistency and significant depth across the board; federalism was referenced both highly consistently and deeply in one of four modes of campaign rhetoric (as well as State of the Union messages), was highly consistent but relatively shallow in two other modes, and enjoyed both consistency and depth in debates as well, if individual debates rather than years were the unit of measurement. There has been a particularly noticeable falloff among perfunctory mentions of the Constitution in televised modes of communication. Platforms have shown little change in the consistency with which perfunctory references are made, but the consistency of such references in candidate messages since 1952 is two-thirds lower among Democrats and three-quarters lower among Republicans than the overall consistency from 1840 to 2004. Ads since 1952 show similar frequencies to candidates' messages. (For a side-by-side comparison of constitutional categories in the four modes of campaign communication from 1952 to 2004, see appendix C, table C1. For the same thing in governing communications, see table C7.)

Although one can observe a number of general tendencies, it is clear (as the trends in perfunctory references demonstrate) that the form of campaign communication matters, sometimes a great deal. It is notable that platforms are consistently endowed with more constitutional references per thousand words, more explicit constitutional rhetoric, a broader range of constitutional topics, and more direct exchanges on constitutional subjects (with one exception) than the other forms of campaign communication studied here. Indeed, one can rank each mode of communication in terms of overall rate of constitutional rhetoric, rate of explicit rhetoric, percentage of references that are explicit, percentage of references devoted to rights (with lower percentages indicating greater breadth of rhetoric), and rate of constitutional exchanges. The results are remarkably consistent. Platforms come out clearly ahead, debates in second, and candidate messages and ads pulling up the rear. The only exception is that debates beat out platforms for the highest rate of exchanges, an unsurprising outcome given the debate format (tables 8.1 to 8.5).

The precise way in which this picture plays out depends upon the indicator. For example, when looking at the average rate of total constitutional references, platforms dominate, ads are far behind (with a rate about 40 percent that of platforms), and debates and candidate messages are clumped close together about halfway between the two extremes. A review of explicit constitutional rhetoric shows platforms in front, ads and messages at the other end, and debates alone standing in the middle. Platforms and debates are in quite close contention for the lead when it comes to breadth of rhetoric and frequency of constitutional exchanges, with messages and ads in close contention for last place. In those instances, there was no middle position, just

Table 8.1. Total constitutional references per thousand words by mode of communication, 1952–2004

Year	Platforms	Messages	TV Ads	Debates
1952	3.30	.26	.18	
1956	2.35	2.21	.13	
1960	2.91	.62	1.88	1.26
1964	1.97	2.88	1.73	
1968	1.90	2.87	1.81	
1972	2.30	.45	1.64	
1976	3.02	2.75	.53	1.97
1980	2.17	.75	.62	1.92
1984	2.53	1.46	.89	2.12
1988	2.33	1.77	.20	1.72
1992	2.73	2.81	.53	1.01
1996	4.64	1.85	1.11	2.14
2000	2.51	1.56	2.45	2.12
2004	2.21	.98	1.05	2.91
Average	2.63	1.66	1.05	1.91
Firsts	10	3	0	1
Lasts	0	4	10	0

Note: Firsts=number of elections in which that mode of communication had the highest rate of constitutional references. Lasts=number of elections in which that mode of communication had the lowest rate of constitutional references.

Table 8.2. Explicit constitutional references by mode of communication, 1952–2004

Year	Platforms Rate*	%	Messages Rate*	%	TV ads Rate*	%	Debates Rate*	%
1952	.74	22	0	0	0	0		
1956	.87	37	.22	10	0	0		
1960	.90	31	.10	17	.81	39	.29	23
1964	.45	23	1.23	43	.30	9		
1968	.15	8	.04	1	0	0		
1972	.54	23	0	0	.92	30		
1976	.77	25	1.19	43	.34	33	.71	36
1980	.49	23	.13	17	.31	9	.83	44
1984	.87	34	.52	35	.52	31	.71	33
1988	.83	35	.30	17	0	0	.15	9
1992	1.24	46	.42	15	1.09	100	.18	18
1996	1.59	35	1.08	58	.45	20	.56	26
2000	.82	32	.26	17	1.21	25	.31	15
2004	.69	31	.20	20	0	0	.99	34
Average	**.78**	**29**	**.41**	**21**	**.43**	**21**	**.53**	**26**
Firsts	**8**	**5**	**2**	**4**	**2**	**3**	**2**	**3**
Lasts	**0**	**1**	**5**	**3**	**9**	**9**	**1**	**1**

Note: Firsts=number of elections in which that mode of communication had the highest rate or percentage of explicit constitutional references. Lasts=number of elections in which that mode of communication had the lowest rate or percentage of explicit constitutional references.
* Rate per thousand words.

Table 8.3. Percentage of constitutional references about individual rights by mode of communication, 1952–2004

Year	Platforms	Messages	TV ads	Debates
1952	45	100	100	
1956	54	53	0	
1960	31	80	73	52
1964	44	44	91	
1968	47	59	80	
1972	53	33	85	
1976	44	44	53	45
1980	49	43	73	51
1984	46	45	46	56
1988	44	69	0	64
1992	54	46	0	11
1996	38	50	80	62
2000	46	73	42	60
2004	60	40	55	51
Average	**47**	**56**	**56**	**49**
Firsts	**3**	**4**	**7**	**1**

Note: Lower rights percentages represent greater diversification of discourse. Firsts=number of elections in which that mode of communication had the lowest percentage of constitutional references about rights.

Table 8.4. Constitutional exchanges by mode of communication, 1952–2004

Mode	Performance exchanges	Policy exchanges	Total exchanges	Avg. exchanges per year
Debates (N=9)	14	23	37	4.1
Platforms (N=14)	15	30	45	3.2
TV Ads (N=14)	2	3	5	.4
Messages (N=14)	0	3	3	.2

Note: "Performance exchanges" are instances in which both candidates or parties refer to the same constitutional issue and agree about what proper constitutional values require but express a disagreement about whether one of them has fallen short in that area. An example would be if one candidate accuses the other of endangering national sovereignty, while the second candidate denies the allegation.
"Policy exchanges" are instances in which both candidates or parties refer to the same constitutional issue and express a disagreement about what proper policy would be. An example would be if one candidate expresses support for a constitutional amendment to restrict abortion while the other candidate expresses opposition to the amendment.

Table 8.5.   Mode of campaign communications ranked by indicator, 1952–2004

Indicator	1st	2nd	3rd	4th
Total references per 1000 words	Platforms	Debates	Messages	Ads
Explicit references per 1000 words	Platforms	Debates	Ads	Messages
Explicit references as % of total	Platforms	Debates	Messages	Ads
% of references not rights	Platforms	Debates	Messages	Ads
Exchanges per year	Debates	Platforms	Ads	Messages

two distinct poles. The difference between the two poles was most striking when it came to exchanges. Both ads and candidate messages since 1952 have offered a trivial number of exchanges—five and three, respectively—though messages contained a healthy number of such exchanges through 1936.

When one examines each mode of communication side by side, it is clear that platforms and debates offer the broadest range of issues that are discussed consistently from year to year. Indeed, platforms and debates are the only forms that have two categories that are both consistently mentioned and discussed in depth. Television advertising—the form of campaign communication that is now most responsible for carrying a campaign's message on a day-to-day basis—is, on balance, the least constitutionally oriented, and discusses a much more constrained set of issues. More generally, it is notable that platforms and debates share a structure of distribution that is quite similar, while television ads and candidate messages share a very different structure. Altogether, in platforms from 1952 to 2004 there were eight categories of constitutional reference that were highly consistent for both parties—that is to say, appeared in at least half of election years—and another four that were highly consistent for one party. Debates had four highly consistent categories and another three that were highly consistent in one party. Candidate messages had only one highly consistent category, plus another that was consistent for one party; and television ads had but one highly consistent category. In this respect, governing rhetoric in inaugural addresses mimics the patterns of television ads and candidate messages, while State of the Union messages mimic platforms (see appendix C, tables C1 and C7).

Of course, there are important exceptions to these generalizations. Candidate messages have been somewhat idiosyncratic, undoubtedly owing to the fact that individual candidates are more likely to change their approach from year to year than are parties. Indeed, candidate messages had more constitutional content than platforms in the mid-1960s (as well as in 1992). Debates had more in 2004. Ads have gone through cycles, maintaining a low but somewhat respectable level of constitutional references from 1960 to 1972 and 1996 to 2004 and extremely low levels otherwise. And in three years, no ads discussed rights. Nevertheless, on the whole, the evidence supports the validity of the generalizations.

Finally, the politics of constitutional rhetoric are not easy to untangle. A higher percentage of Democratic than Republican references are explicit in every mode of communication. However, in recent years, Republicans have consistently made many more constitutional references and more references per thousand words than Democrats in platforms, candidate messages, ads, and debates (they likewise hold this advantage in State of the Union messages). Sometimes Democrats have not trailed by far in references per thousand words, but they usually have trailed. Furthermore, Republicans have typically engaged in a broader constitutional rhetoric emphasizing both rights and federalism, along with (in some venues) issues such as enumeration of powers and constitutional sovereignty. Thus, while both parties have contributed, Republicans have disproportionately fueled the limited reconstitutionalization of campaign rhetoric over the last four decades. The rather sharp decline of Republican constitutional rhetoric (except in debates) under George W. Bush may portend the end of that trend, if it is not reversed by Republicans or compensated for by Democrats.

Aside from the two major parties, third parties have typically had the effect of raising the quantitative level of constitutional rhetoric. Some third parties, like the Southern Democrats of 1860, the Progressives of 1924, the American Independent Party of 1968, have driven big increases in overall constitutional rhetoric. Of fourteen third parties or independent candidates who received at least 5 percent of the nationally aggregated popular vote, only Ross Perot in 1992 had very little interest in constitutional issues. Furthermore, third parties tend to extend their constitutional interests well beyond rights, even when the major parties do not. This pattern is consistent enough that one can add enhanced constitutional rhetoric to the list of things that third parties contribute to American politics.

Interestingly, over time, winning campaigns are less likely to make constitutional platform references than losing campaigns are, though the gap has narrowed in recent years. This is true on its face, when controlled for incumbency, and when controlled for incumbency and party. Party platforms of losing parties make an average of 7.5 references per thousand words, those of

Table 8.6. Major-party-platform constitutional references per thousand words, controlled by incumbency, 1840–2004

	Incumbent party	Challenging party
Winning party	4.6 (N=23)	5.1 (N=19)
Losing party	6.8 (N=19)	8.2 (N=23)

winning parties only 4.8 references per thousand words. When controlled for incumbency, that general pattern holds: although incumbents use fewer references than challengers, winning incumbents use fewer references than losing incumbents and winning challengers use fewer than losing challengers. Winning incumbents use the fewest references, losing challengers the most. When controlled for party, Democrats show an identical pattern. Republicans deviate only insofar as their winning incumbents actually use more references than their winning challengers; but in this case, too, winners of both kinds use fewer constitutional references than losers of both kinds. It is difficult to say whether this phenomenon demonstrates the relative unpopularity of constitutional rhetoric, or a tendency of campaigns that already face an uphill climb to try to fight on more abstract or principled ground. At the very least, it is clear that frequent references to the Constitution are not sufficient to rescue a losing campaign. (See tables 8.6 and 8.7.)

Table 8.7. Major-party-platform constitutional references per thousand words, controlled by incumbency and party, 1840–2004

Democrats	Incumbent party	Challenging party
Winning party	4.3 (N=8)	6.7 (N=9)
Losing party	7.4 (N=10)	8.2 (N=15)

Republicans	Incumbent party	Challenging party
Winning party	4.8 (N=15)	3.5 (N=10)
Losing party	6.0 (N=9)	8.0 (N=8)

Factors Contributing to the Outcome

A natural question arising from these conclusions is: what explains them? As with any important set of social or political trends, the answer is complicated. Of course, one must first assign responsibility to the overall ethos of the age. Candidates and campaigns inherit a particular political environment circumscribed by particular assumptions and expectations about what constitutes legitimate or illegitimate, useful or counterproductive rhetoric. At a certain point, both deconstitutionalization and reconstitutionalization can become self-perpetuating by establishing such constraints. This explanation, however, is too tautological to be really satisfactory. It also falls short of being able to explain the specific contours of constitutional rhetoric.

The facts uncovered in this study might be explained in a variety of ways, some of which have suggested themselves in the course of the book. A thorough consideration of those possibilities can lead us to a better understanding of the condition and potential future of constitutional rhetoric in elections. First, we must survey the factors that might be considered "inputs" into the amount and breadth of constitutional rhetoric. Then we will consider how they interact to produce the outcome that has been documented here. There are at least seven crucial inputs. At the base of American politics always lies public opinion as an ephemeral but pervasive force. Similarly, the intellectual climate establishes a general atmosphere within which campaigns operate, an unseen but powerful influence. Parties and candidates are most directly responsible for campaigns. Interest groups, media forms, and news media coverage of politics all contribute as well, but more indirectly. Each will be examined in turn.

Public Opinion

The most general, and yet most foundational, factor affecting constitutional rhetoric in campaigns is public sentiment, which is not only shaped by political rhetoric but helps to shape it by establishing the parameters of acceptable and successful rhetoric. The starting point of any understanding of the role and possibilities for constitutional rhetoric in campaigns is to assess the public demand or tolerance for such rhetoric.

Prior to the advent of scientific polling in the 1930s, measurement of public opinion depended on interpretation of periodic election results and impressionistic and anecdotal analysis of the public mood. Some of that analysis has come from scholars seeking to trace the deepest relationship of Americans to the Constitution. What they have postulated, generally speaking, is that Americans participate in a vague "Constitution worship," in which the Constitution is conflated with rights, that masks substantial lack of knowledge about the Constitution and substantial ambivalence about how rigidly to follow the Constitution in practice. As Max Lerner argued in 1937, Americans "sought a way by which their revolutionary ideals could be worshipped without being followed. They found their peace in the safe haven of the Constitution."[1] One need not adopt Lerner's cynicism to appreciate his point. Decades later, Larry Baas concludes that the constitutional symbol was, for at least one subject of an intensive study, a matter of hope rather than certainty, and that "other symbols and figures, such as the presidency, are more likely to induce her to accept policy, authority, and to provide her with some security."[2] All of which, if true, would place real limits around the potential for public mobilization on behalf of the Constitution.

Public opinion polls taken on the Constitution since 1935 show a number of interesting patterns which generally confirm the impressionistic view of scholars. The first is that Americans continue to express love and admiration of the Constitution. In perhaps the earliest poll on this topic, a 1939 Roper survey found that 64 percent of Americans agreed with the statement "Our form of government based on the Constitution is as near perfect as it can be and no important changes should be made to it."[3] In a 1997 poll, 71 percent said that they "strongly agreed" with the statement "I am proud of the United States Constitution"; 71 percent also said that they "strongly agreed" that "The United States Constitution is important to me." Fewer than one in ten disagreed with either statement. In the same poll, roughly three in four respondents disagreed that "The U.S. Constitution doesn't impact events today" and that "The Constitution doesn't matter much in my daily life."[4]

One year later, 83 percent of poll respondents contended that it was "absolutely essential" for public schools to teach children to appreciate the freedoms guaranteed by the Constitution and the Bill of Rights.[5] In 1999, a Pew Research Center survey found that 85 percent of Americans considered the Constitution a "major reason" for America's success.[6]

Second, Americans think government should run according to the Constitution, and that it largely does. A 1987 Gallup/Newsweek Poll showed that 69 percent of Americans thought the Constitution was "very important" in determining national policies; another 18 percent thought it was "fairly important."[7] However, Americans have remained open to the possibility that government has strayed from constitutional principles. In mid-1999, two-thirds of those who answered a CNN/USA Today poll held that the signers of the Declaration of Independence, if alive today, would disagree with the way the Constitution is now being followed.[8]

Holding the Constitution in abstract veneration, Americans believe it is important to be knowledgeable about the document. A July 2002 poll showed 76 percent of Americans strongly agreed, and other 14 percent somewhat agreed, that it was "more important than ever to know what our Constitution stands for" in the wake of the September 11th terrorist attacks.[9] However, as a group, Americans freely admit that their actual knowledge of the Constitution is partial rather than complete and general rather than specific. During the 1987 bicentennial of the Constitutional Convention, two polls asked Americans to judge their own knowledge. In a CBS News/New York Times survey, only one in nine claimed they knew what the Constitution said "very well," while 56 percent said "fairly well."[10] Similarly, an ABC News/Washington Post survey found one in eleven saying they knew "a great deal" about the Constitution and its provisions, compared with 56 percent who said they knew "some."[11] A decade later, 6 percent claimed to know "a great deal" about the Constitution, while another 11 percent put themselves in an intermediate category of "quite a bit" of knowledge.[12] Fifty-three percent admitted to only "some" knowledge. In the three surveys, about one-third—31, 35, and 29 percent, respectively—said they knew very little or nothing about the Constitution.

This self-appraisal actually strikes close to the mark. As constitutional scholar Michael Kammen observes, "The Constitution is too often neglected or poorly taught in American schools."[13] A wide range of polling data shows that most Americans have a rough familiarity with the supremacy clause and the First Amendment, and either a majority or a strong minority also share a general understanding of the purpose of the Second Amendment. They have little specific knowledge about the rest of the Bill of Rights or other constitutional provisions. Most Americans—about two-thirds—understand that the Constitution does not specifically guarantee a right to a job or a right to an abortion, but many believe that it confers other nonexistent rights and that it contains a variety of phrases (including "life, liberty, and the pursuit of happiness" and "all men are created equal") that are actually found elsewhere. A 1986 poll indicated that a substantial plurality of 31 percent of Americans believed Thomas Jefferson to have played the biggest role in the writing of the Constitution, despite the fact that he was in Paris serving as U.S. Minister to France during the Federal Convention.[14] More troubling, Americans are on unsure footing when thinking about structural issues. In a 1997 poll, only 58 percent knew there were three branches of the federal government.[15]

There are also at least scattered clues that Americans have internalized the doctrine of judicialism, making them potentially less receptive to campaign rhetoric on the Constitution. Two polls in the late 1980s hinted at this. One survey asked, "Who is the final authority on the interpretation of the Constitution?" About three in five Americans answered "the Supreme Court."[16] Another asked, "Should the Supreme Court have the power to decide that the President or Congress has violated the Constitution and order the violations stopped, or should each branch decide for itself whether its actions are constitutional?" In response, 58 percent rejected the idea of "departmentalism" and said the Supreme Court should have that power.[17]

As will be discussed more thoroughly below, polling questions on the Constitution over the last two decades have been highly skewed toward individual rights, especially First Amendment rights, testing both citizen knowledge and citizen attitudes. Another large cohort of questions addressed constitutional amendments, most notably the Equal Rights Amendment, balanced budget amendment, and school prayer amendment, all of which received majority support most of the time, and the human life amendment and anti-same-sex marriage amendment, both of which had a more mixed reception. It is notable that four of the five high-profile amendments related to individual rights. Modest but recurring sets of questions asked respondents to address the proper mode of constitutional interpretation or to interpret the significance of the Constitution, with Americans seemingly of two minds on how closely constitutional interpretation should be tied to original intent. A mere handful of questions touched on presidential war powers, Supreme Court cases (especially the flag-burning decision in 1989, which was highly unpopular), impeachment (especially in 1998–1999), or federalism.

Altogether, surveys of public opinion consistently show Americans to be imbued with great respect for the Constitution, concern that it be properly applied, and abstract commitment to knowledge about it, coupled with actual lack of specific knowledge and at least mild attachment to judicialism.

Despite popular veneration of the Constitution, however, polls have consistently shown constitutional concerns of any kind to be overwhelmed by questions about the economy, war and peace, and the leadership capacities and other qualities of the candidates. Since 1939, Gallup has been asking Americans what they consider the "most important problem" facing the nation. A review of this open-ended Gallup question in each election year back to 1940 shows that only rarely do constitutional issues penetrate the din of everyday concerns about peace and prosperity.[18] In 1940, for example, fewer than half of 1 percent of respondents volunteered "enforcement of civil liberties" or "Prohibition," the only two clearly constitutional issues on a very long list, as the most important issue. At the top of the list were national defense (25 percent) and unemployment (17 percent). In 1954,

"McCarthyism" was listed by 2 percent; busing by 1 percent in 1972; school prayer, abortion, and the Equal Rights Amendment by 1 percent each in 1984; gun control by 2 percent and abortion by 1 percent in 2000; the judicial system by 1–2 percent in 2002, 2004, and 2006; homosexuality by less than 0.5 percent in 2002 and 1 percent in 2004. "Abuse of power" was also cited by 1 percent in 2004.

Only one constitutional issue attained great prominence in the Gallup surveys: civil rights, especially between the years of 1956 and 1970. During that time, civil rights was the top-ranked issue once (in 1964) and the second-ranked issue three more times (in 1958, 1966, and 1968). It was the only constitutional issue to have broken into the top two issues in any of the surveys reviewed from 1940 to 2006, and the only one to be cited by more than 10 percent of respondents. After peaking in 1964, when 24 percent of respondents rated it the most important issue, civil rights tapered off as an object of attention, falling to 20 percent in 1966, 17 percent in 1968, and 7 percent in 1970. Since 1970, although civil rights or race relations has consistently made the list, it has been cited by only 1–2 percent of Americans as the most important issue.

Two other issues came up often though intermittently. In a number of years, between 1 and 3 percent raised "centralization" or "big government" as a concern (1952, 1964, 1966, 1972, 1976, 1980). After 1968, law enforcement and courts appeared on a number of surveys, being cited by 5 percent in 1970, 2 percent in 1972, 3 percent in 1974, and 1 percent in 1976. Altogether, in twenty-three out of thirty-two election years from 1940 to 2006 all clearly constitutional issues combined did not amount to 5 percent of responses; in the most recent half of that period, from 1972 to 2006, sixteen of eighteen elections did not meet the 5 percent threshold.

Of course, the categories of "constitutional" and "nonconstitutional" issues in this context are more permeable than the above analysis implies. Some respondents citing an apparently constitutional issue might have had their own nonconstitutional reasons for doing so, or might have been thinking of some nonconstitutional aspect of the issue. Conversely, many ostensibly nonconstitutional issues might be thought of by some respondents in a constitutional way. In 1980, for example, Ronald Reagan argued that the economy was troubled (among other things) because government had exceeded its constitutional bounds; there were probably a number of voters who followed his reasoning. For them, the state of the economy was at least partially a constitutional issue. Nevertheless, it is clear that issues that are explicitly and directly constitutional have been almost invariably submerged well beneath other concerns, with the exception of civil rights in the decade and a half starting in the year of Eisenhower's reelection.

It may be an interesting reflection of the ambivalence of public opinion that members of Congress have expressed in recent surveys a greater abstract willingness to challenge the Supreme Court and an increased belief that the constitutional arguments raised by their colleagues are genuine rather than for political show, yet the frequency with which they actually challenge the Supreme Court is not any greater than four decades ago. In general, the evidence from members of Congress and congressional staff is that constituency pressures are assuredly not driving in the direction of greater concern with constitutionality.[19] As Bruce G. Peabody notes,

> [T]he survey data reaffirm the importance of the "electoral connection," even in the context of constitutional matters. Lawmakers appear most likely to heed constitutional issues in political areas closest to their constituents' concerns, including federalism, individual rights, and state- or district-specific matters. Congress's capacities as an independent constitutional interpreter are importantly shaped by public attitudes.[20]

Another recent study indicated—not at all surprisingly, given both public attitudes and campaign rhetoric—that an overwhelming plurality of congressional hearings that touch on constitutional topics relate to individual rights.[21]

Intellectual Climate

If the attitudes and opinions of the broad mass of American society necessarily serve as the foundation of electoral activity, it is also true that the intellectual climate among opinion leaders helps to establish constraints and drive action. That climate, which defines the "respectability" of certain arguments in the public sphere, is established by the aggregate (though not collective) efforts of noteworthy public intellectuals and commentators, influential journals of opinion, the professoriate in institutions of higher learning, and, when it comes to constitutional questions, the legal profession practicing at the bar, in the law schools, and on the bench as judges. Complicating the picture is the fact that political rhetoric both on the campaign trail and governing, when delivered by a skillful leader who is attempting to advance a coherent political worldview, can move the intellectual climate, hence becoming both a cause and an effect of that climate. So, too, can legislative action, if it dramatically breaks the established mold, change people's minds about the location of constitutional boundaries and contribute to establishing a new intellectual climate.

While the intellectual climate is even more ephemeral than public opinion, which at least can be polled, its potential importance should not be underestimated and can be observed in retrospect by example. The progressive revolution in the practice of constitutionalism owed much to the intellectual ground plowed by Herbert Croly and *The Nation*, Charles Beard, the "Muckrakers," Woodrow Wilson in his academic incarnation, and even the direct democracy innovations of the Populist platforms of the 1890s. The New Deal transformation likewise owed much to the Progressives and theorists such as John Dewey. Presidential rhetoric by Theodore Roosevelt, Woodrow Wilson, and Franklin Roosevelt itself became an integral part of the intellectual climate.

There can be no doubt that the elevation and expansive redefinition of rights in the Constitution—the so-called "rights revolution"—was a major intellectual current of the last half of the twentieth century, driven at least partially by change in the law schools.[22] Supreme Court decisions both reflected that revolution and helped define and legitimate it. And it is clear that a conservative legal response to the "rights revolution," the rise of judicialism, and the downgrading of federalism took the form of an intellectual movement attempting to relegitimize a jurisprudence of originalism and judicial restraint.

As scholar Steven Teles points out, in the short term, political actors are constrained by the intellectual (and institutional) climate. They are free, however, to pursue long-term strategies to shift that climate to their benefit, and in the legal and constitutional realm both liberals and conservatives have attempted to do so.[23]

The Political Parties

Political parties are one of the two most important actors with a proximate influence over campaigns, candidates being the other. The relationship of party to candidate has varied over time. It is generally understood by political scientists that the nineteenth century was an era characterized by the power of parties over candidates, while the twentieth century became increasingly candidate-centered.

Nevertheless, even today, party nominations are heavily influenced by the party activists, the relatively small hard core of the party's supporters who heavily engage their time, money, and personal networks on behalf of the party and its candidates. The enthusiasm of the activists is also crucial for success in the general election campaign. Consequently, while small in number, they continue to hold a pivotal position in electoral politics in America.

Numerous studies of the parties in the nineteenth century emphasize how the motivation of the party organizations shifted from principle to patronage after the Civil War. Sidney Milkis argues that the major parties have, since the New Deal, been transformed from decentralized, local entities to instruments of centralized national administration. In the process, they became vehicles of a politics of rights and entitlement. The parties, in Milkis's view, have trivialized the Constitution and constitutional dialogue: "in routinely conferring constitutional status on policies, the new social contract drained partisan debate and resolution of real meaning."[24] These broad brushstrokes must be augmented by a closer look at the activists themselves.

Owing to studies of each party's national convention delegates reaching back to the 1960s, a number of conclusions that bear on our discussion here can be employed. First, party activists and elites as a whole tend to be better informed about politics, more interested in politics, and more ideologically sophisticated and consistent than the mass public.[25] Second, party activists have become more ideological over the last four decades. For example, Democratic National Convention delegates became more ideologically extreme between 1968 and 1972;[26] on most issues both Democratic and Republican delegates in 1972 were more ideologically extreme than their party's voters.[27]

As Aaron Wildavsky points out about 1964 Republicans, activists can be divided into at least two groups, the "professionals" who have typically been relatively more pragmatic and the "amateurs" who are typically the most ideologically driven. Subsequent studies demonstrated that "amateur" activists were indeed more ideological than professionals and have increased their relative weight over time, due first to a series of ideological movements arriving on the scene and then to party reforms in the nominating process.[28] Some studies have indicated that in recent years party "professionals" have caught up with and perhaps even surpassed "amateurs" in their degree of ideological motivation and extremism.[29] Overall, activists are both more ideological than nonactivists and, on balance, more ideological today than they used to be.

It also matters a great deal which party they belong to. Activists are more ideological than they were forty years ago, but they are not of the same ideology. In general, Democratic and Republican party elites grew more ideologically polarized over a wider array of issues from 1956 to 2000, and this process has partially seeped down to the level of the mass voter.[30] The Republican Party has grown more conservative, and Democrats more liberal.

"Ideological," of course, is not synonymous with "constitutional." Nevertheless, constitutional questions comprise a large part of what defines opposing political ideologies in America. In one recent survey of party activists conducted by prominent scholars seeking to measure ideological polarization, the "cultural" dimension of issues was defined by five social issues, every one of which was constitutional in nature; of the three issues in the racial dimension, another one was constitutional. The five cultural issues were abortion, gay rights, school prayer, gun control, and parental consent. In the racial issues category, preferential hiring was the one constitutional issue. [31] More generally, ideological thinking is of a higher level of abstraction, and it is abstract thinking that is required to place a high priority on the Constitution and constitutional issues. Consequently, though more ideological thinking does not automatically lead to more constitutional thinking, it is probably necessary for such thinking and is probably connected to it in actual practice. To look at the same question from the opposite direction, a total loss of ideological thinking would create a climate in which constitutional rhetoric would not find fertile soil.

Candidates

Individual candidates are, for the most part, short-term actors, although a handful aim to change the constitutional debate long after they leave the scene. They have, nevertheless, become the most significant actors in a proximate sense. Presidential candidates have long ago abandoned the reticence that prevented them from directly campaigning for most of the nineteenth century. Today, they help write and then deliver their acceptance speech; they must approve, and often appear in, their television advertisements; and they personally participate in the debates. The party platforms, which once preceded and bound the candidates, are now written by the candidate's supporters with him in mind (although usually in negotiation with important factions of party activists). Even in the nineteenth century, when the candidates' influence was often hidden, it was seldom absent.

Candidates are always constrained by political realities, but they possess considerable freedom of action within those constraints. They are also idiosyncratic, as can be seen by the wild swings in constitutional references from one candidate message to another. They each have their own background, their own convictions, their own peculiar bases of support, their own capacity and propensity for making abstract arguments, their own short-term policy agendas and long-term aims, if any.

William Henry Harrison emphasized his anti-Federalist lineage; it is not clear that Henry Clay would have done so. William Seward would not necessarily have replicated Abraham Lincoln's constitutional argument. James Garfield produced a brief spike in the downward trend of constitutional references in inaugural addresses, for no apparent external reason. He simply wanted to.

Woodrow Wilson virtually stopped using constitutional rhetoric from 1912 to 1920, a falloff consistent with his personal aversion to Constitution worship. His predecessor, William Howard Taft, operating as well in a progressive environment, had no such aversion. Would Robert Taft have run a 1952 campaign as free of constitutional discussion as Dwight Eisenhower's? Would William Scranton or Nelson Rockefeller have devoted as much attention to federalism and enumeration of powers as Barry Goldwater did in his 1964 platform and speech? Since both Ronald Reagan and John Anderson did run in the 1980 general election, it is not difficult to see that Reagan's constitutional arguments as the Republican Party nominee were very different than Anderson's would have been. Reagan's use of constitutional rhetoric in government also stands out in sharp relief next to his late twentieth century and early twenty-first century successors.

It is, of course, difficult to quantify how much difference individual candidates make, and this analysis does not attempt to do so. Nevertheless, no thoroughgoing accounting of the subject can exclude them.

Interest Groups

Interest groups have multiplied vastly in number since the early 1800s, and it is clear that the weight of interest groups in American politics is not often put in the service of constitutional principles. A study of the websites of the top twenty Political Action Committee (PAC) contributors in the 2005–2006 election cycle, compiled as of mid-2006 by the Center for Responsive Politics, found that only five PACs declared anything of a constitutional nature to be within their purview.[32] In all but one of the five cases, the constitutional focus was either quite narrow or very much a secondary concern for the organization. In the former category, the National Beer Wholesalers' Association (the number-two PAC) stated that a primary concern of the organization was maintaining the three-tiered alcohol control system instituted by the Twenty-first Amendment (the amendment repealing Prohibition); the number-fifteen PAC, the National Cable and Telecommunications Association, listed as one of its concerns avoiding government regulation of cable programming content (a relatively narrow application of the First Amendment). Numbers nineteen and twenty, the United Auto Workers and the International Association of Machinists and Aerospace Workers, both cited "civil rights" as an area of concern, a broad constitutional topic but one that was at best peripheral to their primary objectives and undoubtedly consumed few of their resources. Only the Association of Trial Lawyers of America (the number-three PAC) emphasized broad constitutional rights including protection of the Sixth Amendment, the Seventh Amendment, and "the rights of the accused" more generally. Another three corporate PACs on the top twenty list had no easily accessible websites

(AT&T PAC, United Parcel Service PAC, and Verizon Communications PAC) and it seemed unlikely that they devoted much attention, if any, to constitutional questions—at best a handful of specific regulatory issues. This pattern is a longstanding one. A review of top soft-money donors to the parties in 2000, the last presidential election in which such contributions were legally permitted, shows that none of the top ten Democratic soft-money donors and only one of the top ten Republican soft-money donors—the National Rifle Association—focused largely or primarily on constitutional issues.[33] Similarly, a listing of the top fifty spending PACs in the 1997–1998 campaign cycle reveals that only three placed fairly broad constitutional concerns as a high priority: the Trial Lawyers Association (number two), the National Rifle Association (number thirteen), and the Human Rights Campaign, which focuses on gay rights issues (number forty-nine).[34]

Looking at interest groups in another way—that is, by identifying the most visible groups whose agendas *are* largely about constitutional issues—is also illuminating. These are groups that would fall in the category of "ideological" groups, which themselves are a relatively small proportion of all organized political interest groups. For example, only one-quarter of PACs are ideological or "nonconnected." Groups whose task largely entails advancing a constitutional position—some of which are or have PACs, some of which are legal advocacy groups, and some of which are "voter education groups"— would include:

- American Civil Liberties Union: The ACLU focuses its advocacy on First Amendment, equal protection, due process, and privacy rights.
- American Center for Law and Justice: Focusing on the First Amendment freedom of religious expression, the ACLJ declares itself "committed to insuring the ongoing viability of constitutional freedoms."[35] It also expresses an interest in judicial nominations.
- Center for Individual Rights: The CIR is a conservative legal foundation that has taken up the cause of opposing racial preferences in court.
- The Institute for Justice: Another legal advocacy group, IJ aims primarily to protect property rights and freedom of speech, and to "restore constitutional limits on the power of government."[36]
- People for the American Way: Contending that "Our most fundamental rights and freedoms—and even our basic constitutional framework—are at risk,"[37] PAW takes a particular interest in church/state issues and constitutional controversies regarding rights, as well as judicial appointments and judicial power.

- Christian Coalition: Deeply interested in church/state issues and a number of constitutional controversies regarding rights, as well as judicial appointments and judicial power, the Christian Coalition claims to have distributed seventy million voter guides throughout all fifty states in the 2004 campaign.[38] It also takes some interest in United Nations reform and constitutional sovereignty issues.
- National Rifle Association: The NRA aims to protect Second Amendment rights to keep and bear arms.
- NARAL Pro-Choice America: The National Abortion Rights Action League has as its primary purpose the defense of abortion on demand, "protecting the right to choose" and fighting efforts to overturn *Roe v. Wade*.[39]
- EMILY'S List: Founded in 1985, this fundraising network raises money and undertakes other efforts to assist the election campaigns of pro-choice Democratic women; in 2004, the network contributed $120 million to such candidates.[40]
- The WISH List: A Republican equivalent of EMILY'S List, Women In the Senate and House provides at least a million dollars a year in support to pro-choice Republican women candidates.[41]
- National Right to Life Committee: NRLC—formed in 1973—seeks to "restore legal protection to innocent human life" by restricting abortion. It has a PAC that supports pro-life candidates for elective office.[42]
- Concerned Women for America: This group, begun in 1979, is a conservative Christian women's group. It lists six "core issues," five of which are constitutional in character: definition of the family, sanctity of human life (especially regarding abortion), opposition to pornography, support for religious liberty, and defense of national sovereignty.[43]
- National Association for the Advancement of Colored People: Declaring itself "the nation's most significant civil rights organization," the NAACP is concerned with promotion and enforcement of civil rights laws, as well as judicial appointments and judicial power.[44] A number of other civil rights groups would fall into the same category.

These organizations have in common one crucial characteristic: all of them are devoted to the advancement of some conception of individual rights. They also have that in common with the handful of top-spending PACs that maintain some interest in constitutional questions, all of which cited some aspect of rights as their concern. A handful take a broader interest in judicial appointments and judicial power, as well, and will take a stand on constitutional amendments when they affect rights issues. One or two follow issues of constitutional sovereignty.

If one broadens the search to include think tanks and more specialized academic groups, a few more with significant interests in the Constitution emerge—but only a few, and fewer yet for whom the interest can be called dominant. Think tanks might include the Cato Institute, the American Enterprise Institute, and the Heritage Foundation, each of which devote some consistent (though hardly controlling) attention to constitutional questions.[45] Though think tanks do not engage in electioneering, the Heritage Foundation, formed in 1973, has exerted particular influence over policy deliberations of Republican officeholders in Washington. The Federalist Society, an intellectual meeting ground for those in the field of law who share a conservative understanding of the Constitution, is devoted foremost to constitutional concerns, but is limited in direct political effect by its narrow membership base and its scholarly approach. It may well affect nominations of federal judges, but it has no obvious impact on electoral races nor does it seek to exert any.

At the other end of the spectrum of political groups—with a much greater mass base but much more amorphous definition—lie social/political movements. While extending well beyond any single organization, movements can institutionalize themselves by spawning numerous interest groups, legal advocacy groups, or think tanks. In the last half-century, there has been at least one broad grassroots movement aimed primarily at a constitutional issue: civil rights. The pro-life movement might be counted another. Several other movements of varying breadth have addressed constitutional questions without being defined by them, including the feminist movement, the gay rights movement, and the conservative movement, the broadest and oldest of the three.

Of the five movements listed above, four have found their constitutional concerns located wholly or primarily in the realm of rights; only the conservative movement was animated by any significant concern with federalism or other structural issues. Looking as well at the narrower set of interest groups that seek to directly influence elections, notably absent is any group devoted to the advancement of federalism. AFSCME, the powerful union of state, county, and municipal employees which ranks ninth in 2005–2006 PAC contributions, has a considerable stake in the decentralization of governmental power, but makes no point of expressing an interest in federalism questions, and aims its attention instead to things such as strengthening public employee pensions and opposing federal budget cuts. The same can be said of the international firefighters' union. Even intergovernmental groups such as the National Governors Association and National Conference of State Legislatures are far more often supplicants of federal aid than advocates of state authority; only the American Legislative Exchange Council seems to take federalism issues somewhat seriously. While groups such as Americans for Tax Reform and the National Taxpayers Union agitate for lower federal taxes and spending, they rarely take up such issues on constitutional grounds and are in any event wildly outspent by groups of all sorts who want more from government.

It is interesting to note that a very large proportion of the advocacy groups (including interest groups, legal advocacy groups, and think tanks) that do maintain a significant interest in the Constitution were either formed or came to maturity in the last four decades. Pro- and antiabortion groups, People for the American Way, the Christian Coalition, Concerned Women for America, the Heritage Foundation and Cato Institute, the Federalist Society, and the American Center for Law and Justice were all formed during that period. Indeed, generally speaking, almost the entire network of both liberal and conservative legal advocacy groups were formed in that period. Civil rights groups and the National Rifle Association, though they had existed long before, considerably increased their political mobilization and political clout during that period.

At the end of the day, there are not many interest groups that have constitutional concerns to any degree, there are fewer yet whose primary purpose can be defined in constitutional or largely constitutional terms, and those that do are overwhelmingly skewed toward rights rather than structural issues. The rise in the number and influence of interest groups has roughly paralleled the rise of expansive government, a fact which leads to the consideration of an unsettling possibility: Perhaps the growth of government in certain eras of constitutional carelessness has led to the growth of interest groups; the growth of interest groups has contributed to the decline of constitutional rhetoric; and the decline of constitutional rhetoric has led to the normalization of constitutional carelessness.

Media Forms

The means of conveyance of campaign rhetoric is an input that would, on the face of it, seem to be neutral and hence unworthy of examination. One can deliver a message by a variety of means, and yet the content of the message remains the same.

However, that superficial conclusion does not account for an obvious fact. Certain forms of media are sometimes better suited for a particular type of communication than are others. Reading the printed word, for example, is not the best way to experience a play that is written to be performed. To recite verbatim a written paper meant to be read is a recipe for a bored audience, as many a scholar has discovered at an academic conference. Glenn Miller's swing music should not be played by an oompah band. And it is not difficult to imagine that the type of media that one wishes to (or must) use in a campaign might set certain parameters around the character of that communication.

For example, it is clearly the case that the length of some communications must be constrained to fit in a certain media format. Not much can be said in a thirty-second advertisement. State of the Union messages shrank dramatically once presidents began delivering them in the form of a speech; similarly, nomination acceptance letters faced fewer limitations than acceptance speeches given on national television. Platforms, on the other hand, face no intrinsic size constraints, and have metastasized (although growing platform length has undoubtedly affected readership).

Along other lines, it is conceivable that different types of media carry with them inherent biases toward particular styles of communication. As early as the 1960s Marshall McLuhan famously contended that "the medium is the message" and argued that television was a "cool" medium that required the viewer to work hard to draw out its meaning. McLuhan's appraisal has been supplanted by more recent study by communications experts, but they too argue that television is different from other types of communication. To provide just one example of the effect of this phenomenon in practical politics, political journalist Theodore White postulates that Edward Kennedy's 1980 run for the Democratic presidential nomination failed partly because his intense speaking style, honed for stumping at the union hall, was bad for television.[46] Jeffrey Tulis, in his study of presidential rhetoric, argues that "the one-sentence paragraphs so common to presidential messages are consciously designed to accommodate television news," with the consequence that "short aphorisms" have replaced "developed arguments."[47]

The implications of media form on constitutional rhetoric—and indeed campaign rhetoric of any sort—are potentially quite large. To the extent that the peculiarities of each form of communication really do drive the form of campaign communication, they may also drive its content.

Media Coverage

The news media both report political campaigns to voters and help shape the outcome of those campaigns through their coverage. Two indicators offer the possibility that the predilections of modern media have negatively affected constitutional rhetoric.

First, the relative lack of media concern with constitutional questions in general is implied in the record of debate questions presented in chapter five.

To summarize, only 7.1 percent of debate questions from 1960 to 2004 had some constitutional content, and only five questions in forty-four years—1 percent of the total—were explicitly framed constitutional questions. In 1992–2004, citizen questioners in the town-hall debates asked considerably more constitutionally oriented questions than journalists did in the other debates. Indeed, in 1992 and 1996 the town-hall debates were the only debates to feature a constitutional question. In sum, from 1992 to 2004, while about one in eight citizen questions had some constitutional content, only one in thirty-three journalist questions did. About two-thirds of the constitutional questions since 1960 were related to individual rights. One-quarter (a total of nine) had to do with appointments. The remainder was a sprinkling of one to three questions each about constitutional amendments, Supreme Court decisions, and executive powers. There has not been a debate question focusing on federalism since one was asked in 1960.

Second, a quick review of news coverage illustrates the way that Americans receive a great deal more information and stimulation from the media about rights issues than about other constitutional controversies. Using the electronic news database Lexis-Nexis, general news stories from major newspapers were surveyed for the six months prior to late April 2006 using thirty-three key search words. Searches for articles with references to "civil liberties," "civil rights," and "abortion" were interrupted when the computer determined that more than one thousand articles were found for each search word or phrase. The next most common topic was gay marriage, with around 500 hits, followed in order by constitutional amendment and Supreme Court appointments (both with 426 hits), First Amendment (326), *Roe v. Wade* (241), and International Criminal Court, which was selected as a term indicative of constitutional sovereignty issues (134). Federalism had 116 hits, though a large number of them had to do with Canadian federalism. No other term or phrase had as many as one hundred hits, and most remaining terms had fewer than fifty (including six terms with no references).

As one can see, newspaper coverage of constitutional questions suffers from a preoccupation with abortion and expressive rights at the expense of other critical questions. Despite being in a time of war, war powers and executive privilege were relegated to minimal consideration; despite a national uproar, the *Kelo* case on eminent domain was cited in only one article for every seven that discussed *Roe*; despite controversies surrounding government wiretapping, the Fourth Amendment was likewise cited in one article for every seven that mentioned the First Amendment (while the Tenth Amendment went completely unmentioned); despite the Samuel Alito nomination and confirmation falling within the same six-month time period, there were no articles referring to original intent or the "living Constitution," and fewer than twenty citing principles of judicial restraint or of judicial activism.

Going back ten and twenty years, a few details change, but the overall picture remains the same. Civil rights, abortion, and civil liberties were the top terms in 1996 and 1986, while constitutional interpretation, judicial power, and enumerated powers languished at the bottom with little to no attention. Constitutional amendments and Supreme Court appointments were also heavily covered in 1996 (less so in 1986). The rise of gay marriage and constitutional sovereignty as issues can be traced across the three snapshots. Perhaps reflecting the interests of the 104th Congress, federalism references experienced a bulge in 1996, as did the line-item veto. In general, although absolute levels varied somewhat, the relative standing of the terms remained consistent in 1986, 1996, and 2006 (see table 8.8).

One other indirect indicator of media interest in and coverage of the Constitution can be deduced from polling questions over the last two decades. The questions are an indicator for two reasons, both because news organizations conduct many public opinion surveys and because the news media is a voracious consumer of polling data. More than five hundred questions on constitutional topics asked between 1985 and 2004 were accessed from the electronic database of polling questions maintained by the Roper Center for Public Opinion Research at the University of Connecticut. The results cannot be considered definitive, since the search was limited to questions that used the word "Constitution" and some polling questions (like some campaign rhetoric) might frame constitutional questions implicitly. A quick look at explicitly framed polling questions is nevertheless instructive. Of those questions, nearly two-thirds—317 of 503, or 63 percent—were rights-related. Nearly two-fifths dealt with rights simply, while one-quarter of the questions were about constitutional amendments that touched on rights issues (like school prayer, flag-burning, and same-sex marriage). Another one-sixth dealt with non-rights-related amendments, especially the proposed balanced budget amendment, which was heavily polled in the 1980s and 1990s. Small but notable blocks of questions were asked about executive powers, about the Constitution itself in a general way, or about respondents' knowledge of the Constitution outside the specific issues that were already coded otherwise. A negligible smattering of questions were asked about a handful of other constitutional questions, including federalism, separation of powers, and judicial powers.

Going back another two decades to the period 1965–1984, an era that saw less frequent polling, there were far fewer constitutional questions asked

Table 8.8. "Hits" on selected constitutional terms in major newspapers, six months prior to April 2006

Category and term	Hits 2006	Hits 1996	Hits 1986
Individual rights			
Civil liberties	>1000	952	253
Civil rights	>1000	>1000	>1000
Abortion	>1000	>1000	613
Gay marriage	522	119	0
Same-sex marriage	490	178	1
First Amendment	326	350	85
Fourth Amendment	46	13	10
Constitutional amendment			
Constitutional amendment	426	674	49
Electoral College/amendment	6	0	0
Appointments			
Supreme Court/appointment	426	168	41
Supreme Court cases			
Roe v. Wade (ind. rights—abortion)	241	36	7
Kelo (ind. rights—property)	35	N/A	N/A
U.S. v. Lopez (enumerated powers)	0	0	N/A
Constitutional sovereignty			
International Criminal Court	134	26	1
Federalism			
Federalism	116	221	14
States' rights	88	140	26
Unfunded mandates	8	22	0
Tenth Amendment	0	8	0
Executive powers			
Executive privilege	39	41	6
Line-item veto	35	189	6
War powers	29	11	18
Mode of constitutional interpretation			
Judicial activism	19	14	9
Judicial restraint	14	7	2
Original intent	0	22	7
Living Constitution	0	0	0
Enumerated powers			
Enumerated powers	0	1	0
Commerce clause	12	3	1
Judicial power			
Supreme Court/court stripping	1	0	0
Supreme Court/appellate jurisdiction	0	0	0

Note: The 2006 Lexis/Nexis search was conducted April 27–28, 2006, for six months prior; 1996 search conducted May 23, 2006, for references from November 1, 1995 to May 1, 1996; 1986 search conducted May 23, 2006, for references from November 1, 1985 to May 1, 1986. In all cases, terms were searched on headline/lead paragraphs/terms setting in general news/major newspapers.

(168). Of those questions, far fewer questions were asked about simply the First Amendment or other rights, constitutional knowledge, and a number of other issues. Two-thirds of all questions were asked about constitutional amendments related to rights, mostly the proposed Equal Rights Amendment and school prayer amendments, meaning that three-quarters of all constitutional questions from 1965 to 1984 were rights-related. Another fifth were asked about other (nonrights) amendments. This sample found only one question that even touched on federalism, a query asking respondents whether they thought George Wallace was a sincere advocate of states' rights or a bigot.

These polling tendencies since 1965 stand in stark contrast with the tenor of survey questions prior to 1965. In the three decades before 1965, fewer than one in ten questions were rights-oriented. More than eight in ten addressed possible constitutional amendments affecting the structure and powers of government, most notably presidential term limits, Supreme Court size and age limits, or requiring a popular referendum for a military draft or entry into a foreign war. In the 1930s, Gallup questioned Americans about whether Congress should be given additional powers over agriculture and commerce by constitutional amendment (table 8.9).

Perhaps, it might be objected, results would be different if implicit question wording was sampled—that is, survey questions about constitutional questions that did not use the word "Constitution." To test this possibility in a few likely cases, the Roper Center survey collection was subjected to another search, this time using the terms "federalism," "states' rights," and "war powers" without a "constitutional" modifier. In the entire period from 1935 to 2005, the search located thirteen "federalism" questions, all of which revolved around Ronald Reagan's 1982 "New Federalism" proposal; twenty-one "states' rights" questions, most of which used the term in relation to southern third-party activity by Strom Thurmond or George Wallace; and two "war powers" questions.

Inputs and Outcomes

The factors outlined above have interacted to produce the decline and resurgence in the level of constitutional rhetoric in campaigns, the heavy and growing tilt toward rights in that rhetoric, and differences in levels of constitutional rhetoric between modes of campaign communication.

Changes in the intellectual environment and the parties can account for much of the broad decline and modest resurgence of constitutional rhetoric. The intellectual environment has seen waves of pragmatic commercialism,

Table 8.9. Polling questions on constitutional topics, 1965–2004

Topic	1935–1964 questions (%)	1965–1984 questions (%)	1985–2004 questions (%)
First Amendment rights	**2 (2.6)**	**9 (5.4)**	**120 (23.9)**
Constitutional amendments relating to rights	**3 (3.9)**	**111 (66.1)**	**118 (23.5)**
Other constitutional amendments	65 (84.4)	37 (22.0)	83 (16.5)
Bill of rights/all rights/ specific rights other than First & Second Amendment	**2 (2.6)**	**5 (3.0)**	**61 (12.1)**
Misc. constitutional knowledge	0	2 (1.2)	35 (7.0)
General appraisals of Constitution	3 (3.9)	2 (1.2)	24 (4.8)
Second Amendment rights	**0**	**0**	**18 (3.6)**
Executive powers	0	0	18 (3.6)
Mode of constitutional interpretation	0	0	7 (1.4)
Constitutional issues re: impeachment	0	0	5 (1.0)
Federalism	0	1 (.6)	3 (.6)
Supreme Court decisions	1 (1.3)	1 (.6)	3 (.6)
Judicial power	1 (1.3)	0	3 (.6)
Separation of powers	0	0	3 (.6)
Appointments	0	0	2 (.4)
Total	**77**	**168**	**503**
Rights-oriented	**7 (9.1)**	**125 (74.4)**	**317 (63.0)**

Note: bold=rights-related categories
Source: Roper Center for Public Opinion Research, University of Connecticut

Wilsonian progressivism, and New Deal liberalism that corresponded with the long decline of constitutional references after the Civil War. The "rights revolution" subsequently stimulated an increase in constitutional conversation by both its supporters and its opponents, as well as in the weight given to rights issues. The change in intellectual climate fostered by the conservative movement also likely contributed to increased attention to questions of federalism and other structural issues since the 1960s.

To the extent that Milkis is correct about the transformation of the parties, it would help to explain both the post–New Deal trough in constitutional discussion and the subsequent growth of rights talk in campaigns (although this study has excluded references to positive economic rights that some have attempted to constitutionalize). Yet Milkis's framework, though a useful starting point, cannot fully address the trends in campaign rhetoric. The increasingly ideological character of party activists since the 1960s helps to explain the overall resurgence of constitutional rhetoric to the extent that it has occurred. The polarization of those activists has led them in different directions of content, with Democrats emphasizing rights and Republicans often emphasizing structural or interpretation issues. Polarization has perhaps, as well, heightened the anxiety with which they view constitutional issues.

Michael Kammen summarizes the "basic pattern of American constitutionalism as one of "conflict within consensus."[48] For his part, Sanford Levinson notes the "potential of a written constitution to serve as a source of disintegration" and disputes the notion that the symbol of the Constitution would necessarily guarantee national political unity.[49] That the Constitution can be at the center of political polarization is obvious from a moment's reflection on the period leading up to the Civil War. Perhaps less obvious is the possibility that the growing polarization of American politics in the last three or four decades is connected with the revival of constitutional issues and rhetoric during roughly the same period.

However, an examination of the ups and downs of constitutional references in platforms in crucial elections shows how complicated this question can be. In chart 8.1, the vertical lines represent elections in 1860, 1876, 1896, 1912, 1920, 1936, 1948, 1968, 1980, and 2004. In four of ten cases, the line correlates with a peak in constitutional rhetoric—1896, 1912, 1920, and 1936. In two other cases, the line correlates with a deep trough—1860 and 1876, although 1860 came immediately after a significant peak. The 1968 and 1980 elections represented little change, and 1948 occurred in the middle of a downward trend. The 2000 and 2004 elections may have demonstrated again that elite polarization and constitutional fervor in campaign rhetoric are not inextricably linked. Elite polarization is said to have reached new highs in the modern era, but constitutional references fell back. Conversely, however, it may be that the degree of elite polarization in 2000 and 2004 was less than many have claimed, or that a decline in ideological polarization—consistent with the rise of Bush's "compassionate conservatism" or "big government conservatism"—may have been masked by high levels of partisan polarization.

The profusion and character of interest groups has also influenced both the decline and resurgence of constitutional rhetoric. On the one hand, few of the most influential interest groups take constitutional concerns as their focus. In the system of interest group liberalism ushered in by the New Deal, this is a prescription for relatively low political attention to constitutional issues in the polity whether campaigning or governing. On the other hand, most of the interest groups, think tanks, legal advocacy groups, and other or-

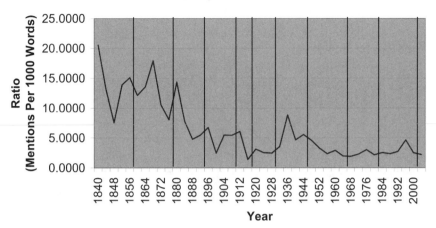

Chart 8.1. Constitutional references per one thousand words in major-party platforms (vertical grid indicates key years)

ganized forces that actually do make the Constitution their business have arisen or grown stronger in the last forty years. Moderately enhanced discussion of constitutional issues in campaigns is one of the plausible consequences of that development. Of those organizations, the vast majority concentrate their energies on individual rights questions such as abortion, civil rights, religious freedom, or gun rights. Many share an overlapping interest in judicial questions. There has clearly been a synergy between interest groups and party activists over the past four decades in those areas.

The print news media powerfully reinforces the focus on rights emphasized by those interest groups that have constitutional concerns. If candidates talk more about rights than any other subject, it may partly be because that is almost the only constitutional subject in which the print media evince a serious interest. Of course, the influence of such coverage may extend indirectly to other actors, as well, up to and including how the public thinks about and prioritizes constitutional issues. If the media spent as much effort covering federalism or separation of powers as it does covering rights (and who can doubt that there is sufficient material?) it seems inconceivable that public concern with those topics would not rise.

Aside from the content of media coverage, twentieth-century trends raise the possibility that the development of new modes of communication that rely more on visual images and emotional appeals than on reasoned argument has had a negative effect on constitutional rhetoric. Most notably, the two forms of campaign communication most thoroughly tied to television—debates and television ads—have contained much lower rates of constitutional rhetoric than have platforms, which are written. Candidate messages, which began as either written missives or speeches transmitted to most Americans by the printed word, experienced a sharp decline in constitutional rhetoric when the nomination acceptance speech began to be delivered at the convention itself with radio (and later television) coverage. The governing communications studied here, which have experienced a similar decline, are now delivered in much the same way. Furthermore, the pure televised modes are the ones that are least likely on the campaign trail to use explicit constitutional references rather than implicit references, and nomination acceptance speeches made their transition to consistently more implicit commentary just as they were becoming mass-media events—in the late 1920s, a full two decades before that transition occurred in platforms. Perhaps an audio or audiovisual medium is inherently less well-suited for the sort of abstract, philosophical, and often complex arguments that surround consideration of the Constitution; perhaps it is less well-suited for the open rather than implicit framing of constitutional issues. As Tulis proposes, television, as a medium that puts a premium on simple, concrete, visually appealing images, may be particularly ill-suited to relatively abstract and complicated constitutional arguments or to the relatively formal, if not confrontational, tack of talking about the Constitution explicitly. Even if the nature of modern media discourages constitutional rhetoric, however, that tendency is clearly not decisive in its influence. For one thing, there is a substantial difference between television ads and televised debates in terms of their usefulness to constitutional dialogue during campaigns. And the decline in constitutional rhetoric has also gone far in platforms, which have not been affected directly by new media forms.

Differences in levels of constitutional rhetoric among varying modes of campaign communication might be explained by the audience—that is to say, by differences between elite and mass opinion in terms both of political knowledge and ideological intensity and consistency. Platforms, which now are aimed most at the activists, are typically the most constitutionally laden. Television ads, which are most aimed at a mass audience, pay the least attention to constitutional questions.

While the style of media may affect the rate and content of constitutional rhetoric, the length of communication probably does not. The rate of constitutional rhetoric in platforms fell at the same time that platforms grew longer, and debate references are often delivered in response segments that are not much longer than television ads.

Undergirding all—though also influenced by all—is public opinion, which is characterized by a mix of veneration for the Constitution, lack of knowledge about many of its specific provisions, relatively strong interest in individual rights, and weak interest in other aspects of the Constitution. These tendencies in public opinion offer several clues to the development of constitutional rhetoric in campaigns in the last half-century. They explain the continued emphasis on rights when other issues have lost their luster. They explain why so few candidates risk frontal assaults on either strict constitutional interpretation or judicial power (which many citizens equate with the Constitution). Public opinion may also help explain the resurgence of constitutional rhetoric after its trough. Perhaps public veneration for the document, however diffuse that veneration might be, establishes a floor below which constitutional rhetoric cannot fall, or cannot fall for long. Too much disinterest in the Constitution on the campaign trail leaves a vacuum that will be filled in a competitive electoral system that is ultimately grounded in the sentiments of the people.

It is, of course, candidates who ultimately must identify and move to fill such vacuums. Although they may be operating within the environment established by the other factors, it is ultimately the candidates and their campaigns who choose in each election how much to discuss the Constitution and in what manner. Each candidate has put his own stamp on campaign rhetoric, each president on governing rhetoric. In the end, by some combination of personal conviction and strategic calculation, candidates over the last four decades have on average made a decision to engage in somewhat more frequent constitutional rhetoric than candidates in the middle portion of the last century. Recently, George W. Bush chose to downplay favorite Republican structural themes in favor of greater relative emphasis on rights and constitutional interpretation issues like judicial appointments, and in general to allow Republican constitutional references to slip from their 1996 high.

The precise way in which these factors have worked together cannot be easily disentangled. Many of them operate not only on the end product but also on each other. There are other possible factors, such as the role of campaign consultants and other campaign staff, that are not even addressed here. Nor should it be forgotten that another, very different sort of factor, can abruptly change the constitutional agenda and alter the constraints formed by the factors already discussed: events.

Clearly, events have played a part in the ups, downs, and specific content of constitutional rhetoric since 1840. The Civil War and the Great Depression and New Deal occasioned considerable commentary and shifted the boundaries of acceptable discourse. More recently, the terrorist attacks of September 11th activated issues of civil liberties, of executive powers, and of constitutional sovereignty. Supreme Court decisions, while in one sense a product of the intellectual environment and linked intrinsically to long-term jurisprudential trends, are nevertheless discrete and contingent events that can jolt the polity at a moment in time. Cases from *Dred Scott* to *Pollock* to *Schecter* to *Brown* to *Roe* have enlivened the constitutional conversation and have stimulated debate over the merits of the decisions, judicial power, and court appointments. Thus, much of constitutional debate in campaigns has been a matter of contingency, revolving around the question of how unforeseen events alter the relationship among the relevant factors and how individual candidates choose to respond.

Is the Glass Half-Full or Half-Empty?

It is tempting to see the glass of American constitutional rhetoric as half-full. Contrary to the expectations fostered by the combination of deconstitutionalization and judicialism, constitutional rhetoric in American elections has survived and even grown since the mid-1960s. Recent party platforms—representing an appeal by and for the party's officeholders and elites and a small substratum of highly informed voters and activists—have contained an absolute number, a rate, and a breadth of constitutional references that can only surprise many who have come to assume that the elected branches have little to say about the Constitution. If campaigns should be viewed as a cumulative exercise in persuasion, it is clear that Americans are cumulatively exposed to a significant amount and variety of constitutional rhetoric from a number of sources in most election years. Furthermore, when constitutional references are put into three broad groupings of rights, structure, and interpretation, rhetoric has appeared relatively balanced most of the time.

To the extent that judicialism is contrary to fundamental precepts of republican government, one might be heartened as well by the degree to which the modest recovery of constitutional rhetoric has come by way of increased discussion about Supreme Court cases, judicial powers, appointments, and constitutional amendments aimed at negating controversial court decisions. The parties and presidential candidates are talking back, or at least talking about talking back.

On the other side of the ledger, there is ample reason to be concerned that the glass is (at least) half-empty. If much of the increase in constitutional rhetoric has been directed toward issues raised by the judiciary, this represents something of bow to judicialism as well. It means that parties and candidates are setting aside constitutional discussion of many issues that Congress and the president decide for themselves most of the time. They may be talking back to the judiciary, but the judiciary is largely setting the agenda.

And the most direct way of repudiating judicialism—by discussing ways of actually limiting the power of the courts—has been largely eschewed by candidates, in comparison to more indirect means such as debating court decisions or appointments.

More generally, it is impossible to gloss over the reality of the deconstitutionalization of political rhetoric, tempered though it may be by recent trends to the contrary. If there has been a revival of such rhetoric, it has started from a much lower base and is far from recapturing lost ground. On balance, American parties and candidates simply talk less about the Constitution than they used to. They talk about it less openly than they used to, and they do the worst job of talking about it in television advertising, from which voters receive campaign messages most regularly. Voters who get everything they know about the candidates' constitutional positions from television ads will wind up knowing next to nothing. Likewise, exchanges on constitutional issues are not often had outside of debates and platforms. It is only a slight exaggeration to say that when it comes to constitutional rhetoric, television advertising is usually a barren wasteland.

The overall loss of explicitly constitutional rhetoric has also exacted a cost. Voters who are less informed or less interested in government and politics have suffered a double blow—not only is the mode of communication that is most directed to the mass public the one with the weakest constitutional rhetoric, but also all modes of communication have used increasingly opaque constitutional argumentation. Well-informed activists may be able to put the implicit references into constitutional context, but the mass public will find it more difficult. It is a good question how much benefit any recent revitalization of constitutional rhetoric has brought in terms of voter education if most of it has been implicit.

Not least, when broken down into the fifteen more specific categories, the content of constitutional rhetoric has become increasingly tilted. Individual rights—the security of which the Declaration of Independence states to be the purpose for which government is instituted—undoubtedly deserve a place of honor in the nation's political debate. Yet a single-minded concern for rights separated from concern for the conditions necessary to secure them is counterproductive. James Madison held both the mechanisms of government and the devotion to liberty of the people as superior to "parchment barriers," or declarations of rights. To the extent that the founders were right about the importance to liberty of sound governmental structure, there can be no question that the glass of political rhetoric has been substantially drained.

On the face of things, by comparison, the decline of the perfunctory reference over time has represented a small loss. Of all the categories of constitutional rhetoric, it is the one that, by definition, possesses no firm substantive content. Its decline can hardly be said to deprive voters of meaningful education about the Constitution, or meaningful choices about its application. However, even the near extinction of perfunctory references in the rhetoric of parties and presidential candidates ought not to be passed by without regret. Perhaps candidates, speechwriters, and strategists consider the form too stilted, too old-fashioned; perhaps they calculate that voters are not interested in such formalistic acknowledgements of the Constitution. In this sense, perfunctory references might be considered a proxy for explicit discussion of the Constitution in general. Indeed, the perfunctory reference is the only time the Constitution is mentioned not as a means to an end, but as the end itself. The loss of such references may say something particular about our political culture, in the manner of a canary in a mineshaft.

Altogether, even candidates openly committed to a renewal of constitutionalism have had difficulty making much of a change in campaign rhetoric. While Barry Goldwater and Ronald Reagan, for example, may have contributed to the general climate driving the limited reconstitutionalization of the last forty years, their campaigns did not stand out as dramatically more likely to use constitutional rhetoric. (They did broaden discussion into areas of federalism and enumerated powers.) It may say something about the constraints of modern campaigns that Reagan's use of constitutional rhetoric as president stood out, while the constitutional rhetoric of his campaigns was relatively lackluster. Further, it can hardly be considered an encouraging sign that winning campaigns are quite a bit less likely to use constitutional rhetoric than are losing campaigns.

Examination of the key campaign inputs can offer not only clues to the past but also insights into the future. It, too, yields a glass that is either half-empty or half-full. On one hand, the character of the party activists—well-informed and increasingly ideological—would militate in favor of a continued upswing in constitutional rhetoric, especially if Republican activists reassert their longstanding concern with such issues after the Bush hiatus. At the moment of this writing, there is no powerful third party operating to augment levels of constitutional rhetoric, but that could change. Even if it does not, there are smaller third parties who, in a closely divided nation, might have an effect even though they win few votes. The Constitution Party, a small party of the right, operates in several states, typically siphoning off some small number of Republican voters and activists with a special concern for limited government, federalism, and conservative views on constitutionalized social issues. The Greens, pushing an uncompromising platform on civil liberties in wartime along with their environmental and anticorporate staple, pull Democrats from the left. Both major parties might try to appeal on different sorts of constitutional issues to Libertarians, a grouping large enough to have swayed a number of statewide races in recent years.

The important symbolic place held by the Constitution in public opinion would seem to invite political candidates to advance their positions on constitutional grounds, and for them to engage in an educational campaign to fill in the gaps of citizen knowledge in a manner most conducive to their own electoral success. Citizen love of the Constitution makes such a campaign conceivable; citizen ignorance of the Constitution would make it both conceivable and challenging.

Yet it is also clear that voters do not naturally think of the Constitution when they think of the problems that most require public attention. To give the Constitution a more prominent place in elections will demand a concerted effort by parties and candidates to raise the salience of clearly constitutional issues and, perhaps more crucially, to explore the constitutional aspects of the issues that voters already think are important. This will demand political leadership. In the absence of such leadership, constitutional rhetoric will atrophy, the result of either neglect (perhaps in the manner of Dwight D. Eisenhower or Lyndon Johnson) or of deliberately downplaying such questions (perhaps in the manner of Woodrow Wilson or George W. Bush).

If such leadership is forthcoming, it will have to overcome the difficulties posed by a mainstream media and an interest group structure that are generally uninterested in constitutional issues. It will also have to overcome a media format that seems to work against constitutional rhetoric, though the growing importance of the "new media" in campaigning may provide a venue that offers the revitalization of thoughtful constitutional arguments in political campaigns. Although the mainstream media is widely uninterested in most constitutional issues, a change in the nature of contemporary media may offer some hope that voters are or will soon be receiving an augmented exposure to those issues. To cite two examples of the "new media," talk radio and Internet blogging both have the potential to broaden the constitutional discussion in the media. Several (mostly conservative) talk radio shows feature fairly frequent discussions of constitutional issues. Hugh Hewitt, for example, has devoted regular segments of his show to an exchange on constitutional issues between conservative legal expert John Eastman and his liberal counterpart Erwin Chemerinsky. Hewitt has paid particular attention to judicial appointments, Supreme Court decisions, and executive powers. Bloggers from across the political spectrum have taken advantage of the decentralized nature of the medium to advance a broad range of legal and constitutional arguments. Candidates themselves have entered the world of blogging, and both blogs and campaign websites offer them the opportunity to engage in written arguments intended for a more general audience than those who read the party platforms. These venues hold open the possibility that well-reasoned constitutional argumentation may find a niche in the new media that has eluded it in the old.

Nevertheless, it will not be easy to rebalance the rhetoric between rights and other issues. When Americans are informed about the Constitution, they seem most informed about rights; when the media does attend to constitutional issues, it attends to rights; when interest groups do place a high priority on the Constitution, they focus on rights. There is virtually no organized constituency in either the media or interest groups for a national discussion about federalism, separation of powers, or the constitutional limits of the federal government's legislative authority, although those topics are surely central to constitutional application. For such topics to find a place in the nation's political discussion, the parties and their candidates will have to work to put them there.

Some might object that constitutional argumentation is not desirable much of the time. As noted above, there is reason to fear that the constitutional content of campaigns can have a positive relationship with political polarization as discussion turns to issues that are closely tied to "first principles." The constitutional debates surrounding the Civil War certainly indicate as much. The cost of rigorous constitutional debate was, in that worst case, very high indeed, and some will even consider the cost of a more modest polarization unwelcome. For example, Donald Grier Stephenson, Jr., concludes his book on the Supreme Court in American campaigns acknowledging that the occasional entanglement of judicial issues with elections is sometimes salutary but contending that we should hope "that it materializes infrequently" to avoid destabilizing the position of the Court in the American system.[50] More broadly, James Madison argues in *Federalist* 49 that stability in the form of the Constitution—perhaps, one might say, our ability to take the Constitution for granted—was important. Thus, it is not unreasonable to hope to tamp down such polarization. At the least, we should be reminded that it is always wise to be careful what one asks for, and that political actors must work to channel constitutional rhetoric and constitutional issues within safe boundaries.

However, the worst case is not likely to be repeated, and we are yet remote from reaching such a repetition. Indeed, as we have seen, the connection between polarization and constitutional rhetoric is uncertain and complex. Madison's admonition was levied against too-frequent efforts to call into question the essence of the Constitution, specifically, Jefferson's call for a new Constitution every generation. Madison's own subsequent career—including authorship of the Virginia Resolutions, arguing for state nullification of the Alien and Sedition Acts on constitutional grounds—should relieve any apprehensions that he intended to absolve political figures from regularly contemplating whether their actions or the actions of others are consistent with the Constitution.

Furthermore, the cost of suppressing constitutional dialogue or allowing it to fall out of use in the name of social peace is high. As Madison also pointed out, conflict and division cannot be divorced from politics in a free society. Any hope of tamping them down by simply refraining from talking about the Constitution is a recipe for a politics of false consensus that is focused only on the low and the mundane. Worse, it is a recipe for the constitutional illiteracy of the American people, and ultimately of their government as well—with all that portends for their freedom and happiness. Constitutional self-government requires a constitutional conversation, not only among judicial and legal elites but also among the people who are supposed to be engaging in self-government.

It remains to be seen how the conflicting tendencies exposed in this study will work themselves out, whether the recovery of constitutional rhetoric will continue and broaden or falter, whether the most recent dip is an aberration, a return to a pre-1996 equilibrium, or the beginning of a new downward trend. In one direction lies a richer political dialogue and a steadier connection between the politics of the day and the enduring demands of our fundamental law. In the other direction lies an impoverished dialogue in which that fundamental law is rendered increasingly mute and irrelevant to the issues of the moment—and hence, in some real sense, less fundamental. In one direction lies a revitalization of the political symbol most responsible for giving the nation purpose and inspiring it to great deeds; on the other, the steady bleeding away of that symbol. No matter where one stands, right or left, no one can think the outcome immaterial to the well-being of the country.

APPENDIX A

~

A Note on the Study Method

Rather than use coding software, which would not easily have been able to account for context or variations in terminology, coding was done manually, by reading and rereading the documents themselves.[1] The basic unit was a *reference* to a constitutional issue that represented a discrete idea. Most of the time, a reference consisted of a full sentence. On some occasions a single sentence might contain more than one reference. This happened in a couple of ways. When a sentence referred in serial fashion to two or more distinct categories of constitutional issues or to distinct ideas within the same category (like a serial listing of distinct constitutional rights), each distinct instance was coded as a separate reference. Sometimes a single phrase as a whole properly belonged in two or three categories; those cases were counted in as many categories as were appropriate, but grand totals were adjusted to eliminate double- or triple-counting. Finally, on rare occasions, consecutive sentences were coded as a single reference when their content presented a consistent whole and their grammatical structure did not allow them to stand on their own.

The relevant campaign documents were coded for fourteen substantive categories of constitutional rhetoric and a fifteenth "perfunctory" category. The fifteen categories were derived from a discussion found in chapter 1, delineating areas in which the elected branches have a constitutional or practical role in interpreting and defining the federal Constitution.

References to these fifteen categories were then subdivided into explicit mentions and implicit mentions, except in the perfunctory and mode of interpretation categories, which by definition could only be explicit. In order to count as an explicit mention, a reference had to contain constitutional language (i.e., "constitutional rights," "Bill of Rights," or the name of specific amendments), quote specific text from the Constitution, or be clearly framed as constitutional. That framing could take the form of ongoing discussion of an issue that had used constitutional language immediately before or immediately after the reference in question. Sometimes it also took the form of a reference being contained within a platform section clearly labeled "The Constitution," "Our Constitutional System," or something along those lines. By and large, explicit references were easy to catalog, and one could expect a high degree of intercoder reliability.

Identifying implicit references was much more complicated, by necessity depending on interpretations of inference and context. Consequently, cataloging of implicit references could be expected to have a greater amount of variation between coders. In an attempt to produce the highest possible degree of reliability for both explicit and implicit references, extensive coding rules were developed for the fifteen categories. This issue raises the broader question of how to assure consistency of coding while reading approximately 390 platforms, letters, and speeches, 24 debate transcripts, and more than 1,000 television advertisement transcripts over a two-and-a-half year period. The platforms, the most comprehensive of the documents, were coded first, and were read over several times in the development of the coding rules. Once the coding rules were developed, they were then applied to the rest of the documents. When all of the documents were finished, about thirty months after beginning, the coding rules were refined to account for issues that arose throughout the course of coding. The entire set of documents was then reread in a one-week period with an emphasis on coding consistency, applying the refined rules. A large set of corrections resulted. Before statistical analysis was done, two smaller sets of corrections resulted from more focused attention to a handful of issues, particularly the handling of civil rights, prohibition, the Equal Rights Amendment, and school desegregation. In those cases, the documents of relevant years were reexamined again for those specific issues. Finally, to avoid double-counting in the total tallies, one last set of corrections adjusted totals to reflect cases of simultaneous multiple references.

The coding rules are summarized below.

Constitutional Amendments (CA)
Explicit: Arguments for or against, or other mention of, a "constitutional amendment" or a particular amendment identified by number. *Implicit*: Arguments made for or against, or other mention of, a change that would re-

quire a constitutional amendment without actually using the term "constitutional amendment." Examples would include calling for abolition of the Electoral College or statehood for the District of Columbia. References to recently ratified amendments were also included for as long as they seemed controversial (for example, the Eighteenth Amendment until it was repealed and the Fourteenth Amendment through 1876).

Appointments (APP)

References to appointments that have an important role in constitutional interpretation (usually attorney general or federal judges), either mentioning this fact (*explicit*) or not mentioning it (*implicit*). Excluded were issues having to do with the president's appointment power, which were categorized as executive power issues.

Enumerated Powers (EP)

Explicit: References to constitutional authorization or lack thereof for a specific federal activity or field of activity, a particular power of Congress, or references to the constitutional doctrine of enumerated and limited powers. These included calls for a "constitutional" bill on a particular subject, by which was meant that the bill would not transgress constitutional limits. *Implicit:* References to a fixed "responsibility," "role," "jurisdiction," "power," or "authority" of the federal or national government. References were excluded if the responsibility or role was not discussed as fixed (i.e., calling for an "increased federal responsibility," which implies a moral or statutory but not constitutional responsibility). Also excluded were limits imposed by the Bill of Rights or other rights guarantees, which were counted in the individual rights category. Finally, references to the role of "government" were excluded if they failed to specify the federal level.

Federalism (FED)

References to the Tenth Amendment (*explicit*). Also references to "federalism;" "rights," "(traditional) role," "responsibility," "prerogative," "authority," "control," or "power" of the states or local governments; restoring or shifting power back to the states; centralizing or decentralizing responsibility; or theories of the federal system; either utilizing constitutional language (*explicit*) or not (*implicit*). Exclusions include references to partnership, coordination, or cooperation between federal, state, and local levels; federal aid to state and local levels; and block grants or revenue sharing if not accompanied by a justification along the above lines. The key question was whether the reference acknowledged a constitutional distinction between the powers and roles of levels of government. Some statements posed coding difficulties to the degree that they could plausibly fall into the categories of either enumeration of powers or federalism. In those cases, the key test was whether the emphasis seemed to be on federal authority (enumeration) or on state/local authority or theories of the interrelationship of the levels of government (federalism).

Individual Rights (IR)

This category was the most difficult to delineate, for a variety of reasons. First, the notion of rights has expanded considerably from so-called "negative rights" of protection from oppressive government to so-called "positive rights" or economic rights to a variety of economic goods or processes. Consequently, the language of rights, which in the 1800s almost exclusively referred to constitutional negatives, can no longer be assumed to be so constrained. Second, even when looking at traditional rights against oppressive government, a variety of Supreme Court cases in the twentieth and early twenty-first centuries radically altered the previous understanding of what those rights meant. Third, there are areas of policy which are themselves partially of a constitutional character and partially not. Perhaps chief among these is the area of civil rights, including voting rights. Civil rights policy is grounded in the Civil War amendments (Thirteenth, Fourteenth, and Fifteenth), as well as the Nineteenth Amendment (women's suffrage), the Twenty-fourth Amendment (abolishing the poll tax), and the Twenty-sixth Amendment (the eighteen-year-old vote). These amendments are often explicated in statutes and court decisions. The Civil Rights Act of 1964, for example, contained sections related to protection of voting rights and to enforcement of school desegregation, which flowed from the Supreme Court's constitutional ruling in *Brown v. Board*. However, pure statutory law or executive order is also crucial in this area (for example, laws against private-sector employment discrimination). Finally, the area of constitutional individual rights overlaps but is not coterminous with the more general idea of individual liberty.

Given this complexity, the following rule was adopted. References to the Bill of Rights or to specific amendments or portions of the original text guaranteeing rights were coded as explicit references to individual rights. Also coded as individual rights were references to specific rights (e.g., freedom of speech, religious liberty), "individual rights," "individual liberties," "personal liberties," "liberties of the citizen," "human rights" (when used in a domestic context), and "civil liberties." References such as "equal protection of the laws," "equality of rights," or "equal justice under law" were also included. References to "voting rights" were counted, as were mentions of "civil rights" unless it was clear that the reference was to purely statutory law. And rights that grew out of Supreme Court interpretations of constitutional rights guarantees were counted, even if those rights were recently "discovered" and highly contentious (e.g., abortion after 1973). In all of these cases, the presence of constitutional language led to an *explicit* coding, and the absence of such language led to an *implicit* coding. References were counted as implicit examples of individual rights when issues were raised that were at that moment in some constitutional controversy, even if this was not made clear within the reference itself (e.g., the death penalty in 1972). There were, indeed, a whole range of contemporary issues that were potentially constitutional but often not discussed in constitutional terms, leaving open the question of whether to count them or not. These included, as mentioned above, abortion and the death penalty, but also included such issues as affirmative action, forced busing, gun control, and school vouchers. To deal with such issues, two factors were taken into account. First, had there been a Supreme Court case firmly asserting that there was a constitutional principle involved? If so, it was counted as implicitly constitutional even if no constitutional language was used. If not, the test was whether the argument in the text itself was practical or constitutional in its presentation. This meant that busing starting in the 1972 election, abortion starting in the 1976 election, affirmative action starting in the 1980 election, and the death penalty in 1972 were always considered constitutional issues, whether explicitly or implicitly framed.[2] Gun control and school vouchers were coded as constitutional issues only when an argument was made on grounds of constitutional principle rather than practicality.

A number of possible types of references were excluded, including references to positive economic rights (e.g., the right to housing), positive legal rights that were clearly not of a constitutional character (e.g., the right to burial in a national veterans' cemetery), the rights of Americans traveling abroad, rights as applied to American possessions abroad, rights of Native Americans unless accompanied by language connecting those rights to citizenship, equality of opportunity (as opposed to equality of rights), and references to individual liberty/freedom or personal liberty/freedom, which implied a more general concept (as opposed to individual liberties/freedoms, which seems to refer to concrete rights), unless clearly made in a constitutional context. References to rights of specified populations, like workers, parents, or the elderly, were assumed to be statutory (or moral) and hence were not counted unless clearly made in a constitutional context.

Impeachment (IMP)

Explicit: All impeachment references that explicitly mentioned a justification for impeachment rooted in constitutional abuse. *Implicit:* All other impeachment references.

Judicial Power (JP)

Abstract theories of judicial power ("an independent judiciary is essential to liberty") or support or opposition for attempts to limit judicial power (through, for example, limitation of appellate jurisdiction or limitation on the use of injunctions) or otherwise shift the boundaries or procedures of judicial power through statute, either framed with constitutional language (*explicit*) or not so framed (*implicit*).

Vetoes (VETO)

Explicit: Vetoes of a constitutionally controversial character, vetoes wielded for constitutional reasons, or vetoes of legislation of an explicitly constitutional character. *Implicit:* Vetoes of legislation of an implicitly constitutional character. All other veto mentions were excluded. General attacks on or defenses of the use of the veto were considered references to executive powers.

Executive Powers (EXEC)

The use, abuse, or form of executive powers by the president, either using constitutional language (*explicit*) or not (*implicit*). This category includes references to specific presidential powers or presidential power in general, the appropriate use of the appointment power and veto power, issues having to do with presidential succession, the president's duty to submit a report on the state of the union and his right to recommend measures to Congress, statutory enhancements of the president's constitutional powers, and issues of civilian control of the military and abuses by executive agencies. Uses of a presidential power as a mere title—such as "commander in chief"—were not counted; discussions of that power were.

Enforcement (ENF)

References to the general constitutional duty of the president to enforce the law, or to the enforcement, administration, or implementation of issues that themselves are constitutional in nature (including treaties), either framed by the use of constitutional language (*explicit*) or not (*implicit*). Excludes references to the enforcement of specific statutes if they have no constitutional import and to "law enforcement" as a term describing police efficiency. The enforcement category is distinct from the executive powers category insofar as the emphasis is on the president's duty rather than his authority; abuse typically takes the form of neglect rather than usurpation.

Separation of Powers (SP)
References to separation of powers, checks and balances, or reassertion of one branch's rightful prerogatives, either framed by constitutional language (*explicit*) or not (*implicit*). The boundary between this category and the categories of executive powers or judicial power was sometimes blurred, in which case the key was to gauge whether the emphasis of the statement was on the executive or judiciary in isolation (which would count as executive powers or judicial power) or on the relationship between the branches (separation of powers).

Supreme Court Decisions (SCD)
Generally, retrospective references to either specific court cases or a general judicial tendency established through a series of prior court cases. This can be either *explicit*, if the reference makes clear the fact that there are constitutional principles at stake, or *implicit*, if this is left unsaid. For example, if a case is cited but the constitutional questions it raises are not explicitly referred to as such, it was counted as an implicit reference. In rare cases, discussion of pending cases was also included, as were occasional mentions of lower federal court or even state court decisions with federal constitutional implications.

Mode of Constitutional Interpretation (MODE)
An *explicit* statement delineating how the Constitution should be interpreted, typically either broadly and in a "modern" way or narrowly and strictly.

Constitutional Sovereignty (CONSOV)
References either asserting or promising to limit the primacy of the U.S. Constitution and the laws of the United States against the claims of international organizations or agreements, either discussing these issues as openly constitutional (*explicit*) or not (*implicit*). Excludes discussions of territorial sovereignty.

Perfunctory (PERF)
Explicit reference to the Constitution in a substantively meaningless manner; use of a constitutional phrase ("We the People") disconnected from any broader constitutional discussion; symbolic reference to some constitutional

feature like the oath of office. Also a handful of miscellaneous references that do not fit in any of the above categories.

Additionally, the constitutional amendment, enforcement, and federal court decision categories could simultaneously entail other substantive categories. For example, references to the Equal Rights Amendment were counted as both constitutional amendment and individual rights; references extolling term limits for presidents were counted as both constitutional amendment and executive powers; promises to enforce voting rights was coded as both enforcement and individual rights; praising or criticizing *Roe v. Wade* counted as both Supreme Court decision and individual rights. When grand totals were calculated, such instances were collapsed into one reference to avoid inflating overall ratios by double-counting.[3]

APPENDIX B

~

Coded Communications

Campaign Communications

1840
- Democratic Party Platform[1]
- Letter from President Martin Van Buren to the Democratic Citizens' Committee, July 4, 1840[2]
- Speech by General William Henry Harrison, September 10, 1840[3]

1844
- Democratic Party Platform[4]
- Letter from James K. Polk to John K. Kane, June 9, 1844[5]
- Acceptance Letter of James K. Polk, June 12, 1844[6]
- Whig Party Platform[7]
- Speech by Henry Clay Upon His Retirement from the United States Senate, Lexington, Kentucky, June 9, 1842[8]

1848
- Democratic Party Platform[9]
- Letter from Lewis Cass to Alfred Osborne Pope Nicholson, December 24, 1847[10]
- Whig Party Platform[11]
- General Zachary Taylor's First "Allison Letter," April 22, 1848[12]
- General Zachary Taylor's Second "Allison Letter," September 4, 1848[13]

- Free-Soil Party Platform[14]
- Acceptance Letter of Martin Van Buren, August 22, 1848[15]

1852

- Democratic Party Platform[16]
- Speech by Minister to Britain James Buchanan, Greensburg, Pennsylvania, October 7, 1952 (D)[17]
- Whig Party Platform[18]
- Acceptance Letter of Winfield Scott, June 24, 1852[19]

1856

- Democratic Party Platform[20]
- Acceptance Letter of James Buchanan, June 16, 1856[21]
- Republican Party Platform[22]
- Acceptance Letter of John Fremont, July 8, 1856[23]
- American Party Platform[24]
- Acceptance Letter of Millard Fillmore, May 21, 1856[25]

1860

- Democratic Party Platform (national)[26]
- Speech by Stephen Douglas on the Admission of Kansas Under the Wyandott Constitution, February 29, 1860 (D)[27]
- Republican Party Platform[28]
- Cooper Union speech by Abraham Lincoln (R)
- Democratic Party Platform (southern)[29]
- Acceptance Letter of John C. Breckinridge[30]
- Constitutional Union Platform[31]
- Acceptance Letter of John Bell[32]

1864

- Democratic Party Platform[33]
- Acceptance Letter by General George McClellan, September 8, 1864[34]
- Republican (Union) Party Platform[35]
- Address by Francis Lieber, New York, April 11, 1863 (R)[36]

1868

- Democratic Party Platform[37]
- Acceptance Letter of Ex-Governor Horatio Seymour, August 4, 1868[38]
- Republican Party Platform[39]
- Speech by Carl Schurz, Chicago, May 20, 1868[40]

1872

- Democratic Party Platform[41]
- Liberal Republican Party Platform[42]
- Acceptance Letter from Horace Greeley to the Liberal Republicans, May 20, 1872[43]
- Acceptance Letter from Horace Greeley to the Democrats, July 18, 1872[44]
- Republican Party Platform[45]
- Speech by Senator Oliver P. Morton, Philadelphia, June 5, 1872[46]

1876

- Democratic Party Platform[47]
- Acceptance Letter of Governor Samuel J. Tilden, July 31, 1876[48]
- Republican Party Platform[49]
- Acceptance Letter of Governor Rutherford B. Hayes, July 8, 1876[50]

1880

- Democratic Party Platform[51]
- Acceptance Letter of General Winfield S. Hancock, July 29, 1880[52]
- Republican Party Platform[53]
- Acceptance Letter of General James A. Garfield, July 12, 1880[54]

1884

- Democratic Party Platform[55]
- Acceptance Letter from Grover Cleveland, August 18, 1884[56]
- Republican Party Platform[57]
- Acceptance Letter from James G. Blaine, July 15, 1884[58]

1888

- Democratic Party Platform[59]
- Acceptance Letter of President Grover Cleveland, September 8, 1888[60]
- Republican Party Platform[61]
- Acceptance Letter of Benjamin Harrison, September 11, 1888[62]

1892

- Democratic Party Platform[63]
- Acceptance Letter from Grover Cleveland, September 26, 1892[64]
- Republican Party Platform[65]
- Acceptance Letter from Benjamin Harrison, September 3, 1892[66]
- People's Party Platform[67]

- Concluding chapter from People's Party presidential candidate James B. Weaver's campaign book[68]

1896
- Democratic Party Platform[69]
- People's Party Platform[70]
- Acceptance Speech by William Jennings Bryan, August 12, 1896[71]
- Republican Party Platform[72]
- Acceptance Speech by William McKinley, August 26, 1896[73]

1900
- Democratic Party Platform[74]
- Acceptance Speech by William Jennings Bryan, August 8, 1900[75]
- Republican Party Platform[76]
- Acceptance Speech by William McKinley, July 12, 1900[77]

1904
- Democratic Party Platform[78]
- Acceptance Letter by Alton B. Parker, August 10, 1904[79]
- Republican Party Platform[80]
- Acceptance Letter by Theodore Roosevelt, September 12, 1904[81]

1908
- Democratic Party Platform[82]
- Acceptance Speech by William Jennings Bryan, August 12, 1908[83]
- Republican Party Platform[84]
- Acceptance Speech by William Howard Taft, July 28, 1908[85]

1912
- Democratic Party Platform[86]
- Acceptance Speech by Woodrow Wilson, August 7, 1912[87]
- Republican Party Platform[88]
- Acceptance Speech by William Howard Taft, August 2, 1912[89]
- Progressive Party Platform[90]
- "Confession of Faith" Speech by Theodore Roosevelt, August 6, 1912[91]
- Socialist Party Platform[92]
- Acceptance Letter of Eugene V. Debs, August 26, 1912[93]

1916
- Democratic Party Platform[94]
- Acceptance Speech by President Woodrow Wilson, September 2, 1916[95]

- Republican Party Platform[96]
- Acceptance Speech by Charles Evans Hughes, July 31, 1916[97]

1920

- Democratic Party Platform[98]
- Acceptance Speech by James M. Cox, August 7, 1920[99]
- Republican Party Platform[10]
- Acceptance Speech by Warren G. Harding, July 22, 1920[101]

1924

- Democratic Party Platform[102]
- Acceptance Speech of John W. Davis, August 11, 1924[103]
- Republican Party Platform[104]
- Acceptance Speech by Calvin Coolidge, August 14, 1924[105]
- Progressive Party (La Follette) Platform[106]
- Speech by Robert La Follette, September 18, 1924[107]

1928

- Democratic Party Platform[108]
- Acceptance Speech by Alfred Smith, August 22, 1928[109]
- Republican Party Platform[110]
- Acceptance Speech by Herbert Hoover, August 11, 1928[111]

1932

- Democratic Party Platform[112]
- Acceptance Speech by Franklin D. Roosevelt, July 2, 1932[113]
- Republican Party Platform[114]
- Acceptance Speech by Herbert Hoover, August 11, 1932[115]

1936

- Democratic Party Platform[116]
- Acceptance Speech by Franklin D. Roosevelt[117]
- Republican Party Platform[118]
- Acceptance Speech by Alfred Landon[119]

1940

- Democratic Party Platform[120]
- Acceptance Speech by Franklin D. Roosevelt[121]
- Republican Party Platform[122]
- Acceptance Speech by Wendell Willkie[123]

1944

- Democratic Party Platform[124]
- Acceptance Speech by Franklin D. Roosevelt[125]
- Republican Party Platform[126]
- Acceptance Speech by Thomas Dewey[127]

1948

- Democratic Party Platform[128]
- Acceptance Speech by Harry S. Truman[129]
- Republican Party Platform[130]
- Acceptance Speech by Thomas Dewey[131]

1952

- Democratic Party Platform[132]
- Acceptance Speech by Adlai Stevenson[133]
- Thirteen Democratic television advertisements[134]
- Republican Party Platform[135]
- Acceptance Speech by Dwight D. Eisenhower[136]
- Thirty-four Republican television advertisements[137]

1956

- Democratic Party Platform[138]
- Acceptance Speech by Adlai Stevenson[139]
- Eleven Democratic television advertisements[140]
- Republican Party Platform[141]
- Acceptance Speech by Dwight D. Eisenhower[142]
- Nine Republican television advertisements[143]

1960

- Democratic Party Platform[144]
- Acceptance Speech by John F. Kennedy[145]
- Ninety-nine Democratic television advertisements[146]
- Republican Party Platform[147]
- Acceptance Speech by Richard M. Nixon[148]
- Twenty-four Republican television advertisements[149]
- Four Presidential debates [150]

1964

- Democratic Party Platform[151]
- Acceptance Speech by Lyndon B. Johnson[152]

- Twenty-eight Democratic television advertisements[153]
- Republican Party Platform[154]
- Acceptance Speech by Barry M. Goldwater[155]
- Fifty Republican television advertisements[156]

1968

- Democratic Party Platform[157]
- Acceptance Speech by Hubert H. Humphrey[158]
- Thirty-four Democratic television advertisements[159]
- Republican Party Platform[160]
- Acceptance Speech by Richard M. Nixon[161]
- Twenty-eight Republican television advertisements[162]
- American Independent Party Platform[163]
- Speech by George C. Wallace, October 24, 1968[164]
- Three American Independent television advertisements[165]

1972

- Democratic Party Platform[166]
- Acceptance Speech by George McGovern[167]
- Forty Democratic television advertisements[168]
- Republican Party Platform[169]
- Acceptance Speech by Richard M. Nixon[170]
- Seventeen Republican television commercials[171]

1976

- Democratic Party Platform[172]
- Acceptance Speech by Jimmy Carter[173]
- Thirty Democratic television advertisements[174]
- Republican Party Platform[175]
- Acceptance Speech by Gerald R. Ford[176]
- Seventy-six Republican television advertisements[177]
- Three Presidential debates[178]

1980

- Democratic Party Platform[179]
- Acceptance Speech by Jimmy Carter[180]
- Eighty-nine Democratic television advertisements[181]
- Republican Party Platform[182]
- Acceptance Speech by Ronald Reagan[183]
- Twenty-four Republican television advertisements[184]

- Announcement Speech by John Anderson[185]
- John Anderson Campaign Brochure[186]
- One John Anderson television advertisement[187]
- Two Presidential debates[188]

1984

- Democratic Party Platform[189]
- Acceptance Speech by Walter Mondale[190]
- Sixty-one Democratic television advertisements[191]
- Republican Party Platform[192]
- Acceptance Speech by Ronald Reagan[193]
- Forty-eight Republican television advertisements[194]
- Two Presidential debates[195]

1988

- Democratic Party Platform[196]
- Acceptance Speech by Michael Dukakis[197]
- Forty-seven Democratic television advertisements[198]
- Republican Party Platform[199]
- Acceptance Speech by George H.W. Bush[200]
- Fifty-four Republican television advertisements[201]
- Two Presidential debates[202]

1992

- Democratic Party Platform[203]
- Acceptance Speech by Bill Clinton[204]
- Thirty-two Democratic television advertisements[205]
- Republican Party Platform[206]
- Acceptance Speech by George H. W. Bush[207]
- Twenty-three Republican television advertisements[208]
- Ross Perot campaign book[209]
- Announcement Re-Entering Presidential Race by Ross Perot, October 1, 1992[210]
- Four Ross Perot television advertisements[211]
- Three Presidential debates[212]

1996

- Democratic Party Platform[213]
- Acceptance Speech by Bill Clinton[214]
- Sixty-two Democratic television advertisements[215]

- Republican Party Platform[216]
- Acceptance Speech by Robert Dole[217]
- Thirty-six Republican television advertisements[218]
- Reform Party Platform[219]
- Acceptance Speech by Ross Perot, August 18, 1996[220]
- Two Presidential debates[221]

2000

- Democratic Party Platform[222]
- Acceptance Speech by Al Gore[223]
- Thirty-one Democratic television advertisements[224]
- Republican Party Platform[225]
- Acceptance Speech by George W. Bush[226]
- Thirty Republican television advertisements[227]
- Three Presidential debates[228]

2004

- Democratic Party Platform[229]
- Acceptance Speech by John Kerry[230]
- Seventy-five Democratic television advertisements[231]
- Republican Party Platform[232]
- Acceptance Speech by George W. Bush[233]
- Fifty Republican television advertisements[234]
- Three Presidential debates[235]

Governing Documents

Presidential Inaugural Addresses, 1841–2005

- www.yale.edu/lawweb/avalon/presiden/inaug

Presidential State of the Union Messages, 1841–2006

- www.presidency.ucsb.edu/ws

These documents are also available in the Public Papers of the President published by the Government Printing Office.

APPENDIX C

~

Data Tables

Table C1. Consistency and depth of categories of constitutional rhetoric by mode of campaign communication, 1952–2004

	Platforms	Messages	Ads	Debates[1]
High consistency/ deep	IR FED R	IR	IR CA	IR
High consistency/ shallow	CA APP EXEC ENF SCD JP SOP R CONSOV R EP R FED D PERF R	FED R		FED APP ENF D SCD D EXEC R
Low consistency/ deep		APP EXEC R PERF R MODE R JP D CONSOV PERF R CA	APP EXEC PERF SCD R JP D CONSOV PERF FED R	
Low consistency/ shallow	IMP VETO MODE SOP D EP D CONSOV D PERF D	IMP VETO FED D SOP EP JP R CONSOV PERF D ENF SCD EXEC D	IMP VETO MODE SOP EP JP R FED D CA ENF SCD D	IMP VETO MODE SOP EP JP CONSOV PERF ENF R SCD R EXEC D

1. Measured by year, not by debate

Table C2.　Constitutional exchanges in major party platforms, 1844–2004

Year	Category	Policy/ performance	Subject
1844	EXEC	Policy	Presidential veto reform
1852	EP	Policy	Internal improvements
1856	EP/FED	Policy	Slavery in Western territories
1856	EP	Policy	Internal improvements
1860	SCD/EP/FED/IR	Policy	*Dred Scott*
1864	EXEC	Performance	Executive abuse occurred?
1868	IMP	Policy	Johnson impeachment
1868	EXEC	Performance	Executive or congressional abuse?
1904	EP	Policy	Protective tariff
1920	CONSOV	Performance	League of Nations & sovereignty?
1920	IR	Performance	Freedom of speech threat?
1928	CA/ENF	Performance	Prohibition enforcement?
1932	CA/ENF	Policy	Retention of Prohibition
1936	EP/FED	Policy	Power of federal govt. vs. states
1940	FED	Policy	Relief returned to states
1952	FED	Policy	Federal aid to education
1952	FED	Performance	New Deal helped or hurt fed.?
1964	FED	Performance	Great Society helped or hurt fed.?
1964	FED	Performance	Fed. education $ controls schools?
1968	CA/IR	Policy	Eighteen-year-old vote
1972	SCD/JP/IR/CA	Policy	Forced busing
1972	EXEC	Performance	Too much executive secrecy?
1972	IR/ENF	Performance	Enough civil rights enforcement?
1976	IR/SCD/CA	Policy	Abortion
1976	SCD/JP/IR	Policy	Forced busing
1976	FED	Policy	State right-to-work option
1976	SOP	Performance	Congress in foreign policy?
1980	CA	Policy	Balanced budget amendment

Table C2. *(Continued)*

Year	Category	Policy/ performance	Subject
1980	SCD/IR/CA/APP	Policy	Abortion
1980	FED	Policy	Welfare returned to states
1980	IR	Policy	Affirmative action
1980	CA/IR	Policy	Equal Rights Amendment
1980	IR/JP	Policy	Forced busing
1984	CA	Policy	Balanced budget amendment
1984	IR	Policy	Affirmative action
1984	JP	Policy	Court-stripping
1984	SCD/IR/CA/APP	Policy	Abortion
1984	APP	Performance	Reagan appointees good or bad?
1984	FED	Performance	Reagan helped states?
1984	IR/ENF	Performance	Reagan civil rights okay?
1988	IR/CA/APP	Policy	Abortion
1988	IR	Policy	Affirmative action
1992	SCD/IR/CA/APP	Policy	Abortion
1992	IR	Policy	Affirmative action
1992	IR/ENF	Performance	Enough civil rights enforcement?
1996	SCD/IR/CA/APP	Policy	Abortion
1996	IR	Policy	Affirmative action
1996	FED	Performance	Clinton good for states?
1996	APP	Performance	Clinton appointees good or bad?
2000	SCD/IR/CA/APP	Policy	Abortion
2000	IR	Policy	Affirmative action
2000	JP	Policy	Court-stripping
2000	CA	Policy	D.C. statehood
2004	SCD/IR/CA/APP	Policy	Abortion
2004	CA	Policy	Federal marriage amendment
2004	CA	Policy	D.C. statehood
2004	IR	Policy	Affirmative action
2004	IR	Performance	Bush civil liberties okay?
2004	IR/ENF	Performance	Bush civil rights okay?
2004	APP	Performance	Bush appointees good or bad?

Table C3. Constitutional exchanges in candidate messages, 1840–2004

Year	Category	Policy/ performance	Subject
1840	EP	Policy	Constitutionality of the national bank
1852	CA/EP	Policy	Naturalization rules
1860	MODE	Performance	South interpreting the Constitution strictly?
1860	IR	Policy	Right to carry slaves into territories
1860	FED	Policy	Power of the federal government to regulate slavery in the territories
1860	SCD	Policy	Dred Scott decision
1868	SOP/EXEC	Performance	Struggles between executive and Congress
1872	FED	Policy	States' rights under Reconstruction
1872	EXEC	Performance	Executive powers under Reconstruction
1904	EXEC	Performance	Abuse of executive powers
	EP	Policy	Constitutionality of protective tariff
1904	IP	Performance	Application of Fourteenth Amendment to Philippines
1908	CA	Policy	Direct election of senators
1920	CONSOV	Performance	League of Nations
1920	SOP	Performance	Senate-president relations on treaty ratification
1920	IR	Performance	Civil liberties and wartime rules
1924	CONSOV	Performance	League of Nations
1932	FED	Policy	State and federal role in relief
1936	PERF	Performance	Restoration/preservation of constitutional government
1992	IR	Policy	Abortion
2000	IR	Policy	Abortion
2004	CA	Policy	Federal marriage amendment

Table C4. Constitutional exchanges in television advertising, 1952–2004

Year	Category	Policy or performance	Subject
1960	IR	Performance	Civil rights progress?
1964	IR	Policy	Civil rights
1972	SCD/IR	Policy	Forced busing
1972	JP	Policy	Court-stripping
2004	CONSOV	Performance	Kerry pro-sovereignty?

Table C5. Constitutional exchanges in presidential debates, 1960–2004

Year/debate	Category	Policy or performance	Subject
1960/1	FED	Policy	Federal aid to education
1960/3	IR	Performance	Eisenhower strong on civil rights?
1960/3	IR	Performance	Eisenhower strong on civil rights?
1976/1	IR	Performance	Ford controlling wiretapping?
1976/1	EXEC	Policy	Federal independence
1976/3	FED	Performance	Revenue-sharing getting to cities?
1976/3	IR/ENF	Performance	Voting Rights Act enforced?
1976/3	CA	Policy	Various proposed amendments
1976/3	APP/IR/SCD	Policy	Court appointments and Warren Court/Burger Court decisions
1980/1	IR	Policy	Abortion/church-state relations
1980/2	CA/IR	Policy	Equal Rights Amendment
1984/1	IR/APP/CA	Policy	Church-state relations/court appointments/school prayer amendment
1984/1	IR/APP	Policy	Abortion/court appointments
1988/1	IR	Policy	Abortion
1988/2	IR	Policy	Abortion
1988/2	APP	Policy	Court appointments
1988/2	APP	Policy	Court appointments
1992/2	CA	Policy	Term limits amendment
1996/1	FED	Performance	Clinton for federalism?
1996/1	EXEC	Performance	Clinton abusing pardons?
1996/2	IR	Policy	Affirmative action/quotas
1996/2	IR	Performance	Church-state: Clinton for free expression?
2000/1	FED	Performance	Gore for local control of education?
2000/1	IR/APP/SCD	Policy	Abortion/court appointments/*Roe v. Wade*
2000/1	IR/APP/SCD	Policy	Abortion/court appointments/*Roe v. Wade*
2000/3	FED	Policy	Local control of education
2000/3	IR	Policy	Affirmative action/quotas
2004/1	CONSOV	Performance	Kerry pro-sovereignty?
2004/2	IR	Performance	PATRIOT Act violates rights?
2004/2	APP	Policy	Court appointments
2004/2	IR	Policy	Abortion
2004/3	CA	Policy	Federal marriage amendment
2004/3	IR	Policy	Abortion
2004/3	APP	Policy	Court appointments
2004/3	CONSOV	Performance	Kerry pro-sovereignty?
2004/3	IR	Policy	Affirmative action/quotas
2004/3	FED	Performance	DOMA protects state rights?

Table C6. Questions asked in debates, 1960–2004

Year	Questions	Const. questions (%)	Subjects
1960	43	3 (7.0)	Local financing of schools (FED) Civil rights x2 (IR)
1976	62	5 (8.1)	Executive intelligence discretion (EXEC) Civil rights & desegregation (IR) Supreme Court decisions and appointments (IR/SCD/APP) Proposed constitutional amendments (CA) Supreme Court appointments (APP)
1980	36	2 (5.6)	Church-state relations x2 (IR)
1984	63	5 (8.0)	Abortion & judges x2 (IR/APP) Abortion x2 (IR) Immigration and rights of citizenship (IR)
1988	44	6 (13.6)	American Civil Liberties Union (IR) Abortion x2 (IR) Abortion & judges (IR/APP/CA) Presidential succession (EXEC) Supreme Court appointments (APP)
1992	49	2 (4.1)	Right to bear arms (IR) Term limits (CA)
1996	42	2 (4.8)	Affirmative action (IR) Equality under law (IR)
2000	96	4 (4.2)	Supreme Court appointments x2 (APP) Supreme Court appointments & abortion (APP/IR) Affirmative action (IR)
2004	63	6 (9.5)	PATRIOT Act (IR) Supreme Court appointments (APP) Abortion x2 (IR) Abortion & *Roe v. Wade* (IR/SCD) Affirmative action (IR)

1. Measured by year, not by debate

Table C7.   Consistency and depth of categories of constitutional rhetoric in governing communications

	Inaugural addresses	State of the Union
Consistent/deep	IR PERF D	IR FED R
Consistent/shallow		EP R EXEC R
Inconsistent/deep	FED EXEC SOP D EP D ENF R PERF R	APP CA D EP D
Inconsistent/shallow	CA VETO IMP SCD JP MODE CONSOV APP ENF D EP R SOP R	CA R VETO IMP SCD JP MODE CONSOV ENF SOP PERF FED D EXEC D

~

Notes

Introduction

1. Keith E. Whittington, *Constitutional Construction: Divided Powers and Constitutional Meaning* (Cambridge, Mass.: Harvard University Press, 1999); Neal Devins and Keith E. Whittington, eds., *Congress and the Constitution* (Durham, N.C.: Duke University Press, 2005); Louis Fisher, *Constitutional Conflicts Between Congress and the President* (Princeton, N.J.: Princeton University Press, 1985); J. Mitchell Pickerill, *Constitutional Deliberation in Congress: The Impact of Judicial Review in a Separated System* (Durham, N.C.: Duke University Press, 2004); David P. Currie, *The Constitution in Congress: The Federalist Period, 1789–1801* (Chicago: University of Chicago Press, 1997); Bruce G. Peabody, "Congressional Attitudes toward Constitutional Interpretation," in Neal Devins and Keith E. Whittington, eds., *Congress and the Constitution* (Durham: Duke University Press, 2005), 39–63; Susan R. Burgess, *Contest for Constitutional Authority: The Abortion and War Powers Debates* (Lawrence: University Press of Kansas, 1992); John J. Dinan, *Keeping the People's Liberties: Legislators, Citizens, and Judges as Keepers of Rights* (Lawrence: University of Kansas, 1998); John Dinan, "The U.S. Congress and the Protection of Rights," (paper presented at the International Conference on Legislatures and the Protection of Human Rights, Centre for Comparative Constitutional Studies, Melbourne, Australia, July 20–22, 2006).

2. Whittington, *Constitutional Construction*, 1.

3. Sidney M. Milkis, *Political Parties and Constitutional Government: Remaking American Democracy* (Baltimore: Johns Hopkins University Press, 1999), 173.

4. John Gerring, *Party Ideologies in America, 1828–1996* (New York: Cambridge University Press, 1998), 13.

5. For example, see especially Roger M. Barrus, John H. Eastby, Joseph H. Lane Jr., David E. Marion, and James Pontuso, who argue that Americans are losing sight of the need for constitutional limits and restraints, a failure that is steadily seeping into the conduct of government. *The Deconstitutionalization of America: The Forgotten Frailties of Democratic Rule* (Lanham, Md.: Lexington Books, 2004).

6. Senator George C. Vest of Missouri, quoted by Edward Campbell Mason, *The Veto Power: Its Origin, Development & Function in the Government of the United States* (Boston: Ginn & Co., 1890), 130–131.

7. See Barrus et al., *The Deconstitutionalization of America*, 50–66; Harvey C. Mansfield, Jr., "Political Parties and American Constitutionalism," in Peter W. Schramm and Bradford P. Wilson, eds., *American Political Parties and Constitutional Politics* (Lanham, Md.: Rowman & Littlefield Publishers, 1992), esp. 10–11.

8. Max Lerner, "Constitution and Court as Symbols," *The Yale Law Journal* 46, no. 8 (June 1937):1313.

9. Stephen M. Griffin, "Constitutionalism in the United States: From Theory to Politics," *Oxford Journal of Legal Studies* 10, no. 2 (1990), 215.

10. Harvey C. Mansfield, Jr., "Our Constitution Then and Now," in Adolph H. Grundman, ed., *The Embattled Constitution: Vital Framework or Convenient Symbol* (Malabar, Fla.: Krieger, 1986), 152–153.

11. Charles Kesler, "Political Parties, the Constitution, and the Future," Peter W. Schramm and Bradford P. Wilson, eds., *American Political Parties and Constitutional Politics* (Lanham, Md.: Rowman & Littlefield Publishers, 1992), 231–232.

12. Sanford Levinson, "'The Constitution' in American Civil Religion," *The Supreme Court Review* 1979 (1979): 151.

13. Gerring, *Party Ideologies in America*; Gerald C. Pomper, "'If Elected, I Promise': American Party Platforms," *Midwest Journal of Political Science* 11, no. 3 (August, 1967), 318–52; J. Zvi Namenswirth and Harold Lasswell, *The Changing Language of American Values: A Computer Study of Selected Party Platforms* (Beverly Hills, Calif.: Sage Publications, 1970); Kathleen Kendall, ed., *Presidential Campaign Discourse: Strategic Communication Problems* (Albany: State University of New York Press, 1995).

14. Peter W. Schramm and Bradford P. Wilson, eds., *American Political Parties and Constitutional Politics* (Lanham, Md.: Rowman & Littlefield Publishers, 1992).

15. Donald Grier Stephenson, Jr., *Campaigns and the Court: The U.S. Supreme Court in U.S. Elections* (New York: Columbia University Press, 1999).

16. See David Adamany, "Legitimacy, Realigning Elections, and the Supreme Court," *Wisconsin Law Review* 3 (1973): 790-846; Richard Funston, "The Supreme Court and Critical Elections," *American Political Science Review* 69, no. 3 (1975): 795; Alan F. Westin, "The Supreme Court, the Populist Movement, and the Campaign of 1896," *Journal of Politics* 15, no. 1 (1953): 3–41; John B. Gates, *The Supreme Court and Partisan Realignment: A Macro- and Microlevel Perspective* (Boulder, Colo.: Westview Press, 1992).

17. William Raymond Smith, *The Rhetoric of American Politics: A Study of Documents* (Westport, Conn.: Greenwood Press, 1969), 423.

18. Jeffrey K. Tulis, *The Rhetorical Presidency* (Princeton, N.J.: Princeton University Press, 1987), 13–14.

19. Milkis, *Political Parties and Constitutional Government*, 186.

20. James L. Sundquist, *Dynamics of the Party System* rev. ed. (Washington, D.C.: Brookings Institution, 1983).

21. David Mayhew, *Electoral Realignment: A Critique of an American Genre* (New Haven, Conn.: Yale University Press, 2002).

22. In general, see Philip E. Converse, "Information Flow and the Stability of Partisan Attitudes," *Public Opinion Quarterly* 26, no. 4 (Winter 1962): 578–599. Some scholars claim television advertisements hold the key to voter learning, for example, Thomas E. Patterson and

Robert D. McLure, *The Unseeing Eye: The Myth of Television Power in National Elections* (New York: Putnam, 1976), while others hold that television news outperforms ads in that respect, for example, Xinshu Zhao and Steven H. Chaffee, "Campaign Advertisements versus Television News as Sources of Political Issue Information," *Public Opinion Quarterly* 59, no. 1 (Spring 1995): 41–65. Likewise, there is a lively debate over whether citizens with high, moderate, or low levels of prior information make the greatest information gains. Some argue that the type of voter who makes the greatest information gain will vary depending on the complexity of the issue discussed in the campaign, and the duration and intensity of the discussion. See Richard Nadeau et al., "Election Campaigns as Information Campaigns: Who Learns What and With What Effect?" Canadian Election Study, Publications—Election 1997. Available at www.ces .eec.umontreal.ca/documents/InformationCampaigns.pdf; Phillip J. Tichenor, George A. Donohue, and Clarice N. Olien, "Mass Media Flow and Differential Growth in Knowledge," *Public Opinion Quarterly* 34, no. 2 (Summer 1970): 159–170; David W. Moore, "Political Campaigns and the Knowledge-Gap Hypothesis," *Public Opinion Quarterly* 51, no. 2 (Summer 1987): 186–200; Thomas A. Kazee, "Television Exposure and Attitude Change," *Public Opinion Quarterly* 45 (Winter 1981): 507–518. Some have argued that voters with higher levels of anxiety or enthusiasm receive more campaign information than those without; George E. Marcus and Michael B. MacKuen, "Anxiety, Enthusiasm, and the Vote: The Emotional Underpinnings of Learning and Involvement in Presidential Campaigns," *American Political Science Review* 87 (1993): 672–685.

23. Michael X. Delli Carpini and Scott Keeter, *What Americans Know About Politics and Why It Matters* (New Haven, Conn.: Yale University Press, 1996), 131.

24. Delli Carpini and Keeter, *What Americans Know About Politics and Why It Matters*, esp. 182–183, 220–224.

25. Lerner, "Constitution and Court as Symbols," 1299, *passim*; Corwin, "The Constitution as Instrument and as Symbol," *American Political Science Review* 30, no. 6 (December 1936):1071–1085; Charles Black, *The People and the Court* (New York: Macmillan, 1960); Sanford Levinson, *Constitutional Faith* (Princeton, N.J.: Princeton University Press, 1988), esp. 10–15; Michael Kammen, *A Machine That Would Go of Itself: The Constitution in American Culture* (New York: Alfred A. Knopf, 1987).

26. Lerner, "Constitution and Court as Symbols," 1294.

27. Keith Whittington carries on some discussion of explicit versus implicit conversation regarding the Constitution, saying, "Explicit discussions of the constitutional text and the use of familiar tools of analysis help distinguish efforts at constitutional interpretation from the mass of political activity. . . . Nonetheless, not all constitutional activity in the United States deals so explicitly and obsessively with the terms of the document itself." *Constitutional Construction*, 9.

28. Tulis, *The Rhetorical Presidency*, 191.

Chapter 1: The Constitution and Electoral Politics

1. See the decisions in *Cooper v. Aaron*, 358 U.S. 1, 18 (1958); *Powell v. McCormack*, 395 U.S. 486, 521 (1969); *United States v. Nixon*, 418 U.S. 683, 704 (1974).

2. Max Lerner, "Constitution and Court as Symbols," *The Yale Law Journal* 46, no. 8 (June 1937), 1303. See also Edward S. Corwin, "The Constitution as an Instrument and as a Symbol," *American Political Science Review* 30, no. 6 (December 1936): esp. 1079–1085; Michael

Kammen, A Machine That Would Go of Itself: The Constitution in American Culture (New York: Alfred A. Knopf, 1987), 8–9.

3. Cited in Charles Warren, Congress, the Constitution, and the Supreme Court (Boston: Little, Brown, 1935), 41.

4. U.S. Constitution, Article III, Section 2.

5. See Warren, 14–15.

6. See Leonard W. Levy, "Judicial Review, History, and Democracy," in Leonard W. Levy, ed., Judicial Review and the Supreme Court (New York: Harper Torchbooks, 1967), 10.

7. Hamilton, Federalist 78.

8. Michael J. Klarman, "How Great Were the 'Great' Marshall Court Decisions?" Virginia Law Review 87, no. 6 (October 2001): 1113–1126.

9. In McCullough v. Maryland, 17 U.S. 316, (1819) the Supreme Court overturned a Maryland statute levying state taxes on federal property, with Chief Justice Marshall famously declaring that "the power to tax is the power to destroy." In Martin v. Hunter's Lessee, 14 U.S. 304, (1816), the Court forcefully asserted the Supremacy Clause by reversing a Virginia state court ruling as contrary to U.S.-British treaties. In Cohens v. Virginia (19 U.S. 264, 1821) the Supreme Court issued a ringing defense of its right to strike down state legislation as well as state judicial decisions, saying "[The Judicial Department] is authorized to decide all cases of every description arising under the Constitution or laws of the United States. From this general grant of jurisdiction, no exception is made of those cases in which a state may be a party."

10. For early examples of this view, see Donald Morgan's chapter on the Bituminous Coal Conservation Act of 1935. Congress and the Constitution (Cambridge, Mass.: Harvard University Press, 1966), 163–183.

11. This is, for instance, Michael A. Bamberger's position in Reckless Legislation: How Lawmakers Ignore the Constitution (New Brunswick, N.J.: Rutgers University Press, 2000).

12. For a discussion of constitutional interpretation by the elected branches in the years from 1789 to 1801, see David P. Currie, The Constitution in Congress: The Federalist Period, 1789–1801 (Chicago: University of Chicago Press, 1997).

13. David P. Currie, "Prolegomena for a Sampler: Extrajudicial Interpretation of the Constitution, 1789–1861," in Neal Devins and Keith E. Whittington, eds., Congress and the Constitution (Durham, N.C.: Duke University Press, 2005), 19–20.

14. See Susan R. Burgess, Contest for Constitutional Authority: The Abortion and War Powers Debates (Lawrence: University of Kansas, 1992).

15. Legal scholar Sanford Levinson presents an extended case for what he calls judicial "protestantism"— that is, refusal to accede to the Supreme Court's constitutional supremacy and infallibility—in "'The Constitution' in American Civil Religion," The Supreme Court Review 1979 (1979): 137–148.

16. U.S. Constitution, Article II, Section 1.

17. http://bensguide.gpo.gov/3-5/symbols/oaths.html

18. "President Jackson's Veto Message Regarding the Bank of the United States; July 10, 1832." The Avalon Project at Yale Law School at www.yale.edu/lawweb/avalon/presiden/veto/veto/ajveto01.htm (accessed April 13, 2006).

19. "James Madison to Thomas Jefferson, October 17, 1788," in Michael Kammen, ed., The Origins of the American Constitution: A Documentary History (New York: Penguin Books, 1986), 370.

20. [Roger Sherman], "A Citizen of New Haven," in Colleen A. Sheehan and Gary L. McDowell, eds., Friends of the Constitution: Writings of the "Other" Federalists, 1787–1788 (Indianapolis, Ind.: Liberty Fund, 1998), 265.

21. "James Wilson, Speech, State House, 6 October 1787, Pennsylvania Packet, 10 October 1787," in Colleen A. Sheehan and Gary L. McDowell, eds., *Friends of the Constitution: Writings of the "Other" Federalists, 1787–1788* (Indianapolis, Ind.: Liberty Fund, 1998), 104.

22. Ralph Ketcham, ed., *The Anti-Federalist Papers and the Constitutional Convention Debates*, reissue ed. (New York: Mentor Books, 1996), Brutus XI, 295, Brutus XV, 305.

23. Those states were Rhode Island, Massachusetts, New York, New Hampshire, and Vermont. Massachusetts and New Hampshire went on to argue that the Alien and Sedition Acts were constitutional and necessary in any event. Another two state legislatures—Delaware and Connecticut—passed resolutions expressing disapproval of the Virginia resolution without explicitly asserting the supremacy of the judiciary. For this entire debate, see Jonathan Elliot, *The Debates in the Several State Conventions on the Adoption of the Federal Constitution Vol. IV*, 2nd edition (Washington, D.C.: U.S. Congress, 1836), 528–580. Page images are available at American Memory, U.S. Congressional Documents and Debates, 1774–1875, at memory.loc.gov/ammem/amlaw/lwed.html.

24. "The Kentucky Resolutions," in Merrill D. Peterson, ed., *The Portable Thomas Jefferson* (New York: The Viking Press, 1975), 281–289.

25. "The Virginia Report," in Marvin Meyers, ed., *The Mind of the Founder: Sources of the Political Thought of James Madison* (Hanover, N.H.: University Press of New England, 1981), 231–273.

26. For an extended discussion of the resolve and replies by other state legislatures, see Herman V. Ames, *State Documents on Federal Relations: The States and the United States* (Philadelphia: Univ. of Pennsylvania, 1911), starting at p. 93, at www.constitution.org/hames/sdfr.htm (accessed January 18, 2007).

27. "Inaugural Address of Abraham Lincoln, March 4, 1861," www.yale.edu/lawweb/avalon/presiden/inaug/lincoln1.htm, 6.

28. For a scholarly but spirited delineation of the antirepublican character of the doctrine of judicialism, see Larry D. Kramer, *The People Themselves: Popular Constitutionalism and Judicial Review* (New York: Oxford University Press, 2004).

29. James Madison, *Federalist 51*, in Clinton Rossiter, ed., *The Federalist Papers* (New York: New American Library, 1960), 322.

30. See Louis Fisher, "Congressional Checks on the Judiciary," in Colton C. Campbell and John F. Stack Jr., eds., *Congress Confronts the Court: The Struggle for Legitimacy and Authority in Lawmaking* (Lanham, Md.: Rowman & Littlefield, 2001), 22.

31. For a good examination of this issue, see Louis Fisher, *Constitutional Dialogues: Interpretation as Political Process* (Princeton, N.J.: Princeton University Press, 1988); Louis Fisher, *Congress Confronts the Court: The Struggle for Legitimacy and Authority in Lawmaking* (Lanham, Md.: Rowman and Littlefield, 2001).

32. See Michael J. Gerhardt, "The Federal Appointments Process as Constitutional Interpretation," in Neal Devins and Keith E. Whittington, eds., *Congress and the Constitution* (Durham, N.C.: Duke University Press, 2005), 110–130.

33. John J. Dinan, *Keeping the People's Liberties: Legislators, Citizens, and Judges as Keepers of Rights* (Lawrence: University of Kansas, 1998).

34. This conclusion can be adduced from several pieces of evidence. First, at the Federal Convention of 1787, two major plans were proposed which would have given Congress plenary power to legislate in all areas it deemed of national importance—the Virginia Plan and the Hamilton Plan. The convention declined to endorse either of those plans, opting for a specific enumeration of powers instead. Second, as with judicialism, it was only the opponents of the

Constitution who argued it could legitimately be read in so expansive a manner. In the ratification debate, the friends of the Constitution vehemently denied any such thing, reiterating that the proposed Constitution was a grant of specific powers that left most powers in the hands of the states. Third, the proponents of limited government have logic on their side in this question. Had the convention meant to make the general welfare clause a plenary grant of power to Congress, the enumeration of powers would have been superfluous. Fourth, the nature of the debate over a bill of rights in the ratification struggle is itself evidence against the modern interpretation. According to *Federalist* 84, enumeration of powers and governmental structure were more central than a bill of rights to the idea of limited constitutional government in America, and made a bill of rights both unnecessary and dangerous. Finally, it is notable that the interpretation advanced by the Kentucky and Virginia Resolutions and by Jefferson's Report on the Constitutionality of a National Bank—that the federal government was a strictly limited government of enumerated powers with the mass of powers retained by the states—was ratified by the nation in the eventual electoral annihilation of the Federalists by the Jeffersonians over the course of several elections.

35. Stephen M. Griffin, "Constitutionalism in the United States: From Theory to Politics," *Oxford Journal of Legal Studies* 10, no. 2 (1990): 214.

36. Quoted by Currie, "Prolegomena for a Sampler," in Neal Devins and Keith E. Whittington, eds., *Congress and the Constitution* (Durham, N.C.: Duke University Press, 2005), 20.

37. Louis Fisher and Neal Devins, *Political Dynamics of Constitutional Law* 3rd ed. (St. Paul, Minn.: West Group, 2001), 46.

38. J. Mitchell Pickerill, "Congressional Responses to Judicial Review," Neal Devins and Keith E. Whittington, eds., *Congress and the Constitution* (Durham, N.C.: Duke University Press, 2005); J. Mitchell Pickerill, *Constitutional Deliberation in Congress: The Impact of Judicial Review in a Separated System* (Durham, N.C.: Duke University Press, 2004).

39. The original study on this was conducted in 1958 by Donald Morgan, who received 203 responses in *Congress and the Constitution*. The most successful recent repetition of Morgan's survey was done by Bruce G. Peabody, who received eighty responses, in "Congressional Attitudes Toward Constitutional Interpretation," Neal Devins and Keith E. Whittington, eds., *Congress and the Constitution* (Durham, N.C.: Duke University Press, 2005). Two other attempts to replicate Morgan's survey were less successful: Bamberger, *Reckless Legislation*, and Andrew E. Busch and Christopher McLemore, "The Constitution and Members of Congress," (paper prepared for the annual meeting of the Midwest Political Science Association, Chicago, Illinois, April 2003). These attempts garnered twelve and twenty responses, respectively.

40. See Edward Campbell Mason, *The Veto Power: Its Origin, Development, and Function in the Government of the United States* (Boston: Ginn & Co., 1890), 129–131; Katherine A. Towle, "The Presidential Veto Since 1889," *American Political Science Review* 31, no. 1 (February 1937): 51–56; Charles L. Black, "Some Thoughts on the Veto," *Law and Contemporary Problems* 40 (Spring 1976): 87–101; Richard A. Watson, *Presidential Vetoes and Public Policy* (Lawrence: University Press of Kansas, 1993), esp. 139.

41. For example, the president's role as "legislative leader" is anchored in his duty to "from time to time give the Congress Information of the state of the Union" and his right to "recommend to their Consideration such Measures as he shall judge necessary and expedient." Today, presidents use those clauses to justify an annual State of the Union address, which is usually a pitch for the president's comprehensive legislative program.

42. Whittington, *Constitutional Construction*, 225.

43. See, among many available sources, Louis Fisher, *Constitutional Conflicts between Congress and the President* (Princeton, N.J.: Princeton University Press, 1985).

44. Max Lerner, "Constitution and Court as Symbols," *The Yale Law Journal* 46, no. 8 (June 1937): 1297.

45. Donald Bruce Johnson and Kirk H. Porter, *National Party Platforms 1840–1972* (Urbana: University of Illinois Press, 1973), 2. (See list of coded documents in appendix B.)

Chapter 2: The Constitution in the Party Platforms

1. See Paul T. David, Ralph M. Goldman, and Richard C. Bain, *The Politics of National Party Conventions* (Washington, D.C.: Brookings Institution, 1960), 29.

2. L. Sandy Maisel, "The Platform-Writing Process: Candidate-Centered Platforms in 1992," *Political Science Quarterly* 108, no. 4 (1993): 676.

3. Of course, it bears noting that rhetoric, if well executed, is never "mere," a point made by both Aristotle and communications experts today.

4. Gerald C. Pomper, "'If Elected, I Promise': American Party Platforms," *Midwest Journal of Political Science* 11, no. 3 (August, 1967): 318–52.

5. See Jeff Fishel, *Presidents & Promises* (Washington, D.C.: CQ Press, 1985).

6. Fishel, *Presidents & Promises*, 27.

7. Maisel, "The Platform Writing Process," 671.

8. Pomper, "If Elected, I Promise," 319–20.

9. For this study, the Douglas (Northern) Democrats' platform was counted as the Democratic platform in 1860, while the Breckinridge Democrats were counted as a third party. In 1840, only Democrats had a platform. Here and in future chapters, the Republican statistical category includes both Republicans since 1856 and a handful of Whig documents before 1856. When appropriate, however, the text delineates between the two.

10. Donald Bruce Johnson and Kirk H. Porter eds., *National Party Platforms, 1840–1972* (Urbana: University of Illinois Press, 1975), 1852, 18. For subsequent platform references other than Johnson and Porter, see appendix B for full bibliographic detail.

11. Johnson and Porter, 1856, 24.

12. Johnson and Porter, 1892, 89.

13. Johnson and Porter, 62, 56.

14. Johnson and Porter, 1884, 67.

15. Johnson and Porter, 1920, 229.

16. Johnson and Porter, 1920, 220.

17. Johnson and Porter, 1940, 389.

18. Johnson and Porter, 1940, 387.

19. Johnson and Porter, 1964, 683.

20. The twelve that saw more explicit than implicit references were 1936 Democratic and Republican, 1940 Republican, 1944 Democratic, 1948 Democratic and Republican, 1960 Democratic, 1976 Democratic, 1984 Republican, 1992 Democratic, 1996 Democratic, and 2000 Democratic. The two close calls were 1976 Republicans and 1988 Democrats.

21. Johnson and Porter, 1840 2; 1844 4; 1848, 11; 1852 17; 1856, 25.

22. Johnson and Porter, 1856, 27.

23. Johnson and Porter, 1876, 53, 49. A similar GOP statement is found on 1880, 61; 1884, 74.

24. Johnson and Porter, 1884, 65.

25. Johnson and Porter, 1924, 249; 1928, 270.

26. Johnson and Porter, 1928, 290–291.

27. Johnson and Porter, 1936, 365.
28. 1996 Republican platform, 11.
29. Johnson and Porter, 1960, 593.
30. Johnson and Porter, 1956, 538.
31. Johnson and Porter, 1880, 61.
32. Johnson and Porter, 1892, 87.
33. Johnson and Porter, 1916, 206.
34. Johnson and Porter, 1952, 487.
35. Johnson and Porter, 1844, 4, 9.
36. Johnson and Porter, 1864, 34–35.
37. 1984 Democratic Platform, p. 47.
38. Johnson and Porter, 1852, 20.
39. Johnson and Porter, 1840, 2.
40. Johnson and Porter, 1964, 677.
41. 1996 Republican Platform, 11, 23.
42. Johnson and Porter, 1936, 362.
43. Johnson and Porter, 1956, 526, 538.
44. Johnson and Porter, 1852, 20.
45. Johnson and Porter, 1884, 67.
46. 1980 Democratic Platform, 1.
47. 1992 Republican Platform, 23.
48. 2004 Republican Platform, 77.
49. Johnson and Porter, 1860, 31–32.
50. 1984 Republican Platform, 29.
51. 1996 Republican Platform, 14.
52. 1984 Democratic Platform, 32.
53. 1984 Democratic Platform, 32.
54. 2004 Democratic Platform, 37.
55. Johnson and Porter, 1972, 865.
56. 1996 Republican Platform, 14.
57. 1980 Republican Platform, 34.
58. Johnson and Porter, 1840, 2; 1844, 3; 1848, 10; 1852, 16; 1856, 24.
59. 1992 Republican Platform, 19.
60. 2000 Republican Platform, 29.
61. 1996 Republican Platform, 35.
62. Johnson and Porter, 1940, 394.
63. 1976 Republican Platform, 23.
64. Johnson and Porter, 1920, 231.
65. Johnson and Porter, 1920, 214.
66. Johnson and Porter, 1956, 546.
67. 2004 Republican Platform, 24.
68. 2004 Democratic Platform, 4.
69. A rough division of platforms into foreign policy and domestic policy components was performed using as foreign policy platform sections anything labeled with foreign policy/national security headings and independent sentences dealing with those issues. So-called intermestic issues (like trade or energy) were counted as foreign policy if the subject was approached predominantly from a foreign policy standpoint. Foreign policy representations were drawn every twenty year period (though the first was taken in 1844), as follows:

Year	D (%)	W/R (%)
1844	7	0
1860	8	0
1880	7	7
1900	38	29
1920	27	36
1940	18	25
1960	26	31
1980	29	35
2000	27	34

70. John Gerring, *Party Ideologies in America, 1928–1996* (Cambridge: Cambridge University Press, 1998).

71. Johnson and Porter, *National Party Platforms*, 1840, 2.

72. Because depth was defined by whether categories represented 20 percent or more of all the constitutional references in a given platform, it was not mathematically possible for more than a few categories to pass that threshold in any platform. It was mathematically possible for no categories to meet the test for depth, if the fifteen categories each had a similarly small share of the total. Because consistency was defined by whether a category achieved at least one reference in more than half of the platforms, it was theoretically possible for every category to be classified as highly consistent.

Chapter 3: The Constitution in Candidate Messages

1. Ellen Fitzpatrick, "History's Lessons," *Online NewsHour*, July 29, 2004, at www.pbs.org/newshour/bb/politics/july-dec04/historians_7-29.html (accessed November 3, 2005).

2. Kathleen Hall Jameison, *Packaging the Presidency: A History and Criticism of Presidential Campaign Advertising* 3rd ed. (New York: Oxford University Press, 1996), xxvi, 522.

3. These have included James W. Prothro, "Verbal Shifts in the American Presidency: A Content Analysis," *American Political Science Review* 50, no. 3 (September 1956): 726–739; Marshall S. Smith, Philip J. Stone, and Evelyn N. Glenn, "A Content Analysis of Twenty Presidential Nomination Acceptance Speeches," in Philip J. Stone, Dexter C. Dunphy, Marshall S. Smith, and Daniel M. Ogilvie, eds., *The General Inquirer: A Computer Approach to Content Analysis* (Cambridge, Mass.: M.I.T. Press, 1966), 359–400; Nancy L. Miller and William B. Stiles, "Verbal Familiarity in American Presidential Nomination Acceptance Speeches and Inaugural Addresses (1920–1980)," *Social Psychology Quarterly* 49, no. 1 (March 1986): 72–81.

4. "Letter of Gen. Scott in Reply," *National Intelligencer*, June 29, 1852, 3. See appendix B for full bibliographical detail of coded documents cited.

5. "Mr. Van Buren's Letter to the Committee of the Buffalo Convention," *The Clarion*, September 13, 1848, 39–40.

6. John Breckinridge's Southern Democratic nomination acceptance letter is treated in chapter 6 as a third-party document.

7. John Hope Franklin, "Election of 1868," Arthur M. Schlesinger, Jr., ed., *History of American Presidential Elections* (hereafter *HAPE*) Vol. II (New York: Chelsea House, 1971), 1286.

8. Franklin, "Election of 1868," *HAPE* Vol. II (New York: Chelsea House, 1971), 1272.

9. William Gillette, "Election of 1872," *HAPE* Vol. II (New York: Chelsea House, 1971), 1361.

10. Charles Richard Williams, *The Life of Rutherford Birchard Hayes, Nineteenth President of the United States* Vol. I (Columbus: Ohio State Archeological and Historical Society, 1928), 461–462.

11. "Governor Tilden's Letter Accepting the Nomination of the National Democratic Convention for the Presidency," John Bigelow, ed., *The Writings and Speeches of Samuel J. Tilden* Vol. II (New York: Harper & Brothers, 1885), 362.

12. "Mr. Blaine's Letter Accepting the Republican Nomination for the Presidency in 1884," in James G. Blaine, *Political Discussions, Legislative, Diplomatic, and Popular, 1856–1886* (Springfield, Mass.: Winter & Co., 1887), 434.

13. "Letter Accepting Nomination for President, Albany, N.Y., August 18, 1884," Albert Ellery Bergh, ed., *Grover Cleveland: Addresses, State Papers and Letters* (New York: Sun Dial Classics Co., 1909), 53.

14. Robert F. Wesser, "Election of 1888," *HAPE* Vol. II (New York: Chelsea House, 1971), 1694.

15. "Madison Square Garden Speech," William Jennings Bryan, *The First Battle*, 316, 319, 337.

16. "Speech of William Jennings Bryan," *Republican Campaign Text-Book 1900* (Philadelphia: Dunlap Printing, 1900), 441, 452.

17. "Speech of Acceptance of Warren G. Harding at Marion, Ohio, July 22, 1920," *Republican Campaign Text-Book 1920* (Washington, D.C.: Republican National Committee, 1920), 43.

18. "Gov. Cox Sounds Battle Summons," *The Democratic Text-Book, 1920*, 57.

19. William Allen, White, *What Its All About*. "Governor Landon's Address," 122–123, 128.

20. "Franklin Delano Roosevelt's Nomination Acceptance Speech—1936," 2.

21. "Acceptance Speech by Senator Barry Goldwater," *HAPE* IV (New York: Chelsea House, 1971), 3669.

22. "August 15, 1996, Remarks by Senator Bob Dole," 4.

23. "Acceptance Speech: Our Nation's Past and Future," 5.

24. Roy and Jeannette Nichols, "Election of 1852," *HAPE* Vol. II (New York: Chelsea House, 1971), 1001.

25. William Nisbet Chambers, "Election of 1840," *HAPE* Vol. I (New York: Chelsea House, 1971), 742–743.

26. William Gillette, "Election of 1872," *HAPE* Vol. II (New York: Chelsea House, 1971), 1357–1358.

27. "Acceptance Letter of General Winfield S. Hancock, July 29, 1880," *HAPE* II (New York: Chelsea House, 1971), 1542.

28. "Address by Francis Lieber, New York, April 11, 1863," *HAPE* II (New York: Chelsea House, 1971), 1186–1187; "Speech by Senator Oliver P. Morton, Philadelphia, June 5, 1872," *HAPE* II (New York: Chelsea House, 1971), 1361.

29. "Acceptance Letter of General James A. Garfield, July 12, 1880," *HAPE* II (New York: Chelsea House, 1971), 1535–1536.

30. "Acceptance Speech by Charles Evans Hughes," *HAPE* III (New York: Chelsea House, 1971): 2294.

31. "Speech of Acceptance of John W. Davis," 115.

32. "Governor Landon's Address," 127, 128.

33. "Dwight Eisenhower Acceptance Speech at the 1956 Republican Party Convention," 3.

34. "Acceptance Speech by Senator Barry Goldwater,", 3669–3670.

35. Chambers, "Election of 1840," 737.

36. For an assessment of the significance of the speech, see Chambers, "Election of 1840," 737. For Harrison's comment, see Chambers, 739.

37. "On Retiring to Private Life," in Calvin Colton, ed., *The Works of Henry Clay* (New York: G. P. Putnam's Sons, 1904), 377.

38. Holman Hamilton, "Election of 1848," *HAPE* vol. II (New York: Chelsea House, 1971), 913.

39. "Letter of Gen. Scott in Reply," 3.

40. R. G. Horton, *The Life and Public Services of James Buchanan* (New York: Derby & Jackson, 1856), 414–418.

41. Franklin, "Election of 1868," 1284.

42. "Speech of Acceptance of Warren G. Harding," 36.

43. "Governor Landon's Address," 126–127.

44. "Acceptance Speech by Governor Thomas E. Dewey," *HAPE* IV (New York: Chelsea House, 1971), 3053.

45. "To Joseph Gurney Cannon," 922–923.

46. "Remarks as Prepared for Delivery by Al Gore," 7.

47. "President Gerald R. Ford's Remarks," 3.

48. "In Acceptance Speech, President Bush Shares His Plan," 5.

49. "Remarks of Senator John Kerry," 8.

50. "Governor Landon's Address," 128.

51. "Cooper Union Speech," 12.

52. "Acceptance Letter of General James A. Garfield, July 12, 1880," 1537.

53. "Acceptance Letter for General James A. Garfield," 1536.

54. Elting E. Morrison, *The Letters of Theodore Roosevelt*, 928–929, 932–933.

55. "Acceptance Letter of General Winfield S. Hancock," 1542.

56. "Acceptance Speech by William Jennings Bryan, Indianapolis, August 8, 1900," *HAPE* III (New York: Chelsea House, 1971), 1947.

57. "Speech of William Jennings Bryan," *Republican Campaign Text-Book 1908*, 479.

58. John Wells Davidson, ed., *A Crossroads of Freedom: The 1912 Campaign Speeches of Woodrow Wilson*, 34.

59. "Gov. Cox Sounds Battle Summons," 58–59.

60. "Acceptance Speech by President William Howard Taft, Washington, August 2, 1912," *HAPE* III (New York: Chelsea House, 1971), 2205.

61. "Speech of Acceptance by Warren G. Harding at Marion, Ohio, July 22, 1920," 51.

62. "Acceptance Speech by President Herbert C. Hoover, Washington, August 11, 1932," *HAPE* III (New York: Chelsea House, 1971), 2794, also 2795.

63. "Governor Landon's Address," 127.

64. "Acceptance Speech by Senator Barry Goldwater, San Francisco, July 17, 1964," 3669.

65. "Acceptance Speech by Senator Barry Goldwater," 3668.

66. "Our Nation's Past and Future," 5.

67. "Address by the President to the Democratic National Convention," 13.

68. "Col. Fremont's Reply," John Bigelow, *Memoir of the Life and Public Services of John Charles Fremont* (New York: Debby & Jackson, 1856), 459.

69. "Judge Parker Accepts His Nomination," 292–293.

70. "To the Democratic Nomination Committee," 595.

71. "Acceptance Speech by President William Howard Taft," 2210, 2219.

72. "Governor Landon's Address," 129.

73. "President Franklin Delano Roosevelt," 2.

74. "Acceptance Letter of General Winfield S. Hancock, July 29, 1880," 1542.

75. "Acceptance Letter of General James A. Garfield," HAPE II (New York: Chelsea House, 1971), 1538.

76. "Gov. Cox Sounds the Battle Summons," 58.

77. "Speech of Acceptance," 29.

78. "Richard M. Nixon, Presidential Nomination Acceptance Speech, August 8, 1968," 8.

79. "Speech of Acceptance," David H. Burton, ed., The Collected Works of William Howard Taft Vol. III (Athens: Ohio University Press, 2001), 22.

80. "Address of Acceptance," Republican Text-Book 1924, 32.

81. "Hon. William McKinley's Letter of Acceptance," Lawrence F. Prescott, ed., 1896: The Great Campaign (New York: Loyal Publishing Co., 1896), 564.

82. "Madison Square Garden Speech," 319–320.

83. "Acceptance Speech by Vice President Hubert H. Humphrey," HAPE IV (New York: Chelsea House, 1971), 3845.

84. "Acceptance Speech by President Herbert C. Hoover," 2801.

85. "Governor Landon's Address," 126.

86. "Acceptance Speech by Governor Thomas E. Dewey, Chicago, June 28, 1944," HAPE IV (New York: Chelsea House, 1971), 3055.

87. "August 15, 1996, Remarks by Senator Bob Dole, Dole Accepts Nomination, San Diego, California," 10.

88. "Remarks of Senator John Kerry, 2004 Democratic National Convention, Thursday, July 29, 2004," 4.

89. "Speech of Acceptance of Warren G. Harding at Marion, Ohio, July 22, 1920," 36.

90. "Franklin D. Roosevelt in a Radio Address to the Democratic National Convention Accepting Its Nomination for President, July 19, 1940," 2.

91. "Acceptance Speech by Senator Barry Goldwater, San Francisco, July 17, 1964," 3669.

92. George H.W. Bush, "Remarks Accepting the Presidential Nomination at the Republican National Convention in Houston," 8.

93. "In Acceptance Speech, President Bush Shares His Plan for a Safer World and More Hopeful America," 5.

94. "Remarks of Senator John Kerry," 2.

95. "Speech by Minister to Britain James Buchanan, Greensburg, Pennsylvania, October 7, 1852," HAPE II (New York: Chelsea House, 1971), 999.

96. H. M. Flint, ed., Life of Stephen A. Douglas, 180.

97. The Works of Henry Clay, 363.

98. "Cooper Union Speech," 13.

99. "In Acceptance Speech, President Bush Shares His Plan," 5.

100. "General Zachary Taylor's First 'Allison Letter,'" April 22, 1848," HAPE II (New York: Chelsea House, 1971), 913.

101. Smith, Stone, and Glenn, "A Content Analysis of Twenty Presidential Nomination Acceptance Speeches," in The General Inquirer: A Computer Approach to Content Analysis (Cambridge, Mass.: M.I.T. Press, 1966), 399.

102. It should be noted here that some of the letters and speeches used in the sample were not available electronically. In those cases, an estimate had to be made of the number of words

in the document. Estimates were reached by manually counting the first five to seven column inches, determining an average number of words per column inch, and multiplying by the total number of column inches.

103. The twenty-three were Polk 1844, Scott 1852, Grant surrogate 1868, Cleveland and Harrison 1892, McKinley 1900, Wilson 1916, Roosevelt 1932, Willkie 1940, Dewey 1944 and 1948, Eisenhower and Stevenson 1952, Eisenhower 1956, Nixon 1960, Nixon and Humphrey 1968, Nixon and McGovern 1972, Reagan 1980, Bush 1988, Clinton 1992, Bush 2000.

104. Excluding perfunctory and mode, in which there is no implicit coding.

105. There were a much larger number of instances in which the candidates either agreed on a constitutional issue or, more often, expressed compatible platitudes about general constitutional principles.

Chapter 4: The Constitution in Television Advertising

1. The very first use of television to advertise presidential candidates came in 1940, but did not include short spot ads. Through 1948, viewership was limited to a handful of markets such as Washington, D.C. and New York City.

2. Kathleen Hall Jameison, *Packaging the Presidency: A History and Criticism of Presidential Campaign Advertising* 3rd ed. (New York: Oxford University Press, 1996), 517.

3. Darrell M. West, *Air Wars: Television Advertising in Election Campaigns 1952–2004* (Washington, D.C.: Congressional Quarterly Press, 2005), 2.

4. See West, *Air Wars*, 16–17; Kathleen Hall Jameison, "Context and the Creation of Meaning in the Advertising of the 1988 Presidential Campaign," *American Behavioral Scientist* 32 (1989): 415–424; Marion Just, Ann Crigler, Dean Alger, Timothy Cook, Montague Kern, and Darrell M. West, *Cross Talk: Citizens, Candidates, and the Media in a Presidential Campaign* (Chicago: University of Chicago Press, 1996).

5. Jameison, *Packaging the Presidency*, xxvi.

6. Thomas Patterson and Richard McClure, *The Unseeing Eye* (New York: Putnam's, 1976); Craig Leonard Brians and Martin P. Wattenberg, "Campaign Issue Knowledge and Salience: Comparing Reception from TV Commercials, TV News, and Newspapers," *American Journal of Political Science* 40, no. 1 (1996): 172–193.

7. Edwin Diamond and Stephen Bates, *The Spot: The Rise of Political Advertising on Television* rev. ed. (Cambridge, Mass.: MIT Press, 1984), 352.

8. For numerous demonstrations of this fact, see Harvard University Institute of Politics' book *Campaign for President: The Managers Look at 2004* (Lanham, Md.: Rowman & Littlefield, 2005), *passim*.

9. See John S. Nelson and G. R. Boynton, *Video Rhetorics: Televised Advertising in American Politics* (Urbana: University of Illinois Press, 1997).

10. West, *Air Wars*, 42.

11. Richard Joslyn, "The Content of Political Spot Ads," *Journalism Quarterly* 57 (1980): 97; C. Richard Hofstetter and Cliff Zukin, "TV Network News and Advertising in the Nixon and McGovern Campaigns," *Journalism Quarterly* 56 (1979): 106–115, 152; Patterson and McClure, *The Unseeing Eye*.

12. West, *Air Wars*, 45–65.

13. The Stanford project included transcripts for the 2000 ads; 2004 ads were available in video form on a website, and were manually transcribed.

14. "The Annenberg/Pew Archive of Presidential Campaign Rhetoric" (2000) [hereafter Annenberg/Pew]; Stevenson, 1952.

15. Annenberg/Pew, Nixon 1960.

16. All of the preceding from Annenberg/Pew, Kennedy 1960.

17. All of the preceding from the Center for Political Communication, University of Oklahoma [hereafter CPC], Goldwater 1964.

18. Annenberg/Pew, Humphrey 1968.

19. All of the preceding from Annenberg/Pew, Ford 1976.

20. All of the preceding from Annenberg/Pew, Mondale 1984.

21. Annenberg/Pew, Reagan 1984.

22. Annenberg/Pew, Clinton 1996.

23. Annenberg/Pew, Dole 1996.

24. Annenberg/Pew, Eisenhower 1956.

25. Annenberg/Pew, Ford 1976.

26. All of the preceding from Annenberg/Pew, Kennedy 1960.

27. Annenberg/Pew, Kennedy 1960.

28. Annenberg/Pew, Carter 1976.

29. Annenberg/Pew, Mondale 1984.

30. Annenberg/Pew, McGovern 1972.

31. Annenberg/Pew, McGovern 1972.

32. Stanford University, "In Their Own Words 2004" [hereafter Stanford 2004], Kerry 2004.

33. American Museum of the Moving Image [hereafter AMMI], Dukakis 1988.

34. AMMI, Ford 1976.

35. Annenberg/Pew, Reagan 1984.

36. Annenberg/Pew, Nixon 1968.

37. Annenberg/Pew, Carter 1980.

38. All of the preceding from Annenberg/Pew, Mondale 1984.

39. Annenberg/Pew, Dole 1996.

40. Stanford 2004, Kerry 2004.

41. CPC, Goldwater 1964.

42. AMMI and Stanford 2004, Bush 2004.

43. AMMI and Stanford 2004, Kerry 2004.

44. Annenberg/Pew, Kennedy 1960.

45. Annenberg/Pew, Kennedy 1960.

46. *The Spot* did provide substantial but incomplete excerpts from a handful of other ads, including a few with constitutional interest: the E. G. Marshall ad for Humphrey, and a Kennedy jingle from 1960 which includes a line about the Bill of Rights guaranteeing his right to be elected "No matter what his creed," p. 302.

47. Two less clear cases can also be considered. The umbrella subject of religious freedom was touched on by both campaigns in 1984, but the specific issues were different: Reagan discussed legislation ensuring equal access to schools for religious groups, while Mondale focused on the alleged threat to religious freedom posed by the "religious right." In 2000, both Bush and Gore claimed fidelity to "local control" of education, but Gores did so only in the superscript, not in the audio portion. Alone among the ads surveyed here, this ad was counted as a constitutional ad in the AMMI sample by itself but not when considered as part of the broader sample. The AMMI sample includes descriptions of superscript, but most sources used in the bigger sample do not. Therefore, superscript was not considered when coding the full sample, since comparability was

impossible. This was the only ad from the AMMI sample that contained a constitutional reference in superscript but not audio text.

48. Diamond and Bates, *The Spot*, 386.

Chapter 5: The Constitution in Presidential Debates

1. The first debate of 1980 featured Republican Ronald Reagan and Independent John
Anderson. Democrat Jimmy Carter declined to participate.

2. The summary description of presidential debates in this section is drawn from Susan A.
Hellweg, Michael Pfau, and Steven R. Brydon, *Televised Presidential Debates, Advocacy in Con-
temporary America* (New York: Praeger, 1992), ch. 5; Edward A. Hinck, *Enacting the Presidency:
Political Argument, Presidential Debates, and Presidential Character* (Westport, Conn.: Praeger,
1978), ch. 1; Stephen Coleman, "Meaningful Political Debate in the Age of the Soundbite,"
in Stephen Coleman, ed., *Televised Election Debates: International Perspectives* (New York: St.
Martin's Press, 2000), 1–24; Kathleen Hall Jameison and Christopher Adasiewicz, "What Can
Voters Learn from Election Debates?" in Stephen Coleman, ed., *Televised Election Debates: International Perspectives* (New York: St. Martin's Press, 2000), 25–42; Kathleen Hall Jameison
and David S. Birdsell, *Presidential Debates: The Challenge of Creating an Informed Electorate*
(New York: Oxford University Press, 1988), ch. 5; Sidney Krause, *Televised Presidential Debates
and Public Policy* (Hillsdale, N.J.: Lawrence Earlbaum Associates, Publishers), ch. 5.

3. See Richard Joslyn, *Mass Media and Elections* (Reading, Mass.: Addison-Wesley Publishing, 1984), 203–217.

4. These studies are cited in Hellweg, Pfau, and Brydon, *Televised Presidential Debates*,
27–29.

5. See Joslyn, *Mass Media and Elections*, 203–217; Jameison and Adasiewicz, "What Can
Voters Learn from Election Debates?" in Stephen Coleman, ed., *Televised Election Debates: In-
ternational Perspectives* (New York: St. Martin's Press, 2000), esp. 28–40; Hellweg, Pfau, Brydon,
Televised Presidential Debates, 101–124; Jameison and Birdsell, *Presidential Debates*, 120–161;
Kraus, *Televised Presidential Debates and Public Policy*, 103–134.

6. See Darrell West, *Air Wars: Television Advertising in Election Campaigns, 1952–2004*
(Washington: Congressional Quarterly Press, 2005), 15–16. In another poll, utilizing a less
stringent standard, 60 percent said the debates helped them make their vote decision, again
higher than for any other mode of media. Kathleen Hall Jameison, *Packaging the Presidency: A
History and Criticism of Presidential Campaign Advertising* 3rd ed. (New York: Oxford University
Press, 1996), xxvi.

7. 1960 Presidential Debate I, 1. For this and future debate citations, see appendix B for
full bibliographic detail.

8. 1960 Presidential Debate IV, 13.

9. 1976 Presidential Debate II, 18.

10. 1992 Presidential Debate II, 13.

11. 2000 Presidential Debate II, 14.

12. 2000 Presidential Debate II, 15.

13. 2000 Presidential Debate III, 16.

14. 2004 Presidential Debate II, 31.

15. 2004 Presidential Debate II, 31.

16. 2004 Presidential Debate III, 29.

17. 2004 Presidential Debate III, 27.
18. 1984 Presidential Debate I, 14.
19. 2000 Presidential Debate I, 7.
20. 2000 Presidential Debate I, 8.
21. 2000 Presidential Debate I, 21.
22. 2004 Presidential Debate III, 24.
23. 1960 Presidential Debate I, 5.
24. 1960 Presidential Debate I, 5.
25. 1980 Presidential Debate I, 8.
26. 1980 Presidential Debate I, 14.
27. 1980 Presidential Debate II, 19.
28. 1984 Presidential Debate I, 16.
29. 1988 Presidential Debate I, 12.
30. 1988 Presidential Debate II, 5.
31. 1992 Presidential Debate II, 11.
32. 1996 Presidential Debate I, 3.
33. 1996 Presidential Debate I, 3.
34. 2000 Presidential Debate II, 21.
35. 2000 Presidential Debate I, 11.
36. 2004 Presidential Debate III, 11.
37. 2000 Presidential Debate I, 22.
38. 1996 Presidential Debate I, 12.
39. 1996 Presidential Debate I, 15.
40. 2004 Presidential Debate I, 22.
41. 2004 Presidential Debate II, 39.
42. 2004 Presidential Debate III, 26.
43. 2004 Presidential Debate III, 26.
44. 2004 Presidential Debate III, 34.
45. 1976 Presidential Debate III, 11.
46. 2000 Presidential Debate III, 23.
47. 1976 Presidential Debate II, 4; 1976 Presidential Debate II, 18.
48. 1980 Presidential Debate I, 12.
49. 1992 Presidential Debate I, 3.
50. 1996 Presidential Debate II, 22.
51. 1976 Presidential Debate III, 14.
52. 1988 Presidential Debate II, 15.
53. 2000 Presidential Debate I, 7–8.
54. 2004 Presidential Debate II, 34.
55. 1980 Presidential Debate II, 20.
56. See 2000 Presidential Debate I, 8.
57. 1976 Presidential Debate I, 16.
58. 1992 Presidential Debate I, 12.
59. 2000 Presidential Debate I, 8.
60. 1960 Presidential Debate I, 1.
61. 1984 Presidential Debate I, 17.
62. For instance, see Mondale, 1984 Presidential Debate II, 15.

63. It was harder than it might seem to count questions. This general rule was followed: Original questions were counted, even if repeated to another candidate; follow-up questions were counted; opening and closing statements were not counted, and invitations for rebuttal were not counted as separate questions. Also, there were a few instances during town-hall debates in which the journalist moderators asked follow-up questions based on questions asked by citizen interlocutors. These were not counted so as to allow a clearer line between journalist questions and citizen questions.

64. One other explicit reference to the Constitution was extraneous to the subject matter of the question. That question, asked of George H. W. Bush in 1988, pressed Bush to reveal the advice he gave Ronald Reagan about the Iran arms sale after rather gratuitously noting that nothing in the Constitution prohibited him from doing so. Another 1988 reference, which was counted, was a close call. It helped frame the subject of the question but was not itself the subject. The question asked Bush to explain his decision to select Senator Dan Quayle as his running mate after reciting the relevant portions of the Twenty-fifth Amendment regarding presidential succession.

Chapter 6: The Constitution and Third Parties

1. John F. Freie, "Minor Parties in Realigning Eras," *American Politics Quarterly* 10 (1982): 42–63; Walter Dean Burnham, *Critical Elections and the Mainsprings of American Politics* (New York: Norton, 1970); Steven J. Rosenstone, Roy L. Behr, and Edward H. Lazarus, *Third Parties in America: Citizen Response to Major Party Failure* 2nd ed. (Princeton, N.J.: Princeton University Press, 1996); Daniel A. Mazmanian, *Third Parties in Presidential Elections* (Washington, D.C.: Brookings Institution, 1974); Paul S. Herrnson, "Two-Party Dominance and Minor-Party Forays in American Politics," in Paul S. Herrnson and John C. Green", eds., *Multiparty Politics in America* 2nd ed. (Lanham, Md.: Rowman & Littlefield, 2002), 27–28; James L. Sundquist, *Dynamics of the Party System* rev. ed. (Washington, D.C.: Brookings Institution, 1983); Paul Allen Beck, *Party Politics in America* 8th ed. (New York: Longman, 1997).

2. Ross Perot, *United We Stand: How We Can Take Back Our Country* (New York: Hyperion, 1992), 21. Full bibliographic details for coded documents can be found in appendix B.

3. "The First Clinton-Bush-Perot Presidential Debate, October 11, 1992." Part I, 3.

4. "The Second Clinton-Bush-Perot Presidential Debate, October 15, 1992," Part I, 16.

5. Charles Kesler, "Political Parties, the Constitution, and the Future of American Politics," Peter W. Schramm and Bradford P. Wilson, eds., *American Political Parties & Constitutional Politics* (Lanham, Md.: Rowman & Littlefield, 1992), 231. For related observations of the constitutionally deprived nature of the 1992 election in general, see Roger M. Barrus, John H. Eastby, Joseph H. Lane Jr., David E. Marion, and James Pontuso, *The Deconstitutionalization of America: The Forgotten Frailties of Democratic Rule* (Lanham, Md.: Lexington Books, 2004), 6–7.

6. Donald Bruce Johnson and Kirk H. Porter, *National Party Platforms 1840–1972* (Urbana: University of Illinois Press, 1975), 13.

7. "Mr. Van Buren's Letter," *The Clarion*, September 13, 1848, 39.

8. Johnson and Porter, 22–23.

9. "Acceptance of the Nomination for President by the American Party, Paris, May 21, 1856," *Publications of the Buffalo Historical Society Vol. XI, Millard Fillmore Papers* Vol. 2, Frank H. Severance ed. (Buffalo, N.Y.: Buffalo Historical Society, 1907), 359

10. Johnson and Porter, 90–91.

11. Johnson and Porter, 176.

12. "A Confession of Faith," 17.

13. Johnson and Porter, 30.

14. "Mr. Bell Accepts," *Political Text-Book for 1860*, Horace Greeley and John F. Cleveland eds. (New York: Tribune Association, 1860), 213.

15. Because of his dual nomination, Greeley is also assessed in major-party chapters.

16. "Acceptance Letter from Horace Greeley to the Liberal Republicans, May 20, 1872," William Gillette, "Election of 1872," Arthur M. Schlesinger Jr., ed., *History of American Presidential Elections* [hereafter HAPE] Vol. II (New York: Chelsea House Publishers, 1971), 1357–1359; "Acceptance Letter from Horace Greeley to the Democrats, July 18, 1872," HAPE II: 1370–1372.

17. Of course, Greeley's death also raised an interesting (but hypothetical) constitutional question. What would have happened had Greeley won but died before the electoral votes were cast? Since electors are constitutionally free to exercise their judgment, Greeley's electors would presumably have coalesced behind an alternative figure agreed upon by the Democrats and Liberal Republicans (if such agreement could be reached). A more difficult issue would have been if Greeley had won and died after the electoral votes had been cast.

18. Johnson and Porter, 104–106.

19. "Madison Square Garden Speech," 336.

20. Johnson and Porter, 190.

21. "Speech of R. Perot on Accepting the 1996 Presidential Nomination of the Reform Party, Valley Forge, PA." (1997) In *Historic Documents of 1996* (Washington: CQ Press). CQ Electronic Library, CQ Voting and Elections Collection, http://library.cqpress.com/elections/hsdc96-0000035228. Document ID: hsdc96-0000035228. Accessed July 15, 2005.

22. See janda.org/politxts/PartyPlatforms/OtherParties/reform.996.html.

23. Johnson and Porter, 31.

24. "Mr. Breckenridge Accepts," *Political Text-Book for 1860*, Horace Greeley and John F. Cleveland, eds. (New York: Tribune Association, 1860), 212.

25. See David Burner, "Election of 1924," in HAPE Vol. III (New York: Chelsea House Publishers, 1971), 2487.

26. Johnson and Porter, 252–255.

27. "Speech by Robert La Follette, New York, September 18, 1924," HAPE III (New York: Chelsea House Publishers, 1971), 2540–2553.

28. Johnson and Porter, 700–706.

29. "New York Campaign Speech by George C. Wallace." In M. Nelson ed. *Historic Documents on Presidential Elections 1787–1988* (Washington, D.C.: CQ Press, 1991).

30. "John Anderson 1980 Campaign Brochure Reprint," at www.4president.org. Accessed July 15, 2005.

31. "The Anderson-Reagan Debate: September 21, 1980," 15.

32. In platforms, the median percentage of third party references that were explicit was 38.5 percent; for Democrats, 41 percent, and for Republicans, 43 percent. The average was third party 40.5 percent, Democrat 42.9 percent, Republican 44 percent. In candidate messages, the median was Democrats 40 percent, third party 43.5 percent, Republican 53.5 percent; the average was Democrats 37.2 percent, third party 45.2 percent, Republicans 46.1 percent.

33. Donald Grier Stephenson, Jr., *Campaigns and the Court: The U.S. Supreme Court in Presidential Elections* (New York: Columbia University Press, 1999), ch. 5 and 7.

Chapter 7: Constitutional Rhetoric and Governing

1. Karlyn Kohrs Campbell and Kathleen Hall Jameison, *Deeds Done in Words: Presidential Rhetoric and the Genres of Governance* (Chicago: University of Chicago Press, 1990), 15; generally, 14–36. See also Mary E. Stuckey, "Presidential Rhetoric in Political Time," Mary E. Stuckey, ed., *The Theory and Practice of Political Communication Research* (Albany: State University of New York Press, 1996), 122–141.

2. John McDiarmid, "Presidential Inaugural Addresses: A Study in Verbal Symbols," *The Public Opinion Quarterly* 1, no. 3 (July, 1937): 79, 82.

3. "Inaugural Address of James Buchanan," 5. Full bibliographic details of coded documents are found in appendix B.

4. "Inaugural Address of James Garfield," 3.

5. "Inaugural Address of James Garfield," 2.

6. "First Inaugural Address of Grover Cleveland," 2.

7. "Inaugural Address of Benjamin Harrison," 1.

8. "Inaugural Address of William Howard Taft," 11.

9. "Inaugural Address of Warren G. Harding," 2.

10. "Second Inaugural Address of Franklin D. Roosevelt," 2.

11. "First Inaugural Address of Ronald Reagan," 3.

12. "Second Inaugural Address of William J. Clinton," 2, 6.

13. This is, of course, as defined by the categories laid out in the introduction. Obviously, Lincoln touched on many themes that might be considered constitutional in a broad sense, but none fit within the specific categories used as a basis for this study.

14. In historical narrative, Jeffrey Tulis traces the same decline. Jeffrey K. Tulis, *The Rhetorical Presidency* (Princeton, N.J.: Princeton University Press, 1986), 47–51.

15. Campbell and Jameison, *Deeds Done in Words*, 55; generally, 52–75.

16. Campbell and Jameison, *Deeds Done in Words*, 73.

17. "President Roosevelt, 1937 State of the Union Address," 3.

18. "President Roosevelt, 1935 State of the Union Address," 1.

19. "President Eisenhower, 1955 State of the Union Address," 10.

20. "President Eisenhower, 1956 State of the Union Address," 11.

21. "President Eisenhower, 1957 State of the Union Address," 3.

22. "President Johnson, 1966 State of the Union Address," 5.

23. "President Nixon, 1974 State of the Union Address," 8.

24. "President Reagan, 1982 State of the Union Address," 6.

25. "President Reagan, 1987 State of the Union Address," 6.

Chapter 8: Conclusion

1. Max Lerner, "Constitution and Court as Symbols," *The Yale Law Journal* 46, no. 8 (June 1937): 1299; see also Edward S. Corwin, "The Constitution as Instrument and as Symbol," *American Political Science Review* 30, no. 6 (December 1936); Michael Kammen, *A Machine*

That Would Go of Itself: The Constitution and American Culture (New York: Alfred A. Knopf, 1987).

2. Larry R. Baas, "The Constitution as Symbol: The Interpersonal Sources of Meaning of a Secondary Symbol," *American Journal of Political Science* 23, no. 1 (February 1979): 115.

3. Survey by *Fortune*, conducted by Roper Organization during December 1939, sample of 5,214 adults. Data provided by Roper Center for Public Opinion Research, University of Connecticut.

4. Survey by the National Constitution Center, conducted by Shephardson Stern & Kaminsky during September 1987, sample of 1,000 adult U.S. citizens. Data provided by Roper Center for Public Opinion Research, University of Connecticut.

5. Conducted by the Public Agenda Foundation, September 3–16, 1998, national sample of 801 parents of public school children. Data provided by Roper Center for Public Opinion Research, University of Connecticut.

6. Survey by Pew Research Center, conducted by Princeton Survey Research Associates, April 6–May 6, 1999, national sample of 1,546 adults. Data provided by Roper Center for Public Opinion Research, University of Connecticut.

7. Survey for *Newsweek*. Conducted by Gallup Organization, May 17–18, 1987, national adult sample of 812. Data provided by Roper Center for Public Opinion Research, University of Connecticut.

8. Survey by Cable News Network and *USA Today*, conducted by Gallup Organization, June 25–27, 1999, national sample of 1,016 adults. Data provided by Roper Center for Public Opinion Research, University of Connecticut.

9. Survey by National Constitution Center, conducted by Public Agenda Foundation, July 10–24 2002, national sample of 1,520 adults. Data provided by Roper Center for Public Opinion Research, University of Connecticut.

10. Conducted by CBC News/*New York Times*, May 11–14, 1987, national sample of 1,254 adults. Data provided by Roper Center for Public Opinion Research, University of Connecticut.

11. Conducted by ABC News/*Washington Post*, April 9–13, 1987, national sample of 1,509 adults. Data provided by Roper Center for Public Opinion Research, University of Connecticut.

12. Survey by National Constitution Center, conducted by Shepardson Stern & Kaminsky, September 1997, national sample of 1,000 adult U.S. citizens. Data provided by Roper Center for Public Opinion Research, University of Connecticut.

13. Kammen, *A Machine That Would Go of Itself*, 24.

14. Conducted by NBC News/*Wall Street Journal*, September 20–22, 1986, national sample of 2,139 adults. Data provided by Roper Center for Public Opinion Research, University of Connecticut

15. Survey by National Constitution Center, conducted by Shepardson Stern & Kaminsky, September 1997, national sample of 1,000 adult U.S. citizens. Data provided by Roper Center for Public Opinion Research, University of Connecticut. One indirect indication of the lesser thought given by Americans to institutional questions can be found in a series of open-ended survey questions testing respondents' knowledge of the content of the First Amendment. While respondents made a wide variety of errors, one error they did not make (or made so rarely as to constitute a negligible response) was to mistakenly put any connotation of federalism or other structural features of the Constitution onto the First Amendment.

16. Survey by Hearst Corporation, conducted by Research & Forecasts, October 20–November 2, 1986, national sample of 1,004 adults. Data provided by Roper Center for Public Opinion Research, University of Connecticut. Perhaps worse, the polling firm, to be helpful for subsequent analysis, labeled the 59 percent answer "correct."

17. Conducted by CBS News/*New York Times*, May 11–May 14, 1987, national sample of 1,254 adults. Data provided by Roper Center for Public Opinion Research, University of Connecticut.

18. In recent years, Gallup polled this question more than once in an election year. In those cases, the poll closest to election day was used (usually September or October) except in a few cases when answers were excessively consolidated to give a much larger than usual residual "other" category. In those cases, the nearest suitable election-year Gallup survey was used instead. World War II survey years of 1942 and 1944 were excluded. The Gallup surveys used were from August 1940, June 1946, June 1948, March 1950, June 1952, March 1954, October 1956, September 1958, October 1960, October 1962, October 1964, October 1966, October 1968, October 1970, October 1972, October 1974, October 1976, October 1978, September 1980, October 1982, September 1984, July 1986, September 1988, August 1992 (first mention), August 1994, July 1996, September 1998, October 2000, September 2002, October 2004, and April 2006.

The survey results reported here were obtained from searches of the iPOLL Databank provided by the Roper Center for Public Opinion Research, University of Connecticut, at www.ropercenter.uconn.edu/ipoll.html (accessed May 2006).

19. Bruce G. Peabody, "Congressional Attitudes toward Constitutional Interpretation," in Neal Devins and Keith E. Whittington, eds., *Congress and the Constitution* (Durham, N.C.: Duke University Press, 2005), 39–63; J. Mitchell Pickerill, *Constitutional Deliberation in Congress* (Durham, N.C.: Duke University Press, 2004), esp. 133–137.

20. Peabody, "Congressional Attitudes Toward Constitutional Interpretation," in Neal Devins and Keith E. Whittington, eds., *Congress and the Constitution* (Durham, N.C.: Duke University Press, 2005), 59.

21. Keith E. Whittington, "The Constitution in Committees," in Neal Devins and Keith E. Whittington, eds. *Congress and the Constitution* (Durham, N.C.: Duke University Press, 2005), 100–103.

22. See Charles Epp, *The Rights Revolution: Lawyers, Activists, and Supreme Courts in Comparative Perspective* (Chicago: University of Chicago Press, 1998).

23. Steven M. Teles, *Parallel Paths: the Conservative Legal Movement versus Legal Liberalism* (Princeton, N.J.: Princeton University Press, 2007).

24. Sidney M. Milkis, *Political Parties and Constitutional Government* (Baltimore, Md.: Johns Hopkins University Press, 1999), 185.

25. M. Kent Jennings, "Ideological Thinking among Mass Publics and Political Elites," *Public Opinion Quarterly* 56, no. 4: 419–441; Richard Herrera, "Understanding the Language of Politics: A Study of Elites and Masses," *Political Science Quarterly* 111, no. 4 (1996–1997): 619–637. It should be pointed out that here and elsewhere, Herrera argues for a narrower gap than some, both because most mass voters have some significant understanding of ideological terms like "liberal" and "conservative" and because the party elites exhibit far from perfect ideological consistency. See Herrera, "Understanding the Language of Politics" and "Cohesion at the Party Conventions: 1980–1988," *Polity* 26, no. 1: 75–89.

26. John W. Soule and Wilma E. McGrath, "A Comparative Study of Presidential Nomination Conventions: The Democrats 1968 and 1972," *American Journal of Political Science* 19, no. 3: 501–517.

27. Jeane Kirkpatrick, *The New Presidential Elite: Men and Women in National Politics* (New York: Russell Sage Foundation, 1976), esp. ch. 9.

28. Aaron Wildavsky, "The Goldwater Phenomenon: Purists, Politicians, and the Two-Party System," *Review of Politics* 27 (July 1965): 393–399; Soule and McGrath, "A Comparative Study of Presidential Nomination Conventions"; Harold D. Clarke, Euel Elliott, and Thomas H. Roback, "Domestic Issue Ideology and Activist Style: A Note on the 1980 Republican Convention Delegates," *Journal of Politics* 53, no. 2: 519–534.

29. Thomas Carsey, John Green, Rick Herrera, and Geoffrey Layman, "The New Party Professionals? An Initial Look at National Convention Delegates in 2000 and Over Time," Paper presented at the 2003 annual meeting of the American Political Science Association, August 28–31, 2003.

30. Warren E. Miller, *Without Consent: Mass-Elite Linkages in Presidential Politics* (Lexington: University Press of Kentucky, 1988); Walter J. Stone, Ronald B. Rapoport, and Alan I. Abramowitz, "The Reagan Revolution and Party Polarization in the 1980s," in L. Sandy Maisel, ed., *The Parties Respond: Changes in the American Party System* (Boulder, Colo.: Westview Press, 1990), 67–93; Geoffrey C. Layman and Thomas M. Carsey, "Party Polarization and Party Structuring of Policy Attitudes: A Comparison of Three NES Panel Studies," *Political Behavior* 24, no. 3: 199–236; Geoffrey C. Layman and Thomas M. Carsey, "Party Polarization and 'Conflict Extension' in the American Electorate," *American Journal of Political Science* 46, no. 4: 786–802.

31. Carsey, Green, Herrera, and Layman, "The New Party Professionals? An Initial Look at National Convention Delegates in 2000 and Over Time." Similarly, Warren E. Miller's study of 1980 and 1984 elite and mass party electorates defined ideological dispositions by reference to three or four "domestic social issues" which included abortion, busing, the Equal Rights Amendment, and prayer in school, along with domestic spending and foreign-policy dimensions.

32. "Top 20 PAC Contributors to Federal Candidates, 2005–2006," The Center for Responsive Politics, at www.opensecrets.org/pacs/topacs.asc?txt=A&Cycle=2006 (accessed April 28, 2006).

33. As determined by the Center for Responsive Politics, the top ten Democratic soft-money donors were (in order) New York Senate 2000; AFSCME; Service Employees International Union; Carpenters & Jointers Union; Communications Workers of America; United Food & Commercial Workers Union; International Brotherhood of Electrical Workers; American Federation of Teachers; Slim-Fast Foods/Thompson Medical; and Saban Entertainment. The top ten Republican Party contributors were AT&T; Philip Morris; Bristol-Myers Squib; National Rifle Association (concerned with the Second Amendment); Pfizer Inc.; Freddie Mac; Republican Party of California; Microsoft Corporation; Enron Corporation; Amway/Alticor Inc. Cited in Paul S. Herrnson, "National Party Organizations at the Dawn of the Twenty-First Century," in L. Sandy Maisel, ed., *The Parties Respond: Changes in American Parties and Campaigns* 4th ed. (Boulder, Colo.: Westview Press, 2002), 59.

34. GovSpot.com, www.govspot.com/lists/top50pacs.htm (accessed May 13, 2003).

35. American Center for Law & Justice,

36. www.aclj.org/About/default.aspx?Section=9.

37. Institute for Justice, www.ij.org/profile/index.html. Another legal-advocacy group worth noting is Judicial Watch. While it is largely interested in issues of government secrecy and corruption, Judicial Watch also includes judicial accountability (in criminal, civil, and constitutional cases) as one of its missions. However, the group does not give a defense of the Constitution as a primary objective. (www.judicialwatch.org/about.shtml).

38. People for the American Way, www.pfaw.org/pfaw/general/default.aspx?oid=163.

39. Christian Coalition of America, www.cc.org/about.cfm.

40. NARAL Pro-Choice America, www.prochoiceamerica.org/about-us/.

41. Emily's List, www.emilyslist.org/about/what-we-do.html.

42. WISH List, www.thewishlist.org/Mission.htm.

43. National Right to Life, www.nrlc.org/Missionstatement.htm; www.nrlc.org/about/nrlctoday.html.

44. Concerned Women for America, /www.cwfa.org/coreissues.asp.

45. National Association for the Advancement of Colored People, www.naacp.org/about_index.html.

46. For example, see Gene Healy and Timothy Lynch, *Power Surge: The Constitutional Record of George W. Bush* (Washington, D.C.: Cato Institute, 2006).

47. Theodore H. White, *America in Search of Itself: The Making of the President 1956–1980* (New York: Warner Books, 1982), 300.

48. Jeffrey K. Tulis, *The Rhetorical Presidency* (Princeton, N.J.: Princeton University Press, 1986), 187.

49. Michael Kammen, *A Machine that Would Go of Itself: The Constitution and American Culture* (New York: Alfred A. Knopf, 1987), 29.

50. Sanford Levinson, "'The Constitution' in American Civil Religion," *The Supreme Court Review* 1979 (1979), 125.

51. Donald Grier Stephenson, *Campaigns and the Court: The U.S. Supreme Court in Presidential Elections* (New York: Columbia University Press, 1999), 240.

Appendix A: A Note on the Study Method

1. Reading the documents also allowed for a refinement of coding definitions. For example, it turned out upon examination that nineteenth-century political texts often used terms like "the fundamental law" or "the organic law" to refer to the Constitution, thus framing a number of references.

2. Abortion presented a particularly difficult challenge for coding, for the reason that much campaign rhetoric discussing abortion is either euphemistic or reflective of personal moral sentiments rather than public policy considerations. The following rule was adopted, counting references that indicate a position toward the question of whether abortion should be considered a constitutional right and counting a handful of "code words" that are almost universally recognized as representing a position on that question, essentially promising fealty to "the sanctity of human life," "choice," or some variations thereof.

3. Beyond explicit and implicit references to issues directly constitutional, at least two other categories offered themselves as possibilities, forming a ring of concentric circles outside the core. It was possible to imagine a third circle, neither explicit nor direct, of issues that were related to those in the first and second circles. This category of derivative topics might include such references as positive economic rights, which not only use the language of individual

rights but also have been held in some Supreme Court minority opinions to have constitutional standing; vetoes, appointments, or enforcement actions not directly related to constitutional issues, on the grounds that they represent sometimes controversial exercises of constitutional powers; references to federal, state, and local cooperation or federal aid to lower levels, insofar as they promote a particular type of constitutional relationship between the levels; or mentions of active, limited, bigger, or smaller government, as a kind of indirect metaphor for enumeration of powers.

Yet farther removed from the core constitutional rhetoric might be a realm of constitutional values, general commitments that are crucial to the Constitution and in many ways define the Constitution but which only imperfectly overlap the Constitution itself. These might include principles such as freedom, liberty, equality, or consent of the governed. As might be imagined, there are a large number of references to these values contained in campaign documents throughout American history.

While it might be defensible to include these two outer circles of constitutional rhetoric within this study, such a decision would have broadened the scope of inquiry so far as to jeopardize its essence. Indeed, by the time one would reach the outermost circle, that of constitutional values, there would remain only the most tenuous and general connection between the references and the Constitution itself. The third layer might provide more useful information, but proved upon examination to be such a fluid gray zone, itself unanchored in the Constitution, that it was entirely unclear whether such references could be coded reliably. Consequently, this study was limited to the first two rings of the concentric circles.

Another coding question also presented itself: should an attempt be made to divide references on the basis of additional substantive content? Three possibilities were considered and rejected. First, references could have been divided into categories of "principles" versus "policies," to distinguish between statements of conviction ("The Constitution should be interpreted strictly") and advocacy of particular actions ("We support passage of a constitutional amendment to ensure women the right to vote"). However, it is not clear that such a distinction can be made successfully, as statements of conviction generally are laden with policy consequences. A proclamation in defense of strict construction can easily be read as a call for action in the area of judicial nominations. Conversely, a call for adoption of a constitutional amendment can become more a statement of principle than of policy, especially when repeated failures to achieve the policy and shrinking prospects of success give the statement a mostly symbolic quality. (For example, Democratic platforms continued endorsing the Equal Rights Amendment long after it was defeated.) Second, a division might have been made on the basis of the "Hamiltonian" or "Jeffersonian" content of the reference. However, not all issues are converted into these terms easily or without controversy; Republicans and Southern Democrats each laid claim to Jefferson in the 1850s, as did both New Deal Democrats and Goldwater Republicans in the twentieth century. Furthermore, the technocratic liberalism of the Great Society and beyond saw itself as rising above Jeffersonianism and Hamiltonianism, and its opponents saw themselves as defenders not only of Jefferson but also of the whole tradition of the American founding. Finally, one could apply a more general test of whether a reference seemed to advocate an empowering of government or a restraint of it. This scheme, however, would run afoul of the fact that the same position—take, in the last quarter of the twentieth century, support for abortion on demand—could simultaneously expand the notion of individual rights and deal a blow against governmental decentralization and accountability by imposing a federal solution on the people of the states through judicial decree. Whether on balance this change represented a limitation or expansion of governmental power remains a question hotly debated by adherents of each side.

Appendix B: Coded Communications

1. Donald Bruce Johnson and Kirk H. Porter, National Party Platforms 1840–1972 (hereafter NPP) (Urbana: University of Illinois Press, 1975), 2.

2. William Nisbet Chambers, "Election of 1840," in Arthur M. Schlesinger Jr., ed., History of American Presidential Elections (hereafter HAPE) Vol. I (New York: Chelsea House, 1971), 733–736.

3. Chambers, "Election of 1840," HAPE Vol I (New York: Chelsea House, 1971), 737–744.

4. NPP, 3–4

5. Charles Sellers, "Election of 1844," HAPE, Vol. I (New York: Chelsea House, 1971), 853.

6. Charles Sellers, "Election of 1844," HAPE, Vol. I (New York: Chelsea House, 1971), 854.

7. NPP, 8–9.

8. "On Retiring to Private Life," in Calvin Colton, ed., The Works of Henry Clay (New York: G. P. Putnam's Sons, 1904), 359–384.

9. NPP, 10–12.

10. Holman Hamilton, "Election of 1848," HAPE vol. II (New York: Chelsea House, 1971), 906–912.

11. NPP, 14–15

12. Hamilton, "Election of 1848," HAPE vol. II (New York: Chelsea House, 1971), 913–914.

13. Hamilton, "Election of 1848," HAPE vol. II (New York: Chelsea House, 1971), 915–917.

14. NPP, 13–14.

15. "Mr. Van Buren's Letter to the Committee of the Buffalo Convention," The Clarion, September 13, 1848, 39–40.

16. NPP, 16–18.

17. Roy and Jeannette Nichols, "Election of 1852," HAPE Vol. II (New York: Chelsea House, 1971), 995–1002.

18. NPP, 20–21.

19. "Letter of Gen. Scott in Reply," National Intelligencer, June 29, 1852, 3.

20. NPP, 23–27.

21. R. G. Horton, The Life and Public Services of James Buchanan (New York: Derby & Jackson, 1856), 414–418.

22. NPP, 27–28.

23. "Col. Fremont's Reply," John Bigelow, Memoir of the Life and Public Services of John Charles Fremont (New York: Derby & Jackson, 1856), 456–459.

24. NPP, 22–23.

25. "Acceptance of the Nomination for President by the American Party," in Frank H. Severance, ed., Publications of the Buffalo Historical Society Volume XI, Millard Fillmore Papers Volume Two (Buffalo, N.Y.: Buffalo Historical Society, 1907), 358–360.

26. NPP, 30–31.

27. "On the Admission of Kansas Under the Wyandott Constitution," H. M. Flint, ed., Life of Stephen A. Douglas, United States Senator from Illinois, with His Most Important Speeches and Reports (New York: Derby & Jackson, 1860), 172–187.

28. NPP, 31–33.

29. *NPP*, 31.

30. "Mr. Breckinridge Accepts," Horace Greeley and John P. Cleveland, ed., *Political Text-Book for 1860* (New York: Tribune Association, 1860), 211–212.

31. *NPP*, 30.

32. "Mr. Bell Accepts," Horace Greeley and John P. Cleveland, ed., *Political Text-Book for 1860* (New York: Tribune Association, 1860), 213–214.

33. *NPP*, 34–35.

34. "To the Democratic Nomination Committee," Stephen W. Sears, ed., *The Civil War Papers of George B. McClellan, Selected Correspondence 1860–1865* (New York: Ticknor & Fields, 1989), 595–596.

35. *NPP*, 35–36.

36. Harold M. Hyman, "Election of 1864," *HAPE* Vol. II (New York: Chelsea House, 1971), 1182–1189.

37. *NPP*, 37–39.

38. John Hope Franklin, "Election of 1868," *HAPE* Vol. II (New York: Chelsea House, 1971), 1282–1286.

39. *NPP*, 39–40.

40. Franklin, "Election of 1868," *HAPE* Vol. II (New York: Chelsea House, 1971), 1272–1273.

41. *NPP*, 41–42.

42. *NPP*, 44–45.

43. William Gillette, "Election of 1872," *HAPE* Vol. II (New York: Chelsea House, 1971), 1357–1359.

44. Gillette, "Election of 1872," *HAPE* Vol. II (New York: Chelsea House, 1971), 1370–1372.

45. *NPP*, 46–48.

46. Gillette, "Election of 1872," *HAPE* Vol. II (New York: Chelsea House, 1971), 1360–1363.

47. *NPP*, 49–51.

48. "Governor Tilden's Letter Accepting the Nomination of the National Democratic Convention for the Presidency," John Bigelow, ed., *The Writings and Speeches of Samuel J. Tilden Vol. II* (New York: Harper & Brothers, 1885), 359–373.

49. *NPP*, 53–55.

50. Charles Richard Williams, *The Life of Rutherford Birchard Hayes, Nineteenth President of the United States* Vol. I (Columbus: Ohio State Archeological and Historical Society, 1928), 460–462.

51. *NPP*, 56–57.

52. Leonard Dinnerstein, "Election of 1880," *HAPE* Vol. II (New York: Chelsea House, 1971), 1542–1543.

53. *NPP*, 60–62.

54. Dinnerstein, "Election of 1880," *HAPE* Vol. II (New York: Chelsea House, 1971), 1535–1538.

55. *NPP*, 65–68.

56. "Letter Accepting Nomination for President, Albany, N.Y., August 18, 1884," Albert Ellery Bergh, ed., *Grover Cleveland: Addresses, State Papers and Letters* (New York: Sun Dial Classics Co., 1909), 51–55.

57. *NPP*, 72–74.

58. "Mr. Blaine's Letter Accepting the Republican Nomination for the Presidency in 1884," in James G. Blaine, *Political Discussions, Legislative, Diplomatic, and Popular, 1856–1886* (Springfield, Mass.: Winter & Co., 1887), 420–434.

59. *NPP*, 76–78.

60. Robert F. Wesser, "Election of 1888," *HAPE* Vol. II (New York: Chelsea House, 1971), 1683–1690.

61. *NPP*, 79–83.

62. Wesser, "Election of 1888," *HAPE* Vol. II (New York: Chelsea House, 1971), 1691–1696.

63. *NPP*, 86–89.

64. H. Wayne Morgan, "Election of 1892," *HAPE* Vol. II (New York: Chelsea House, 1971), 1765–1769.

65. *NPP*, 93–95.

66. Morgan, "Election of 1892," *HAPE* Vol. II (New York: Chelsea House, 1971), 1746–1750.

67. *NPP*, 89–91.

68. "Chapter XX, Danger and Duty," James B. Weaver, *Call to Action*, reprint ed. (New York: Arno Press, 1974), 441–445.

69. *NPP*, 97–100.

70. *NPP*, 104–106.

71. "Madison Square Garden Speech," William Jennings Bryan, *The First Battle*, 315–337.

72. *NPP*, 107–109.

73. "Hon. William McKinley's Letter of Acceptance," Lawrence F. Prescott, *1896: The Great Campaign* (New York: Loyal Publishing Co., 1896).

74. *NPP*, 112–116.

75. "Speech of William Jennings Bryan," *Republican Campaign Text-Book 1900* (Philadelphia: Dunlap Printing, 1900), 441–452.

76. *NPP*, 121–124.

77. "Speech of President McKinley," *Republican Campaign Text-Book 1900* (Philadelphia: Dunlap Printing, 1900), 437–441.

78. *NPP*, 130–135.

79. "Judge Parker Accepts His Nomination," Col. John R. Grady, ed., *The Lives and Public Services of Parker and Davis*, 1904 (Philadelphia: National Publishing Company, 1904), 288–301.

80. *NPP*, 137–140.

81. "To Joseph Gurney Cannon," Eltin E. Morrison, ed., *The Letters of Theodore Roosevelt* (Cambridge, Mass.: Harvard University Press, 1951), 921–943.

82. *NPP*, 144–151.

83. "Speech of William Jennings Bryan," *Republican Campaign Text-Book* (Philadelphia: Dunlap Printing, 1908), 476–484.

84. *NPP*, 157–163.

85. "Speech of Acceptance," David H. Burton, ed., *The Collected Works of William Howard Taft Vol. III* (Athens: Ohio University Press, 2004), 5–35.

86. *NPP*, 168–175.

87. "Speech of Acceptance," John Wells Davidson, ed., *A Crossroads of Freedom: The 1912 Campaign Speeches of Woodrow Wilson* (New Haven, Conn.: Yale University Press, 1956), 15–36.

88. *NPP*, 183–188.

89. George W. Mowry, "Election of 1912," *HAPE* Vol. III (New York: Chelsea House, 1971), 2204–2219.

90. *NPP*, 175–182.

91. Theodore Roosevelt, "A Confession of Faith," at www.theodore-roosevelt.com/trarmageddon.html (accessed June 8, 2005).

92. *NPP*, 188–191.

93. Mowry, 2237–2241.

94. *NPP*, 194–200.

95. Arthur S. Link and William M. Leary Jr., "Election of 1916," *HAPE* Vol. III (New York: Chelsea House, 1971), 2308–2317.

96. *NPP*, 204–207.

97. Link and Leary, 2294–2307.

98. *NPP*, 213–223.

99. "Gov. Cox Sounds Battle Summons," *The Democratic Text Book 1920* (Washington, D.C.: Democratic National Committee, 1920), 45–70.

100. *NPP*, 229–238.

101. "Speech of Acceptance of Warren G. Harding at Marion, Ohio, July 22, 1920," *Republican Campaign Text-Book 1920* (Washington, D.C.: Republican National Committee, 1920), 35–53.

102. *NPP*, 243–252.

103. "Speech of Acceptance of John W. Davis," *Democratic Campaign Book 1924* (Washington, D.C.: Democratic National Committee, 1924), 107–124.

104. *NPP*, 258–265.

105. "Address of Acceptance Delivered by President Coolidge at Washington, D.C., August 14, 1924," *Republican Campaign Text-Book 1924* (Washington, D.C.: Republican National Committee, 1924), 21–34.

106. *NPP*, 252–255.

107. David Burner, "Election of 1924," *HAPE* Vol. III (New York: Chelsea House, 1971), 2540–2553.

108. *NPP*, 270–278.

109. "Address of Acceptance," *Campaign Addresses of Governor Alfred E. Smith* (Washington, D.C.: Democratic National Committee, 1928), 1–26.

110. *NPP*, 280–291.

111. *The New Day: Campaign Speeches of Herbert Hoover 1928* (Palo Alto, Calif.: Stanford University Press, 1928), 9–44.

112. *NPP*, 331–333.

113. Frank Freidel, "Election of 1932," *HAPE* Vol. III (New York: Chelsea House, 1971), 2784–2791.

114. *NPP*, 339–351.

115. Freidel, "Election of 1932," *HAPE* Vol. III (New York: Chelsea House, 1971), 2792–2805.

116. *NPP*, 360–363.

117. Franklin D. Roosevelt, at www.geocities.com/rickmatlick/nomafdr36.htm (accessed February 9, 2004).

118. *NPP*, 365–370.

119. "Governor Landon's Address," William Allen White, *What It's All About: Being a Reporter's Story of the Early Campaign of 1936*, New York: Macmillan, 1936), 117–130.

120. *NPP*, 381–388.

121. Franklin D. Roosevelt, at www.geocities.com/rickmatlick/nomafdr40.htm (accessed February 9, 2004).

122. *NPP*, 389–394.

123. "Speech of Acceptance by Wendell Willkie," *This Is Wendell Willkie: A Collection of Speeches and Writings on Present-Day Issues* (New York: Dodd, Mead & Co., 1940), 259–280.

124. *NPP*, 402–404.

125. Leon Friedman, "Election of 1944," *HAPE* Vol. IV (New York: Chelsea House, 1971), 3062–3065.

126. *NPP*, 407–413.

127. Leon Friedman, "Election of 1944," *HAPE* Vol. IV (New York: Chelsea House, 1971), 3053–3057.

128. *NPP*, 430–436.

129. Harry S. Truman, at www.geocities.com/rickmatlick/nomatruman48.htm (accessed February 9, 2004).

130. *NPP*, 450–454.

131. Thomas Dewey, at www.cfinst.org/eguide/PartyConventions/speeches/1948r .html (accessed January 31, 2005).

132. *NPP*, 473–487.

133. Barton J. Bernstein, "Election of 1952," *HAPE* Vol. IV (New York: Chelsea House, 1971), 3293–3296.

134. Annenberg School of Communications, *The Annenberg/Pew Archive of Presidential Campaign Discourse* CD-ROM (2000). [Hereafter APCD.]; American Museum of the Moving Image, "The Living Room Candidates" online exhibit at www.ammi.org. [AMMI hereafter]; Edwin Diamond and Stephen Bates, *The Spot: The Rise of Political Advertising on Television*, rev. ed. (Cambridge: MIT Press, 1984) [hereafter *The Spot*].

135. *NPP*, 496–505.

136. "Texts of Eisenhower and Nixon Addresses to the Convention," *New York Times*, July 12, 1952, 4.

137. *APCD; The Spot.*

138. *NPP*, 523–542.

139. Malcolm Moos, "Election of 1956," *HAPE* Vol. IV (New York: Chelsea House, 1971), 3413–3418.

140. *APCD; AMMI; The Spot.*

141. *NPP*, 545–562.

142. Dwight D. Eisenhower, at www.geocities.com/rickmatlick/nomaike56.htm (accessed February 9, 2004).

143. *APCD; AMMI; The Spot.*

144. *NPP*, 574–600.

145. John F. Kennedy, at www.cs.umb.edu/jfklibrary/j071560.htm (accessed February 9, 2004).

146. *APCD.*

147. *NPP*, 604–621.

148. Theodore C. Sorenson, "Election of 1960," *HAPE* Vol. IV (New York: Chelsea House, 1971), 3549–3558.

149. *APCD; The Spot.*

150. Presidential debates, at www.debates.org/pages/trans60a.html; www.debates.org/pages/ trans60b.html; www.debates.org/pages/trans60c.html; www.debates.org/pages/trans60d.html (accessed October 29, 2003).

151. *NPP*, 641–672.

152. Lyndon B. Johnson, at www.geocities.com/rickmatlick/nomalbj.htm (accessed February 9, 2004).

153. *APCD*.

154. *NPP*, 677–690.

155. John Bartlow Martin, "Election of 1964," *HAPE* Vol. IV (New York: Chelsea House, 1971), 3664–3670.

156. University of Oklahoma, Center for Political Communication; AMMI; *The Spot*.

157. *NPP*, 718–743.

158. David S. Broder, "Election of 1968," *HAPE* Vol. IV (New York: Chelsea House, 1971), 3841–3847.

159. *APCD; AMMI.*

160. *NPP*, 748–763.

161. Richard M. Nixon, at www.4president.org/speeches/nixon1968acceptance.htm (accessed October 8, 2003).

162. *APCD; AMMI.*

163. *NPP*, 700–718.

164. New York campaign speech by George C. Wallace. (1991). In M. Nelson, ed. *Historic Documents on Presidential Elections 1787–1988* (Washington D.C.: CQ Press), from CQ Electronic Library, CQ Voting and Elections Collection, at library.cqpress.com/elections/hdpres-149-7148-391040. Document ID:hdpres-149-7148-391040 (accessed July 15, 2005).

165. *AMMI; The Spot.*

166. *NPP*, 782–820.

167. "The Acceptance Speech," George McGovern, *An American Journey: The Presidential Campaign Speeches of George McGovern* (New York: Random House, 1974), 16–24.

168. *APCD; AMMI; The Spot.*

169. *NPP*, 847–882.

170. Richard M. Nixon, at www.geocities.com/rickmatlick/nomanixon72.htm (accessed February 9, 2004).

171. *APCD; AMMI; The Spot.*

172. Democratic Party, at www.presidency.ucsb.edu/site/docs/print_platforms.php?platindex=D1976 (accessed October 7, 2003).

173. Jimmy Carter, at www.4president.org/speeches/carter1976convention.htm. (accessed October 13, 2003).

174. *APCD; AMMI; The Spot.*

175. Republican Party, at www.presidency.ucsb.edu/site/docs/print_platforms.php?platindex=R1976 (accessed October 7, 2003).

176. Gerald R. Ford, at www.4president.org/speeches/ford1976convention.htm (accessed October 13, 2003).

177. *APCD; AMMI.*

178. Presidential debates, at www.debates.org/pages/trans76a.html; www.debates.org/pages/trans76b.html; www.debates.org/pages/trans76c.html (accessed October 29, 2003).

179. Democratic Party, at www.presidency.ucsb.edu/site/docs/print_platforms.php?platindex=D1980 (accessed October 7, 2003).

180. Jimmy Carter, at www.4president.org/speeches/carter1980convention.htm (accessed October 13, 2003).

181. *APCD; AMMI.*

182. Republican Party, at www.presidency.ucsb.edu/site/docs/print_platforms.php?platindex=R1980 (accessed October 7, 2003).

183. Ronald Reagan, at www.4president.org/speeches/reagan1980convention.htm (accessed October 13, 2003).

184. *APCD; AMMI.*

185. "John B. Anderson announces candidacy for presidency," in M. Nelson, ed. *Historic Documents on Presidential Elections 1787–1988* (Washington: CQ Press) from CQ Electronic Library, CQ Voting and Elections Collection, at library.cqpress.com/elections/hdpres-149-7148-391147. Document ID:hdpres-149-7148-391147 (accessed July 15, 2005).

186. "John Anderson for President 1980 Campaign Brochure," www.4President.org (accessed July 15, 2005).

187. *AMMI.*

188. Presidential debates, at www.debates.org/pages/trans80a.html; www.debates.org/pages/trans80b.html (accessed October 29, 2003).

189. Democratic Party, at www.presidency.ucsb.edu/site/docs/print_platforms.php?platindex=D1984 (accessed October 7, 2003).

190. Walter Mondale, at www.cfinst.org/eguide/PartyConventions/speeches/1984d.html (accessed January 31, 2005).

191. *APCD; AMMI.*

192. Republican Party, at www.presidency.ucsb.edu/site/docs/print_platforms.php?platindex=R1984 (accessed October 7, 2003).

193. Ronald Reagan, at www.4president.org/speeches/reagan1984convention.htm (accessed October 13, 2003).

194. *APCD; AMMI.*

195. Presidential debates, at www.pbs.org/newshour/debatingourdestiny/84debates/1prez1.html (accessed October 29, 2003).

196. Democratic Party, at www.presidency.ucsb.edu/site/docs/print_platforms.php?platindex=D1988 (accessed October 7, 2003).

197. Michael Dukakis, at www.4president.org/speeches/mikedukakis1988acceptance.htm (accessed October 13, 2003).

198. *APCD; AMMI.*

199. George H. W. Bush, at www.presidency.ucsb.edu/site/docs/print_platforms.php?platindex=R1988 (accessed October 7, 2003).

200. George H. W. Bush, at www.4president.org/speeches/georgebush1988convention.htm (accessed October 13, 2003).

201. *APCD.*

202. Presidential debates, at www.debates.org/pages/trans88a.html, www.debates.org/pages/trans88b.html (accessed October 29, 2003).

203. Democratic Party, at www.presidency.ucsb.edu/site/docs/print_platforms.php?platindex=D1992 (accessed October 7, 2003).

204. Bill Clinton, at www.cfinst.org/eguide/PartyConventions/speeches/1992d.html (accessed January 31, 2005).

205. *APCD.*

206. Republican Party, at www.presidency.ucsb.edu/site/docs/print_platforms.php?platindex=R1992 (accessed October 7, 2003).

207. George H.W. Bush, at www.4president.org/speeches/georgebush1992convention.htm (accessed October 13, 2003).

208. *APCD; AMMI.*

209. Ross Perot, *United We Stand: How We Can Take Back Our Country* (New York: Hyperion, 1992).

210. "Statement by Independent Presidential Candidate R. Perot on Ending, then Reviving, His Candidacy in 1992," in M. Nelson, ed., *Historic Documents on Presidential Elections 1787–1988* (Washington: CQ Press) from CQ Electronic Library, CQ Voting and Elections Collection, at library.cqpress.com/elections/hsdc92-0000090880. Document ID:hsdc-0000090880 (accessed July 15, 2005.)

211. *AMMI.*

212. Presidential debates, at www.debates.org/pages/trans92a1.html; www.debates.org/pages/trans92a2.html; www.debates.org/pages/trans92b1.html; www.debates.org/pages/trans92b2.html; www.debates.org/pages/trans92c.html (accessed October 29, 2003).

213. Democratic Party, at www.presidency.ucsb.edu/site/docs/print_platforms.php?platindex=D1996 (accessed October 8, 2003).

214. Bill Clinton, at www.4president.org/speeches/clintongore1996convention.htm, (accessed October 13, 2003).

215. *APCD; AMMI.*

216. Republican Party, at www.presidency.ucsb.edu/site/docs/print_platforms.php?platindex=R1996 (accessed October 8, 2003).

217. Robert Dole, at www.4president.org/speeches/dolekemp1996convention.htm (accessed October 13, 2003).

218. *APCD; AMMI.*

219. "1996 Reform Party," at janda.org/politxts/PartyPlatforms/OtherParties/reform.996.html (accessed July 15, 2005).

220. "Speech of R. Perot on Accepting the 1996 Presidential Nomination of the Reform Party, Valley Forge, PA." 1997). In *Historic Documents of 1996.* (Washington, D.C.: CQ Press) from CQ Electronic Library, CQ Voting and Elections Collection, at library.cqpress.com/elections/hsdc96-0000035228. Document ID: hsdc96-0000035228 (accessed July 15, 2005).

221. Presidential debates, at www.debates.org/pages/trans96a.html; www.debates.org/pages/trans96b.html, (accessed October 29, 2003).

222. Democratic Party, at www.presidency.ucsb.edu/site/docs/print_platforms.php?platindex=D2000 (accessed October 8, 2003).

223. Al Gore, at www.4president.org/speeches/gorelieberman2000convention.htm (accessed October 13, 2003).

224. Democratic Party, *In Their Own Words: Sourcebook for the 2000 Presidential Election.* CD-ROM. Stanford University, 2000; *AMMI.*

225. Republican Party, at www.presidency.ucsb.edu/site/docs/print_platforms.php?platindex=R2000 (accessed October 8, 2003).

226. George W. Bush, at www.4president.org/speeches/bushcheney2000convention.htm (accessed October 13, 2003).

227. Republican Party, *In Their Own Words: Sourcebook for the 2000 Presidential Election.* CD-ROM. Stanford University, 2000; *AMMI.*

228. Presidential debates, at www.debates.org/pages/trans2000a.html; www.debates.org/pages/trans2000b.html; www.debates.org/pages/trans2000c.html, (accessed October 29, 2003).

229. *Strong at Home, Respected in the World: The 2004 Democratic National Platform for America* (Washington, D.C.: Democratic National Convention Committee, 2004).

230. John Kerry, at www.4president.org/speeches/kerry2004acceptance.htm (accessed May 24, 2005).

231. *In Their Own Words: Sourcebook for the 2004 Presidential Election*. CD-ROM. Stanford University, 2000; *AMMI*.

232. *2004 Republican Party Platform: A Safer World and a More Hopeful America* (Washington, D.C.: Republican National Committee, 2004).

233. George W. Bush, at www.4president.org/speeches/georgewbush2004convention.htm (accessed May 24, 2005).

234. *In Their Own Words: Sourcebook for the 2004 Presidential Election*. CD-ROM. Stanford University, 2000; *AMMI*.

235. Presidential debates, at www.debates.org/pages/trans2004a_p.html; www.debates.org/pages/trans2004c_p.html; www.debates.org/pages/trans2004d_p.html (accessed May 24, 2005).

Bibliography

A complete bibliographical listing of the coded documents can be found in appendix B.

Adamany, David. "Legitimacy, Realigning Elections, and the Supreme Court." *Wisconsin Law Review* 3 (1973): 790–846.

Ames, Herman V. *State Documents on Federal Relations: The States and the United States.* Philadelphia: University of Pennsylvania, 1911.

Baas, Larry R. "The Constitution as Symbol: The Interpersonal Sources of Meaning of a Secondary Symbol." *American Journal of Political Science* 23, no. 1 (February 1979): 101–120.

Bamberger, Michael A. *Reckless Legislation: How Lawmakers Ignore the Constitution.* New Brunswick, N.J.: Rutgers University Press, 2000.

Barrus, Roger M., John H. Eastby, Joseph H. Lane, Jr., David E. Marion, and James Pontuso. *The Deconstitutionalization of America: The Forgotten Frailties of Democratic Rule.* Lanham, Md.: Lexington Books, 2004.

Beck, Paul Allen. *Party Politics in America* 8th ed. New York: Longman, 1997.

Black, Charles L. "Some Thoughts on the Veto." *Law and Contemporary Problems* 40 (Spring 1976): 87–101.

Black, Charles. *The People and the Court.* New York: Macmillan, 1960.

Brians, Craig Leonard, and Martin P. Wattenberg. "Campaign Issue Knowledge and Salience: Comparing Reception from TV Commercials, TV News, and Newspapers." *American Journal of Political Science* 40, no. 1 (1996): 172–193.

Burgess, Susan R. *Contest for Constitutional Authority: The Abortion and War Powers Debates.* Lawrence: University Press of Kansas, 1992.

Burnham, Walter Dean. *Critical Elections and the Mainsprings of American Politics.* New York: Norton, 1970.

Busch, Andrew E., and Christopher McLemore. "The Constitution and Members of Congress," Paper presented at the annual meeting of the Midwest Political Science Association, Chicago, Ill., April, 2003.

Campbell, Karlyn Kohrs, and Kathleen Hall Jameison. *Deeds Done in Words: Presidential Rhetoric and the Genres of Governance.* Chicago: University of Chicago Press, 1990.

Carsey, Thomas, John Green, Rick Herrera, and Geoffrey Layman. "The New Party Professionals? An Initial Look at National Convention Delegates in 2000 and Over Time." Paper presented at the annual meeting of the American Political Science Association, August 28–31, 2003.

The Center for Responsive Politics. "Top 20 PAC Contributors to Federal Candidates, 2005–2006." The Center for Responsive Politics at www.opensecrets.org/pacs/topacs .asc?txt=A&Cycle=2006 (accessed April 28, 2006).

Clarke, Harold D., Euel Elliott, and Thomas H. Roback. "Domestic Issue Ideology and Activist Style: A Note on the 1980 Republican Convention Delegates." *Journal of Politics* 53, no. 2 (May 1991): 519–534.

Cohens v. Virginia, 19 U.S. 264 (1821).

Coleman, Stephen. "Meaningful Political Debate in the Age of the Soundbite." In *Televised Election Debates: International Perspectives,* edited by Stephen Coleman, 1–24. New York: St. Martin's Press, 2000.

Converse, Philip E. "Information Flow and the Stability of Partisan Attitudes." *Public Opinion Quarterly* 26, no. 4 (Winter 1962): 578–599.

Cooper v. Aaron, 358 U.S. 1, 18 (1958).

Corwin, Edward S. "The Constitution as an Instrument and as a Symbol." *American Political Science Review* 30, no. 6 (December 1936): 1071–1085.

Currie, David P. "Prolegomena for a Sampler: Extrajudicial Interpretation of the Constitution, 1789–1861." In *Congress and the Constitution,* edited by Neal Devins and Keith E. Whittington, 18–38. Durham, N.C.: Duke University Press, 2005.

Currie, David P. *The Constitution in Congress: The Federalist Period, 1789–1801.* Chicago: University of Chicago Press, 1997.

David, Paul T., Ralph M. Goldman, and Richard C. Bain. *The Politics of National Party Conventions.* Washington, D.C.: Brookings Institution, 1960.

Delli Carpini, Michael X., and Scott Keeter. *What Americans Know About Politics and Why It Matters.* New Haven, Conn.: Yale University Press, 1996.

Devins, Neal, and Keith E. Whittington, eds. *Congress and the Constitution.* Durham, N.C.: Duke University Press, 2005.

Diamond, Edwin, and Stephen Bates. *The Spot: The Rise of Political Advertising on Television,* rev. ed. Cambridge, Mass.: MIT Press, 1984.

Dinan, John J. *Keeping the People's Liberties: Legislators, Citizens, and Judges as Keepers of Rights.* Lawrence: University of Kansas, 1998.

Dinan, John. "The U.S. Congress and the Protection of Rights." Paper presented at the International Conference on Legislatures and the Protection of Human Rights, Centre for Comparative Constitutional Studies, Melbourne, Australia, July 20–22, 2006.

Elliot, Jonathan. *The Debates in the Several State Conventions on the Adoption of the Federal Constitution Vol. IV.*

Epp, Charles. *The Rights Revolution: Lawyers, Activists, and Supreme Courts in Comparative Perspective.* Chicago: University of Chicago Press, 1998.

Fisher, Louis, and Neal Devins. *Political Dynamics of Constitutional Law.* St. Paul, Minn.: West Group, 2001.

Fisher, Louis. "Congressional Checks on the Judiciary." In *Congress Confronts the Court: The Struggle for Legitimacy and Authority in Lawmaking,* edited by Colton C. Campbell and John F. Stack, Jr., 21–35. Lanham, Md.: Rowman & Littlefield, 2001.

Fisher, Louis. *Constitutional Conflicts between Congress and the President.* Princeton, N.J.: Princeton University Press, 1985.

Fisher, Louis. *Constitutional Dialogues: Interpretation as Political Process.* Princeton, N.J.: Princeton University Press, 1988.

Fitzpatrick, Ellen. "History's Lessons." *Online NewsHour,* July 29, 2004. www.pbs.org/newshour/bb/politics/july-dec04/historians_7-29.html (accessed November 3, 2005).

Freie, John F. "Minor Parties in Realigning Eras." *American Politics Quarterly* 10, no. 1 (1982): 47–63.

Funston, Richard. "The Supreme Court and Critical Elections." *American Political Science Review* 69, no. 3 (1975): 795–811.

Gates, John B. *The Supreme Court and Partisan Realignment: A Macro- and Microlevel Perspective.* Boulder, Colo.: Westview Press, 1992.

Gerhardt, Michael J. "The Federal Appointments Process as Constitutional Interpretation." In *Congress and the Constitution,* edited by Neal Devins and Keith E. Whittington, 110–130. Durham, N.C.: Duke University Press, 2005.

Gerring, John. *Party Ideologies in America, 1828–1996.* New York: Cambridge University Press, 1998.

GovSpot Lists. "Top 50 PACs." Govspot.com at www.govspot.com/lists/top50pacs.htm (accessed May 13, 2003).

Griffin, Stephen M. "Constitutionalism in the United States: From Theory to Politics." *Oxford Journal of Legal Studies* 10, no. 2 (1990): 200–220.

Hamilton, Alexander, James Madison, and John Jay. *The Federalist Papers,* edited by Clinton Rossiter.

Healy, Gene, and Timothy Lynch. *Power Surge: The Constitutional Record of George W. Bush.* Washington, D.C.: Cato Institute, 2006.

Hellweg, Susan A., Michael Pfau, and Steven R. Brydon. *Televised Presidential Debates, Advocacy in Contemporary America.* New York: Praeger, 1992.

Herrera, Richard. "Cohesion at the Party Conventions: 1980–1988." *Polity* 26, no. 1 (Autumn 1993): 75–89.

Herrera, Richard. "Understanding the Language of Politics: A Study of Elites and Masses." *Political Science Quarterly* 111, no. 4. (Winter 1996–1997): 619–637.

Herrnson, Paul S. "Two-Party Dominance and Minor-Party Forays in American Politics." In *Multiparty Politics in America* 2nd ed., edited by Paul S. Herrnson and John C. Green. Lanham, Md.: Rowman & Littlefield, 2002.

Herrnson, Paul S. "National Party Organizations at the Dawn of the Twenty-First Century." In *The Parties Respond: Changes in American Parties and Campaigns* 4th ed., edited by L. Sandy Maisel. Boulder, Colo.: Westview Press, 2002.

Hinck, Edward A. *Enacting the Presidency: Political Argument, Presidential Debates, and Presidential Character.* Westport, Conn.: Praeger, 1978.

Hofstetter, C. Richard, and Cliff Zukin. "TV Network News and Advertising in the Nixon and McGovern Campaigns." *Journalism Quarterly* 56, no. 1 (1979): 106–115.

Institute of Politics, Harvard University. *Campaign for President: The Managers Look at 2004.* Lanham, Md.: Rowman & Littlefield, 2005.

Jackson, Andrew. "President Jackson's Veto Message Regarding the Bank of the United States; July 10, 1832." The Avalon Project at Yale Law School. www.yale.edu/lawweb/avalon/presiden/veto/ajveto01.htm (accessed April 13, 2006).

Jameison, Kathleen Hall, and Christopher Adasiewicz. "What Can Voters Learn from Election Debates?" In *Televised Election Debates: International Perspectives*, edited by Stephen Coleman, 25–42. New York: St. Martin's Press, 2000.

Jameison, Kathleen Hall, and David S. Birdsell. *Presidential Debates: The Challenge of Creating an Informed Electorate*. New York: Oxford University Press, 1988.

Jameison, Kathleen Hall. "Context and the Creation of Meaning in the Advertising of the 1988 Presidential Campaign." *American Behavioral Scientist* 32 (1989): 415–424.

Jameison, Kathleen Hall. *Packaging the Presidency: A History and Criticism of Presidential Campaign Advertising*, 3rd ed. New York: Oxford University Press, 1996.

Jefferson, Thomas. "The Kentucky Resolutions." In *The Portable Thomas Jefferson*, edited by Merrill D. Peterson, 281–289. New York: The Viking Press, 1975.

Jennings, M. Kent. "Ideological Thinking among Mass Publics and Political Elites." *Public Opinion Quarterly* 56, no. 4 (Winter 1992): 419–441.

Joslyn, Richard. "The Content of Political Spot Ads." *Journalism Quarterly* 57, no.1 (1980): 92–98.

Joslyn, Richard. *Mass Media and Elections*. Reading, Mass.: Addison-Wesley Publishing, 1984.

Just, Marion, Ann Crigler, Dean Alger, Timothy Cook, Montague Kern, and Darrell M. West. *Cross Talk: Citizens, Candidates, and the Media in a Presidential Campaign*. Chicago: University of Chicago Press, 1996.

Kammen, Michael. *A Machine That Would Go of Itself: The Constitution in American Culture*. New York: Alfred A. Knopf, 1987.

Kazee, Thomas A. "Television Exposure and Attitude Change: The Impact of Political Interest." *Public Opinion Quarterly* 45, no. 4 (Winter 1981): 507–518.

Kendall, Kathleen, ed. *Presidential Campaign Discourse: Strategic Communication Problems*. Albany: State University of New York Press, 1995.

Kesler, Charles. "Political Parties, the Constitution, and the Future of American Politics." In *American Political Parties and Constitutional Politics*, edited by Peter W. Schramm and Bradford P. Wilson. Lanham, Md.: Rowman & Littlefield Publishers, 1992.

Ketcham. Ralph, ed. *The Anti-Federalist Papers and the Constitutional Convention Debates* reissue ed. New York: Mentor Books, 1996.

Kirkpatrick, Jeane. *The New Presidential Elite: Men and Women in National Politics*. New York: Russell Sage Foundation, 1976.

Klarman, Michael J. "How Great Were the 'Great' Marshall Court Decisions?" *Virginia Law Review* 87, no. 6 (October 2001): 1111–1184.

Kramer, Larry D. *The People Themselves: Popular Constitutionalism and Judicial Review*. New York: Oxford University Press, 2004.

Krause, Sidney. *Televised Presidential Debates and Public Policy*. Hillsdale, N.J.: Lawrence Earlbaum Associates, Publishers.

Layman, Geoffrey C., and Thomas M. Carsey. "Party Polarization and Party Structuring of Policy Attitudes: A Comparison of Three NES Panel Studies." *Political Behavior* 24, no. 3 (2002): 199–236.

Layman, Geoffrey C., and Carsey, Thomas M. "Party Polarization and 'Conflict Extension' in the American Electorate." *American Journal of Political Science* 46, no. 4 (2002): 786–802.

Lerner, Max. "Constitution and Court as Symbols." *The Yale Law Journal* 46, no. 8 (June 1937): 1290–1319.

Levinson, Sanford. "'The Constitution' in American Civil Religion." *The Supreme Court Review* 1979 (1979): 123–151.

Levinson, Sanford. *Constitutional Faith*. Princeton, N.J.: Princeton University Press, 1988.

Levy, Leonard W. "Judicial Review, History, and Democracy." In *Judicial Review and the Supreme Court*, edited by Leonard W. Levy, 1–42. New York: Harper Torchbooks, 1967.

Madison, James. "James Madison to Thomas Jefferson, October 17, 1788." In *The Origins of the American Constitution: A Documentary History*, edited by Michael Kammen, 369–370. New York: Penguin Books, 1986.

Maisel, L. Sandy. "The Platform-Writing Process: Candidate-Centered Platforms in 1992." *Political Science Quarterly* 108, no. 4 (1993) 671–698.

Mansfield, Harvey C., Jr. "Our Constitution Then and Now." In *The Embattled Constitution: Vital Framework or Convenient Symbol*, edited by Adolph H. Grundman, 151–157. Malabar, Fla.: Krieger, 1986.

Mansfield, Harvey C., Jr. "Political Parties and American Constitutionalism." In *American Political Parties and Constitutional Politics*, edited by Peter W. Schramm and Bradford P. Wilson, 1–16. Lanham, Md.: Rowman & Littlefield Publishers, 1992.

Marcus, George E., and Michael B. MacKuen. "Anxiety, Enthusiasm, and the Vote: The Emotional Underpinnings of Learning and Involvement during Presidential Campaigns." *American Political Science Review* 87, no. 3 (1993): 672–685.

Martin v. Hunter's Lessee, 14 U.S. 304 (1816).

Mason, Edward Campbell. *The Veto Power: Its Origin, Development & Function in the Government of the United States*. Boston: Ginn & Co., 1890.

Mayhew, David. *Electoral Realignment: Critique of a Genre*. New Haven, Conn.: Yale University Press, 2004.

Mazmanian, Daniel A. *Third Parties in Presidential Elections*. Washington, D.C.: Brookings Institution, 1974.

McCullough v. Maryland, 17 U.S. 316 (1819).

McDiarmid, John. "Presidential Inaugural Addresses: A Study in Verbal Symbols." *The Public Opinion Quarterly* 1, no. 3 (July, 1937): 79–82.

Milkis, Sidney M. *Political Parties and Constitutional Government: Remaking American Democracy*. Baltimore, Md.: Johns Hopkins Press, 1999.

Miller, Nancy L., and William B. Stiles. "Verbal Familiarity in American Presidential Nomination Acceptance Speeches and Inaugural Addresses (1920–1980)." *Social Psychology Quarterly* 49, no. 1 (March 1986): 72–81.

Miller, Warren E. *Without Consent: Mass-Elite Linkages in Presidential Politics*. Lexington: University Press of Kentucky, 1988.

Moore, David W. "Political Campaigns and the Knowledge-Gap Hypothesis." *Public Opinion Quarterly* 51, no. 2 (Summer 1987): 186–200.

Morgan, Donald. *Congress and the Constitution*. Cambridge, Mass.: Harvard University Press, 1966.

Nadeau, Richard, Neil Nevitte, Elisabeth Gidengil, and André Blais. "Election Campaigns as Information Campaigns: Who Learns What and With What Effect?" Canadian Elections Studies Publications–Election 1997. Available at www.ces.eec.montreal.ca/documents/InformationCampaigns.pdf

Namenswirth, J. Zvi, and Harold Lasswell. *The Changing Language of American Values: A Computer Study of Selected Party Platforms*. Beverly Hills, Calif.: Sage Publications, 1970.

Nelson, John S., and G. R. Boynton. *Video Rhetorics: Televised Advertising in American Politics*. Urbana: University of Illinois Press, 1997.

Patterson, Thomas E., and Robert D. McLure. *The Unseeing Eye: The Myth of Television Power in National Elections*. New York: Putnam, 1976.

Patterson, Thomas, and Richard McClure. *The Unseeing Eye*. New York: Putnam's, 1976.

Peabody, Bruce G. "Congressional Attitudes toward Constitutional Interpretation." In *Congress and the Constitution*, edited by Neal Devins and Keith E. Whittington, 39–63. Durham, N.C.: Duke University Press, 2005.

Pickerill, J. Mitchell. "Congressional Responses to Judicial Review." In *Congress and the Constitution*, edited by Neal Devins and Keith E. Whittington, 151–172. Durham, N.C.: Duke University Press, 2005.

Pickerill, J. Mitchell. *Constitutional Deliberation in Congress: The Impact of Judicial Review in a Separated System*. Durham, N.C.: Duke University Press, 2004.

Pomper, Gerald C. "'If Elected, I Promise': American Party Platforms." *Midwest Journal of Political Science* 11, no. 3 (August, 1967): 318–352.

Powell v. McCormack, 395 U.S. 486, 521 (1969).

Prothro, James W. "Verbal Shifts in the American Presidency: A Content Analysis." *American Political Science Review* 50, no. 3 (September 1956): 726–739.

Rosenstone, Steven J., Roy L. Behr, and Edward H. Lazarus. *Third Parties in America: Citizen Response to Major Party Failure*, 2nd ed. Princeton, N.J.: Princeton University Press, 1996.

[Sherman, Roger]. "A Citizen of New Haven." In *Friends of the Constitution: Writings of the "Other" Federalists, 1787–1788*, edited by Colleen A. Sheehan and Gary L. McDowell, 263–271. Indianapolis, Ind.: Liberty Fund, 1998.

Smith, Marshall S., Philip J. Stone, and Evelyn N. Glenn. "A Content Analysis of Twenty Presidential Nomination Acceptance Speeches." In *The General Inquirer: A Computer Approach to Content Analysis*, edited by Philip J. Stone, Dexter C. Dunphy, Marshall S. Smith, and Daniel M. Ogilvie, 359–400. Cambridge, Mass.: M.I.T. Press, 1966.

Smith, William Raymond. *The Rhetoric of American Politics: A Study of Documents*. Westport, Conn.: Greenwood Press, 1969.

Soule, John W., and Wilma E. McGrath. "A Comparative Study of Presidential Nomination Conventions: The Democrats 1968 and 1972." *American Journal of Political Science* 19, no. 3 (1975): 501–517.

Stephenson, Donald Grier, Jr. *Campaigns and the Court: The U.S. Supreme Court in U.S. Elections*. New York: Columbia University Press, 1999.

Stone, Walter J., Ronald B. Rapoport, and Alan I. Abramowitz. "The Reagan Revolution and Party Polarization in the 1980s." In *The Parties Respond: Changes in the American Party System*, edited by L. Sandy Maisel, 67–93. Boulder, Colo.: Westview Press, 1990.

Stuckey, Mary E. "Presidential Rhetoric in Political Time." In *The Theory and Practice of Political Communication Research*, edited by Mary E. Stuckey, 122–141. Albany: State University of New York Press, 1996.

Sundquist, James L. *Dynamics of the Party System*, rev. ed. Washington, D.C.: Brookings Institution, 1983.

Teles, Steven M. *Parallel Paths: the Conservative Legal Movement versus Legal Liberalism*. Princeton, N.J.: Princeton University Press, 2007.

Tichenor, Phillip J., George A. Donohue, and Clarice N. Olien. "Mass Media Flow and Differential Growth in Knowledge." *Public Opinion Quarterly* 34, no. 2 (Summer 1970): 159–170.

Madison, James. "The Virginia Report." In *The Mind of the Founder: Sources of the Political Thought of James Madison*, edited by Marvin Meyers. Hanover, N.H.: University Press of New England, 1981.

Towle, Katherine A. "The Presidential Veto since 1889." *American Political Science Review* 31, no. 1 (February 1937): 51–56.

Tulis, Jeffrey K. *The Rhetorical Presidency*. Princeton, N.J.: Princeton University Press, 1987.

United States v. Nixon, 418 U.S. 683, 704 (1974).

Warren, Charles. *Congress, the Constitution, and the Supreme Court*. Boston: Little, Brown, 1935.

Watson, Richard A. *Presidential Vetoes and Public Policy*. Lawrence: University Press of Kansas, 1993.

West, Darrell M. *Air Wars: Television Advertising in Election Campaigns 1952–2004*. Washington, D.C.: Congressional Quarterly Press, 2005.

Westin, Alan F. "The Supreme Court, the Populist Movement, and the Campaign of 1896." *Journal of Politics* 15, no. 3 (1953): 3–41.

White, Theodore H. *America in Search of Itself: The Making of the President 1956–1980*. New York: Warner Books, 1982.

Whittington, Keith E. "Hearing about the Constitution in Committees." In *Congress and the Constitution*, edited by Neal Devins and Keith E. Whittington, 87–109. Durham, N.C.: Duke University Press, 2005.

Whittington, Keith E. *Constitutional Construction: Divided Powers and Constitutional Meaning*. Cambridge, Mass.: Harvard University Press, 1999.

Wildavsky, Aaron. "The Goldwater Phenomenon: Purists, Politicians, and the Two-Party System." *Review of Politics* 27, no. 3 (July 1965): 386–413.

Wilson, James. "James Wilson, Speech, State House, 6 October 1787, Pennsylvania Packet, 10 October 1787." In *Friends of the Constitution: Writings of the "Other" Federalists, 1787–1788*, edited by Colleen A. Sheehan and Gary L. McDowell, 102–108. Indianapolis, Ind: Liberty Fund, 1998.

Zhao, Xinshu, and Steven H. Chaffee. "Campaign Advertisements versus Television News as Sources of Political Issue Information." *Public Opinion Quarterly* 59, no. 1 (Spring 1995): 41–65.

Index

~

About the Author

Andrew E. Busch is professor of government at Claremont McKenna College. He has authored or coauthored ten books on American politics and government, including *Reagan's Victory: The Presidential Election of 1980 and the Rise of the Right, Red Over Blue: The Elections of 2004 and American Politics*, and *The Front-Loading Problem in Presidential Nominations*. He received his PhD from the University of Virginia.